BEGGING FOR CHOCOLATES
A Story of World War II Italy
Edited with commentary by Richard Allison

Published by Hellgate Press
(An imprint of L&R Publishing, LLC)
PO Box 3531
Ashland, OR 97520
email: sales@hellgatepress.com

Book design: Michael Campbell
Cover design: L. Redding

ISBN: 978-1-55571-862-6

BEGGING FOR CHOCOLATES

A story of World War II Italy

A COMPILATION OF LETTERS,
JOURNAL ENTRIES, INTERVIEWS,
POEMS, CARTOONS AND HISTORY

—◠◠◠—

EDITED WITH COMMENTARY BY

RICHARD ALLISON

ALSO BY THE AUTHOR

Operation Thunderclap and
The Black March: Two Stories
From the Unstoppable
91st Bomb Group (2014)

—⚏—

"When I see the people here, I am thankful you folks have the food, fuel and shelter and live in a country where there is enough for all. I took so much for granted before coming here. I have also observed that the closer men live to danger and suffering, the more grateful they are for things that ordinarily go unnoticed."

Bill
Christmas Eve, Signa, Italy 1944

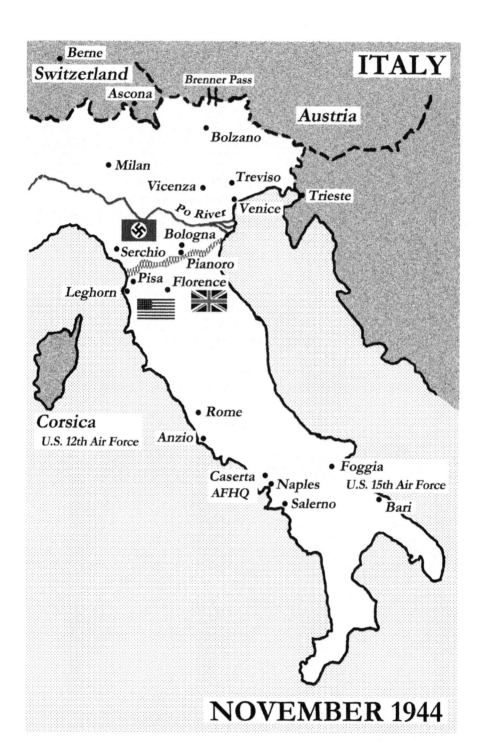

DEDICATION

This book is dedicated to the Italians whom Bill saw close up, to those he described as decent and hard-working in the face of adversity, to those who were not *Fascisti* but rather just ordinary people trying desperately to survive in the midst of a horrible situation. It is also dedicated to the citizen American soldiers depicted in the story: Mark Renick, Jack King, John Lesesne, Dick Stroud, Bill Newnan, Leon Weckstein, Wade McCree and thousands more like them; to those who manned the snow posts and those who dug their shelters into the sides of hills for protection; to those who typed and those who directed mortar fire; to those who lived in the big house; to those who saw the angry enemy up close; to the poets and roosters; to the Americans who wrote **H**ome regularly whether or not there was news to report.

And also to my father Bill Allison.

Richard Allison
Grosse Pointe Woods, Michigan
May 2017

"This was the most heavily fortified area along the entire front—held by German forces not materially inferior in strength to those which would be attacking. Under unfavorable conditions of weather and terrain it seemed to me an appalling undertaking. Even with overwhelming support of our air forces, I thought it would be a difficult and costly venture even if it could succeed."

LIEUTENANT GENERAL LUCIEN K. TRUSCOTT, JR. CRITICIZING THE PIANORO BATTLE-PLAN OF HIS SUPERIOR GENERAL MARK W. CLARK FOR THE FINAL CAMPAIGN IN ITALY. FUTA PASS, ITALY, DECEMBER 1944

"A certain division in Italy has had 400 days of actual combat, casualties have been heavy and eventually the men get into a frame of mind in which the only future they see is death."

CONGRESSWOMAN CLARE BOOTHE LUCE, QUOTED IN *STARS AND STRIPES MEDITERRANEAN*, ROME, ITALY, JANUARY 4, 1945

"Today, March 16, [1945] I am in receipt of a letter from you which shows that the United States Government is barring the Soviet representatives from the Berne negotiations. The U.S. Government's refusal to admit Soviet representatives to the Berne negotiations came as a complete surprise to the Soviet Government and is inexplicable in terms of the relations of alliance existing between our two countries."

PEOPLE'S COMMISSAR FOR FOREIGN AFFAIRS OF THE USSR VYACHESLAV MOLOTOV, PROTESTING THE SOVIET UNION BEING EXCLUDED FROM PARTICIPATING IN SECRET NEGOTIATIONS WITH SS GENERAL KARL WOLFF OVER THE SURRENDER OF THE GERMAN ARMY IN ITALY (LETTER RESPONSE TO U.S. AMBASSADOR W. AVERELL HARRIMAN)

"We can let the work cover the romance, and the romance cover the work."

OSS DIRECTOR ALLEN W. DULLES TO EMPLOYEE/SPY/MISTRESS MARY
BANCROFT. BERNE, SWITZERLAND, 1942-45

If I were an artist, with nothing to do,
I'd paint a picture, a composite view,
Of historic Italy, in which I'd show,
Visions of contrasts, the high and the low.
There'd be towering mountains, a deep blue sea;
Filthy brats yelling "Carmella" at me,
High plumed horses, and colorful carts;
Two toned tresses on hustling tarts.

AUTHOR UNKNOWN, ALLIED FORCES HEADQUARTERS
CASERTA, ITALY 1944-45 (TO BE CONTINUED)

"Let those at **Home** see Rome."

BILL—SOMEWHERE IN ITALY, 1945
(*ALSO TO BE CONTINUED*)

CONTENTS

BEGGING FOR CHOCOLATES

Allied Forces Headquarters shoulder patch

INTRODUCTION

December 24, 1944

"What have I gotten myself into?" Captain William "Bill" Allison despaired, as he sat at a table and watched the crude, wire-suspended incandescent light bulb flicker. This latest mess resulted when Army electricians jury-rigged a lighting system up to a new generator that was promised to work better than the one it replaced.

Bill sighed. "There are many challenges here," he thought. "Self-inflicted ones."

A month and one-half had passed since Bill left Detroit for Europe. Now he was alone in a small upstairs office in a drafty baron's mansion in Signa, Italy, not far from Florence to the southwest, and also not far from the Nazi army to the north. "I might as well be in China," Bill wailed, slowly shaking his head as he thought of how the war had turned a popular resort area into an empty and desolate wasteland. He fantasized about phoning home.

Bill shuffled papers on the table before him, a partial draft of his second military report for his superior, Major Renick. He had struggled with it for two hours this morning and now in the afternoon was back at it. His first report, done the week earlier had been easy for him to write. Since then Bill had completed additional inspection trips to different forward supply areas, but he was at a temporary loss now for new ideas to submit. Renick, three hundred miles to the south at theater headquarters at "MTOUSA" was due this second report in a couple of days.

"MTOUSA" Bill thought. Who came up with that acronym?

Bill glanced at the nearby "log sheet" of letters he had written to his wife Dotty and two-year old son, Davy, and also to his parents. He had mailed out a total of fifty-seven letters and had received none in return. He knew this was not due to the failure of his family to write. "They are waiting for me at Caserta," Bill thought, or rather imagined (or desperately hoped). "Batches of letters." "MTOUSA."

Bill ruminated upon the circumstances that had brought him here. Part of it was complaints, he knew, complaints written in the form of scores of angry letters to Congress, authored by G.I.s (or the parents of G.I.'s) serving in the Apennine

Mountains on the Italian Front. With the advent of cold weather these soldiers suffered. They needed more stoves and the fuel to run them, more tents and building materials to bolster the tents from slashing winter winds, more protective wool clothing, boots, greatcoats and raincoats. They needed more of everything, including the "Three Bs" — bread, bandages and bullets. The gist of their grievance was that from D-Day forward the U.S. Fifth Army in Italy had become a "forgotten army," an army that for one reason or another (be it impassable roads or the re-allocation of precious resources to a more vital warfront in France) was not being restocked adequately. The U.S. Fifth Army and British Eighth Army still faced a determined foe in Italy — approximately 300,000 Waffen-SS and Wehrmacht soldiers. The issue had sprouted political legs and the U.S. Congress was now directly involved in the plight of the U.S. Fifth Army. Bill had followed the news stories about this controversy before coming over.

Bill thought of his son Davy at the Detroit Zoo shortly before he left. An elephant enchanted the boy, and it was a most endearing moment to watch his son attempt to formulate a new three-syllable word. "Elphant" Davy said, gleefully. "Elphant, elphant!" When the boy heard his parents affectionately correct him enough times, out popped "Elephant!"

While Bill was stationed in Detroit, the word came down the chain of command from Headquarters, U.S. Army Transportation Corps, Washington D.C., that an officer was to be sent overseas from the Automotive Tank Command to assess the transport of supplies to the Italian front. "I drew the short straw," Bill laughed to himself, mentally reliving this event. Bill had not been "ordered" to go, it had been subtler than that. Because he was an eleven-year Army reservist, it was suggested to Captain Allison that it might look good on his record if he "volunteered," so he did so in lieu of being commanded to go.

Bill reflected on his parting. What a surreal experience, he thought, and not an easy one. First, there had been the farewell with his youngest brother's widow and her year and one-half old son, Jim, or "J.B." Dick Allison, J.B.'s father, a P-47 fighter pilot died in a 1943 airplane accident in Wales five days after J.B. was born. Then there was the farewell to his parents who lived on a small farm in western New York State. They feared for Bill, of course, as they had for Dick, and moreover were unsettled about whether the draft might take their other two sons, teachers and married with children. "I'm not going over in a combat status," Bill told them.

Bill tried to convince Dotty to believe the same. As a good soldier's wife, what choice did she have? She reminded him however, of that affidavit he signed in 1942 consenting to go on active duty. Active duty for Bill had turned out easy for the first couple of years, all stateside with his family, first teaching courses in Chicago for an Army Signal Corps school and then working on vehicle inventions at the Tank Command in Detroit, something he loved to do. "Sorry it didn't last, Dotty," Bill acknowledged to his wife, imagining wistfully she could now hear him at a distance of 5,000 miles.

Bill reminisced on the many times he played soldier for two weeks during the summers at Camp Grayling, Michigan. It had been spit and polish inspections, tenting, maneuvers and war games. Bill graduated from the University of Michigan College of Engineering in 1933 (being elected to Tau Beta Pi Honor Society) and was commissioned through R.O.T.C. He needed the tuition assistance that R.O.T.C. provided and two careers seemed a good idea at the time. He would end up with two pensions he reckoned, one civilian and the other military. He did not envision another world war, however.

Camp Grayling and reserve army life had been nothing like Italy, 1944. Bill was re-thinking things, and particularly whether he wanted to stay in the Army for a full term reserve career. He did not wish to experience what he now experienced ever again.

Bill glanced at the red, white and blue shoulder patch on his officer's blouse hanging on a nearby hook. He had worn this blouse the previous evening for the first time since leaving the States, the occasion being a Christmas party at "the big house," his name for the mansion he now lived in on a temporary basis. The patch bore two stitched letters in the art deco style, "AF," and he carried this blouse today to this room should he need it for extra warmth. "Allied Forces Headquarters" Bill mumbled. "MTOUSA, Mediterranean Theater of Operations United States Army." What a mouthful, he thought.

Most of the other officers and men at the big house wore a similar patriotic-colored shoulder patch only rectangular shaped, slightly tapered at the top, with a large letter "A" and a smaller number "5" on it, signifying U.S. Fifth Army. The background for this patch was the silhouette of a mosque, symbolic of the victorious African campaign. The U.S. Fifth Army had been engaged in continuous combat operations since being formed in early January 1943, and Bill was keenly aware that to many of the officers at the big house this mosque patch, along with sleeve hash marks signified almost two years of very arduous duty. Bill respected these long-term veterans and was careful about what he said in their presence, being mindful of his rookie status as a G.I. overseas. These men served at a time when his command MTOUSA had been "NATOUSA — North African Theater of Operations U.S. Army."

Bill mentally laughed at the length of the upper combat chain of command. Americans Lucien Truscott and Mark Clark, Britain Harold Alexander, Eisenhower, Marshall... and the lowest of these was three stars! Bill's commanding general (MTOUSA himself) was in administrative command with three stars: Lieutenant General Joseph T. McNarney, USA. The other major military leader in the theatre was British General Richard McCreery who commanded the British Eighth Army and reported to Clark.

Bill had been instructed to make his reports to MTOUSA only, that is, he was not to share any of his findings and recommendations with members of the U.S. Fifth Army Transportation Section, his host at the big house. MTOUSA expected an independent evaluation from Bill, also from a Major Cowan who accompanied Bill on his trip north. This circumstance was known to the commanding officer of the U.S. Fifth Army Transportation Section, who had cooperated with the officers from MTOUSA. There was a built-in tension created by this requirement, however, and Bill had to be mindful of it, and also respectful of the seniority of the officers on the U.S. Fifth Army staff. His and Major Cowan's jobs were not to ruffle feathers, but rather report and recommend in the manner instructed.

The Christmas party he had gone to the night before had been inappropriate, Bill believed. There was Army brass dining, drinking, smoking and making merry, couples "dating" and at least one notable member of Congress making the rounds, someone who had stayed behind after the Congressional Committee on Military Affairs had gone home. Bill had been to the war front and seen with his own eyes how G.I.s struggled in horrible conditions. The rear echelon lived well, he saw. It had been a real Saturday night event, with a tinge of glitz and no-holds-barred partying.

Of course none of this could go into his weekly reports.

A blast of cold winter wind buffeted the massive outside window-shutters that were closed snugly. The giant window hung in French door fashion and was covered on the inside by highly-polished hinged wooden doors that were latched shut. For all intents and purposes, Bill felt as if he was sealed inside a cell of a fortress. The room was small, almost nook-like, but had a high ceiling. Bill marveled at the degree of Italian craftsmanship that had gone into the making of the tight-fitting wooden fixtures that sealed the windows. He had seldom seen anything handmade of wood of that high quality before. The same could be said for the cabinetry, table and sole chair in the room. Still, the small chamber could not escape being drafty, even with its tight-fitting window joinery. A heating vent in the floor opened to a larger downstairs room, one with a small fire burning in it; this helped some but not much. The room that he slept in with its own fire was less humid but lacked privacy. Bill had sought out this closet-office to be alone; he needed to spread out his notes, collect his thoughts and prepare his not-to-be-shared report.

As Bill pondered what to write, not too far away nineteen-year-old Specialist 4th Class Sergeant John L. "Jack" King of Bellefontaine, OH, a railroad town of 6,000, thought of the Christmas that his parents and five-year younger brother, Dan, were about to have. Jack missed his family and wished he could be home to celebrate the holidays, as did soldiers everywhere, but Jack was not unhappy. He had been in Italy for six months now and his division, the 91st Infantry, referred to as the Old West "Powder River Division," or variously nicknamed "Pine Tree Division" after its shoulder patch, had participated in the liberation of Rome, Florence and Pisa and even partially breached the Gothic Line at Futa Pass, elevation 3,000'. As a member of this hard-fighting outfit, one of eleven U.S. Fifth Army divisions now facing-off against the Germans, Jack, who had a year of college at the University of Dayton, had been exempted from combat duty due to a happenstance of fate that played to his benefit. While training to become a "dogface rifleman" at Camp Adair, Oregon, the Army checked Jack's service record and discovered that he had taken high school courses in typewriting and shorthand. Without his asking, Jack was assigned to the 91st Division Headquarters Company, promoted to sergeant and placed in charge of two enlisted men. He worked in the adjutant general's office, a heated space with 150 others approximately fifteen miles behind the line, primarily typing up leave and travel orders.

Favorable duty status notwithstanding, wartime Italy had been no vacation. Like everyone else Jack wondered what would happen to him next and he knew there were no assurances. On the positive side, things European had intrigued Jack. He had taken to maintaining a diary, being careful not to write about wartime-prohibited subject matters, but rather recording the names and tidbits about places he stayed at or visited. He purchased his small diary book (entitled "My Life in the Service") likely at a PX and every page contained a motivational quotation such as this: "Every man thinks meanly of himself for not having been a soldier" — *Samuel Johnson*.

As regards the wintertime lull, as year-end approached Jack recorded men being given time off: "Issued leave orders for 375 men to visit Florence," he wrote. "We have been here in Pietramala on Route 65 for a month and one-half," he added, "a winter resort in peacetime." "I hope we can stay [here] during the winter." "If all we do is hold the line maybe I'll learn how to ski."

Jack loved and missed his family, yes, but Italy had opened horizons for this nineteen year-old. Alpine skiing in Dayton had not been an option! Gary Cooper-like in appearance and standing 6' 5", Jack wore a perpetual grin and possessed the optimism of youth.

Shivering, Bill reached for his blouse and slipped it on. Since he wasn't wearing a necktie and his gabardine dress pants, which he left on a hanger in his bunkroom, he was technically out of his "pinks" uniform. This did not concern him, however. The door was closed and no one would see him. Last night had reminded him how comfortable his heavy Army blouse could be. It should be comfortable to wear, he thought — he had paid a pretty price to have it made to order at Hart Schaffner & Marx in Chicago. Bill tried to be a snappy dresser when he could. The same was true for his wife, Dotty. The two made for a strikingly handsome couple; Dotty was ten years younger than Bill, and Bill was proud of that.

His status at the Christmas party had been unusual, Bill reflected. Here he was only a captain, a junior officer, but that small special shoulder patch singled him out. "I see you are from headquarters," someone would invariably say, starting a conversation, and the next question invariably would be, "What are you doing here?"

In the receiving line at the Christmas party Bill stuck close to Major Cowan and let him do most of the talking. Then Bill was introduced to the Congresswoman. "I see you're in the Transportation Corps," she said, focusing on his lapel insignia after spotting his shoulder patch. "Here to review the supply situation, are you?" Bill blushed and nodded affirmatively. "What is your assessment as to why our troops aren't getting what they need?" Grinning defensively, Bill mentioned road conditions due to terrible winter weather and managed to deflect her follow-up questions about "inadequate" planning.

A moment later, moving down the reception line, Bill smiled as he remembered this politician giving a fiery keynote speech at the 1944 Republican National Convention in Chicago. He had heard it on the radio. Roosevelt had chosen to run for a fourth term and the Republicans were spike hot about it. Over the airwaves she vehemently accused the President of mismanaging the war and causing undue American fatalities. To wild cheers she harangued delegates about FDR's turning American democracy into a "dictatorial bumbledom." Later, during the campaign, she went even further and accused Roosevelt of lying to the American people. She argued that he had set up the war on hapless China by furnishing Japan with the oil to fight it, and then invited the attack on Pearl Harbor by precipitously cutting Japan off from the same oil. Bill remembered well her most vitriolic charge: that FDR was "the only American President who ever lied us into a war because he did not have the political courage to lead us into it." The no-holds-barred rhetoric of 1944 had been unprecedented, Bill remembered.

And the Roosevelt camp retaliated with its own cheap shot: "A sharp-tongued glamor girl of forty," they branded this Congresswoman.

The volleys between the Republican "glamor girl" and traditional cigar-smoking southern Democrat "good ol' boys" proved to be something fresh for U.S. politics, and Bill did not know exactly what to make of it. Election day was over but if the conduct of the war in Italy was now to be a continuation of political mud-throwing, then Bill, a Republican himself, had no desire to become either a named or unnamed source. The lady from Congress did have moxie, Bill appreciated — and she was vivacious, even at her "advanced" age. Bill thought of her in her black silk from the night before — unique for a warfront, he knew. The other females at the party, USO girls, WACs, Army nurses and civilian employees, many younger and some quite attractive, did their best at sprucing-up but did not stand a chance against the well-fitting black silk.

Nor for that matter, did they against Clare Boothe Luce's smile, wit, unending laughter and aura of self-confidence.

Bill knew of the politician's circumstances. Prior to becoming elected Luce had been editor of *Vanity Fair* society magazine and the Broadway scriptwriter• who wrote the fabulously successful avant-garde play *The Women*. He knew she was married to one of the most powerful men in America, a die-hard leading Republican contributor, and that she had "stolen" this man, Henry "Harry" Luce from his wife and mother of his two young sons, delightfully scandalizing New York society.

Bill thought again of her rousing convention speech; he had liked it at the time.

Bill believed that she had done nothing wrong in asking him the questions that she did, that in fact these were the same questions he had been sent to ask. He was not at liberty to provide her with information, however, and the subtlety did not escape Bill that she might be the real reason he was here. What the sixteen double-chinned fuddy-duddy male members on the Military Affairs Committee had to say about their inspection visit to the war fronts would probably not get much reported, Bill reckoned — but definitely would in her case. Her husband Harry Luce controlled huge parts of the publishing industry, and the words of his wife would be read.

Bill and Dotty Allison, newlyweds, December 1939

"Luce" was a married name that worked well for her, Bill knew, but he also appreciated that she went by Clare Boothe Luce and never Clare Luce. Using her maiden name sent a message that she was her own person, that she had an identity apart from her husband's.

The wind outside howled.

Bill reflected on what he had recently witnessed in the mountains and knew that the same strong wind now bore down on others who lacked his good fortune to experience only draftiness in a baron's mansion. "I will finish this report," he resolved, again looking at the flickering light bulb, "by candlelight if necessary." "I've got to help those guys," he thought. This, his second weekly report was more of a challenge than the first. Was he running out of ideas? Bill knew that as a lowly captain he was not likely to change the outcome of this war. Still, there had to be *something* he could do to improve living conditions at the front.

Bill's family worried about his being painfully underweight and possibly not physically strong enough to endure what might be asked of him. He promised that he would try to eat heartily and take care of himself. Bill had left Dotty and Davy with his parents in New York State, but expected that by now she and Davy were back in Detroit.

Bill had seen the mid-December 1944 newsreels of Mussolini's "Il Duce" spewing forth vitriolic hatred while rallying his base in Milan. The dictator's reformed *Fascisti* divisions had been trained by Hitler's forces properly this time, and would soon be spilling southwards, hoping not only to destroy the Allied armies but also to kill Italians loyal to the Italian King, who had turned against Mussolini. God, what a mess, Bill thought. It was an Italian bloodlust *vendetta*, a civil war within a world war. Bill had flown north and witnessed from the air a country half-destroyed. How much more destruction would there be before peace came?

What neither Bill nor the American people had seen or read about were the many behind-the-scenes efforts going on: the involvement of religious leaders, industrialists, the neutral Swiss and the secret Allied intelligence communities, the American OSS and British SIS. The censored news outlets did not report on these activities.

As Bill contemplated what to put in his report, Captain John M. Lesesne was grateful for a peaceful Christmas Eve. The 1941 honors graduate of The Citadel had stayed at his command post most of this day. Jerry had been mercifully quiet. With time to reminisce, John looked at the first pages of a small pocket diary that he had started on November 4, 1944, the day before he led his command, Company "B" of 100th Chemical Mortar Battalion up Highway 65 to take its position on the line. John and his platoon leaders had made an inspection trip to the forward areas earlier that day during the daylight hours. On this, the date of a baptism to "firing," as mortar crews referred to it, platoons two and three were inserted on the line. First Platoon remained temporarily behind at what was known as "company rear." Normally a company would have four platoons and four companies would constitute a battalion, but in the case of the 100th Chemical Mortar Battalion the organization was done in threes — Companies "A", "B" and "C" constituted the 100th, with each company initially having three platoons. The intent was to bring the number of platoons up to four per company.

Thinking back to that eventful day, John uttered under his breath: "A month and a half finished." After a pause he asked himself: "How much longer?" wondering when offensive operations might commence. There had been considerable talk and some preparation but so far no orders.

John, who had briefly attended Episcopal seminary prior to joining the Army (but had no intention of going back) made a Christmas Eve prayer of thanks to the Lord that none of his men ("boys" as he called them) had become a casualty. A couple of Purple Hearts had been awarded, yes, but for minor wounds only. John knew that this string of good luck was not the case with the other mortar companies and the infantrymen in the area, or for that matter, even the far off artillerymen who waged daily duels with their enemy counterpart. There had been action since coming up and yes, John himself had experienced close calls and was aware of Germans and Americans killed, but again, no one from Company "B" had been seriously hurt.

And what a relief it was, he admitted to himself that the action now seemed to be tapering off with the onset of winter. John had no reservations about what he was doing and the need to do it; he had wanted to go to West Point but could not do so because of his eyesight. The Citadel, near where he had been raised in Charleston, SC, had been his second choice for a military education. John had volunteered for overseas duty and he wanted to be and was in command. The lives of approximately 155 "boys", the Company "B" strength, were in his care[1] and on top of that another twenty-three attached to his command from the 100th Chemical Mortar Battalion — his ammo detail. These boys looked up to him, at age twenty-four, as the "old man."

Glancing at his diary John read what he wrote about that first day, the date of insertion. He knew censorship rules prohibited soldiers from keeping diaries, but he kept one anyway. If it was not in his pocket, he kept it hidden and locked. John's handwriting was so compact that even if one did chance upon the tiny booklet, reading it would be extremely difficult without eyestrain.

Sunday 5 Nov. 1944 A rather odd experience, moving up to the front
for the first time, me heading a convoy of jeeps, no lights at all, dark as
H — except for gun flashes and searchlights. We had to cross one stretch

of road on which Jerry was placing interdiction fire. I wondered if the boys were scared — they should have been — riding thru the dark, not knowing what they were going into or when they would be shelled.

Mortar work was dangerous, and one knowledgeable on this kind of warfare opined, "The guys who operate them [Ed: the mortars] are at a big disadvantage. Because of the mortar's limited range, they have to work so close to the front that they are a favorite target for snipers..."[2] That said however, belonging to a chemical mortar battalion was not as perilous as being an infantry mortar man or even more dangerous, a *patrolling* infantryman where daily probes to find the enemy resulted in casualties. The winter had given a partial respite for the patrollers, but not much of one.

The U.S. Army history for the 100th Chemical Mortar Battalion reflected that when organized in August 1944, the strength authorized was thirty-nine officers and 556 enlisted men including medical. John had no way of knowing at this time that when the war ended in early May 1945, only five would be killed and five wounded from his battalion.[3] Had this information been available to him, he likely would not have backed off his statement that his "boys" should have been scared on the day they inserted. That drive in the dark, as he indicated, had been eerie.

The range for all classes of U.S. Army mortars was between 200 and 4,500 yards and the longer distance might be extended some depending on the lay of the land. The mainstay of the U.S. heavy mortar arsenal was the 4.2-inch diameter chemical mortar, that weighed 333 lbs. and could deliver high explosive or white phosphorus shells weighing up to twelve lbs. at a maximum rate of fire of five rounds a minute.[4] The 4.2" had a riffled barrel that was unusual for a mortar, and the spinning shells required no stabilizing tailfins. One of John's platoons might operate three to five of these mortars at a time, and a dramatic photograph showing a nighttime firing of one of these behemoths reveals a crew of five, all backs turned away from the muzzle at the moment of detonation. These men bent over as far as possible. A mortar blast in one's face was definitely something to avoid!

The 4.2" could also be used to deliver toxic liquid fillings such as mustard or phosgene gas — the agents that made World War I trench warfare uniquely horrible. John was thankful that gas warfare had not erupted in the present war, at least so far. In case the enemy resorted to poisonous gas, however, John was

aware that the U.S. Army maintained stockpiles of chemical shells near the front
for retaliation.

The other weapon used by mortar battalions was the more portable 81 mm (3.19
inch) M1 Mortar that weighed 130 lbs. and was designed to deliver conventional
rounds, smoke and sixty-second illuminating star shells.[5] Finally, U.S. infantrymen used the M2 Mortar, a 60 mm muzzle-loading tube weighing forty-two lbs.
that could shoot a three pound shell 2,000 yards (a peashooter when compared
to a 4.2"). John never fired these little ones, but he heard them fired in combat.

The shoulder patch the 100th wore was as ugly as it was cleverly vulgar: the
number "14020" appeared with the "100" in gold weave and "4.2" in pink, both
numbers set against an olive background. It was the outside striping, however,
that gave it a masculine identity: a pointy mortar shell thrust upwards nestled
between two balls.

100th Chemical Mortar Battalion sleeve patch

The 100th had been commanded by Major Russell E. McMurray since late
November and John consistently referred to him in his dairy as "Maj. Mac." The
command post for the 100th was at Filigare and would remain there until the
North Apennines campaign commenced in mid-April 1945. John's command
post for Company "B" would move twice during this period, but he did not
know this yet.

Thinking about last summer when he knew little about mortars but had been
on active duty for two and one-half years, John chuckled. Now he was an expert!
Why, he even worked on an invention to improve the 4.2" baseplate that was prone
to shift or even buckle under the heavy repeated recoil of the powerful charges.
His unit would be called into action when the situation required the lobbing in
of these charges at close range and it was impractical to use field artillery, say a
105 mm howitzer for example.

On this Christmas Eve, Captain Lesesne completed his diary entry from the day before: "We reorganized the command post," he started, referring to the winterization of the small room where he and nine others slept. "Set up the stove in the bedroom."

> *It had been snowing lightly all day and… about dark the snow began to fall heavily and it became quite cold. Tonight Pappy and I took supplies to Jimmy's platoon. We couldn't see the moon, but outside everything was quite bright. Under different conditions with a lovely gal such as Miss Jackie Sumner beside me, this would have been a beautiful ride. The snow covered mountains… We made the trip there and back without incident.*

Bill focused on the current military situation, and the reason why he had been sent over. He had been advised before leaving that the U.S. Fifth Army was stalemated before another Nazi-built battle line, this time the "Gothic Line," and the most formidable fortification yet. A defensive system of entrenchments, razor-wire fences and bunkers crisscrossed rolling country and a number of treacherous mountain slopes. In some places this line was miles deep. The Gothic Line snaked across the Northern Italian boot between U.S.-occupied Florence and Nazi-occupied Bologna. U.S. forces fought on the western side of the Italian boot and the British and other allies, the eastern side. The Germans were of course to the north, with the Waffen-SS facing the Americans and the Wehrmacht, the British.

At the Gothic Line in some places the Germans had constructed elaborate dugouts into mountainsides that penetrated into the rock some seventy-five feet. In addition to housing artillery, these dugouts could shelter up to twenty men. Barbed wire in front of the German guns was often twenty-five feet deep, one foot high and placed on any given mountain side at hundred meter intervals — designed to slow an Allied advance while German machine gunners and artillerymen fired.[6]

By the time he arrived fighting would likely be light, Bill was told. The onset of winter would determine that. It was no secret that the Allied master plan called for a huge coordinated final offensive against the Nazis in Italy. First, a few key mountain positions, not specified to Bill, needed to be secured. Then troops had to bring stockpiles of supplies forward and place them in special spots, close enough to access quickly but disbursed widely enough not to reveal a grand strategy. At the same time vehicles needed to be readied and positioned and troops massed. Unseasonable weather could be an obstacle to preparations. The Allied goal was simple and the Nazis knew it: break through the Gothic Line, blow past the German defenders and bottleneck them from retreating over the Alps into the Fatherland. Once out of the mountains, the U.S. and British Armies could finally, after more than a year of frustration, do some downfield running. A stretch of flat lands and good roads lay to the north. The Transportation Section's job was to provide the means for the mass of the U.S. Fifth Army to get there. The Po Valley waited ahead.

Headquarters, Allied Forces, specifically the Transportation Section of MTOUSA offices at the Royal Palace of Caserta near Naples, was a good place to be stationed, Bill appreciated. He looked forward to returning there soon. His immediate superior, Major Renick, seemed like a good person to work for. Bill liked working in the *really* big house, a major European palace, no less!

Bill thought of the Christmas tree he knew would be up and decorated and in a corner of the small Detroit apartment shared by Dotty and Davy. Davy reacted wondrously to Christmas 1943 as a one and one-half year old. "What must Davy be like this Christmas?" Bill asked himself, longing to be with his son to share the joy expressed on his face. Since Davy had arrived he and Dotty had talked frequently about the need for a real home with a big backyard but the war had put their dream on hold.

The last ten days had been perhaps the most stressful of his thirty-six-year life. Bill had inspected the war front and was now back at the headquarters of the U.S. Fifth Army Transportation Section. No one had shot at him, true, but he had seen both civilian and military misery that had shocked and emotionally upset him. And he had never been so cold in his life. He had inspected a plethora of international units in addition to regular U.S. Army divisions, to wit: a large Brazilian Expeditionary Force and South African and Indian forces. One U.S. division he visited was unique in character — the almost all-African-American 92nd Infantry Division, new to the front. Each sector of the Gothic Line had its individual supply challenges. Depots might or might not be convenient to troops in an area depending on the road situation.

Bill had formed preliminary opinions on a few matters that he might recommend to help the supply situation, but was not overly confident of a good result. Still, he would try. He believed that sufficient material supplies were now pouring into Italy at the northern port of Leghorn and that the U.S. Fifth Army

Transportation Section and other units were doing the best they could do in the face of deplorable winter conditions for trucking operations. Larger, more powerful vehicles had been requisition by MTOUSA, but requesting and receiving were different matters. Between the mud, snow, ice, winding mountain roads, dangerous loose rocks, potholes and slickened steep drop-offs, more G.I.s now perished driving trucks than at the hands of the Nazis. If the war front remained quiet for a time, however, the transportation problem would solve itself, Bill believed — in spite of the horrible situation. For the Americans the front line extended a distance of some ninety tortuous miles from a slim coastal plain upwards in an easterly direction to rugged centrally located Monte Grande, where the British were.

In addition to the U.S. Fifth Army Transportation Section, a large separate U.S. Army command known as the Peninsular Base Section ("PBS") provided for the rear area transportation of supplies. PBS's job was to get material from port areas to near where the fighting was. U.S. Fifth Army would then allocate the supplies among its units on the line, based on need and battle planning. PBS had its own fleet of trucks for long haul operations and coordinated truly a team effort: quartermaster, engineer, ordinance, weapons, transportation, medical, signal, petroleum, oil and lubrication components all came under its jurisdiction. The Transportation Corps of course maintained and drove the trucks.

The QMC light truck company — "QMC" for Quartermaster Corps — was the unit to haul in, time and time again, everything from toilet paper to mortar shells. A standard QMC light truck company had forty-eight assigned vehicles.[7] The G.I. nickname for this truck, based on tonnage of payload, was "Deuce and a Half," and it was produced mostly by GMC. This truck, the workhorse of the Army, could travel at forty-five mph and in a pinch could transport approximately two-dozen soldiers, and at the same time tow a heavy gun. Its operational range was 300 miles.

PBS had approximately twice the number of supply carrying vehicles as the U.S. Fifth Army, over two thousand. MTOUSA's job was to ensure that the two commands worked together for the common good. Rail lines could not reach U.S. Fifth Army troops at the mountain front, so trucks, large and small, were essential for the war effort. Ultimately, however, it was the mule that delivered needed provisions from forward supply areas over the most rugged tracts of mountain. All in all, over 10,000 pack animals were used in the Italian campaign.

On average each could carry 220 lbs. Bill laughed at the thought of a descendant of Eeyore the Donkey being the ultimate fighting machine in the day and age of blitzkrieg. Italian mules were different from American mules — they fed off homegrown hay and chopped straw known as tibben, while the American animals ate only grain and hay. At the onset of the campaign only Italian mules were used; this would change.

"What a terrain to pick for a fight," Bill muttered to himself. "Mules." "Gee-haw."

Bill toyed with an idea for a new truck trailer, one that might make transport more efficient and safer for heavy, larger loads, up to and including tanks. Bill was a tinkerer, and using cardboard, glue and bits of sawed-off pencils (the only materials available) he quickly dummied up a working model with multiple moving axles. "I must send this design to the Tank Command," Bill said to himself. "It might be patentable." In submitting this invention proposal, Bill responded to a call that came from the top of his section's chain of command. Bill's chief called "to increase lift capacities of the truck companies by means of truck-tractors, semitrailers and heavy duty trucks capable of carrying eight-ten tons."[8] Bill knew his invention idea would not come into being in time to affect the outcome of the Italian campaign, but maybe it might be of use against the Japanese.

In Naples, Italy, three hundred miles to the south, First Lieutenant Richard E. "Dick" Stroud was desperate to receive a Christmas letter from his wife, Sue. Along with their two-year-old son, Richard, Jr., Sue had moved into her parent's home in Garland, Texas. In her letters their son sometimes went by the endearing familial name "Dickie," but more often than not "Pumpkin." Dick, like Bill, was a recent arrival to Italy and in the employ of MTOUSA only on the Air Forces side. He worked as a supply officer at the 18th Depot Supply Squadron of the Air Service Command, and was frequently on the phone, most often to Pisa in the north and Bari in the south, near where the two U.S. Army Air Forces, the Twelfth and the Fifteenth, operated.[9] A high school chemistry teacher prior to the war, Dick was a few years older than Bill and had been married ten years. The Army had found him, commissioned him and trained him for this new line of work while his wife continued to teach high school and raise Pumpkin.

The 18th Depot was tasked with keeping track of available airplane stocks throughout the MTO and requisitioning deliveries of needed supplies from the United States. When Dick was not on the phone, he was at a Teletype machine placing orders. By the time he arrived, the supply situation from port to port was well in hand, but one always had to think ahead and consider the time factor involved for the delivery of *thousands* of needed parts. Dick knew well what price might be paid in American lives if he or members of his unit failed to process orders timely. Planes wore out from stressful usage or returned shot-up from missions and were repaired and serviced on a twenty-four-hour basis. Supplying two U.S. Army Air Forces was a huge operation. Most of the work Dick did was for the Twelfth — the fighter-bombers that operated over enemy occupied Northern Italy. The office he worked in was staffed with four officers and twenty-two enlisted men, and headed by a captain.

Like Bill, Dick was shocked by what he saw. He witnessed a seriously battle-damaged Naples and a civilian population ravaged by war from the year before. He knew the same sad process was now taking place in Northern Italy. Dick harbored no illusions about the importance of his job. The only thing to do was to win this war as soon as possible and then he could go home.

Anticipating Christmas, Dick wrote to Sue: "There is not much of the spirit in evidence here, but in imagination I can be at home with you wrapping packages, fixing up Pumpkin's things and probably explaining to an astute youngster just what it's all about. Maybe next year, Darling."[10]

In a few weeks Bill would fly back to Caserta where the temperature would be slightly warmer and the pace more routine. He would commit to work long hours there, but also be able to relax somewhat and better savor the cartoons of Bill Mauldin and leisurely read the news reports from *Newsweek* and *Time* magazines and the *Stars and Stripes* newspaper, clipping his favorite items for the file he had started. At the Royal Palace of Caserta he would also catch up on the local poetry competition and maybe even pen a few stanzas himself. Maybe enter a checkers or chess tournament? Most important, he would read and re-read letters from "**H**ome," as Bill usually wrote the word. There was a heated room in the palace where he could do these things after work, a special place for him to be temporarily away from his daily activities involving the war. And as painfully thin as Bill was, being in a heated room served him well.

The incandescent light bulb flickered again, and Bill wondered if the new generator might be going out — again. There was a knock at the door. Bill stood and removed his blouse so he would not be seen wearing it for additional warmth over his work uniform. "Come in," he said.

"Captain Allison," the soldier replied, "You have a letter from home, Sir. It came in with the air pouch from Caserta."

Bill thought as his pulse spiked: "Major Renick, God bless you!" MTOUSA had come through. "Thank you," Bill said to the soldier, grasping the letter. Bill's second report would have to wait a little while longer, but that was OK. He had several more days to complete and mail it in. It would be finished early as Bill's spirits now soared; he had renewed energy for everything, as the letter pipeline from his loved ones had finally begun. This was the boost he needed; the best Christmas present he ever received.

CHAPTER ONE:

A VOYAGE

October–November 1944

21 October 1944

HAMPTON ROADS PORT OF EMBARCATION

It is requested that the necessary orders be issued moving Captain William D. Allison to Camp Patrick Henry, Virginia, so as to arrive during the daylight hours on 6 November 1944.

On Sunday November 12 before embarking Bill made a long distance phone call to Dotty to share what had to have been an emotional and difficult goodbye. During the course of the conversation he uttered to his wife: "Remember our secret, Hon, just as soon as I get there."

Maintaining confidentiality of movement was critically important during World War II. U.S. Army Air Forces supply officer Dick Stroud shipped out from Greensboro, North Carolina for Italy the month before Bill got underway from Virginia, and Dick was ordered not to reveal to anyone the day and hour of his departure ("loose lips sink ships"). Bill was undoubtedly under the same constraint when he phoned Dotty from Hampton Roads. Dick got around the gag rule by "code talking." On the day of his departure he phoned his wife Sue in Garland and told her that his sister Edith had been hospitalized and also the time of day that she was admitted. Sue immediately appreciated that this would be Dick's last phone call to her for the duration of the European war.[11]

How Bill orally communicated his departure information to Dotty is unknown, but surely he did something similar to Stroud. Bill and Dotty's "secret" pertained to the way Bill would identify his port upon arrival.

On the same day Bill mailed a few lines to his parents: "Dear Dad & Mother: Just a note to tell you how much you have always meant to me. Few men have enjoyed as great a privilege. I hope you will do everything in your power to remain well and not overdo. Take care of yourselves and God bless you both. Love, William."

Captain William D. ("Bill") Allison, Transportation Corps, U.S. Army Reserve made the crossing aboard the *USS Monticello*, an Italian flagged passenger ship that had been interned as a war prize by Brazil and subsequently purchased by the United States and converted into a troop carrier. The liner was 650 feet long and displaced 26,000 tons, but more important it could make twenty knots which, when combined with a zigzag course, made it practically impervious to submarine attack. Speed and maneuverability were critical since the ship had been converted to a military transport to carry approximately 7,000 troops (including 200 officers) at a time. Prior to the war, the ship had been the *SS Conte Grande* and had a maximum passenger capacity of 1,700. Armaments had been added at the Philadelphia Naval Shipyard making the *Monticello* an official auxiliary ship of the U.S. Navy — the ship took on one 5" gun, three 3" guns, sixteen 20 mm AA guns and an assortment of machine guns, and (of course) a mandatory coat of grey paint.

Being a commissioned officer, Bill was assigned a stateroom on "B deck" along with three other U.S. Army captains. In his first shipboard letter to Dotty, written on the third day of the voyage from a rear deck (letter No. 8 since seeing her last) he wrote, "I will tell you as much as I can about the trip without violating censorship." Bill was careful not to mention names of fellow officers, the identity of military units, the number of troops being transported and the destination, and equally important — the name of his ship. As Dick Stroud put it in a quaint shipboard letter to his wife: "I'm somewhere, I'm fine and I love you, is about all that is legal just now..."[12]

"We have our own private bath with limited fresh water," Bill wrote Dotty, and he noted that the two double bunk beds came with clean linen, a warm blanket and "even bedspreads." The cabin was positioned amidships, providing for a superior ride, and had a porthole window. There was also an officer's lounge nearby within the ship.

"Since we have an outside stateroom, we have no lights from about six p.m. until seven the next morning," Bill wrote. "One is not even allowed to use a flashlight." Security regulations did not permit evening strolls on a promenade deck;

cigarette lightings or careless door openings might hazard a ship; the interior officer's lounge remained open and was accessible by an interior passageway.

If Bill and his roommates retired to their stateroom after the evening meal, there was nothing for them to do other than talk, take turns looking out of their porthole window or sleep. As regards the nighttime view from his stateroom, Bill noted: "The salt water here is full of tiny phosphorescent bodies which glow in the dark." Describing the water as "luminous," looking aft Bill undoubtedly saw the propeller-churned curved track of the ship caused by the zigzags.

The day before Bill made his train trip to Hampton Roads, in central Italy not too far from Nazi occupied Bologna, Captain Lesesne experienced warfare for the first time. He recorded in his diary about moving his company into position just south of the town of Livergnano (a place the G.I.s referred to as "Liver an' onions" he wrote[13]) and being attached for fire support purposes to the 361st Infantry Regiment of the 91st Infantry Division, which belonged to II Corps. He wrote this about it:

> The first night only 2nd Platoon fired — harassing fire only. The next day we got a call for counterbattery fire on a suspected German mortar position. Second Platoon (Lt. Jay Staley) was out of range; so 3rd Platoon (Lt. Herb Labiliaty) quickly got ready. He had not even registered previously, but the first round was close — fifty yards short. The next was on target. The whole platoon was then brought in to fire five volleys (twenty rounds) of mixed high explosive and white phosphorus [shells]. The Infantry observer reported good coverage of target. A doughboy later told Lt. Bob Oathoff our liaison officer that when a second round of phosphorus came over and hit a haystack, Jerrie's [German soldiers] scattered in all directions. Good firing, Lippy!

The first two days at the front had proved easy for Company "B" but on the third day the Germans shot back. Two sergeants out of John's command post narrowly missed disaster (a "close escape" John termed it) while driving a jeep over a "hot road" during daylight hours. Three Germans shells, seemingly out of nowhere, exploded near these men. This incident explains why jeep convoys traveled at night and without lights, but there was danger in that too — accidents. The greater danger, however, remained German artillery directed with observation.

A German 88 mm anti-tank gun could shoot nine miles but its effective range was a little over two miles. This gun was bad news for the Allies on every front.

On November 9, four days into it, the war became personal for John:

> Jerry shifted fire to the road and then to us. The front part of the house from which I was observing was partly knocked down and offered little protection. One round hit just in front of me, causing bricks to fall on my head and hurting my ears; so I retreated to the rear of the house. The house was shelled on all sides, but none hit us. Probably 88's firing. 170's [Ed: the large German 17cm Kanone] opened on a house 300 yards away and got two direct hits. Burned about four G.I.'s. We couldn't go to their rescue. It was impossible to move during daylight. After dark we sent a man over and he found one of the burned men still alive (he was later removed).

As horrible as this event had to have been for John and everyone else involved (on both sides) John was able to put it behind him and four days later complain: "My female correspondents have really dropped off. Sally Schall my old high school & college gal married, Mary Robertson, old 'steady' and Citadel sponsor engaged, and now lovely Jackie Sumner hasn't written for quite a while."

The third day into the crossing Bill reported: "Sunshine every day and gentle breezes — air so warm no coats are necessary." He seemingly enjoyed the roll of the ship, and spent every moment outside that he could ("crowded" he recorded). He indicated that his two daily meals (7:00 a.m. and 4:30 p.m.) were "large." Summarizing the totality of his circumstances he wrote: "I don't mind it at all. The clear salt air is like June."

Something was beginning to weigh on Bill, however. He very much missed being able to get in touch with members of his family. The reality was that he and Dotty could not communicate with each other, even in a personal emergency. A war was on and ship radio traffic would be limited to military necessity only.

This sunny third day out, November 15, 1944 was a special one for Dotty. Bill wrote:

> "On your twenty-sixth birthday we are many miles apart but very close all other ways."

> "I long for the day when we can make the trip together."

> "… Give Davy a three-way hug."

On the same day, John received good news: "Got a letter from Mother today," he wrote, "saying Mrs. Early had met Mary Robertson in Columbia and Mary had told her she was far from being engaged — Bueno!" That John was ecstatic to learn this news about a former girlfriend reflects upon his high degree of optimism. As special as Mary may have been, however, John most certainly was not committed to her or anyone else. Indeed, the next day he started his diary: "Jackie's Birthday."

On November 17 Bill reported rough seas and "several hard rainstorms." The ship rolled, pitched, pounded and creaked: "When the stern comes up the propeller cuts the surface and sets up a severe vibration," he wrote. Bill did not become seasick, but rather worried about the possibility: "[I] am not the least bit overconfident." In a subsequent communication he stated: "The bunks are provided with handrails for a good reason."

As uncomfortable as Bill may have been from time to time he was nevertheless fortunate to make the crossing on a swift converted ocean liner. Specialist 4th Class Sergeant John L. "Jack" King started his voyage the previous spring from Hampton Roads as a member of the advance party of 91st Infantry Division aboard a Liberty ship.[14] "It had a huge hold," Jack recollected, "full of bunks, and I was lucky to get a top bunk five tiers up." Jack explained his good fortune: "I never got puked on." Liberty ships were turned out cheaply at the incredibly fast rate of three a day by mid-war; needed for victory these ships were known for bathtub-type rides. At a flank speed of only eleven knots, Jack went over as part of a convoy guarded by the U.S. Navy. Like Bill, Jack never got seasick.[15] On April 3 Jack recorded in his dairy: "Now at sea — destination as yet unknown." The name and class of ship that Dick Stroud crossed over on is unknown; John Lesesne, for the Newport News to Oran leg of his trip to Italy, voyaged aboard the USS General A.E. Anderson (AP 111) a troop transport commissioned in 1943 capable of twenty-one knots.

Bill passed the time playing checkers ("Competition is not too tough.") and various card games like bridge and cribbage. In 1939 Bill won a checkers tournament while on a trip to the Bonneville Salt Flats for Hudson Motor Car Company, and he fancied himself to be a superior player. One game Bill did not play on the voyage, but rather watched "in the joint" (his chosen term for the officer's lounge) was poker. "Several officers with the urge spent all their cash and wrote a few checks," he recounted. The lounge had to have been blue with cigarette smoke but there was no alcohol served (U.S. Navy ships retained prohibition).

In the officer's lounge Bill perused an issue of *Life* magazine, November 7, 1944, that came out the day before U.S. elections were held. Practically everything in the magazine was politically charged, and all of it old news: Roosevelt had won a fourth term and that was that.

Life magazine's owner and publisher, Harry Luce (who also owned *Time* and *Fortune* magazines) had failed to get his man, Dewey, elected. The political fight had not gone out of Mr. Luce, however. The Democrats had lost a major political contest to defeat his wife, Clare Boothe Luce, in her bid for reelection (her margin of victory had been a scant 2,000 votes). The Luces resided in affluent Greenwich, Connecticut but their district, the 4th on Long Island Sound and within commuting distance to Manhattan, had many well-heeled liberals. It had been a hard-fought, nasty congressional battle and the winner and her spouse were heartened and energized by the outcome. This contest had gotten personal.

"Clare and Harry" practically worshiped each other but their physical romance had evaporated. Harry viewed his wife as if on a pedestal: a successful writer, politician and style-setter and the most fun, best-looking companion in the world! For her part, Clare held her husband's accomplishments in an equal reverence. She was proud of the fact that Harry's phone calls — even those to his opponents — always got returned. That meant real power.

A paragraph in a *Life* editorial page caught Bill's eye.

> *As Americans in Italy noted with bewilderment, the delegation of technicians Russia sent to the Advisory Council on Italy not only made our delegation seen amateurish; it also surpasses any team that could be put together from all the men now trained as experts in Italian matters in the entire U.S. government.*[16]

Reading this, Bill thought: what is going on in Italy now involves more than just the Nazis. Bill knew that many of the Italian partisans were communist. "Not my problem," Bill said to himself. "At least I hope so," he added.

Bill delved further into the magazine and found a photo of a crooning and very handsome Frank Sinatra who declared he was a common man. "To elect Roosevelt I'm willing to give everything, every cent I earn," Sinatra was quoted as saying. To counterbalance Sinatra, a nearby photo of Shirley Temple appeared. The wholesome-looking sixteen-year-old smiled broadly and wore a bonnet containing small American flags. The caption read: "[Temple] who according to movie bosses should be impartial, got into some trouble by producing a Dewey button."

Bored, Bill put the magazine down and watched a "B" movie double-header. He had seen these movies with Dotty, but there was little else to do. He then wrote home about how time was "passed" noting: "Some officers who play musical instruments have formed a little orchestra and go around entertaining the troops." Another activity was to navigate: "Everyone is trying to plot our course. I will know in a few days how accurate my calculations are."

Dining was "gratis" Bill reported to Dotty, and this was something that surprised him. "There will be no [pay] deductions," he wrote. This would not be the case when he arrived in Italy and participated in the U.S. Army Food Services Program. Dress at dinner aboard *Monticello* was informal; a tie was worn but no blouse.

As Bill approached the warm Straits of Gibraltar, winter was about to set in in the Northern Italian Apennine Mountains, where the warfront was, and Bill appreciated that he would likely experience the blast of cold weather soon enough. He wrote to his wife: "Each passing day brings our reunion one day closer. We each have a big job to do."

Bill spoke about the enlisted men who cleaned his cabin: "I feel sorry for them. They do all the work and the quarters they are crowded into are unbelievably small. The men (some of them) get very dirty and just seem to give up trying to keep clean. Ventilation down in the lower decks is very poor."

As an aside, the army rule was the lower the rank the fewer the privileges. While transiting First Lieutenant Dick Stroud wrote to Sue about his "sharing" experience: "My [state] room is not as large as your bathroom yet there are six beds…"[17]

As Bill was approximately two-thirds through his ocean voyage, in Berne, Switzerland the station chief of the American Office of Strategic Services (OSS), Allen W. Dulles, the man who would become the first civilian director of the CIA, peered out of his office widow and pondered when something big might break. Dulles, who had worked at this post since late 1942, was pleased with the progress the Allies had made in the war but could not understand why the Nazis continued to resist so ferociously when they had no chance at victory. Dulles had hoped to establish contact with a high up Nazi leader who recognized that the war was irretrievably lost and who had the courage to defy Hitler and, most important, the military authority to surrender unconditionally a large number of German troops. So far he had had no luck.

The role of peace seeker was new to Dulles. Heretofore he had done all of the usual things expected of a regional spy chief in a time of war; he had waged psychological and political warfare, sabotage and guerilla activities. America was at the forefront of "techniques of unconventional warfare,"[18] and Dulles managed a principal station in the chain of OSS stations set up across Europe. If killing needed to be done away from the battlefront, Dulles was up to the task of arranging for it, but he would not go off half-cocked as a maverick operator. He was in regular communication with the OSS station at Caserta, Italy and also his boss in Washington, D.C., the World War I military hero and now director of the OSS, William J. "Wild Bill" Donovan.

Dulles' preferred method for disposing of a German double agent was to give the man his first and final assignment in France. The resistance there had no compunction about carrying out a Dulles execution directive.[19] With the liberation of France the previous summer, however, Dulles now had to rely on Italian partisans to do his bidding, and they, many being anti-American leftists, were more challenging to deal with.

In the World War II spy game Dulles worked alongside of, learned from, and was occasionally aggravatingly at odds with his British counterparts at MI6. It was the British who first urged the United States before it entered the war to establish a professional spy agency along the lines of what they themselves were doing. Two British naval intelligence service officers, Admiral John Godfrey and his aide, Lt. Commander Ian Fleming met with President Roosevelt in the Oval Office in early 1941 to discuss the compelling need to do this in order to counter the threat posed by the Nazi *Abwehr* and the Imperial Japanese Intelligence Service.[20]

A child prodigy from a prominent family and educated at Princeton, Dulles entered the diplomatic service in 1916, following the public-spirited tradition of a grandfather who had been U.S. Secretary of State for eight months under Republican President Benjamin Harrison (who failed at reelection). Serving in Europe as a young man, Dulles became well-traveled and wise to the ways of the world. He obtained a law degree from George Washington University in 1926 and became a partner at the prestigious Wall Street law firm of Sullivan and Cromwell; he was a writer with two books to his credit (the first book written at age eight about the Boer War was reviewed by the *New York Times*[21]). He reentered government service in 1942.

While overseas, Dulles missed the company of his wife of twenty-five years, Clover, and their three children, but at the same time very much enjoyed being back at his old haunts (and habits). The truth was Dulles and his wife had had a challenging marital relationship that they somehow managed to hold together, with little credit going to Dulles the husband. As a bride, there had been none prettier than Clover Todd Dulles, but Dulles was unable to contain his wanderlust. He and Clover argued heatedly over his many infidelities, and Dulles did not attempt denial. Dulles won these exchanges simply by shutting his wife out; after a period of cold silence Clover would cave.

Back in Europe, Dulles appreciated and took double advantage of the special freedoms offered by his incognito profession. He could be absent for short, but long enough, periods of time to do what he enjoyed doing and no one would question his activities or whereabouts. His late father, a renowned theologian, Yale educated Presbyterian pastor, and a leading American seminarian would not have approved of his son's behavior.[22] His older brother, John Foster (who would become U.S. Secretary of State at the same time Allen directed the CIA) was cut from a different cloth — he was prim and proper and scrupulously moral. Allen role-played the typical younger brother "going my own course," cad-but-well-liked gentleman pattern to perfection. He was lively, thin, handsome ("ruddy looking") witty, engaging and forever eastern preppy at all passages of adulthood. As an additional plus for his chosen undercover lifestyle, the OSS had a reputation for "*Oh… So… Social*," owing to a very generous (and almost impossible to account for) government monetary allowance.[23]

The family money came from his mother's side.

Dulles enjoyed his espionage work and was generally good at it — but not always. In early 1944 he predicted the Nazis were "near collapse" and that D-day would be an easy landing for the Allies. On the productive side, however, he located the town and plant where Nazi vengeance weapons were being manufactured, Peenemünde, and this intelligence enabled an Allied bombing raid that set V-1 and V-2 rocket production back for a month or more. Dulles also ran agents deep inside Germany who obtained and delivered Nazi documents assessing the effectiveness of Allied air attacks; he learned of and advised that *Operation Valkyrie* was coming — the July 1944 attempted assassination of Hitler.[24] One of the plotters had managed to communicate with him and inquired: if the scheme succeeded would the Allies perhaps reconsider their "unconditional surrender" policy agreed upon the previous year at the Casablanca Conference? With direction from the top Dulles reportedly issued a sharp-tonged response: "Unconditionally, no."

In World War II, neutral Switzerland was like Canada had been during the American Civil War: a place where intriguers, spies and operatives from both sides continuously plotted and schemed, a country where the individual or individuals sitting at a nearby restaurant table might well be the enemy. If a contact was made through the nearby American Embassy, Dulles knew that the matter would be referred to him for handling. The Gestapo watched the U.S. Embassy too closely for it possibly to be secure. The Gestapo knew who Dulles was and what kind of work he did (as Dulles knew the same about his enemy counterpart in Switzerland) but the rules of neutrality were generally respected.

One thing that Allen Dulles believed strongly in, and he believed it early on, was that America had two enemies to confront, fascism and communism. Indeed, when the unconditional surrender policy was being contemplated for approval at Casablanca, Dulles had reservations about the wisdom of it as he felt the German people, if given the ability to negotiate some terms, might be relied upon to fight enemy number two. Dulles did not back away from punishing Nazi war criminals; he argued this had to done but only on the basis of due process where innocent Germans would be protected. He put forth his views on this subject in a letter to Donovan dated December 6, 1942 that contained this:

> *There is a widespread apprehension that we in America may be too distant and the English too weak to prevent Soviet Russia from taking advantage of the temporary social chaos which is likely to follow our victory over Germany and imposing its own type of domination on Europe.*[25]

Dulles slowly paced his office with his hands clasped behind his back, pipe in mouth, pondering. Soon it would be martini time, he reflected, looking forward to it, and following that time to decide what scrumptious menu items to select. A war was on, but it was still good to have all the comforts that Berne provided.

"Gout be damned!" Dulles explained under his breath; despite his doctor's orders, tonight he would drink and eat his rich fill.

—⁀ᴍ—

By day #8 Bill was sincerely fed up. He complained: "It's increasingly hard to kill time." He reported on the mundane things he did that day just to make time pass: "... polished two pairs of shoes, got clean bed linen and made up my bunk, went to the PX and got two candy bars" [Ed: by this juncture Bill felt he needed more than two meals a day]. He took a cold shower "... when the water was turned on at noon," and concluded: "And so the day drags on." Additionally Bill's ego had been deflated. "Played checkers last night and found I have much to learn..." he lamented, "... an expert defeated me easily."

On November 21, disgusted, Bill wrote: "More water, more water, more water." This was followed by: "We don't hear much news. Nearly every day a bulletin is issued, carefully edited for military consumption. I miss the news broadcasts."

As an aside, the daily troop-transport news bulletins were not the only "edited" publications at the time. Newsmagazines routinely carried the notice: "All material which in the opinion of the editors involves military security has been submitted to competent military or naval authority for review as to security."[26] Undoubtedly the radio broadcasts that Bill thought were more forthcoming were in fact more revealing, but also subject to the same subjective self-censoring wartime prior restraint on free speech. It was all a matter of degree, with NBC and CBS winning out (but only slightly) over the U.S. Army writers. Where a reporter was supposed to draw the line could be a difficult issue to determine.

On the day Bill grumbled about too much water, November 21, John Lesesne complained to his diary about the lack of a commodity he knew he needed to keep the Germans at a distance: "Nothing much doing today," he wrote. "No ammo." He would make similar complaints on November 24 and 26, especially noting on the latter date: "Lots of artillery firing on both sides early this morning, but we didn't fire for lack of ammo." John recorded that he spent that day working on his "baseplate gadget," which he tried out unsuccessfully two days later: "Stayed in place, but shattered," he wrote. " '1 / 4'' armor plate — I'll try again..."

John contemplated recommending Private DeLallo, a radio operator with Second Platoon (Lt. Jay Staley) for the Silver Star medal. The full story of what

DeLallo had done on the night of November 15 had filtered in from various sources, and the private was no doubt a hero. In the darkness two German soldiers demanded the surrender of the platoon observation post at Gneppe, stating that the post was surrounded. DeLallo had the presence without being ordered to immediately smash his radio. Two American soldiers went "out with the Jerries, to talk over the situation," John wrote ("I imagine to see their C.O." he opined) and were never seen again. It was what DeLallo did next that was brave. He went outside and re-established the hardwire link that the Germans had cut. "He fixed a communications line when the infantry boys wouldn't do it," John recorded in his diary. "He had two riflemen to cover him, but one went over the hill."

The fact that a "dogface" infantryman skedaddled while this communications man stayed and performed a critical task had to have been a source of pride for John. There existed a hierarchy of risk within the fighting forces of the U.S. Fifth Army and the combat infantry understandably let everybody know about it. In 1999 former infantry staff sergeant Leon Weckstein (who served with the 363rd Infantry Regiment an outfit John's mortar company would be called upon to support) wrote a compelling account of his combat experiences entitled, *Through My Eyes: 91st Infantry Division in the Italian Campaign.* He observed: "When there finally was time to tally the Fifth Army losses after the war was over, they found that of the 3,000 men originally in my regiment, 1,564 men had been wounded and 535 killed in action. Of my own small section of men — the ten I started out with — most of them were lost."[27] Weckstein served with the 1st Battalion Combat Team that was commanded by Lieutenant Colonel Ralph N. Woods.[28]

John received the phone call at 11:00 p.m. that night (when he was just about asleep) from Colonel Reynolds, the commanding officer of Red Battalion, to prepare for a firing on S. Ansano where it was thought the Germans had gone. "Jerry pulled a fast one on us," John noted. "We knew they wanted prisoners badly — just as we did."[29]

In Washington D.C. on November 21, a three-star general officer in the U.S. Army heard plenty of very specific news at a morning Pentagon briefing. Lieutenant General Lucien K. Truscott, Jr., had been asked to attend the briefing by U.S. Army Chief of Staff General George C. Marshall. "It was intensely interesting,"

recollected Truscott in his memoirs, *Command Missions*, "learning concisely, and in detail the military deployment of our forces in all parts of the world." Truscott had been granted a short period of home leave to be with his wife and family and wondered why he had been summoned to Washington. He had been aware that the senior ranks of the British military needed to be reshuffled due to the recent passing of a field marshal in Washington D.C., but he had no idea that this would personally impact him.

After the briefing, Marshall came to the point: "How do you feel about going back to Italy?" he asked. Truscott, taken by surprise, hemmed and hawed a bit before responding. He replied to Marshall that if given a choice he would prefer to remain in France, only to learn that his response was not what the Chief of Staff desired to hear.[30]

Bill wrote Dotty the following day: "I read the book *A Tree Grows in Brooklyn* and enjoyed it very much. It helped pass some time."

On a side note, when Dotty received this letter a month later she was nonplussed. She mailed it to Bill's mother with an acerbic note attached. "I had the book Bill mentions here for three months and told him all about it," she wailed, "and he doesn't even remember!"

An "abandon ship" drill was conducted and Bill wrote about being crowded into a mess hall: "The passengers are corralled [here] while the crew prepares everything on the outside." He added, quaintly: "Sure hope the practice will remain practice." That evening Bill attended entertainment put on by the USO: "It was fairly good but the room was extremely hot." The officer's lounge, or "the joint" was growing old to Bill no matter what amusement might be held there.

Bill became even more irritable and one of his roommates got on his nerves. "[He] practically lives here," he bemoaned, referring to the small, shared stateroom. "Everyone anxious to get some place."

Complain as he might, Bill often ended his letters to Dotty on a positive note usually pointing to a good, shared future. One example was: "One of the men last night said his ambition was to find a huge, very ornate soup tureen and send it home, the object being to have a large bowl of soup on Sunday evenings. He said he had experienced that in Europe once and had always been trying to find one since. He said it just radiated warmth & comfort. Would you like that?"

As the *Monticello* snaked its way towards land, Captain John Lesesne settled further into the daily routine of being a commanding officer of a chemical mortar company. His command post was located in the little town of La Guarda that was approximately seven miles down the road from enemy-held Pianoro. He wrote about it: "One living room and bedroom for the ten of us. A fireplace makes the living room quite cozy. We have a radio and are quite comfortable here — despite the fact that Jerry can see our house."[31]

Two of John's platoons were deployed at "positions" on the line in the country-side while the third was at "company rear" where there was shelter and warmth. A rotation schedule had been set up so each platoon would get a period of rest in the rear area. "The men of both platoons [at the front] will be in the open," John wrote, "in foxholes & under shelter halves and the weather is chilly. Wish they could be in houses." A shelter half is a pup tent.

An important part of John's job was to find good defensive positions for his platoons and also observation posts, or "O.P.s" in the vicinity that could spot enemy activity in the area. John and his mortar men/observers had plenty of U.S. help when looking for the enemy. The area infantry commander was in frequent communication with Company "B" and directed fire support missions based upon radio requests made by platoons or squads who patrolled the area in front.

The nine "boys" who lived with John were enlisted communications special-ists who crawled nightly on their hands and knees to put down or string up wire connecting O.P.s to various headquarters — platoon, company, battalion and regimental. Wires often needed replacement due to enemy shellfire and the labor to do this was continuous, dangerous, exhausting and often performed during severe weather conditions. To John's thinking, these young men were heroes.

Thus far John and Company "B" had had quite a November. John and a com-panion survived a serious nighttime jeep accident: "We came to a fork in road and didn't see it," John wrote.[32] First Lieutenant Jay Staley's 2nd Platoon achieved a white phosphorus firing success: "Hell of a thing to be elated at having killed several men," John recorded.[33] His men Patton & Schmidt survived a late after-noon strafing run. "A Jerry plane on way up from company rear."[34] John and another soldier named Key had desperately jumped into the same foxhole during an artillery barrage.

About this last, John joked: "Split my trousers trying it. Somebody had taken a crap in this, but it didn't stop Key — he hopped in anyway and threw it out. Key said he thinks I split my trousers on purpose."[35]

By mid-November Company "B" was up to full strength with four platoons. John himself went out on reconnaissance and used maps and aerial photographs to search out new platoon positions, invariably pressing a bit forward each time. It was all in a day's work; by a couple of weeks and with guidance from an infantry commander John had become an old hand. His company had fired upon targets in Caravetta, C. Nuova, Orta Nova, Zula, Brenta and S. Ansano.

At Brenta a German machine gun nest killed a U.S. infantry soldier on patrol; the request came in from the 361st for white phosphorus shells, a fierce burning incendiary that ignited clothing. John tasked Jay's platoon for this job, but there was a forty-five minute delay encountered due to "... shifting mortar baseplates in the dark, rain and mud." John wrote in his diary, "I was very much afraid that our tardiness may have caused casualties." To his relief, he learned the following morning that this was not the case; that the mission succeeded.[36]

War is brutal. That German machine gun crew undoubtedly quickly sensed it had been "ringed" by the buddies of the U.S. infantrymen who it killed and that it would be suicide to attempt surrender. When these machine gunners heard the unmistakable sound of mortars going off forty-five minutes later, they knew that in a short moment — the time required for a parabolic arc in the sky to be completed — they would be incinerated.

Both sides used phosphorus and often. American combat infantryman Leon Weckstein described the horror: "... the rain of white-hot particles, that, having once entered the skin, didn't stop burning for many minutes as they smoldered and singed their way deep into the flesh."[37]

John now knew that a good position for a mortar platoon was on a ledge on the reverse slope of a mountain. The enemy could not observe such a position from the ground, fast moving artillery shells would fly harmlessly overhead and enemy mortars on the other side of the mountain, if located at a lower altitude, might have difficulty obtaining the range required for shooting back. Having an "O.P." on top of the mountain helped matters — it made it difficult for the enemy to sneak-up. John recorded getting a hit on top of a house at the very long distance of 4,700 yards;[38] on another occasion he spotted "...the flash of a Kraut gun behind a hill ..."[39] and was quickly able register on it and fire off four rounds.

On November 19 John learned from the 100th Chemical Mortar Battalion Headquarters that Company "B" would be temporarily attached to the 34th Infantry Division just east of the 91st. Such a reassignment was routine and John recorded in his diary: "We will probably remain here [Ed: not relocate] which suits us fine." The 34th was one of the longest serving in the MTO, having first experienced combat in French Algeria during early November 1942.

—ᴍ—

For Bill Allison on the eleventh day out there was this: "It is a beautiful day here. I am sitting on deck watching the rugged shoreline." The *Monticello* passed through the Straits of Gibraltar.

23 Nov 1944 2:00 p.m.
Letter No. 13

Dear Dotty:

I grow a little awestruck when I think of all the famous people who have sailed over these waters." The sea is very calm…. It is so wonderful to know that those you love are waiting for the day of your return. It gives an objective to living.

"We are celebrating today by having three meals… "It feels wonderful to have a full stomach at mid day."

A celebration of sorts that afternoon was held on an aft deck. "The ship's orchestra played before the boxing started," Bill wrote. "The bouts are Army versus Navy. From the cheering the Army is doing OK or maybe it is because more soldiers than sailors are watching."

There were no U-boats operating in the Mediterranean at this stage in the war, but the Allies could not be sure of this, and all waters had to be considered dangerous. Indeed, when Jack King cleared the Straits earlier in the year his slow-moving convoy was attacked at night by German E-boats. "They were shooting torpedoes," Jack said. "We were ordered up on deck and to put on our life preservers," he continued. "We stood for three or four hours while the Navy swept the area." The E-boat, 115 feet long, had a range of 700 nautical miles and was capable of bursts of speed up to forty-eight knots. These attackers had come from Nazi-occupied Southern France and obviously knew that the convoy was on the way and when it would transit the Straits, a confined area. Fortunately for the Americans that night no torpedoes hit. "I heard some shooting," Jack said, "in the distance but never saw any flames." Jack thought that maybe two, possibly three boats were involved.

As an aside, the portion of Jack's transit from the U.S. to Gibraltar, although uneventful, could have been otherwise. Three Liberty ships on the same route were sunk during April 1944.[40]

Another anecdotal episode relating to Jack's passage to Italy is worth recounting as it shows how the U.S. Army treated casualty reporting in World War II. Jack said that during the entirety of war only one member of 91st Division Headquarters Company was killed and it happened on the way over in Algeria when the 91st stopped at Oran for a short period of amphibious training.[41] "He was a tech sergeant in charge of a number of people and he went for a walk along the beach and was killed by a landmine," Jack recounted. Asked if he had attended the man's funeral, Jack responded, "No. I don't think they [Ed: the 91st command authority] even announced it to the troops." Today this would not happen.

It was a positive thing for Bill and his fellow passengers that all wartime safety rules had been enforced aboard *Monticello*, e.g., securing the weather decks at nightfall, darkening ship, zigzagging, life boat drills and the like. At approximately 6:00 p.m. on Christmas Eve, 1944 the *SS Léopoldville*, a Belgium passenger liner converted into a troop carrier, while in route to Cherbourg from Southampton and carrying over 2,000 American servicemen on their way to join in the Battle of the Bulge was torpedoed. The ship sank slowly by the stern and rescue operations were impeded by high seas. Seven hundred and sixty-three G.I.s perished. At the time the torpedo struck approximately 200 seasick U.S. soldiers sang Christmas carols on deck, desperate to avoid the stench of vomit below.[42] The attack happened close to port and wartime precautions had been loosened due to the heavy seas; press censors hushed the details of the disaster.

Owing to its continuous turning the *Monticello* made slow progress across the Mediterranean despite its continued flank rate of speed. As Bill's transport neared its port destination, nine mule ships moved from the Indian Ocean towards the U.S. east coast. Ultimately these ships would arrive in Italy; thousands of animals had been requisitioned from the United States by MTOUSA to help the serious supply problem at the mountainous front.[43]

—᠊ᦙ᠊—

In Washington D.C. members of the of the House of Representatives Committee on Military Affairs, consisting of sixteen men and one women, Representative

Clare Boothe Luce, boarded an airplane that would take them first to England and then to all the battle fronts of western Europe. This was a first of a kind war inspection by members of a Congressional committee, and there was some skepticism expressed by the American public as to whether the cost of the trip constituted a good use of taxpayer money. The trip promised good political theater, however: there would be strong conflicting opinions to come from it. The public appetite for such stuff would be quenched.

The Committee was scheduled to meet first in the ETO with Eisenhower, Bradley, Patton, Spaatz and second with Mark Clark in the MTO.[44] As regards Italy, a charge had been made in Congress that the war there had been mismanaged; that it was a *forgotten front* and as such the U.S. soldiers there suffered needlessly. Many eyes and ears of the nation would be on the Committee's last scheduled inspection visit, and most particularly the reaction that would emanate from the strong-willed, popular, outspoken and curvaceous Republican Representative from Connecticut. Luce embodied a new wave in American national politics, and she was by far *the* most interesting Committee representative to report on, her junior status as a member notwithstanding.

—⁂—

During the early morning semi-dark hours of November 25, 1944, four days after General Marshall informed General Truscott that he was going to Italy, General Mark Clark was awakened by a knock on the door of his small sleeping van at his command post at Futa Pass. A British signal officer had a message for Clark from the Prime Minister. "It gives me the greatest pleasure," Churchill wrote Clark, "to tell you that the President and his military advisers regard it as a compliment that His Majesty's Government should wish to have you command the Fifteenth Group of Armies under General Alexander who becomes supreme commander owing to…" Clark stopped reading as his heart joyfully skipped a beat. He was being given double the responsibility! For the first time Clark would be in overall charge of not only the U.S. Fifth Army but also the British Eighth Army, representing the whole of the Italian front! The unexpected death of Field Marshal Sir John Dill in Washington D.C., the British representative on the Combined Chiefs of Staff, had resulted in his replacement being selected from the British high command in the Mediterranean. This in turn opened the door for Alexander and Clark to each move up a notch. Clark's counterpart at the British Eighth Army, General McCreery would now report to him.

In his haste Clark raced down the Prime Minister's letter until he came to the part where Churchill announced that General Lucien Truscott had been released by U.S. authorities from duty in France at the request of Great Britain and would become commanding general, U.S. Fifth Army. About Truscott's appointment, the Prime Minister noted to Clark: "I expect this will be agreeable to you and General Alexander specially desires it."[45]

Nine months earlier in a crisis situation Clark made Truscott a corps commander and put him in charge of the stalled Anzio beachhead. The landing there had not gone well and Truscott had been called in to replace a sacked commander. At the time Clark characterized Truscott, based upon his service in Africa and Sicily as "most outstanding… quiet, competent and courageous," someone who "… inspired confidence in all with whom he came in contact."[46] Then in the summer of 1944 after Truscott broke out of Anzio and the U.S. Fifth Army liberated Rome, Eisenhower tapped Truscott for duty in the upcoming invasion of Southern France.

Upon re-reading Churchill's letter Clark now focused on the words pertaining to Truscott's selection: "… Alexander specially desires it."

Clark thought of a slang expression in play at the time that he had grown fond of using: "A rooster one day and a feather-duster the next." [47] It was used to describe someone who wavered between confidence and uncertainty. He knew from his previous experience with Truscott that this general officer was no feather-duster.

—〰—

Thanksgiving Day 1944 passed for the protagonists of this story. Jack's diary makes no mention of the holiday but rather records that near this time frame he purchased presents — earrings for his mother and a cameo ring for his brother, Dan. The motivational quotation printed at the bottom of his G.I. diary for the holiday reads like like a Chinese fortune cookie: "He who is not prepared today, will be less so tomorrow" — *Ovid*.

Dick's Thanksgiving letter (surely he wrote one) does not survive. Bill reported his wristwatch being set four and one-half hours ahead on the ship and knowing that at the time he wrote his letter Dotty would be "getting ready for Thanksgiving dinner at the Wingerts." John recorded this: "We (the nine men & I) had just gotten up and I was putting some toast over the fire when a shell knocked our chimney down." His men asked why Jerry had waited so long since their house was in clear view and John replied, "Thanksgiving." A prayer of gratitude for no one becoming a casualty undoubtedly followed.

The USS Monticello made port Naples on November 26, having crossed 4,000 nautical miles of ocean. For this fourteen-day passage, it made 286 nautical miles per day, equating to twelve knots per hour, port to port. By comparison, the liberty ship Jack King rode on, also likely in a zigzag pattern only in convoy, traveled 3,500 nautical miles to Oran, Algeria over a period of 19 days making for eight knots per hour.

—m—

At the time Bill arrived in late November 1944 a practically all African-American infantry division, the 92nd, greatly expanded its manpower base with the arrival of three new untried combat regiments. Proceeding to an area known as Serchio Valley that abutted the Ligurian Sea on the Mediterranean side of the Italian boot, these regiments took up positions in the mountains north of the valley in what had been a relatively quiet section of the front.[48] Awaiting the arrival of these regiments on the line was the veteran African-American 370th Infantry Regiment of the 92nd that had served in Italy since August 1944 and acquitted itself with distinction at the Arno River crossing.

Something novel was in the making: for the first time in U.S. history an almost all African-American combat infantry division, some 15,000-plus men strong, would fight as a cohesive unit. The 92nd went by the nickname "Buffalo Soldiers," a holdover from African-American cavalry days of the American West. The 92nd would fight a racist enemy, as was done by African-Americans in the Civil War, only now on a much larger scale. The manpower influx was part of a build-up to replace troops taken out of Italy for the invasion of Southern France. Also arriving at the same time was the 25,000 men-strong Brazilian Expeditionary Force, to be positioned inland not far from the 92nd.

Lieutenant Wade McCree, an African-American who served with the 92nd, observed in later life: "Politically, you could not leave negroes home when white boys were going to war." Early in the war the U.S. Army sent scores of thousands of African-Americans soldiers overseas, but only a small number were committed to combat. The vast majority of black soldiers were employed as dockworkers, truck drivers or mess cooks, and the mainstream U.S. press had given these G.I.s so little recognition for their contribution to the war effort that the term "invisible soldier" came into usage by African-Americans. This was about to change with them taking on a full and important combat role.

On the movement north into the mountains, these three African-American regiments passed through or near the medieval village of Lucca (that had been liberated by the 370th) and also the charming historic town of Barga located in the middle of the valley. As tranquil as these environs may have been, the Buffalo Soldiers were on edge even more than one might expect for those approaching a combat zone for the first time.

The last of these infantry regiments to arrive in the area, the 366th, had been greeted in an unexpected manner. Major General Edward M. Almond, a Virginia Military Institute graduate and son of the Old Dominion State, brother-in-law to Army Chief of Staff George Marshall, and Commanding General, 92nd Infantry Division, welcomed this regiment with the words: "I did not send for you. Your Negro newspapers, Negro politicians, and white friends have insisted on your seeing combat and I shall see that you get combat and your share of casualties."[49]

The euphoria over his selection for oversight command of the U.S. Fifth Army and British Eighth Army soon settled, and General Mark Clark was back at planning where and how to smash the Gothic Line and bring the war in Italy to a successful conclusion. Clark favored an attack in force up central Highway 65 to take the town of Pianoro that had been 99% destroyed by recent bombings and combat, but only partly liberated. Clark believed that the Germans would not be expecting an all-out go-for-broke frontal attack, and that if Pianoro could be quickly seized, then Bologna and the entire Po Valley would fall. Clark put out the word to prepare for the assault, and the commanding officer of Company "B" recorded in his diary: "[I] went down to company rear and thence to battalion. Big push coming soon."[50]

Upon arrival in Naples Bill used an agreed upon "letter code" to confirm his location:

Can the reader break Bill's code?*

---

* *Answer:* Start with the first letter of the last paragraph and then the first letter of the next to last paragraph, and move one more up to spell "NAP." "Another officer did it smarter than me," Bill related. "He used onionskin airmail stationery specially pre-cut to fit over a small map of Europe, a map that he and his wife both possessed. He'd put a pinhole in his letter to denote his location, and his wife knew exactly where he was throughout the war."

CHAPTER TWO:
A WAR PRIMER
BEFORE BILL'S ARRIVAL

WHEN NAZI GERMANY invaded Poland on September 1, 1939 starting World War II, Italy chose to watch from the sidelines. As a member of the Axis Powers, Italy could have and probably should have come to the defense of its ally, Germany, when Britain and France declared war on it. Instead, Benito Mussolini and his principal military advisers, Marshals Pietro Badoglio and Italo Balbo (of trend-setting "Balbo beard" fame — the standalone mustache atop a modified goatee), watched as Hitler quickly gobbled up the part of Poland he wanted. Then Italy and the rest of the world waited through an unsettling winter of military inactivity called the "phony war." For years Mussolini had boisterously extolled the natural right and even moral obligation of Italy to reclaim its Roman Empire through aggression if necessary, but when it came down to actually attempting to do so (much beyond Ethiopia that is) Il Duce was reticent to confront *alone* the real power in the Mediterranean: Great Britain.

In May 1940 the successful German blitzkrieg through Belgium into France enabled the Germans to flank the British Expeditionary Force, thus separating it from the French Army and pinning it to the seashore. Following this military event, Mussolini thought he saw opportunity for Italian conquest.

Italy declared war against both France and Great Britain on June 10, 1940 — shortly after the British evacuated its forces in disarray from Dunkirk (leaving behind all heavy equipment) — and on the same day the French government abandoned Paris as its capital. Advised by Badoglio and Balbo that Italy was ill prepared to enter the war, the Italian dictator Mussolini scoffed: "I only need a few thousand dead so that I can sit at the peace conference as a man who has fought."[51]

A five-day shooting war between Italy and France started June 20 and it did in fact end in a negotiated armistice, brokered by Hitler as Mussolini had hoped. Although Italian troops performed poorly in the mini-war, Mussolini was awarded a small occupation zone in Southern France, permission to occupy the island of Corsica and given other minor concessions. For Hitler there was a return gift: German troops were permitted to deploy inside Italy as a wartime "ally." Italian sovereignty was compromised, but this did not get noticed much in the euphoria over "defeating" France.

There was widespread international condemnation for what Italy had done with perhaps the sharpest words booming from across the Atlantic. Viewing Mussolini's bald-faced treachery, Franklin Roosevelt spoke for the American people when he called out the leader of Italy as a thug and murderer: "The hand that held the dagger has stuck it into the back of its neighbor."[52]

Italo Balbo, age forty-four, a charter-member Black Shirt and world-renowned transatlantic aviator, who served as Italy's Marshal of the Air Force and Governor General of Libya was killed at Tobruk on June 28, 1940 by Italian anti-aircraft gunners who mistook his airplane as enemy. This event is arguably significant to history for Balbo was an Italian World War I military hero (on the Allied side) and one who early on expressed concerns to Mussolini over his alliance with Nazi Germany. Balbo was someone who might have counseled against what was next being contemplated by Mussolini for Italy.

In regard to Italy's last minute hasty invasion of France, it is probably not an exaggeration to state that not often in the history of armed conflict had so little been gained for putting so much at risk. Because of Dunkirk, Mussolini assumed that the British Empire was done, finished. Counseled by Marshal Badoglio (who had served Mussolini fifteen years as Supreme Chief of the Italian General Staff) and unconcerned with international reaction, Mussolini did something that Bill would later write about: "[He] went crazy in the head." After years of providing stable, albeit non-democratic government, doing many beneficial public works, weathering the worldwide Great Depression and achieving the almost impossible — making Italian trains run on time — Il Duce (undoubtedly to show off to Hitler) invaded Greece.

From its onset on October 19, 1940 this Italian military aggression was a disaster, and it resulted in the Nazis attacking Greece in April 1941 to preclude an Italian rout. The Nazis defeated the Greek army, yes, but the Greeks went down with pride. Before Stalingrad and D-Day it was the Greeks who showed the world how to stand up against fascist military aggression. The little country that brought forth democracy in the world fought bravely to defend its sovereignty. The poor performance of the Italian Army in this campaign forced Badoglio to resign his office in December 1940. Unfortunately for the Italian people, however, this would not be Badoglio's last service to King and country. Badoglio was a well-connected hanger-on, and he knew the teachings of the book *The Prince* by Machiavelli.

Great Britain did not hold back. The Italian dictator had misjudged the resolve of this major power, and had not paid sufficient attention to the capabilities of the aircraft carrier and seaborne radar. The British Royal Navy made short work of the major Italian fleet, or *Regia Marina,* in two decisive engagements. On November 11, 1940 torpedo bombers from the aircraft carrier *HMS Illustrious* attacked anchored Italian warships at Taranto seriously damaging two battle-ships and sinking a third. Four months later off the coast of Greece, acting on cypher intelligence and using radar (which the Italian navy lacked), during a night engagement the British substantially annihilated the remaining portion of the Italian surface fleet at the Battle of Matapan — the Italians were defeated to the point that the *Regia Marina* would never sally forth again.

Great Britain, with firm posts at Gibraltar, Malta and the Suez Canal, never lost control of the Mediterranean and managed to hang on during the extremely close-run contest that followed. The German *Afrika Korps* went across in March 1941 to join the Italians already fighting there; by May 1943 it had been defeated largely because it could not be replenished with men and material. Malta proved to be the unsinkable aircraft carrier that controlled the sea lanes. Also, the arrival of the Americans in North Africa during November 1942 made it impossible for the Germans and Italians to win. When Bill signed that document in 1942 agreeing to go on "extended" active duty (i.e., service for the duration) millions of other Americans stepped up to the challenge by volunteering or accepting the draft. Roosevelt and Churchill quickly agreed that the European fascists and not Imperial Japan posed the larger threat, and they planned accordingly. In mid-July 1943 the Americans and British invaded the island of Sicily.

With the war not going well for Italy and nearing her shores, on July 24 the Fascist Grand Council voted no confidence in Mussolini and the next day King Victor Emmanuel III had him arrested and confined. The upshot of this was the naming of Pietro Badoglio Prime Minister of Italy. Two days later Badoglio told an incredulous Albert Kesselring, the field marshal that Hitler appointed to hold Italy, that he did not know where Mussolini was detained; he also assured him that the new Italian government would remain loyal to the German/Italian treaty of alliance. Kesselring described the meeting as, "… chilly, reticent and insincere."[53]

Allied leadership (and particularly American leadership) distrusted both the morality and competency of Badoglio. He had led the murderous conquest of hapless Ethiopia (1935-36), the 1940 military "stab in the back" of down-on-its-knees France, the unprovoked attack on Greece and had served the despot Mussolini faithfully for all those years. To the Americans, Badoglio was a latter-day Cassius; to the British he was a slightly nobler version of Brutus. Once appointed Prime Minister, Badoglio could not constrain himself from perpetrating further military follies. Through intermediaries Badoglio communicated to Eisenhower that Italy wanted to surrender but on condition that the Allies swiftly take Rome to avoid its destruction. Eisenhower, desirous of fighting only one opponent, the Germans, reluctantly agreed. A commentator described it thusly:

> *Thus was born* Giant II, *a near disaster that came very close in resulting in the destruction of the 82nd Airborne Division.... Badoglio's plan was that the allies would air-drop a large force onto airfields around the city where they would be joined by Italian units. The Allies were assured by the marshal's emissaries that the combination of the two elements would insure the control of Rome against the German forces in the area.*[54]

As a precaution Eisenhower directed that two U.S. Army officers (one of whom was Brigadier General Maxwell Taylor, deputy commander of the 82nd) be secreted into Rome to find out firsthand what the situation on the ground would be when the drop was made. Spirited in on an Italian corvette boat, the American officers were escorted into the city under guard posing as captured Allied airmen. Taylor was aghast at what he learned. Face to face with the seventy-two year-old shifty-eyed smiling Badoglio on September 8, the agreed-upon day for the Italian surrender to take place, and the day before the Salerno invasion was scheduled (which Badoglio had not been informed about) Taylor was mortified to discover that the Italians had changed their minds about *Giant II*, that they now feared there were too many Germans in the area. The Italians had not made any troop dispositions to do battle alongside the 82nd nor made an effort to inform Eisenhower. Taylor managed to get a message out to Eisenhower calling off the airborne operation at the very last moment. Sixty-four U.S. planes circled in the air above Sicily when his message finally arrived; Taylor's commander General Mathew Ridgeway wore a parachute expecting to take off.

No one had been killed and the British perceived that Badoglio still might be of some use and wanted to work with him; the Americans reluctantly went along and agreed to keep their hands off him. Badoglio was just beginning his incompetence, however!

The Sicily campaign had gone well for the Allies and by early September as the Allied invasion fleet approached the Italian coastal city of Salerno, a short distance southeast of the port of Naples, the Italian government did in fact surrender effective September 8. In anticipation Eisenhower released the following message: "All Italians who now act to help eject the German aggressor from Italian soil will have the assistance and support of the United Nations."[55]

In signing an armistice agreement with Eisenhower on 4 September 1943, many Italians hoped beyond hope that Italy might be somehow spared the wholesale violence that was planned to come its way. On September 8, the big day, as new leader of the Italian government, Badoglio broadcast on the radio "Italian soldiers will resist all attacks from whatever quarter they come." Italian military commanders did not know what to make of this broadcast; they telephoned the War Office in Rome for clarification and were told (hope upon hope), "If the Germans are leaving the country, let them. Try not to provoke them."[56]

A memorandum previously agreed upon by the new Italian government "instructing Italian Army Corps and Division Commanders to face the Germans" was never activated, nor did the new Italian government, having surrendered the day before, apparently think to rescind its standing order "to resist an Allied invasion." Italian commanders were flummoxed, and U.S. commanders were less than impressed by the lack of coordination and resolve on the part of the new Italian government.

The commentator continued acerbically:

> "At least one [Italian] submarine approached the Allied invasion fleet at Salerno and was prevented from attacking only at the last moment. On the rest of the mainland of Italy, the unprepared Italian army had no chance against the Germans. After celebrating the hoped-for end of the war with manifestations of joy on the night of 8 September... masses of [Italian] soldiers took the Badoglio broadcast as their signal to desert

and go home by bus, train, bicycle, tram or on foot and put on plain clothes."[57]

What Badoglio had done was far worse than described above.

The reaction of the Nazis to the turn of events was swift and clearly articulated. Propaganda minister Dr. Joseph Goebbels spoke for his nation: "The Italians have abandoned us in our moment of crisis... their treachery has turned all our plans upside down... If we could use the divisions now needed in Italy for the Russian front, we could throw the Bolsheviks back."[58] Scores of thousands of Nazi troops poured into Italy over the Brenner Pass to join other German military units already there. The aggressive Kesselring (who was already in Italy impatiently waiting for this event) wrote happily: "It was a blessing I no longer had to pull my punches with the Italians..."[59] One of the new arrivals from Germany was SS Obergruppenführer Karl Wolff, a favorite of Hitler, who would report to Kesselring and among other duties command the Waffen SS, numbering approximately 150,000 troops.[60]

As the Germans approached Rome, Prime Minister Pietro Badoglio and figurehead King Victor Emmanuel III fled for their lives to the southeast — to the protection afforded by the British Eighth Army then at Brindisi. Those capital residents who were unable to likewise escape, being most of the city, had gone from grappa-induced mental joy to a sober state of abject horror and hopelessness.

In a revealing book written in 1966 by Peter Tompkins who served with the OSS in Italy during 1944 entitled *Italy Betrayed*, it comes out that Badoglio was, in addition to being incompetent and treacherous, a coward; that the Prime Minister had *intentionally* delayed issuing orders that might cause the Germans to press more hastily into Rome; he did this, per Tompkins, so he and the King would have time to make good their escape.

> *At last, and with unparalleled gall, late in the evening of September 11, [Ed: when the escape was accomplished] Badoglio finally issued orders for the Italians to attack the Germans everywhere. He then informed the local press that OP44 had just been put into effect and that this was a carefully planned order of the High Command to guide the armed forces in a fight against the Germans.*
>
> *Unfortunately, by this time almost the entire land forces of Italy had been captured, had dispersed or were being passed before execution squads. Worse, Badoglio had failed to accompany his order with a formal*

*declaration of war, thus making it legally (and understandably) possible
for the Germans to shoot Italian soldiers as rebels and traitors.*[61]

In its rush south the German Army bypassed an estimated 200,000 Northern Italian civilians who remained sympathetic to the Royalist cause. Many of these individuals would become partisans and take up arms against the Nazis and those Italians who supported them. These partisans had to hide in cellars and attics or in the open countryside, however, to avoid being hunted down by fellow Italians who remained loyal to Mussolini. The *Fascisti* often knew the individual identities of partisans on the basis of past expressed political persuasions; lists of names of traitors to Il Duce were prepared for round-ups. A vicious small-scale cloak and dagger hit-and-run civil war ensued.

At the time this civil strife started up, approximately 80,000 Allied POWs, mostly British and British Commonwealth captured in Africa, were held in Italian Army-run prison camps spread across Italy, with a number of large camps situated in the north. When the Italian prison camp guards left their posts following the first Badoglio announcement these POWs had little doubt that the Germans would come for them, but when? During the few days that the POWs had the freedom of choice, that is to stay put or flee, many Senior British Officers ("SBOs") in the camps, concerned over how the Germans might react, "advised" against escaping.[62] Many chose to ignore this advice and make a run for it. Those who stayed (being the majority of POWs including the SBOs) ended-up in prison camps inside Nazi Germany; quite a number of these captives wished later that they had risked a chance traveling south in the Italian countryside, or attempted a hike northward through the mountains into neutral Switzerland (as many had successfully done). The Italian people by in large helped those British who attempted escape and this did much to mend torn relations between the two countries.

As stated, Mussolini had been arrested on July 25, 1943; the Germans rescued him on September 12 in a daring mountain plateau raid involving ninety glider-borne commandos.[63] On October 13 Italy finally declared war on Germany. Many Italians, however, particularly in Northern Italy (Milan most notably) remained loyal to Mussolini and continued to fight for him at the side of the Germans. Undoubtedly very late into the war some of the "enemies not so long ago" (as would be referred to by Bill) viewed themselves as enemies of the Allies.

Commentators used the term "co-belligerents" to describe the split Italian nation after its surrender to the United Nations.[64]

It should be noted that in selecting Southern Italy for the invasion, the Allied command arguably made a poor military choice. After the rapid conquest of Sicily (only thirty-eight days) the Allies may have thought that Italy could be taken quickly from the south — for the first time in its history. In 1800 after overrunning the country Napoleon said, "Italy is a boot that you enter from the top."[65] His point was that an invasion from the north could trap an enemy army in the south (one without a navy that is) but not vice versa. On this point Hitler agreed. Hitler acknowledged to Mussolini on April 22, 1944 that an Allied invasion at Leghorn (named today Livorno) or further north at Genoa would have required him to withdraw to the north.[66] Additionally although perhaps not a priority to the Allies, an invasion in the far north would have precluded the widespread destruction of much of the country.

The lack of a naval presence explains why the Germans did not put forward a major effort to hold Sicily. When the Germans ascertained the invasion at Salerno was the real thing, they took affirmative military action accordingly. A commentator noted:

> When the invasion of Sicily started in July 1943, the Germans had about four divisions there to bolster the Fascist garrison, with three more on the Italian mainland. By mid-October, shortly after the Allies took Naples, the Germans had nineteen divisions in Italy, eight more than the Allies. Obviously, they intended to hold Italy if they could... [67]

In either direction north or south, the terrain of Italy favored the defender. One writer described it as follows: "... a chain of precipitous mountains, wall after wall, running up the spine of the peninsula, rising in places to 10,000 feet [Ed: these would be the Alps] and traversed by rivers cutting through deep valleys to the sea."[68]

The invasion at Salerno in September 1943 proved costly for the U.S. Fifth Army. Salerno was General Mark Clark's first experience as an invasion force commander, and it went so badly during the early hours that Eisenhower not only lost confidence in Clark, but also feared for his own job. Landing craft were hit by shellfire or blown up by harbor mines and the Luftwaffe put up "the heaviest aerial resistance ever encountered during the war in the Mediterranean."[69] The

82nd Airborne commanded by General Ridgeway saved the day by dropping 1,300 troops near the beachhead at an early and very critical moment in the battle. Hundreds of USAAF heavy and medium bombers under the control of Northwest African Air Forces were brought into emergency action to attack Nazi units approaching the beachhead.[70] More 82nd Airborne paratroopers jumped into the fray and finally, after five days of ferocious fighting, troop reinforcements arrived by sea, averting total calamity. The U.S. Army suffered 13,000 casualties including 2,149 killed in action — approximately four times what their opponent experienced.[71] In the Allied press the invasion was depicted as a successful breach of Hitler's "Fortress Europe" and the fact that the Nazis were dug in and waiting was downplayed.

Winston Churchill described the months that followed as "scandalous stagnation."[72] The British and Americans forces found themselves stalled before a formidable set of Nazi defenses that ran across the entire peninsula known as the Gustav Line. This line was best defended through the Cassino area. Naples had been taken, yes, and heavily damaged in the process — but the prize, Rome, remained elusive to the Allies for the better part of a year. Repeated Allied assaults resulted in heavy Allied casualties. The "scandal" Churchill referred to stood for the large loss of life, with little or no territorial progress to show for it. The public euphoria over the total victories in North Africa and Sicily began to be replaced by pessimism. In the East, the Red Army was making good progress, and the international press reported this.

One fortunate event for the Americans and British happened fairly early on after the invasion. In the Nazi rush to occupy territory after the Italian surrender, 12,000 German troops were dispatched to the island of Corsica. The French resistance on the island rose up and the Italian occupying forces (most of them anyway) remained loyal to King Victor Emmanuel III. These Italians fought alongside the French resistance as the Germans poured in more troops and the Allies hurriedly landed available Free French forces. The island was liberated on October 4, 1943 (the Germans evacuated having suffered approximately 1,000 casualties). This victory proved immediately beneficial for the Allies. Corsica was situated close to the coast of Northern Italy allowing for tactical air sorties to be flown from the island over much of the mainland. This would prove a huge advantage to the Allies in the coming months.

Stalemated before the Gustav Line, the Americans and British launched a seaborne initiative on January 22, 1944 code-named "Operation Shingle." Fifty thousand men and 5,000 vehicles came ashore at the port cities of Anzio and Nettuno located forty-five miles northwest of the major fighting and 30 miles south of Rome. Most of the Allied leadership strongly favored this audacious plan. A notable exception was General George S. Patton who told U.S. General John Lucas, who would lead the assault: "John, there is no one in the army I'd hate to see killed as much as you, but you can't get out of this alive."[73] Patton himself was still out of favor, however, over the G.I. slapping incident the previous year in Sicily. No one listened to Patton when he advised (correctly) before the Salerno invasion that the plan called for the American and British forces to be too far apart; that the Germans would exploit this circumstance to drive a wedge between the two armies.[74] And no one was about to listen to Patton now when he talked about terrain, firepower and most important, the constant need for movement. General Clark, who selected Lucas for the command (with British commander Alexander's agreement) listened least of all. Clark and Patton had competed with each other during the Sicily campaign, and resentments may have lingered.

General Lucas had his own grave concerns about Shingle — particularly whether 50,000 men — only two divisions identified as VI Corps, was strong enough to do the job. He confided to his diary "These battles of the Little Big Horn aren't much fun…" and made a reference to Churchill's involvement: "… this whole affair has a strong odor of Gallipoli…" referring to the World War I Dardanelles disaster that Churchill, then First Lord of the Admiralty, was key in setting up. In that seaborne operation Australian and New Zealand soldiers got hopelessly pinned to the beach by the Turks.[75]

Still — the faithful soldier — Lucas took the assignment.

To Lucas' astonishment the Anzio landing went off without a hitch. The few Germans defending the seashore were taken completely by surprise. An intense rocket barrage from the Allied fleet starting in the early morning hours went unanswered; eighty landing craft then went to work, shuffling back and forth, safely conveying troops to the shore. Amphibious ships successfully put off trucks, heavy weapons and supplies. Maybe this "end-run" behind the German lines might work after all?

To the south, however — at the Gustav Line — Mark Clark's attempt to cross the Rapido River, part of the overall plan to draw enemy reserves away from Anzio, met with disaster. It turned out the Germans didn't need reserves to defeat Clark. The U.S. Fifth Army suffered 1,681 casualties and had nothing to show for it.[76]

On that first morning at Anzio an American junior officer, an Army engineer, performed reconnaissance duty north of the town. With a driver he took a jeep to the outskirts of Rome and saw the Tiber River. The two Americans stayed for about an hour and observed a few enemy vehicle movements but nothing suggesting that wholesale preparations were underway for a counterattack. Returning to the beachhead, the lieutenant made his report accordingly.[77]

At Anzio, General Lucas dug in and secured his position. He was not about to be rushed or made to do anything rash. His orders were to seize and secure a beachhead and then advance to higher ground, specifically the Alban Hills approximately twenty miles away in the direction of Rome. He had no orders to advance on Rome itself. If Lucas made a mistake, it was not appreciating the opportunity afforded by what reconnaissance had discovered that critical first day. The Appian Way into Rome was undefended! If this intelligence had been acted upon promptly then additional backup forces could have been easily landed at Anzio and the Gustav Line could have been bypassed by sea. In his defense Lucas had no way of knowing that only 1,500 German soldiers then defended the Eternal City; but that was in fact the case on invasion day, January 22, 1944.[78]

The terrain in Italy as a whole did not favor tank warfare as the lowlands tended to be swampy. The German lightweight, easily moveable, rapid firing long-range 88 mm antiaircraft gun was perfectly adaptable for ground combat in Italy, however. German forces wasted little time in removing these weapons from the capital city and ringing them around the invading Anzio force. Anzio turned into a bloodbath, with both sides pouring in additional soldiers. By February 12, three weeks into it, the U.S. Army history noted: "All 96,401 Allied soldiers were required to hold the thirty-five-mile perimeter against an estimated ten German divisions in the 14th Army, totaling 120,000 men..."[79] Lucas, for negligently allowing the enemy time to seize the high ground for the placement of deadly artillery, had caused a great loss of Allied life and put the entire Anzio operation in danger. He was relieved of command on 23 February, to be replaced by General Lucian Truscott. Overwhelming air superiority saved the American and British forces, but not without a high price being paid in casualties on the ground.

The artillery barrages going both ways continued for months on end during which time Adolf Hitler repeatedly pointed with pride to the non-growing pimple-blip on the map. Der Führer derogatorily referred to it as the "Anzio abscess."[80] And to add insult to injury, the Germans brought in two huge rail guns to the Alban Hills to pound, at their leisure, the beachhead (Bill would be involved in moving one of these guns after the war — more to follow).

During February 1944, on the Gustav Line in the south things did not improve for the Allies. In frustration and arguably wrongfully, on February 15 the U.S. Army Air Forces was ordered to use heavy bombers to obliterate the 1,400 year-old Benedictine Abbey on top of Monte Cassino to preclude the Germans from using it for military purposes. Bill had occasion to visit these blasted ruins. Years later he related how conflicted he felt upon viewing what had been done in the name of "military necessity."

One historian noted "… the Germans declared that they had ordered their forces to stay away from the Monastery," but that "some Allied observers reported sighting enemy troops in the building, and among these were Generals Eaker and Devers."[81] Another historian suggested that the rubble left from the American bombing made for *a better defensive enemy position* than the standing building itself would have been.[82]

The Vatican was of course aghast over this bombing.

If such destruction could be wrought on this magnificent historic abbey, what might be in store for Rome? Papal authorities maintained close contacts with both the Allied and Axis powers. In occupied Rome the high-up German who was most sympathetic and responsive to Vatican requests for moderation on the part of German troops and the Gestapo was, perhaps surprisingly, SS General Karl Wolff. In addition to being a major military commander in Italy Wolff also had superintending police powers. One of the first things Wolff had done after arriving in Italy the year earlier was to dispel the rampant rumor that the Pope and his inner circle would be kidnapped and held hostage in Germany.[83] This assurance set well with the Italian people.

On a side note, in regards to the abbey today, it has been rebuilt magnificently. It sits tranquilly on top of where it was before but now overlooks something special on an adjacent slope. A large Christian cross outlined by planted trees stands atop more than 1,000 graves of free Polish soldiers who gave their lives in the May 1944 Battle of Monte Cassino. The Poles singularly recognized at Cassino earned the honor. The U. S. Army history reads: "…the Polish Corps assault on

Monte Cassino failed with more than 50 percent of the attacking force counted as casualties."[84]

The small and unassuming entrance to the enormous abbey has the Latin word "*Pax*" carved in stone over it, its script letters painted in light blue. A more fitting memorial to mankind's tragic folly could not be better presented. Bill would walk through this door in 1972; his second visit to the mountaintop religious community was to be a happy one.

The Italian conflict witnessed many war crimes and on March 24, 1944 the largest took place. On orders from Berlin, the SS chief in Rome, Colonel Herbert Kappler had 335 Italians taken to the Ardeatine Caves on the outskirts of Rome where they were murdered by a bullet to the head. This was done in retaliation for the bombing of a bus by communist partisans that killed thirty-five South Tyrolean German policemen. Many of the victims of this decimating reprisal — the taking of ten lives for one — were Jews who had been earlier arrested and awaited transportation to the death camps. Political prisoners were shot and when the Nazis ran out of those, lists of suspects were rounded up and finally, individuals taken randomly off the streets.[85] The SS had been in a big hurry; it had been ordered that the reprisal had to be completed within a day's time.

On the same day that the Ardeatine massacre occurred, Italian Fascist and Wehrmacht soldiers captured fifteen U.S. soldiers some 250 miles behind the line. These Americans had landed by sea with the intent of blowing up a strategic railroad tunnel connecting La Spezia and Genoa. The men were properly dressed in U.S. Army field uniforms and possessed no civilian attire. During the course of their interrogation one of the U.S. officers revealed the target of the mission. On orders received from a Wehrmacht General Anton Dostler, a corps commander, the fifteen were executed by firing squad on the morning March 26, 1944.[86]

For Italy there would be no "sense of peace and goodwill" again until the war was over. The Axis combatants were determined to deal harshly with those they considered "saboteurs and commandos." A book written by James Holland entitled *Italy's Sorrow* contains a number of photographs of Italian partisans and civilians murdered by German and Italian Fascisti starting in 1944. They were hanged, shot at stakes or mowed down en masse in trenches. One photo shows an attractive female partisan hanging in a town square with her legs completely exposed. Her clothes had been torn off. There were hundreds of massacres. Innocent people were rounded-up and murdered in public in reprisal for surprise attacks waged by non-uniformed partisan fighters many of whom were communists.[87]

For his part, Kesselring remained lifelong unapologetic about the treatment the partisans received at the hands of his troops and Axis partners. Following the war he wrote:

> Altogether the Partisan groups presented a picture of a motley collection of Allied, Italian and Balkan soldiers, German deserters and native civilians of both sexes of widely different callings and ages with varying ideas of morality, with the result that patriotism was often merely a cloak for baser instincts.[88]

Kesselring believed the partisans violated international law, specifically the Hague Convention, and he had no compunction about executing them. The ranking SS General in Italy, Karl Wolff, at Kesselring's behest issued a standing order: "Whoever knows the place where a band of rebels is in hiding and does not immediately inform the German Army, will be shot."[89] Wolff would become a major player in the surrender process and despite his standing order, Holland noted as the war dragged on Wolff developed a reputation for trying "... to temper the brutality of Kesselring's anti-partisan measures ...".[90] It is possible Wolff moderated his behavior knowing that a legal reckoning loomed for war crimes committed. A gregarious man ("... famously handsome, very tall, a true Siegfried," per one account[91]) Wolff had his own secret from earlier in the war that he hoped to finesse from becoming public.

The Italian people were in the middle of a man-made hell and there was hatred over the United Nations being involved. Exhorting his troops in his usual fascist style, on April 24, 1944 Mussolini harangued the San Marco Division of the newly re-formed (and patently misnamed) "Republican Army" at Grafenwohr, Bavaria:

> The shame of our betrayal [i.e., the royalist Italian government switching sides] will not be expunged unless we fight the invader who contaminates our soil. Beyond the Garigliano [Ed: a river near Cassino] you will find not only the bivouacs of the hard-faced British but Americans, French, Poles, Indians, South Africans, Canadians, Australians, New Zealanders, Moroccans, Senegalese, Negroes and Bolsheviks. You are to have the privilege of fighting this witches' cauldron of bastard nations who respect nothing and nobody as they invade Italy.[92]

In his exhortation Mussolini neglected to include the Japanese-Americans who fought as a U.S. Army infantry combat regiment; he probably chose not to smear them for concern over offending an Axis partner.

Try as he might to generate enthusiasm for military aggressiveness, Mussolini obtained poor results. One authority noted: "According to a German report, the men [Italian Republican Army soldiers] deserted in numbers ranging from ten to twenty-five percent per division."[93] Mussolini was acutely aware of this. Working closely with his Nazi partners, he knew that he had to rebut the perception of Italian military ineptness. He desperately needed a victory. Any victory would do to show the world that the reformed fascist Republican Army was a force to be feared. Mussolini and his German advisors poured over maps of Italy, thinking strategically for the future.

On May 10, 1944 the Pope granted a private audience at the request of SS General Karl Wolff. Following the war Wolff wrote about what he said to the Pope for publication in an Italian magazine: "I declared my readiness to do whatever was in my power for the rapid conclusion of the war, should an honorable opportunity present itself." He also (earlier in the same paragraph) told of how the audience came about: "His Holiness Pius XII had been informed by cardinals and bishops of the way I carried out my duties, my efforts to avoid harshness, and my efforts towards shortening the war."[94]

The planned Allied breakout from Anzio in the springtime caused disagreement between Clark and Alexander, and Truscott got pulled into the dispute. Clark recounted in his memoirs that Truscott reported to him that Alexander ordered him [Truscott] to await his [Alexander's] decision as to the timing of the launch of U.S. Fifth Army assault. Learning this from Truscott, Clark became angry. "This message [from Truscott] made me fear that Alexander had decided to move in and run my army," Clark wrote, complaining. Clark confronted Alexander directly about this, requesting him to, "... please issue orders through me instead of dealing directly with my subordinates."[95]

According to Truscott the cause of this brouhaha was because Clark feared, "... the British might beat him into Rome."[96] Rome did fall to Clark on June 4, 1944 but the event was quickly overshadowed in the public eye by press coverage of the D-Day landings at Normandy two days later. "Mark Clark's Fifth Army" (as it referred to itself in its press releases) had little afterglow for its accomplishment in outracing the British. *All* Italians were overjoyed, however, that their Eternal

City had changed hands largely without damage; the declaration of "open city" the year earlier had been respected and the Pope's prayers for intercession, answered. As an additional plus for the Italian people, on June 9 the leader of the Labour Democratic Party, Ivanoe Bonomi, replaced the despised Pietro Badoglio as Prime Minister of Italy.[97] Badoglio would find a new role, however, as he always somehow managed to do. The disliked King Victor Emmanuel III held weakly onto his crown, if by force of title only, with most of his regal functions being transferred to his less loathsome son Prince Umberto.[98] The Italian government was a complete mess and would remain so for quite some time.

The breakout from Anzio ultimately was a success but the long delay there had been bloody; the U.S. Army history records: "During the four months of the … campaign the Allied VI Corps suffered over 29,200 combat casualties (4,400 killed, 18,000 wounded, 6,800 prisoners or missing) and 37,000 noncombat casualties."[99] The Germans never drove the Allies into the sea, and Rome was taken.

On a side note, Jack King had an early adventure in the "open city," being one of the first from his division to enter it. The 91st Infantry Division Headquarters Company traveled by sea and made land at Civitavecchia, the Port of Rome some fifty miles northwest of the city on July 3. Two days later Jack was ordered by his major to find a jeep and fetch the headquarters mail that was being held in central Rome. Jack obtained the jeep and headed off with "… a Private Hunter from the Post Office," he recorded. For personal protection the men had carbines. "We went through downtown Rome and it was eerie," Jack explained many years later. "There was not a soul, not a person, in Victor Emmanuel Square." The thought did not escape the two G.I.s that the good citizens of Rome might be inside because it was unsafe to be outside, and that at any one of the *hundreds* of surrounding windows a sniper might be waiting. "Apprehensive," Jack admitted to being with a chuckle. Fortunately for Jack and Private Hunter the episode ended without incident and their mission was completed. Jack rode under the nearby window balcony from which Mussolini made his harangues and stiff-arm salutes. A month had passed since Rome's liberation when Jack experienced this; the likelihood is that the close association of this particular section of the city with the fascist rule caused the citizens of Rome to stay away.

The 361st Regimental Combat Team from the 91st Infantry Division did not arrive by ship but rather fought its way north after landing at Anzio on June 1. Heavy casualties were sustained by the 361st but it succeeded in its mission, and a reputation for a Regiment was in the making. Colonel Rudolph W. Broedlow, a no nonsense guy, commanded the 361st, consisting of approximately 3,000 infantrymen.

Captain John Lesesne recorded in his diary about having dealings with Broedlow. About their first meeting, the day after Company "B" assumed positions along the line, John introduced himself to the Colonel at his regimental command post. On that day, November 6, John recorded that the Colonel was "really tough, even a bit sour." Of all the many depictions of senior officers in John's 104-page war diary, this is the only arguably negative one. In comparison John added that the other officers at the regimental command post had been "quite friendly and cooperative." Four days later, on November 10, the day after John had endured the flying bricks-on-his-head incident, he was ordered to report to Broedlow. John described what happened:

> He chewed me a bit. He wanted observers up all the time and mortars moved up more. After leaving him I went to the platoons, got Jay & Lippy [Ed: platoon leaders] and we started forward, over the encampment and along the side of ridge running almost due north — towards Jerry. We had to crawl as we were exposed and didn't know quite how far away Jerry was. Finally reached the forward end of ridge… we had an excellent view — Bologna, and across the Po Valley we saw what we figured were the Alps (probably were). On the way back crawling through bush I smelled something — it smelled like a dead man, but I couldn't see him. Lippy, moving along below me didn't smell him, but suddenly came face to face with him — a dead Jerry. We got back to platoons about 2:30, having found no prospective mortar positions, but a good O.P. [observation post].

Colonel Broedlow had tested the metal of John Lesesne and his officer reports no doubt. He had sent (or rather induced) John and two of his top men out on a dangerous reconnaissance mission to see something that he undoubtedly intended for them to see. Following this mission John reported back to Broedlow:

> I saw the C.O. told him where we'd been and that we'd have an observation post there with wired communications, but that we had found no mortar positions. He was interested in where we had been, asked many questions and seemed satisfied with job we were doing.

What is telling about this incident is the fact that the Colonel knew from John's answers and descriptions that he had in fact seen the Alps. No doubt John left the Colonel's presence vowing to remain wary of him, yes, that is until they got to know each other better, and no doubt Broedlow intended it that way. Lesesne and Broedlow would interact again.

What eventually enabled the Allies to move northwards after Rome fell?

More than anything else, it was airpower.

The Allies used "tactical air" as effectively as it has ever been arguably used. Northern Italy was a "target rich" environment, that is, a good hunting ground for low flying, fast swooping "prowling" fighter-bombers or higher-flying medium bombers.

For the Americans it was the Twelfth Air Force that ran the tactical show in the north. It used medium (two engine) bombers, most often the A-20 Douglas Havoc and also fighter-bombers, usually the P-47 Republic Thunderbolt (this model sported a devastating arsenal of eight powerful .50 caliber machine guns). Flying sorties from Corsica (and later in the war Pisa and other places) the Twelfth regularly hit bridges, communication centers, rolling stock, barracks, houses, guns, defensive positions, battle areas, ammunition dumps, vehicles, marshaling yards, railroads, highways and "targets of opportunity" including tunnel entrances. About the only thing that could stop the Twelfth was bad weather and this happened mostly during the winter. The distance over water when the bombing was done from Corsica was only sixty miles and targets could be hit as far north as 150 miles above the Gustav Line.

An anecdotal example of how feared U.S. tactical air was can be found in an account of American Army Ranger Lieutenant William Newnan who had been taken prisoner by the Germans in Italy in early 1944. Awaiting rail transportation to a POW camp inside Nazi Germany, Newnan chose to escape his captors and risk his chances far behind the lines in the Italian countryside rather than board a train. He later wrote about why he decided to escape: "...to take that [train] trip was hazardous because our own air force was in complete control of the air, machine gunning and bombing everything that moved." After his escape Newnan learned that he had made the correct decision. The next train out, the one he would have been on, was repeatedly hit by U.S. fighters and ultimately destroyed on a collapsed bridge.[100]

Flying tactical missions was dangerous work for Allied pilots and aircrews. Getting down low to dive bomb a bridge or some other target meant being exposed to 20 mm Nazi anti-aircraft guns that had a four-gun configuration cyclic rate of fire of up to 1,800 rounds per minute.[101] There also were the standard 88 mm flak guns that could put up on average seventeen exploding rounds per minute aimed at higher-flying targets. P-47 Thunderbolts typically started their dive-bombing from 10,000 feet. Speed meant safety, and pulling out routinely caused pilots to briefly black out. Two 500 lb. wing bombs in addition to rockets could be delivered, and if the target was a bridge and the pilot was successful in landing his bombs to straddle it, the countervailing shock waves through the ground might spectacularly drop an entire span.

A USAAF documentary filmed during early to mid 1944 entitled *Thunderbolt* shows how one fighter group employed tactical air.[102] The film depicts low flying P-47 fighter-bombers scattering herds of animals and strafing farmhouses; if a farmhouse blew up that was proof of munitions within; not all farmhouses shown blew up, however. This strafing activity was widespread and continuous until war's end. One of the young pilots depicted in the film had 170 missions to his credit. He would never become a fighter ace (there was no Luftwaffe opposition) but rather honored within his group by the title "Wheel." A strafing pilot did not have much time to make a discerning decision respecting military versus civilian aiming points; to linger in an area for a longer look or a second pass might spell disaster. These fighter-bombers took a large toll of innocents, no doubt.

It was the bombing of bridges that was most effective. Increasingly it became more difficult for the Germans to resupply the Gustav Line, and particularly by rail. The American tactical air campaign was appropriately named "Operation Strangle." Seven hundred bridges were destroyed, and a number of them had been built in the days of the emperors. The U.S. Twelfth Air Force became particularly adept at demolishing bridges attached to tunnels in the narrow river gorges where temporary repair was more of a challenge. Following the bridges and rail lines, highways were hit. The British and Free French (supplied with airplanes by the Americans) flew tactical sorties as well. The film documentary claims 10,000 enemy vehicles destroyed by tactical air. And while this went on, weather permitting, the U.S. 15th Air Force based in Foggia, Italy to the south flew high altitude strategic heavy bomber missions over Germany and other countries. It was all that Dick Stroud and many like him could do to keep the supplies coming so that these tactical and strategic air missions could continue and even increase in intensity.

After the liberation of Rome progress up the boot northwards was slow and bloody. Perched on high in machine gun pillboxes and camouflaged artillery dugouts, the Germans shot down at the advancing Allies. In the mud and dirt of the Allied path the Germans planted thousands of land mines. With the fall of Rome, Luftwaffe Field Marshal Albert Kesselring (known as "smiling Albert" to the Allies) anticipated that the Allies would move swiftly northwards. He wrote that he "... expected a rapid thrust across the Apennines beyond Florence." Instead, to his satisfaction, he watched as "a slow attrition" set in.[103]

Kesselring was *the* master of attrition warfare. On his retreat north, he arranged for a series of temporary lines or defensive positions to be set up — the Trasimene and Arno among others.[104] These lines held up long enough to give the Wehrmacht and Waffen-SS time to fully prepare the Gothic Line. In the first year of fighting in Italy the Allies advanced, on average, less than one mile a day.[105]

The British Eighth Army fought on the eastern side of the boot and the U.S. Fifth Army, the western side. The Royal Italian Army, loyal to the King, fought alongside the British and this was soon to expose a schism between the Allies. U.S. leadership had little confidence in Italian combat capability. In mid-July 1944 the Royal Italian divisions ran short of war materials and the scant industrial production in liberated southern Italian cities could not begin to make up the shortfall. A commentator noted:

> "Accordingly, at General Alexander's suggestion Churchill agreed to equip
> them [the anti-fascist Italian soldiers] from Allied sources. Immediately
> Roosevelt complained, and ordered that no U.S. equipment of any sort
> was to be issued to the Italian Army. Churchill decided the British would
> go it alone, and Alexander was authorized to equip four Italian divi-
> sions... entirely from British sources."[106]

Word of this spread to the American rank and file — i.e., that the Italian contribution to the war effort to liberate their country was not worth materially supporting. The situation was such that General Clark felt burdened in having to sustain so many United Nations forces, and he drew the line at supporting additional troops, and particularly those of a recent enemy; Eisenhower, Marshall and Roosevelt backed him up. Additionally, the long-term aims of the U.S.

Government towards Italy may have been (were) different from what the British had in mind — the Americans were thinking of going home, the British, not. The brashness that Bill would observe on the part of American soldiers against Italians had been tacitly encouraged from the topside down.

To make matters even more challenging for the United Nations forces in the summer of 1944, Eisenhower siphoned off 100,000 men from Italy for *Operation Dragoon*, the invasion of Southern France.[107]

When Bill would inspect trucking operations at the front, U.S. Fifth Army morale was really low. Now confronting it north of Florence was the Gothic Line, in places almost fifty miles deep; a series of ditches, barbed wire fences and bombproofs built into daunting mountain inclines. Spread out across half of Italy, the Americans faced an unbeaten, still powerful and waiting enemy.

Perhaps the best news for the Allies in Italy at this time was that Field Marshal Kesselring was in Germany recuperating from a serious head injury. On October 25, 1944 while driving rapidly to visit units in the field he collided with a field gun crossing the road. His loyal troops put out the story "… the Field Marshal was doing well, but the gun had to be scrapped."[108] The large gash to his left temple and resulting concussion would sideline him until mid-January; in his absence his command duties would be performed by his deputy, Wehrmacht General Heinrich von Vietinghoff.

The policy adopted by the U.S. Army for managing its largely African-American 92nd Division was upside down from what it had been during the U.S. Civil War, when white commissioned officers who led black enlisted men were often known for their strong desire to end slavery (with perhaps the best personal example being Bostonian Colonel Robert Gould Shaw who died in 1863 while leading the all-black 54th Massachusetts). With the 92nd Infantry Division in Italy the senior commissioned officers were white, yes, but most were *purposely recruited into the 92nd because they were native to the Old South.* The "Negro Press" had argued strongly for a black general for the 92nd but this had been rejected outright by the U.S. Army.

The prevailing thought in the U.S. Army in late 1944 was that tough talk was necessary to keep "colored" troops in line; that Southern born and bred military leaders were best suited to maintain discipline among high-spirited African-American combat troops. One historian noted that Almond rationalized his bias by arguing that the "frequent contacts" that Southerners had with blacks taught them how they might be managed.[109] An African-American sergeant who heard Almond's harangue had a different view of the reason behind the tough talk: "Hell, they [the whites] didn't want us to succeed."[110] A black warrant officer with the 92nd alluded to a special situation that sprung up: "Rapport between black and white officers was very poor. There was almost a race riot between them in Viareggio, about the usual thing, girls in the area."[111]

Italian women, those who would date American soldiers, did not discriminate on the basis of race, and this enraged the white command structure of the 92nd.

Even with the additional manpower provided by the African-Americans and Brazilians, the U.S. Fifth Army would be reduced by almost 50% from its original strength — down to only 153,000 men.[112] Adding in the British Eighth Army, the total number of Allied combatants was approximately 300,000, a number roughly equal to the opposing Axis forces.

On November 18, John Lesesne recorded in his diary:

A terrible thing happened last night. About midnight I got a call from the operations officer of the 361st Infantry Division saying that a round of W.P. [white phosphorous] had landed directly in one of our foxholes and killed the man inside. This was just this side of Canovetta. I checked with Jimmy and he said he'd been firing at Canovetta and had gotten a short round of W.P. The infantry are so very close to our place. It's hard to say how I felt and I knew Jimmy felt the same. It was definitely us. I told the S-2 [operations officer] about it. Didn't sleep too well last night. To think that we had killed one of our own boys! It's true that we've killed many Jerries and thereby saved just as many G.I's, and also true that there was evidently no carelessness or neglect involved, but still we feel a certain responsibility. Jimmy and I went up to Regimental Hq (361st) early in the morning to report to the C.O. — I have thought him a sour--------, but I'll "eat" that now. He was very nice about it — didn't say much. I won't forget that.

I've somewhat gotten over my remorse already — what things war does, one becomes so calloused that he quickly forgets even the taking of human life — the life of an American boy. Of course, we think nothing of killing Jerries — this long-range killing isn't hard. Jimmy's platoon somewhat redeemed itself today when it fired a mission and a little later a mule cart hauled the dead Jerries (about twelve, I think)...

Got a letter from Jack S. — expects to come over soon — he won't come if he can possibly get out of it — guess he's wise at that... Would like to go to church tomorrow. The boys here are most considerate — always doing some little service for me. Last night when we got the bad news and they knew I was feeling pretty bad about it, they did their best to cheer me up. Being the only officer here with 10 men and living with them, the discipline is very informal, but they never take advantage of this — I think a lot of these boys.

The following day Company "B" continued to fire on or near Canovetta and it stopped a German tank on Highway 65 and German mortars behind a house from firing. John reported a visit from his commanding officer, Major Russell McMurray and he wrote this about it: "Major Mac. told me that Col Reynolds, C.O. 1st Bn 361st Inf., was most enthusiastic over our work."

This was significant as Colonel Reynolds reported to Colonel Broedlow.

CHAPTER THREE:

A TENT AND A PALACE

November–December 1944

BILL HAD WRITTEN eighteen letters to his wife and son by the time he arrived in Italy; additionally, four to his parents. From Naples he cabled Dotty, undoubtedly using the only words permitted: "Arrived safely. Love, Bill." Bill's first V-mail to his parents contained no code indicating where he might be: "My address is CAPT WILLIAM D. ALLISON, 0-306464 Trans Sec. AFHQ APO No. 512 c/o Postmaster New York, NY. I am writing this sitting on my cot in a tent. It rained most of the night and there is plenty of mud. I have not joined my outfit yet but expect to soon. Every place is so busy and crowded."

The Royal Palace of Caserta

The mud that Bill mentioned was from a dairy farm formerly owned by Mussolini's son-in-law, Count Ciano, who had been executed the previous January for treason against the fascist government (he voted for the ouster of his father-in-law in July 1943). The U.S. Army had converted Ciano's farm, located at Caserta north of the Port of Naples, into a tent city for incoming and outgoing U.S. troops.[113] Getting there involved a short train ride for Bill from the port.

Army tally records show that at this place Bill was issued standard items for duty in Italy: helmet, M-1 carbine, ammo, rifle cleaning equipment, gas mask, four tubes of "Ointment, Protective," tent poles and pins, "Bar, Mosquito," suspenders, first aid kit, "Fork/Spoon," various blankets, mattress cover and "Roll Bedding, Canvas W/Straps."

Bill's dog tags now had importance as he was in a warzone. The stamped metal I.D.s were tied together on a shoelace but spaced apart so as not to rattle and possibly alert an enemy soldier within earshot. Bill knew that in the event he got killed, one tag would remain with his body and the other be removed by Graves Registration for processing. In addition to his name and serial number, the tags contained his blood type ("A"), religion ("P" denoting protestant) and next of kin. If something were to happen to him (like in the case of his brother who died in that 1943 plane accident) Bill had arranged for someone other than his wife to receive the casualty telegram notice. He designated his father "S.B. [Sam] Allison, R.D. [rural delivery] Franklinville N.Y." as next-of-kin with the intent that Sam telephone Dotty's parents in Detroit some 300 miles away (Dotty's parents lived in the same apartment building as she and Davy).

That was how it was most often done in World War II; someone in the family other than the military spouse would learn first of a death, wounding, accident or illness; that way a wife would not suffer the shock of encountering a telegraph delivery boy at her doorstep. Lieutenant Dick Stroud did it like Bill; he designated a sister, Nell, as next-of-kin on his dog tags; Nell resided in Longview, Texas some 125 miles distant from Dick's wife Sue in Garland. In Dick's case it would turn out that Nell had a job to do.

In a letter to Dotty, Bill described living conditions in the five-man tent that he shared at the U.S. Army Replacement Depot, Naples: "I am fortunate in having one of the two dry corners… The streets are a soggy mass of mud with stone and gravel for paths connecting the tents. The puddles sometimes come over the paths and once in a while there is no gravel — just mud." In another letter he described the *quality* of Italian mud, perhaps not yet fully appreciating that this was a good part of the reason that he had been sent to Italy in the first place: "It's a slippery, sticky mud that sticks on everything like cement."[114]

As for heat, he and his fellow campers had none: "One of the men in the tent was trying to burn some trash for a little heat. He just about smoked us out." Bill reported wearing "my helmet liner and wool cap" and "a lot of heavy clothing" including two pairs of wool socks.

As Bill huddled for warmth with nothing to do, 300 miles to the north another G.I. experienced something akin. "Now that the first thrill of being in the line is over and things are rather quiet," John Lesesne wrote, "I'm beginning to find it pretty dull — even boring."[115]

Bill soon appreciated the abysmal situation that was wartime Naples. He wrote Dotty: "It is difficult to realize there is such a difference between the people here and in the U.S. Everyone, the natives, appears so dirty and tattered. … Last night the men were throwing cigarettes down on the dock from the ship to a crowd of the boys of all ages. There was a mad scramble for each cigarette. They looked like a football team going after a fumble."

Bill managed to leave the base and see some things. About the local transportation he observed: "Most civilian transportation is by high two-wheeled carts… they balance the load over the single axle and sometimes it looks like the loads would almost lift the horse!"[116] On another occasion he recorded: "It will take me some time to get used to such extremes of wealth and poverty."[117]

Bill was not the only American to be shocked. He wrote: "One soldier said, 'He would much rather be over here fighting than to have the Germans wrecking things at **H**ome.'"[118] The use of the word "home" (or "**H**ome" as Bill wrote it) had a special reverence for G.I.s. "I have all of everything that one needs except home," Dick Stroud wrote Sue (Dick was not in the habit of bolding and capitalizing the first letter but like all G.I.s he used the word frequently).[119]

By November 29th the rain had stopped but the wind had created a problem for Bill and his camping companions: "This morning found all of us driving tent stakes and lacing the tent down," he reported. "It sure did slap around last night." Camp life was primitive, and being a commissioned officer at the rank of O-3, or captain, did not allow for orderlies. "We use the steel shell of our helmets for laundry buckets…", Bill observed. "They are most useful." He also offered they were used for washbasins.

On the same day John's boredom came to an abrupt halt. Jimmy's platoon blew up an enemy ammo dump using white phosphorous (scoring a direct hit on the second round) and then it attacked "Jerries running about the area" with high explosives. The "area" became so target rich that the infantry called in the artillery to join the firing. It happened that that day was payday ("one day early" John wrote) and while John and others were "taking money up to Jay's platoon," presumably riding a jeep, the enemy tried to get even. John and his boys got shelled but escaped unhurt.

Bill's mail call was at 4:00 p.m. daily and during this first week he suffered a false hope: "One man in our tent got ten letters today," he wrote Dotty, "so I guess mine will be coming soon."

Dick Stroud had been fortunate. Camping at the same dismal place, on December 5 he wrote Sue: "On my arrival here I found thirty-two letters... an orgy of letter reading... was wonderful." It happened that there was a specific reason that Dick had all these letters waiting for him. On the transit over Dick's ship experienced a major mechanical problem forcing almost a month's' stay in Bermuda, a place Dick described (in his first letter mailed from Naples) as, "beautiful... with quaint streets, horse and bicycle transportation... *White Horse Inn* St. George... soccer, rugby...". Because of this repair stop the voyage to Italy had taken approximately forty days and during this period his mail accumulated at repple-depple Naples.

While the unscheduled stop at an island vacation spot had proved to be good fortune for Dick (and no doubt reinforced the time honored military adage "*luck counts*") unbeknownst to Dick his wife Sue paid a psychological price worrying for his safety. When Dick finally got to Naples he soon learned from one of Sue's letters that she had yet to receive *any* of the letters and presents that he had mailed to her from Bermuda. The Army did not tell Dick (and undoubtedly all others embarked) that mail from Bermuda had been intentionally delayed.[120] The reason for this of course was because it would not do for a solder to unthinkingly write, "It looks like our repairs will be completed in a day or two..." and have such a communication fall into the wrong hands.

Dick first learned of this circumstance on December 12 when he wrote Sue from Naples: "I am much put out ..." Dick was upset with the Army but this was the way it was done in World War II: information that might pertain to a ship's casualty repair and scheduled movement was strictly blocked; loved ones at home suffered anxiety accordingly.

To the north the war was going at a slower pace for Captain John Lesesne with the onset of colder weather. At his command post at La Guarda, with a small fire burning in the stove, John had taken to playing poker for money with his enlisted contingent, a thing a commissioned officer (and especially one in command!) should not have done, but how else could he relieve the monotony?

John enjoyed the company of his "boys" (whom he sometimes referred to as "comm men") and wrote about some of them. Corporal Billy Key of Texas caught a couple of chickens one day and these, along with potatoes dug out of a nearby patch were prepared by Sergeant "Pappy" Gordon Stem of Brillion, Wisconsin "... for a fairly good supper." Other names mentioned are McGuinness, Hoffman, Grennan, Dunn, Fluet, Budgake and Schalow. John reported positive things about his charges, an example being:

> Joe Fluet comes from way up in Maine — a little fellow of French Canadian descent. I understand that when he first came into the Army he spoke no English, only French. His accent together with a dry humor, give us many laughs. He is another whom I didn't consider as non com material until we got up here.[121]

These men shared a dangerous job, one requiring considerable time outside of a foxhole. John wrote about them connecting lines to the same platoon four times over the span of one week. "Shell fire quickly knocks them out," he observed. John undoubtedly chortled when he recorded: "Played a little poker with the boys tonight. Won $38.00." No doubt these G.I.s, all of them, enjoyed and supported each other as teammates. About Budgake from New Jersey, John wrote: "Clean, high morals, wants to be a pro baseball player." About the Texan, Key: "... a poor garrison soldier, but a good one up here."

Letter writing at repple-depple Naples was a main activity. "Four of us are here now writing letters," Bill wrote. "Each is sitting on his cot with a candle providing light. We closed the tent flap and the candles give us a surprising amount of warmth." Bill also indicated how thankful he was to be "rationed" a candle every third night which would burn "from six to eight hours." He wrote: "I am grateful for that after the early blackouts on the ship." Thinking about a person, any person, being issued only one candle every three days is telling about how material resources were closely managed in World War II.

Growing up on a farm, Bill learned to shoot at a young age and he enjoyed hunting rabbits and pheasants for sport and food and also popping off varmint woodchucks. At R.O.T.C. Bill won a marksmanship award that he was proud of. A shooting range had been set up at the replacement depot and it was undoubtedly no surprise to Dotty when she read: "Tomorrow I am going to request permission to fire my carbine for practice and to adjust the sights correctly. The other men want to do the same." In a subsequent letter he embellished: "It is a fine little gun and easy to shoot. It is quite accurate and also easy to carry."[122]

As an aside, Jack King, like Bill a behind the lines soldier, had also been issued this model weapon for personal protection; infantry soldiers carried the more powerful and heavier M-1 Garand.

Commissioned U.S. infantry officers were often offered the carbine as a symbol of officer status akin to British officers carrying only a revolver or swagger stick. Many, wishing not to be specially targeted while on patrol, declined this visible display of "rank class," opting instead to carry the heavier M-1 Garand.[123]

At the end of a letter to Dotty Bill apologized, as if he were having an active conversation with her: "I have written the whole letter about myself… I wish you would tell me everything you and Davy do, all your activities with your friends." A day later he would write her and tell her that he hoped to send a considerable portion of his officer pay home using a free system run by the Army where deposits made in Italy were converted to checks mailed to dependents from Washington, D.C.

"As you know we receive ten percent extra on our base pay for Foreign Service," Bill wrote. "That amounts to twenty or so dollars a month. For this part of a month it was twelve dollars. I would like for you to set aside that money each month to be used on our vacation immediately after the war." The U.S. Army paid soldiers in "invasion money," Bill observed in another letter, which undoubtedly was a method of currency control.

In a letter to his parents Bill explained the calamity that had crippled Italy beyond the death and destruction caused by widespread combat: "The Italian unit of currency is the lira, which at present has a value of one cent. In normal times before the war the value of the lira was about five cents. Those inhabitants who had some money saved up were suddenly poor people when the value dropped."[124]

This devaluation created a humanitarian disaster. Bill expounded on one of its immediate brutal consequences: "There is a great shortage of milk here. All of it is rationed to children under one-year old. There is not enough even for that. In 1943 almost one-half of the children born died before they were one-year old from malnutrition." The non-farming Italian population had great difficulty in obtaining food; money was practically worthless.

In addition to the sustenance crisis, Dick Stroud identified another calamity brought on by the war and this one involved the onset of winter: "No heat of any kind in most of the places," he observed. "Fuel I'm sure is imported, thus 'no fuel."[125] In another letter written during the winter he described his experience: "Imagine if you can going to bed in your garage on a cold night."[126]

Bill confirmed to his parents that U.S. soldiers ate well at the repple-depple: "[Army] food has been good ... three adequate meals a day," he wrote. "The men are forming already in the 'chow line.' The doors open at five o'clock. I will wait a while before going and thus avoid some standing ..."

In another letter to his wife, Bill amplified on the subject of the Army Food Service, ending his description with a tongue-in-cheek: "The cooking and most of the work here is done by the residents [and] most everything is chopped up real fine. There is no tendency to overstuff as on the ship when there were only two meals. When we go to the mess, we each carry our own tin cup and silverware, a knife, fork and spoon. We are served on a metal tray having six various sized pockets. After eating we each wash our own cup and silverware. They heat three huge tubs of water to the boiling point over a gasoline fire. The first tub has soap solution, the second something to take the soap off and the third to rinse. The water is so hot that the utensils dry in air almost immediately. I think a system like that would be good at home, don't you?"[127] When Bill became permanently stationed, he joined an officer's mess. "Meals will cost about $1.00 a day," he wrote.[128] This is consistent with what Dick Stroud reported, who indicated to Sue that he could get by on a budget of $40 a month, total,[129] allowing him to set up an allotment to her of much of his pay.

On December 1 Bill first mentioned in a letter to Dotty something that would trouble him throughout his year abroad. A legislative proposal was being considered at the time calling for compulsory military training at age eighteen. Thinking of Davy, Bill wrote: "To be of value rather than degrading it will have to be on much higher standards than Army morals." What irked him was the fact that some of his officer tent-mates had boasted about their downtown Naples exploits. The abject poverty brought on by the war had caused many native women, particularly in Southern Italy, to do things they otherwise would not have done. In a letter the day earlier Bill mentioned that he had declined to go into Naples with certain tent-mates. He also mentioned a young officer who was devoted to his wife and devastated by their separation, who stayed away from Naples and wrote letters home.

Bill must have gotten out of the tent camp for some excursions, however. While still at the "repple-depple" he expressed a concern over something that he witnessed that would irritate him continuously: "Motorized equipment here sure gets abused," he complained to Dotty referring to the unnecessary rapid accelerations, clutch-riding and excessive braking. Of this driving trip outside the compound he wrote: "I saw people picking olives today. They pick them with ladders and also shake the trees."

—m—

As Bill languished in the repple-depple, the seeds of racial discord planted by General Almond at Serchio Valley began to germinate. In the days before deployment to the line some black soldiers elevated goofing off to an art form. One staff sergeant recorded:

> By now my friend and I had no false ideas about the white man's army
> so it became a game of seeing just how much we could avoid doing. We
> found out one of the most effective little gimmicks was to take a clip
> board, pad, and pencil and go up to the headquarters area and just walk
> around. No one ever bothered to ask us what we were doing up there.[130]

No doubt this sort of shirking took place in all units of the army but what was different was the "white man's army." Almond was referred to as "the great white father."

The 92nd's insertion through the Valley proved difficult; it involved land mines, combat and a climb into the mountains over terrain that vehicles could not traverse. Advance planning by the U.S. Army had been inadequate; pack animals had not been provided beforehand and as a consequence the countryside was hurriedly scoured for private purchases from the local populace. Three hundred and seventy-two Italian mules and 173 horses were procured,[131] an inadequate number for the better part of a combat division on the move. A supply crisis was endemic to the entire U.S. Fifth Army at this time, but to the minds of the Buffalo Soldiers, they had been singled out for special mistreatment. They placed the blame on their commanding general and his white staff. One African-American sergeant would observe thirty years after the fact: "I felt then, and I still do, that the military did not want black combat units, particularly as large as a division."[132]

Reaching a pinnacle in the mountains, units of the 92nd met the enemy. Almost immediately the Buffalo Soldiers felt they were about to be nonsensically sacrificed. "Our position on the mountain was exactly face-to-face with the

Germans," wrote a second lieutenant from the 370th Combat Regiment. "The only thing separating us was a mound of rock. We could almost toss cigarettes back and forth..."

> *"Two paths led around the mound. One was convenient for us to get to their position and the other equally convenient for them to get to ours... The Germans appeared to have settled for this Mexican standoff. Not our command, they kept calling to throw us into that meat-grinder. The guys had tried at night, in the rain, in fog, and they had paid for it. Nevertheless, these calls would come in regularly, like our probes and attempts had been a howling success."*[133]

Again, the same comment might have been penned by any white second lieutenant serving down the line in one of the all-white divisions. World War II was a colorblind meat-grinder when it came to the subject of infantry patrols. The purpose of these incursions was to preclude the enemy from establishing new weapons positions and the laying of land mines. In the minds of those separated on the basis of skin color, however, the perception was that the 92nd was being set-up to become cannon fodder.

An anecdotal book first published in 1975 by Wayne State University Press entitled *The Invisible Soldier* (compiled and edited by Mary Penick Motley) relates occurrences that are troubling.

> *"The captain told him not to ever give an order to a white officer."*

This dressing down, according to African-American Staff Sergeant David Cason, Jr., 365th Regiment, occurred when a black first lieutenant dared to offer directions to a white second lieutenant. It happened in front of the men.[134] Other Buffalo Soldier's statements echo this event repeating itself at different units.

> *"Interesting point: our battalion commander and our company commander had both been evacuated. Neither man had been hit, for they had not been in the vicinity of the fire protective line."*

Staff Sergeant Charles Brown, 370th Regiment [Ed: absence of white leadership in the combat area was a recurring complaint][135]

> *"We had ten white lieutenants come into this outfit and only one was sent to a rifle company, but all black lieutenants go to rifle companies."*

Warrant Officer Robert Millender, 371st Regiment[136]

If you saw a black captain or someone in field grade, you could be sure he was a doctor or chaplain, neither of which had command functions.

First Lieutenant Wade McCree, 365th Regiment[137]

The Invisible Soldier contains statements from a dozen or so former Buffalo Soldiers; their recollections of World War II army race issues are uniformly bitter.

Bill's frustration at being stuck in the tent city began to boil over. On December 2 he complained: "I came over here to work and not sit around." Later in his overseas tour Bill would reflect back upon his stay at this place: "Many of the officers over here spend months in the replacement depot. Sometimes their units are dissolved, or reduced in numbers and they are sent to the depot to await a re-assignment. They really become forgotten men… I would not wish to be there again."[138] Replacement depot Naples had a notorious reputation in the U.S. Army as an inefficient, festering mud hole. One account had 30,000 U.S. soldiers "temporarily" stationed there. Indeed, the *New York Times Magazine* in 1945 referred to "repple-depples" in general as "dreary places."[139]

Dick Stroud wrote to Sue: "For once in the Army Lady Luck was on my side. I was the first one out of the replacement depot." Dick had been quartered with a Neapolitan family that had an extra bedroom in their fifth floor apartment; he would take his meals, most of them at an officer's mess "which was at one time a very nice hotel." He worked at a nearby office in the procurement side of Army Air Forces supply, telling Sue that he prepared requisitions and controlled stock levels.[140] Dick noted that the group he shipped over with had been "really scattered" all over Italy,[141] but he seemed pleased with his overall personal set-up. On the day he moved into the apartment he wrote: "This afternoon as I was unpacking the family immediately pressed my wool shirts and pants."[142]

Jack King from 91st Infantry HQ had been spared the repple-depple altogether. Landing at Port of Naples Jack camped out for a few days on a marble floor inside a University of Naples building before proceeding to Rome by water. This had been his introduction to Italy, one with a roof over his head!

John Lesesne arrived in Italy around the same time as Jack and had a whole month at repple-depple Naples. John did not complain about this, however, perhaps because he had earlier experienced a month at repple-depple Canastel,

Oran, Algeria, a place he referred to as a "hell-hole." At least while at repple-depple Naples John could and did visit the city and also see Pompeii, Sorrento and Vesuvius.

On a side note, the diary that John started on November 4, 1944 contains a short preamble detailing his approximate two and one-half years of active military service prior to arriving in Italy. Entering the Army in February 1942 he served a year and one-half in the Panama Canal Zone and then was rotated to Fort Bliss, Texas, a place he disliked. In January 1944 he and eight other captains volunteered for overseas duty to avoid additional duty at this "tiring station" (John's words). On his way to Italy John had had some good times in North Africa, in fact upwards of two-months' worth after he was processed out of repple-depple Canastel. He found Tunisia beautiful and rented a villa there along with some other G.I.s that was formerly occupied by General Jimmy Doolittle. Female members of the U.S. military served as dance partners; the music was provided by a Victrola.

When John arrived at Naples he had no idea how or where the Army might use him. He did not belong to a unit and had little or no experience with mortars. Being a captain with solid evaluations the Army decided to make John commanding officer of Company "B" of the 100th Chemical Mortar Battalion. Jay Staley who had been with John in Oran was made one of his platoon leaders. John would be responsible for the lives of many men, but first he needed to be trained-up. He recorded how this was done:

> [We] left Caserta early in Sept for Follonica [Ed: a region of Tuscany] where we were to be trained as the 100th Chemical Mortar Battalion. Our training area was General Balbo's country estate, looking across the water at Elba and Monte Christo. We had an officer's club in 'Balbo Castle,' but I had little time for this. We trained very hard — speed marches (five miles in fifty-one minutes), cross-country hikes, Me & My Pal courses [Ed: working in pairs for live fire exercises], snap shooting and obstacle courses. We also did firing problems with 4.2"s. The last week was "kill drills" — four night exercises.
>
> Twice we acted as infantry while the 99th Battalion was mortar, and then vice versa. The grand finale was for us an infantry problem of marching across mountains and occupying positions on the other side.

We left camp at 4:45 PM and marched steadily through the cold rain until 2:45 AM. What a night! We could use no lights and had trails only, part of the time. Once when I went to put my right foot down in the path (I could see nothing — only feel), it went into nothingness and I landed head first in a rocky creek bed. Only my steel helmet saved my skull. Finally reaching our objective, we spread out raincoats on the wet ground, wrapped in a blanket and drawing shelter halves over us, went to sleep — despite being soaking wet and very cold. McGuiness loaned me one of his blankets as I had none — God Bless him. We stayed there until dawn when we came down out of the hill to the road and were camel back to camp by jeeps. On arriving my 1st Sgt. (Norm Rasmussen) and I had a big drink of my whiskey ration (Lord Calvert), the most enjoyable drink I've ever had.143

During this training John honed his skills as a map-reader. Battle maps were prepared daily for officers of the U.S. Fifth Army; it was critical to use the most current map available and also to be able to locate precisely the coordinates communicated in for a firing. A mistake could result in tragedy. After he had gained some experience, John wrote, "this long-range killing isn't hard," but by this he did not mean that it was without professional stress. His men would often shoot over the heads of U.S. infantrymen. A defective charge such as would happen on November 17 with white phosphorous could not be avoided; to be negligent in registering because a map was misread was another matter entirely. There was no margin for error. Information communicated describing a target was checked and re-checked and if possible ranges were confirmed by triangulation — geometry.

As Bill waited impatiently for the army snafu that had made him a tent prisoner of sorts to be cleared up, Allen Dulles assessed the complete lack of progress in peace seeking. Dulles had learned that the British had earlier in the month received what Dulles sarcastically termed "the same German dream" — that is, the Nazis joining the British and Americans in a glorious "common front against the Russians."[144] This, of course had been rejected out of hand — as it would be again later on — it was simply too late for that. Dulles liked the idea, however of stopping the communists. During his formative years as a cub diplomat he had followed the Bolshevik revolution, and he believed that the fault for the turmoil and suffering that it brought on was with those who proffered a utopian world based on the government control of all capital and the abolition of naturally occurring class distinctions. Dulles was from the school of thought that regarded the Soviet Union as, "... the emblem of torture and persecution."[145]

Following the British contact there had been a more recent tête à tête. The OSS had garnered that the Cardinal of Milan had secretly tried to mediate a deal between the Nazis and the Italian partisans. Essentially His Eminence hoped to broker a deal whereby German troops might be allowed safe conduct out of the country in exchange for their promise not to destroy Italy's industrial infrastructure while on the way out.[146] The partisans would have none of this of course — they smelled blood and were hell bent to show the world that they were a fighting force capable of liberating Italy. Dulles knew better, of course, but he was not part of this parley and he also knew there was nothing he could do to dissuade the partisans who were hotheads. Also, he was not unmindful that the mission of Allied forces in Italy was to *prevent* the German forces from leaving the country.

There was relative quiet now on the Italian front. With nothing going on as regards peace inquiries, Dulles nevertheless made a significant decision. Dulles had been told by his most trusted advisor, OSS agent Gero von Schulze Gaevernitz, that it was too dangerous to send an OSS man behind enemy lines to discuss surrender. Gaevernitz further advised that the Gestapo daily policed the activity of important German military commanders; any attempt on their part to wave a white flag would likely be discovered. Gaevernitz had at his disposal an underground network into and out of Nazi Germany and based on his input, Dulles directed Gaevernitz to put the word out in Germany that surrender discussions could be conducted in secrecy in neutral Switzerland. All any high-up Nazi official had to do to initiate the process would be to use intermediaries to contact Swiss intelligence; the Swiss would remain neutral but also cooperate at the border; Dulles would then set up the meeting at a safe house. Swiss Major Max Waibel would be most helpful in the role of facilitator.

Gaevernitz, of German-Jewish descent, had become a naturalized U.S. citizen before the war. Debonair, cordial-to-a-fault and in his early forties, Gaevernitz had been born into a prominent German family. His father Gerhart (who died in 1943) had been a member of the Weimar Parliament and a renowned college professor. It had been both the wealthy Jewish-American mother and the pacifist father who influenced the son to actively resist Nazism, that is, to do more than just protest. Gaevernitz himself at one time had dared to travel through Nazi Germany, but he stopped doing that when it declared war on the United States in December 1941.

Gaevernitz had family business interests in Switzerland and the use of two villas at the Swiss municipality of Ascona belonging to a brother-in-law who left Europe when the war approached. One dwelling was on the shore of beautiful Lake Maggiore, and the other high above it on a hillside. Gaevernitz was initially hired to screen those desiring to meet with Allen Dulles; as the war progressed he became the director's right hand man. One commentator noted that he divided his free time "between skiing and reading Seneca"[147]; another, a female member of the OSS, observed," "Gero was so extremely handsome!"[148]

Dulles knew that Gaevernitz could keep a confidence, and that he was the kind of individual all people — most important the enemy — could easily talk to. Gaevernitz's personal forte was to effectively advocate a strong position, yes, but to also to do it in a friendly manner. Dulles decided to compartmentalize his most important agent — some OSS office personnel in Berne knew that Gaevernitz was the personal assistant to the Director, but Dulles permitted only two agents other than himself to know what Gaevernitz now attempted to do. The availability of dwellings at Ascona was kept strictly secret. Much of Gaevernitz's spy work was done at Ascona, a 275-mile drive from Berne, a quiet out-of-the-way place on Lake Maggiore. This lake was shared by Nazi occupied Northern Italy and neutral Switzerland, with Ascona being on the Swiss side.

At Berne, security was tight at the bustling OSS station. Only three-digit numbers identified OSS agents; personal names were not used in meetings or correspondence. The British had instructed the Americans to do this before the United States entered the war. Dulles was agent #110.

With the liberation of France in 1944 Switzerland was accessible again to Americans. Clover Dulles hoped to join her husband in Berne in late 1944 but the poor health of Clover's mother delayed her departure. In the meantime, Dulles continued to enjoy the company of his mistress, Mary Bancroft, who wrote a tell-all book about Dulles in the 1980s. Dulles hired Bancroft in 1942 stating (per Bancroft): "We can let the work cover the romance and the romance cover the work."[149]

Dulles' lifestyle was the stuff of secret agent legend. His apartment at 23 Herrengasse, located in the medieval, most charming section of Berne, was perched high atop a ridge overlooking the horseshoe turning River Aare and had a balcony view of the Bernese Alps crowned by the Eiger massif in the distance. It was at the end of a beautifully arcaded cobblestoned cul-de-sac.

The butler was named Pierre.

For those wishing to enter from its front, Dulles had provided some measure of privacy by prevailing on the city authorities to turn off a nearby streetlight. For those entrants needing more anonymity, there was always the rear door, access to which involved a steep climb up from the river through terraced vineyards. Dulles used his apartment for meetings and did not attempt to hide the fact where he resided. He knew that the Germans knew. And he also knew where *they* resided. A small sign next to his front door read: "Allen W. Dulles, Special Assistant to the American Minister."[150]

—⁂—

On December 4, 1944, nine days after arriving in Italy, Bill was finally "found" by his not-too-far-away command. The MTOUSA Transportation Section "called the camp to find out what the holdup was in my reporting," Bill noted dryly in a letter to his parents. "I just completed my first day on my new job… I believe I will like it. My work will involve considerable travel and I should see a lot of this part of the world." He further described: "My job will be mostly observation, reports and recommendations."

Not everything was satisfactory for the new MTOUSA staff officer, however. To his dismay Bill learned *with certainty* that he would not receive mail for "three or four weeks." Bill gave no explanation for this but likely a communication announcing his arrival at AF Headquarters had to be mailed to "APO" (Army Post Office) New York to start the process. At this point Bill had not heard from his loved ones for three weeks.

As for accommodations, Bill's were arguably better than a tent: "I now have quarters in what formerly was part of a hospital," he wrote. "There is no heat in the rooms… it is hard to get used to the cold weather… damp and cold at night." Bill would soon learn, again to his dismay, that although he did not have a human roommate he was not alone.

Bill made no mention in his early letters of his direct superior Major Renick, but he would later. Renick would prove to be a bright spot in Bill's Italy experience.

The day that Bill reported to MTOUSA, December 4, was the same day that John learned that the big push was coming. If he had been startled by this revelation his diary does not reflect it: "Won seven bucks at poker tonight and I feel a bit badly about taking the boy's money, but I guess that's better than their taking mine."

Two days later Bill was issued an "ARMY EXCHANGE SERVICE RATION CARD" good for eight weeks. The markings on this card show that he used up his candy, chewing gum and smoking rations, but took only one beer (holders were entitled to eight beers, issued at the rate of one a week). Bill later wrote to Dotty: "We are given six packs [of cigarettes] a week and I use about two. I wish I could send you some of my extras but they are tax-exempt and we are not permitted to send them back. The natives... are so grateful for a few or a pack."[151] Bill often mentioned the young children put out to beg on the streets of Naples. Cigarettes had value on the black market; they could be bartered for other commodities, and Bill wrote of giving away his extra cigarettes.

Lieutenant Dick Stroud worked in an elaborate residence in downtown Naples that had been converted into an office.[152] Army-purchased folding chairs and tables were in sharp contrast to the home's highly polished wooden trim. A wall niche behind where Dick sat displayed a white marble Roman bust. The 18th Depot Supply Squadron was a material artery for two major fighting commands, one in the south at Foggia (Bari) where many long-range bombers were located, and in the north, Pisa, the most recent location selected for fighter-bomber squadrons. Boxes containing file cards — inventory control — were everywhere. Stroud, used to Texas flatlands had an adjustment to make as regards the ups and downs of Old World buildings. "These interminable stairs," he complained in a letter to his wife Sue, "... one level to the next."

As an aside, when outside Dick wore a "crush hat" that identified him clearly as air force. Aircrew officers started this trend by removing their steel hat rings so that earphones could be worn in flight; it was not long before the practice became popular with most USAAF officers regardless of flight status. The crush hat was symbolic — it distinguished wearers from the "lowly" ground forces.

Like Bill, Dick would see much of Italy.

In the north John Lesesne breathed a sigh of relief. "Got in three loads of ammo before daylight," he recorded in his diary on December 7. This welcome event had followed his 4:00 a.m. successful reconnaissance to find positions for two 81 mm mortars "on Highway 65." John noted that these new positions could not be approached during daylight hours: "Jerry is 1,500 yards away and has observation." The guns and ammo were there, however ready to be fired the following night before beating a hasty retreat.

Mortar work required stealth.

A few days earlier members of John's command post had captured two geese that were being fattened for Christmas and today there was this: "Key, McGuiness, and Hofmann went out for meat — found a hog and butchered it; so we'll have pork — this with the geese will fix us up pretty well."

—⁓—

On December 8 Lieutenant General Truscott and members selected by him to serve on his staff reported for duty at the Army Command Post at Futa Pass a few miles south of where John was. Truscott had been scheduled to relieve General Mark Clark as commanding general of the U.S. Fifth Army, the American fighting arm in Italy on December 16, and he would use this first week to familiarize himself with the military situation at the Italian front. As stated, General Clark was to be "bumped up" to the Fifteenth Army Group position, that is, promoted to take charge of both the British Eighth Army and the U.S. Fifth Army and he would report operationally to contemporaneously minted "Field Marshal and Supreme Commander," Harold Alexander. Truscott, a non-West Pointer, was an old hand in the MTO and his return involved a reunion with many of the men that he had previously served with.

Truscott focused immediately on Clark's "Pianoro Plan" — the frontal assault (or "push" as John called it) on a German strongpoint to breach the Gothic Line at the village of Pianoro on Highway 65 for the purpose of gaining favorable terrain. Later in his memoirs, he recorded discretely: "I came to learn that General Clark was very sensitive to any criticisms or suggestions pertaining to the Pianoro Plan."

The distance the U.S. Fifth Army would have to travel to reach Bologna from Pianoro using the highway was only twelve miles,[153] Truscott noted, and if Highway 64 to the west were used, the distance would be twice as long.

Additionally, Highway 64 was defended from a nearby ridge occupied by well-armed Germans. Clark advocated hard for attacking over the shortest distance.

As Truscott studied the plan details, he could not help but think back to the tug of war he had waded into the previous May between Alexander and Clark over the Anzio breakout. Sensing possible command decision conflict again for his future, Truscott resolved to be mentally prepared. The General had the same leadership style for subordinates and superiors alike: respectful but also dominant.

One of the immediate problems facing Truscott in his new command position involved the low morale of his men. Organizationally the Fifth United States Army consisted of four corps. One of these, "II Corps," consisted of three infantry divisions, the 34th, 88th and 91st, [154] and was commanded by Major General Geoffrey Keyes. Shortly after Truscott arrived, Keyes delivered to him a copy of an extraordinary letter that he had written to General Clark dated November 28, pertaining to the performance of one of his divisions. The letter had been written in response to a Congressional inquiry.

> *After an exhaustive study of the disciplinary and morale status of the 34th Infantry Division I am of the conclusion that certain personnel of this division should be withdrawn from combat. The division has maintained a consistently high AWOL and Courts Martial rate for some time. An inordinately large percentage of the Courts Martial cases have been for misbehavior before the enemy, disobedience of orders, aggravated AWOL, and related offenses. The division has a high "exhaustion" rate. Investigation discloses that all of these conditions are traceable, either directly or indirectly, to a common, motivating influence: a deep conviction by the older or original, officers and men of the 34th Division, that they have done their part in the war, that they should be permitted to return to the United States and the struggle left to those who have not been absent from home for two years. After periods of rest, rehabilitation, and reorganization in the rear areas, the unit displays little, if any, increased efficiency when again committed to action. The attitude of the men would seem to stem, not from "combat" weariness, but from general "war" weariness.[155]*

Truscott had been in the army long enough to know that the problem described by Keyes was not endemic to the 34th Infantry Division alone; that the 34th had been selected for this special recognition since Congress was now involved, and at this particular point in time the 34th division had plenty of company among other long-serving units. One of the problems was if a deserter could make it to a major city like Rome or Naples, or possibly even a lesser city, he had a reasonable chance at hiding out the war.[156] Indeed, a G.I. who happened to serve in the same outfit as Dick Stroud, the 18th Depot Supply Squadron, in an oral history project explained how easy it was to lose oneself in Naples towards war's end, even if wearing a U.S. uniform! "If I took off my tie," former Sergeant Anthony Abilo told his interviewer, "I would be one of the locals." Abilo explained that Italian soldiers had been issued U.S. uniforms at this stage of the war, but without neckties.[157] As the war dragged on desertions happened more and more all over Europe. From a morale standpoint this was devastating to the U.S. Army.

Truscott favored returning men to the United States who had served in combat for three years, but knew that the devil was always in the details and that in any event, it would be the War Department that would make this decision.

When Truscott took over command of the U.S. Fifth Army he knew he would have eleven combat divisions reporting to him (or in some cases the equivalent of divisions e.g., a Brazilian Expeditionary Force) through the corps-structured chain of command. He also knew that he would need the entirety of this force for what was coming; that he could hardly afford to send even one soldier home. He decided what to do with the Keyes letter; he would forward it to MTOUSA, General McNarney, for disposition. This was not a tactical problem, after all!

Truscott wrote to McNarney that he had "no personal knowledge as of yet" about the 34th Division; he also suggested a three-year rotation home for all U.S. combat troops.[158]

As an aside, John Lesesne (who then supported the 34th) made his own observation about the division. "... [M]ost of them have 'the big head,' " he wrote, describing the 34th officers, "on the whole, the 91st Division was much better to work with."[159]

In Southern Italy Bill settled in and familiarized himself with the Naples area. On December 9, he wrote Dotty: "Rode about forty miles in a jeep yesterday… have seen many foreign makes of cars and trucks. There are about as many broken down along the road or out of gas as there are running. The people are very careless about traffic and many of the natives get killed in traffic accidents."

"The Italian people are friendly and eager to help out and cooperate with the Allies. I am beginning to learn a few Italian words. The Latin of high school is slightly valuable after all." He ended with: "I expect to start on a trip next week and will be gone for about a month …" Bill knew he would soon be going to the front to inspect the delivery of supplies by the Transportation Corps but due to censorship he could not mention his destination to Dotty.

There is no doubt that Bill immediately appreciated that the Royal Palace of Caserta was far preferable to the repple-depple! Among his memorabilia are to be found several documents pertaining to the palace: a newspaper clipping, a postcard, a small pamphlet entitled *Historical and Architectural Guide*, and (something amusing considering a war was on) a "Programme" for an opera listing British officers stationed at the palace as opera directors for the "SEASON 1944-45." British Field Marshal The Honorable Sir Harold R.L.G. Alexander, Supreme Allied Commander of the Mediterranean Theater of Operations, was the senior opera director.

Built in the mid-18th century for the King of Naples with 1200 rooms and fifty-six stairways and sometimes called "Bourbon Palace," the Reggia di Caserta was intended to rival Versailles. The palace ran some 800 feet in length and most, like Bill, worked on the fifth, or top floor.

As classically beautiful as this palace was, many of the working spaces there — the British offices being located at one far-end and the Americans, at the other — were *not* luxurious. Beaverboard, or plywood had hastily been erected in order to section off small beehive-like compartments. A large number of workers, military and civilian alike toiled at the palace and this space partitioning needed to be done in order to provide some minimal degree of privacy. For a wartime foreign duty-station, however, Bill had still hit a jackpot. He had a royal roof over his head; Caserta was a good place for a home base.

There was a special thing that Bill immediately appreciated above all else about AFHQ. He found a special room that he could retreat to during off hours, a quiet reading room for the enjoyment of newspapers and magazines and also the writing of letters home. "It is heated," he wrote.[160]

At Company "B" in the north comfort was harder to find. John described visiting platoons three and four in mid-December on a rainy day and his jeep stalling out in one of the eleven streambeds to be crossed. "The water almost took me out of the jeep," he recorded. Soaking wet up to his waist, John slogged to his C.P. and "drank the flask of whiskey I'd been saving for such an occasion." He gave his only dry pair of pants to another wet traveler and put on his "leg handles" — leggings.

The following day, December 9 John learned from Headquarters, 135th Infantry Regiment, 34th Division, that during the "pending operation" Company "B" was to "...do plenty of firing — unlimited ammo" he noted in his diary. This entry was followed a day later by: "This morning I went to company rear and thence to Battalion [Ed: 100th Chemical Mortar HQ] to get the straight ammo situation. It's still very confused." The situation was not confused. There was no ammo available.

—⋙—

In one of the spacious offices at the royal palace, MTOUSA — General McNarney — worked on a reply to General Truscott's letter about the manpower and morale needs of the U.S. Fifth Army. McNarney wrote tersely, pointing out that the problem was being worked on and that the problem was a big one. "The build-up overseas in 1942 had been so rapid that rotation at the end of three years would soon effect several hundred thousand men," McNarney declared. He then slammed the 34th Infantry Division directly, pointing to its "command failure particularly at the lower echelons"; he specifically named several other better performing U.S. divisions that had served as long as or longer than the 34th and were just as or even more deserving of relief.

"Some misguided individual introduced a bill in Congress to require the 34th Division to be returned to the United States," McNarney lamented. He further stated, crustily: "proper public relations" should be applied to "... convey to the home areas of the 34th Division [Ed: meaning to convey to the loved ones of longest serving soldiers] and to the public at large, the inestimable damage that is done by this over-sympathetic and pitying attitude."[161]

In regard to rotating men back home Truscott had no choice but to accept McNarney's position in the matter. He had done his best for his longest serving men, however, and (undoubtedly) they knew it. As regards the 34th, well, enough had been said. Truscott resolved to limit his fighting to the field and steer clear of Congress and recrimination. Whether the two generals collaborated on a "good guy — bad guy" management approach Truscott did not mention in his memoirs.

As for his relationship with Clark, Truscott had learned from a top aide to Eisenhower that Winston Churchill had personally asked that he, Truscott, take command of the U.S. Fifth Army for the final campaign.[162] Truscott must have appreciated that it was good to have the confidence of those in the highest positions, but being an old-line soldier he also knew not to ask for help outside of the chain of command; he could not, would not, bypass his new boss.

Above all else Truscott sensed the U.S. Fifth Army desperately needed a victory — one that would be swift, decisive and most important, from a military leadership perspective, competently planned and led. The ultimate remedy for the 34th would be to win this war, Truscott knew. There was no substitute for triumph.

—⁂—

It did not take Naples long to wear on Dick Stroud. Shortly after he arrived, he wrote to his wife: "Theft is punishable by a fine of twenty cents, so it is almost a profession, as is begging an art. The women have a profession too, a *respected one,* if you can imagine." The schoolteacher turned supply officer had entered the middle ages and knew it. Describing the streets as "very narrow" he noted: "Food markets are as a rule from a cart in the street or a hole in the wall sort of thing... no windows, no refrigeration, all in the open."[163] In the end, like Bill, however, he would feel pity for the Italians especially ravaged by a deep poverty freakishly brought on by war.

Also like Bill, there was a recurrent theme in Dick's letters about a specific hope for a stable future in one special place with one special spouse. This thirty-nine year-old wrote about the subject of permanence to his wife: "Your description of the apartment made me homesick indeed, but I'll bet our home will be a lot more attractive."[164] As an aside, Dick's daughter (who was born after the war) would write seventy years after-the-fact: "I keep getting the feeling that the letters he wrote — when he couldn't reveal much — were a link to the sane and 'normal' world. As long as he could write, that was still tangible."

Bachelor John Lesesne's focus during this time frame was different than the older married men. On December 14, the twenty-four year-old recorded in his diary:

> *I wish I had a gal like Mary R. to talk with sometimes. We've been*
> *friends a long time, despite Quassela... Have never been really in love*
> *with her like with Sally or Jackie but have always felt a certain affection*
> *for her — she is the kind of gal I can tell my troubles to — I must seem*
> *awfully fickle!*

One of the documents that Bill retained after the war is a mimeograph copy of a typed poem entitled, *Panorama of Italy.* A barely legible word appearing to be "Choruole" is handwritten on the poem in pencil, possibly the autograph of the author. It is a grim poem, but a telling one.

No record could be located that this poem was published,[165] and unless noted, the same may be said for the other poems appearing in this story. World War II witnessed considerable poetry writing by military personnel. Chances are this particular poem was written for the benefit of loved ones at home and also the enjoyment of the AFHQ staff. Its title notwithstanding, it is likely *Panorama* was written more with Naples in mind than Italy as a whole.

Panorama of Italy

If I were an artist, with nothing to do,
I'd paint a picture, a composite view,
Of historic Italy, in which I'd show,
Visions of contrasts, the high and the low.

There'd be towering mountains, a deep blue sea;
Filthy brats yelling "Carmella" at me;
High plumed horses, and colorful carts;
Two toned tresses on hustling tarts.

I'd show Napoleonic cops, the carabiniere;
Dejected old women, with too much to carry;
A dignified gentleman, with a "Balbo" beard;
Bare-breasted bambino, both ends smeared.

Castel and palace, opera house too;
Hotel on a mountain, glorious view;
Homes made of weeds, brickbats and mud;
People covered with scabs, scurvy and crud.

Fine old homes, pride of the nations,
Beautiful to see, but no sanitation;
Well-equipped schools, without a scholar;
Temples of learning, surrounded by squalor

Chapels and churches, great to behold;
Each a king's ransom, in glittering gold;
Poverty and want, men craving for food;
Picking through garbage practically nude.

[Ed: to be continued]

12 December 1944
Letter # 34

Dear Hon and Davy,

This evening I am acting as Duty Officer. The job consists of sitting in the head office and answering the phones. Another duty is to go through the Section late in the afternoon, collect all the classified papers to be destroyed and then supervise their destruction by fire. It was about the first time I have been real warm since arrival.

The Sergeant on duty tonight is also writing a letter and just about burning up the other typewriter. Perhaps one can think faster after a couple of years over here? Most of the men here went through the African campaign. They all say they liked Africa much better than Italy.

For a little while each evening, or at least some evenings, some of the Officer's Clubs have beer for sale. After that is gone they sell several kinds of mild poisons. The men complain about it but keep right on drinking the stuff.

The Colonel just came in, whipped out his portable typewriter and finished a V-mail letter. By comparison the Sergeant is the tortoise. I guess many years of hard work in the Army makes one a good typist.

In another letter done while serving as duty officer, Bill added, "I hope you don't mind the typewriter... My stock goes up every time the Colonel sees me working at it."[166]

Bill was correct about the typewriter being essential to the war effort. A commentator noted: "Among the ships sunk off Normandy during the D-Day invasion was a cargo ship carrying 20,000 Royal and Underwood typewriters intended for the use of the Allies."[167] This was a big deal when it happened.

As a typist Jack King tested out at fifty-five when he joined the army,[168] which put him within the range for a *professional* typist — fifty to eighty wpm. And when Dick Stroud typed his letters to Sue, they were practically letter perfect. Dick had learned to type early on when during his youth he temporarily moved from Dallas to Detroit where he supported himself by working two jobs both requiring typing skills: as a bellhop at the Book Cadillac Hotel and a security guard at the General Motors Building. While traveling in Italy, which Dick would do frequently in February and March of 1945 to inventory supply stocks, Dick put his typing skills to good use in hammering out dozens of V-Mails to Sue. On the road, blank V-Mail sheets would be provided at every depot and a typewriter could pack in more words than handwriting.

—∾—

In Northern Italy General Truscott was having a devil of a time trying to justify launching the Pianoro Plan. The plan called for five infantry divisions and one-armored division to advance upon four mountains with, "enormously rugged features," Truscott recorded. He further observed:

> This was the most heavily fortified area along the entire front — held by German forces not materially inferior in strength to those which would be attacking. Under unfavorable conditions of weather and terrain it seemed to me an appalling undertaking. Even with overwhelming support of our air forces, I thought it would be a difficult and costly venture even if it could succeed.[169]

Truscott needed more information and more time. He dug his heels in and resolved not to let General Clark badger him into doing something that he did not believe in. He appreciated he needed a bona fide *reason*, more than just his military opinion alone, for Alexander to become actively involved.

"Remember that warm, soft mud last summer?"

CHAPTER FOUR:
LEGHORN AND SNOW POSTS

December 15–19, 1945

BY MID-DECEMBER a winter battlefront lull had set in over parts of northern Europe with the assumption being that fighting would resume when the weather warmed, unless of course the Nazis somehow finally came to the realization that absent their surrender Germany would be completely demolished by Allied air power. Hitler remained in control, however, intransigent to reality and scheming to win. Certainly there was no expectation on the part of the Allies that the Germans had the capability of launching a substantial offensive, and the British, who regularly intercepted German military message traffic using their code-breaking Ultra machine, had learned nothing suggesting that a new Nazi war planning effort was afoot for the western front.

As the southern spearhead of the Red Army neared Budapest, Hungary, some 280 miles from the Italian border, Yugoslav communist forces scored solid successes moving northwards along the Adriatic.

In Italy, Bill traveled north.

> *Dec 15, 1944*
> *Letter No. 10*
>
> *Dear Folks,*
>
> *... Had a safe trip yesterday, required about two hours by air. I can see snow-capped mountains from here and the air is much cooler.*
>
> *Our quarters here are in a mansion or large dwelling of a former Baron — beautiful building and grounds situated on top of a hill. Most rooms have fireplaces. We heat with a combination of oil, gas, and a little wood in small army stoves... You should see the furniture, Mother... great massive chests of drawers, bureaus, bookcases...*

...We will be up here about a month and then return to our permanent station. [Ed: the next paragraph was partly cut out by ARMY EXAM-INER 0619]

The country is very pretty from the air... We flew directly over [Ed: word removed by scissors] and I was able to identify [Ed: word removed]. Hope to visit it while here.

The Army travel orders issued to Bill to place him on this military flight are not to be found in his service record. One may surmise, however, that Bill's flight was northward from Naples, and that "Examiner 0619" cut out the word "Rome" and also a Roman landmark, probably either the Vatican or Coliseum. With respect to his military assignment, in a letter to Dotty Bill made an intriguing comment: "The request by the Chief that I submit a weekly report direct to him was somewhat [of] a surprise to others here."[170] The "Chief" referred to was Colonel Lastayo who was in charge of the MTOUSA Transportation Center and Major Renick's boss.[171]

Bill's letters to both his parents and Dotty dated December 16 (that were not opened by an examiner) reveal his exact location and not in a subtle manner: He mentions climbing a famous leaning tower! As an aside, it was a common practice in World War II (almost a game for G.I.s) to attempt to slip locations past a censor. Dick Stroud for instance used, "Tomb of Virgil" to denote the City of Naples to Sue who as a Latin teacher quoted Virgil and knew well what city he was buried in.[172]

The town of Pisa is approximately twenty-five miles inland from the western Italian port of Leghorn (again today known as Livorno) and is approximately three quarters north up the Italian boot. Per the *Office of History, U.S. Army Corps of Engineers*, Leghorn, the third largest port facility in Italy was a major staging and supply area for the U.S Fifth Army. Rome lies directly in line between Naples and Leghorn. It was the city of Rome that Bill flew over, no doubt.

On the Etruscan Coast in Tuscany, Leghorn was the most completely demolished port in the Mediterranean during World War II. Both the Germans on the ground and the Americans in the air destroyed the port and much of Leghorn itself before the U.S. Army captured it on July 19, 1944. For the German's part, they erected barricades, blew up bridges and sank twenty ships in the harbor to make the port unusable. The U.S. Army Air Forces hit the city with fifty raids, dropping thousands of tons of bombs. When the Americans arrived they confronted a high number of deadly landmines planted by the retreating Nazis.

The *U.S. Army Center of Military History* summed up the transportation situation in this area succinctly and suggested why Bill, a car and truck expert, had been ordered north: "Although they [Ed: the American forces] had captured Leghorn and begun restoring its harbor before the beginning of the North Apennines Campaign, the supplies off-loaded there moved slowly and tortuously through the mountains to reach the men on the front line."[173]

On the day that Bill flew north John made a telling entry in his diary:

> *Got call from Lippy that 135th had found some 4.2" ammo. Went over to find out where it was — about 350 rounds in a rather accessible place. Agreed with S-3, 135th [Ed: Operations Officer, 135th Regiment, 34th Infantry Division] that if he would have a mule team bring it to road I'd have jeeps pick it up and we'd fire it for his regiment "off the record" — to be fired during the push. I say "off the record" for ammo expenditures as well as withdrawals from the dump are specified. Have just been notified that our allocation from the fifteenth to twentieth is zero — ammo critical. Of course that will be changed if the push comes off on schedule. I hear its been postponed again — originally the 8th and even now several days to go — bad for morale of the rifle doggies I imagine.*

In the evening after the first day of his new assignment in the north, writing in a makeshift bunkroom in the baron's mansion (that Bill would later refer to as "the big house") and using his knee as a table, Bill described to his wife his first impression of Italy from the air and then what he saw on the ground. He was conflicted by what he experienced that day. Bill's odyssey, related below, could be appropriately titled: "The Ecstasy and Agony." In the latter part of his letter for the first time Bill really detailed the grief of war.

> *Italy is very pretty from the air… Every hill and [many] mountain peaks are crowned by a village, city, or a large house or castle. Most of the villages have a church with a tall tower, dome or steeple, and nearly all have high walls through or around them. All of the land [that] can be farmed is neatly laid out in small patches separated by rows of small trees. The hillsides are terraced and every square inch of land is used. Many large stone houses cover the country between the villages. Most of the roofs are red tile and have less pitch than ours at home. Courtyards*

in the buildings are popular. The country is green in the valleys, gray on the mountain slopes and white on the mountaintops. They have a huge species of pine tree [that] has a top like a giant umbrella. The lower limbs appear to be trimmed for wood; the trees grow large and so tall they are beautiful when seen against the sky along the tops of the hills.

When one comes down to the ground though, he realizes there is a war on and the people have a desperate struggle to live. Two of us came from the Transportation Section, a Major Cowan and myself. He is interested in rail and water shipping. I am convinced now I have a real job to do and feel confident I can do some good.

Today I rode 155 miles in a command reconnaissance car... On the highway, one comes in close contact with the people. I feel so sorry for them. Up here the children beg for chocolate instead of cigarettes. I know from their faces many of them are not friendly towards the Allies. Their homes have been ruined, their stock stolen, their families torn apart, their public buildings, factories, bridges, roads, schools, canals, docks, airports and practically everything except their churches have become partly or completely demolished. Now they are forced to scrape for a living as best they can. This evening we passed many of them carrying bundles of shrub-bery, small sticks, twigs and pieces of rotting timber for fuel. Even up here where it is considerably cooler, bare knees on the small children and boys up to older ages seems the rule. Seldom [are there] any hats. The little kids' legs look so red and cold and their noses all run... I don't know how they endure it. The old people look so small, withered and tired. They seem to have lost all hope.

On the roads there are thousands of bicycles ridden mostly by men and women of the middle class and ages. So much traffic from the Army makes it very dusty and dirty in the cities. Many of the paved sections are dusty from driving over and through the debris. We passed a refuse dump today and it was being carefully combed for bits of wood, cardboard, metal scraps and anything that might be eaten.

The buildings here are nearly all of stone, reinforced by some steel and wood rafters, etc. The walls are thick and rebuilding them seems such a hopeless task.

[I] am wondering what the Congressional Committee on Military Affairs sees as they tour this region in their C-54 luxury planes… I would be interested in any reports they print [up] back home. I doubt if they see what I have seen.

It turned out that Bill was only half-correct about churches being protected from destruction. The U.S. Fifth Army had a policy not to billet soldiers inside churches, one that Captain John Lesesne learned about the hard way. The month earlier soon after arriving John wrote about he and another officer seeking out a bivouac spot for some of his men to spend the night. "Very hard to find place," he recorded. "We finally decided on a cemetery with a small chapel even though under enemy observation." John elaborated: "In fact a big shell had landed here shortly before, but we were desperate. Just before moving in we received an order from Headquarters, Fifth Army saying churches would not be used for quarters."[174]

Bill was only partially correct because the U.S. Army routinely used church steeples and towers for observation posts. The Germans targeted many as a consequence (John would later write about this).

As stated, the restructuring of the Allied Mediterranean chain of command went into effect on the day that Bill wrote his impassioned letter. General Mark Clark, who had commanded the U.S. Fifth Army since it was activated in North Africa on 5 January 1943, moved up to become Commander Fifteenth Army Group responsible for all British and American fighting units in Italy. As scheduled, on December 16, 1944 Clark departed U.S. Fifth Army Headquarters at Futa Pass near the Gothic Line for a new headquarters in the woods near Florence. The *Fifth Army History* reflects the compliment that it paid to General Clark upon his departure:

> *"… General Clark had guided the destinies of Fifth Army through many months of hard campaigning. Like the Gothic Line fighting of the past fall, it had been a campaign marked by brilliant victories and bitter disappointments. Fifth Army would take pride in being the first American army to invade Hitler's Fortress Europe; the first Allied Army to capture a European capital; and until 6 June 1944 [D-Day] the only American army opposing the Wehrmacht.*[175]

This reorganization had little direct impact on Bill but likely had a positive impact for the U.S. Fifth Army. The nice write-up notwithstanding, over time a number of military leaders as well as the rank and file had come to question Clark's competency as a tactician and his ability to motivate fighting men. Promoted "up" in Clark's situation may have had the effect of placing him in the chain of command between two individuals who thought differently than he did about the subject of military tactics.

In any event, the commander selected to replace Clark (and also report to him but whose stated preference was to serve in France) was well known and respected by all members of the U.S. Army. Truscott wisely eschewed playing to the press (as Clark had been accused of doing repeatedly) and he created a persona among the men that was favorably received. Like Patton he dressed up for his star role; his sartorial trademark underneath his leather jacket was a white silk scarf; he also wore his "lucky" cavalry boots to show off before the troops. He was proud of the fact that in his early army days he had been a horse soldier, and that he had excelled in the very rough and tumble manly sport of polo. Unlike Patton, Truscott prided himself at being only "a little bit of a son of a bitch," not a big one, and then only sometimes, which again struck a chord with the men. He was aggressive yes, and constantly expressed that there was no substitute for winning.

When he trained soldiers he expected much: the "Truscott trot" meant a four mph infantry march — not unlike what Confederate General Stonewall Jackson expected of his "foot cavalry." This was a challenging pace for any infantry soldier to sustain and in any century. By one account Truscott had a very "gravelly" voice; by another, "very soothing" (this was caused by accidently putting acid into his mouth as a child). The General enjoyed plentiful spirits and tobacco and was forty-nine years old when he assumed command of the U.S. Fifth Army. Not classically handsome, perhaps, and carrying a few pounds ("stocky") he had an engaging smile and could turn on the charm when he wanted to. Truscott had the gift of communication, no doubt.

In an irony of sorts, Bill's accommodations near the front were by *far superior* to those of the commanding general of the U.S. Fifth Army! At the time, the Army Command Post was housed in "trailers, tents, and a few prefabricated buildings" on the north side of lonely Futa Pass off Highway 65 where there were "a few scattered trees" but for the most part only barren and windy mountain slopes, that in the distance rose to as high as 5,000 or 6,000 feet. Truscott had his own small van for sleeping and personal use, like Clark before him, but in it he slept on an army cot the same as Bill and all "dog face" infantry soldiers. For conferences there was a prefabricated building known as "The Hut"[176] that lacked amenities and space. It was a grim place to spend a winter but a symbolically appropriate one for a commander who would lead soldiers spread out all over the mountains and encamped in terrible conditions.

The big house at nearby Signa fascinated Bill, no doubt, with its spectacular views and timeless charm. He wrote to Dotty: "I don't believe I've told you much of the place where we are staying. It is a mansion of perhaps forty or fifty rooms, three or four stories high and U-shaped. [The] ceilings are high [with] many large beautiful fireplaces and some of the original furniture. Some of the bookcases, highboys and cupboards are as nice woodwork as I have ever seen. The big stone stairways are impressive but lost in the enormous hallways." In a subsequent letter Bill noted the house had a roofed bell tower "with balconies in all directions" and that women drew drinking water from a stone well in the courtyard by lowering a bucket on a rope.

Bill's personal accommodations were not pampering: "I share a large room with five other captains," he wrote. "The civilian help place cans of water in the room every day and help keep the place clean. A bathroom down the hall may be used for No. 1 but No. 2 requires a short hike down the side hill to the open air, surrounded by burlap and covered by canvas. We may take a shower in the former swimming pool about 100 yards from the house."

When Bill was stationed in Chicago he and Dotty frequented a department store there that he now mentioned to Dotty. Being thin and perpetually cold Bill was proud of the fact that he had come prepared. He effused: "I brought... the big canvas bedroll with *five* army-blankets..." and then noted: "Two blankets issued to me in the States are stamped 'Marshall Field' so I enjoy them more." Bill additionally brought with him a comforter, sheets, and a pillow with case; he indicated the U.S. Fifth Army provided the cot. "I sleep very warm and enjoy my rest," he wrote. He added: "I make my own bed. They would do it if I left it and also polish shoes if the polish and brush is handy."

Three days later, Bill wrote how the business offices at the big house ran on a twenty-four-hour basis, with two shifts of twelve hours each: "Of course a shift includes three meals, time out for chores, etc., which brings it down to about a normal day of work."

All and all the big house was not a bad set-up Bill observed: "Our mess here is about the best I have had in the Army.... They make excellent soup and have fresh meat. The air here is more invigorating. It is cold enough that a small fire is provided, and our room where I am writing this is quite comfortable. We have electric lights of low power but enough. The power is generated by Army equipment. This building is the first dry place that I have [stayed] in since I got off the boat."

Bill reminisced as he recounted his experiences: "Last night ... after I went to bed the night was filled with strange noises — snoring in at least four keys, a very bad catfight outside and squirrels jumping across the roof. Remember how the acorns used to fall on the cottage roof up at Ashland? Those were wonderful days."

"I am to go out on an all-day trip again tomorrow. The men here seem eager to cooperate and give me all possible help. Col. H _ _ _ was here a few months ago (we are not allowed to name anyone in letters with the rank of Colonel and above). He was quite impressed by the operations."

As an aside, the prohibition against using colonel's and above names in letters apparently did not apply to diaries or journals, or at least John didn't think so. John mentioned Colonel Brown (34th Infantry Division Assistant C.O.), Colonel Boyle (Chemical Warfare Services Officer) and the aforementioned Colonels Broedlow and Reynolds several times.

Bill's letter contained a premonition: "If there is to be a little new member of our family, I will be so happy and proud." Bill could not have been aware that Dotty was pregnant when he left to travel to Italy, but she was. "My mail will be another week now in reaching me," he wrote due to his temporary assignment in Northern Italy. I have about given up receiving any before the New Year."

The Italian front was quiet in the west during this time frame but not so in the east. In the Eighth Army sector the 10th Indian Division secured Pergola, the New Zealand 2nd Division established bridgeheads over the Senio River and the British V Corps advanced on Faenza.[177]

"The Headquarters Company for the 91st Infantry Division at Pietramala was located on a plain south of the mountain range," Jack explained. "It was a home of fifteen or more rooms used by the adjutant general's staff. We had stoves in the office rooms with chimneystacks sticking out the windows."

The army orders that Jack and his reports generated there were important government documents. Many were recreational leave orders — a few days in Florence or Rome or some nearby resort spot. The government often provided free transportation and shelter on an availability basis. The orders were important as they served as written proof that the carrier had permission to be away from his unit. MPs on the street might well ask (and often did) to see a serviceman's "papers."

If temporary duty orders were needed to send someone to a different location, in addition to identifying the who what when where and why, an order prepared would normally contain: "… the travel involved is chargeable to …". It was a critical function that this accounting data be inputted correctly, and this Jack and his reports did. When interviewed Jack never claimed to be anything more than a typist; the 91st had selected and promoted him for more than just this manual ability, however. Telling is his diary entry of May 17, 1943, written four days after going on active duty: "Took I.Q. test got 150 the highest in our group."

"The sleeping rooms were unheated and it could get below zero some nights," Jack said. He added, unrelated: "I need size fifteen overshoes, and the Army could not supply me with them. My mother mailed me my own." The circumstance was that Jack's large feet forestalled his military career from the onset. His diary confirms he was delayed from processing out of Fort Benjamin Harrison, IN, for the better part of a month in the spring of 1943 waiting for special order size fifteen boots to arrive in the mail.[178]

The commanding general of the 91st, Major General William G. Livesay had started his army career before World War I as a buck private. Typical for his generation, Jack had respect for authority and perhaps doubly so for someone who had come up through the ranks. "General Livesee had a good reputation," he observed. Jack could not recall often seeing the General, however. "He was usually at the front," Jack observed.

Judge advocates (army lawyers) and quartermasters worked and lived in the same place as Jack, and rounded out an administrative command that supported 13,000 to 15,000 combat infantry soldiers. Each army division had a similar company HQ.

At this place while near the Gothic Line, Jack's only enemy encounter had been an airplane that would fly over every evening at the same time, presumably to take photographs. "He never dropped any bombs," Jack recollected. "We nicknamed him *Bed Check Charlie*." Jack was open about his good fortune to have the assignment that he had: "I did not see a real fighting German during the entirety of the war!" he exclaimed. As stated, he readily agreed with the military axiom *luck counts*. In this regard, it might be noted that Jack had also been lucky in that Pietramala was only forty miles north of Florence.

In Naples Dick Stroud was not enjoying his off-duty experience as much as Jack. Being in the Old World was an eye-opener for Dick, and apparently not an uplifting one: "The streets, or should we call them alleys, are very narrow..."[179] In letter after letter Dick related how Naples was overpopulated, dark in places, impoverished, smelly, seriously battle-damaged and lacking in artistry. The view of Naples Bay from upon high and Mount Vesuvius was spectacular, however; Dick liked that.

Bill's observation that the Italian people suffered "stock stolen" was spot on. Hungry American soldiers (undoubtedly British too) were the culprits. A second lieutenant from the 92nd used humor to describe the circumstance: "... the men often supplemented our rations with chickens that strayed out in the fields of the villages further down the mountain and climbed up the mountain into our kitchen." On one occasion headquarters called him about a complaint registered by a villager regarding the theft. "This I emphatically denied, quite indignant that anyone would dare impugn the reputation of the American soldier, as I content-edly munched on a chicken bone ..."[180]

The African-Americans comprising the 92nd experienced pretty much what all combat infantrymen along the Gothic Line endured at this time frame. Bless-edly, the enemy in the mountains north of Serchio Valley remained relatively calm. The Germans held the high ground and had excellent positions for artillery observation.

In Switzerland Allen Dulles' frustration grew — he continued to wait for some-thing "useful" to break. "Useful" was a descriptor that Dulles liked to employ, and he had not been able to speak this word for some time now; it denoted the receipt of valuable intelligence information. Dulles was aware that the *Fascisti* rallied in Milan and that there was nothing he could do about it. He was also alarmed by a report coming out of Belgium — apparently the Germans had launched a large counter-attack in the Ardennes area. Being taken by surprise was not a good thing for a spy chief. How had Hitler and his Nazi regime pulled this off without him learning?

Apparently it did not occur to Dulles, or if it did he did not write about it in his book *Secret Surrender*, that the fascists might attempt a thrust south in Italy. Nor did he ask himself: whom might the Master Race attack to show off its superiority?

This was a difficult period for Dulles. No big Nazis had contacted Swiss Intelligence to discuss surrender. And on top of this, his trusted subordinate, Gaevernitz, had submitted a recommendation to the Pentagon that had been rejected outright. Gaevernitz proposed that a committee be formed to include captured German generals who were cognizant of the calamity Hitler now senselessly inflicted for a lost cause and also who might be willing to work with the Allies to end the war. If a way could be found for these POW generals to communicate with their counterparts inside the Third Reich, Gaevernitz reasoned, what harm could this do? The Pentagon took a hard line, replying that it would be inappropriate to use "... German militarists to defeat German militarism."[181] Gaevernitz, ever the pragmatist, vowed to continue in his efforts to communicate *with anyone* to achieve peace, but he was also discouraged that his underground network seemed not to be producing results.

On December 17 Bill wrote his eleventh letter to his parents. It was a "warm-up" to a more detailed and impassioned letter he would subsequently write to Dotty describing what he saw on that date and how he felt about it. "4:50 p.m.... It is getting dark outside and a heavy fog is closing in. Our electric lights went out a few minutes ago and the boys just brought around candles. I never knew how nice candlelight could be until this trip... I am able to stay warm..."

"I have never seen so much mud. It snows on the mountaintops nearly every night and melts during the day. It seldom gets cold enough to freeze so there is perpetual mud. We were provided with overshoes so I am able to keep dry. The men up there have a real problem just living... There is not much fuel and many of them have rigged up little gasoline stoves. Water and mud covers the floors of the tents and dugouts. Those men with all their coldness and miserable conditions do far less complaining than those having all the luxuries..."

"I don't know how much good I can do here," he continued. "This is a well-run organization and they have learned a lot during the past two years. The information has not gone out to the Theatre though, and perhaps I can help where it will do the most good." Bill then wrote something favorable for the benefit of his mother that was not quite truthful but rather something she would want to be reassured about: "The officers here conduct themselves far better than many groups in which I have been assigned." Bill would qualify this statement in a subsequent letter to Dotty. Bill's mother was prim and proper and viewed the world from a tiny church-going farm community. Dotty was prim and proper too, but her perspective was from an urban, big city.

"They are putting on a big Christmas party Saturday night ... This will be the third Christmas away for many of the men here. Most of them have families and some have children they have not seen. Many have had misfortunes at home." [I] will be glad when the days start getting longer. If we can complete the [European] war by next summer, good weather will help. They say it rains all winter here."

"The mountain roads are very slippery from the mud carried on to them by the heavy truck traffic. Trucks here need power on all the wheels. When they get in too deep, a big 10-ton wrecker comes and drags them out with its boom or winch."

Although mules ultimately delivered supplies to men in the mountains, the two and one-half ton QMC trucks brought critical services to *near* where the men were. Some trucks were configured as surgical vans, other dental offices and still others chemical decontamination units (up to the end of the war the Allies remained concerned that a desperate Hitler would resort to the employment of chemical weapons). Wood slats could be installed as benches for seating and Jack King referred to these as 6' X 6' trucks, denoting the fact that they could uncomfortably seat six men with full gear and that the trucks were six-wheelers.

Bill concluded by describing the plight of the Italian civilians: "I don't know how they [the natives] manage to live. They look so hungry and discouraged ... The children clop around in wood soles with a little cloth or leather over the toes and no sides or back around the heel. They look so cold. [I] must stop now ... Sure hope you are well. Just keep on writing and we'll come **H**ome soon. Don't worry about me."

Bill's next letter written to Dotty four and one-half hours later could be fairly titled, "Band of Brothers":

No mail yet ... but I don't expect it to arrive until about January 1, 1945.

... We covered ninety-five miles in a jeep. I am not sure whether I am getting used to the bumps or paralyzed where I sit down. Uphill and

down, sharp hairpin curves, the road surface covered with slimy mud and almost slippery as grease… Army installations of all kinds… everywhere trucks can go. The Congressional Committee on Military Affairs visited the same area today. I did not see them [as] they passed a corner while we were inside eating at a post.

When we started out [I] saw many people in the villages in their best clothes, going to and coming from church. The church is one of the best things in their meager lives… It provides some education and little groups of children gather all day long for their lessons.

[I] saw some things I cannot write, Dotty. The nurses and Doctors have their hands full just living… let alone caring for the wounded…

Men in the lonely outposts are so grateful for the necessities. One of the Captains in the party sent up a little lumber to a certain small group. Two of them today worked [in] the mud nailing the boards together to hold a canvas tent in place so they could cook and eat their meals together. [They] said to the Captain, "We sure thank you for the lumber." The wind had broken their other framework and torn their tent apart. They dig their shelters into the side of the hill for wind and protection and then slide down the banks in the mud to reach them. I sure used my overshoes today.

… I have noticed the closer one gets to the serious side of the war, the cleaner the language of the officers and men, a complete difference in conduct, a willingness to live in miserable circumstances, sometimes hungry, always cold and usually wet and a reliance and close friend- ships for each other. It makes me feel that when people have things easy, they are most likely to be discontented. These men are so busy living they cannot waste time worrying about it.

Bill continued his letter by describing what these front line soldiers did to cel- ebrate the season: "Would you believe that up on top of a high mountain, where the Germans can see it, the Americans have decorated a huge Christmas tree with over 400 lights and have erected a gigantic sign saying "Merry Christmas." As of yet it has not been disturbed. It looked out of another world — standing there with mud on all sides."

As an aside John Lesesne indicated in his diary that the Christmas tree Bill mentioned was located ten miles back of the line; Bill had been well north of that tree however, the living conditions he described are unmistakably of the front.

Bill finished his long and informative letter of December 17th on a light note, describing two varied meals at stations he visited: "This noon we had lunch at a Traffic Control Post. An officer and several enlisted men are stationed there. They had a couple of Italian boys cooking for them. We had a meal new to all of us: a mixture of potatoes, chocolate, milk (condensed) and sugar. Ugh! This evening we found better at another post — we had hamburgers, string beans, cheese, coffee and canned pears."

At the time Bill wrote the above Dick Stroud had thoroughly immersed himself into his work as a supply officer for the U.S. Army Air Forces. "I am happy to be in my present location and work," he wrote Sue, "it is wonderful to be really busy..."[182] At the time Dick wrote this, weather permitting, the U.S. Fifteenth Air Force hit military targets inside Nazi Germany with upwards of 500 heavy bombers a day, and the U.S. Twelfth Air Force used smaller fighter bombers to paste targets all over Northern Italy. It was the heavy bombers that the Luftwaffe went after, and this enabled Allied troops on the ground in Italy to (for the most part but not always) fight without fear of air attack.

On December 18 John and three of his "boys" came as close to getting killed as they ever would and celebrated their survival in a special way that deserves to be enshrined today for posterity. The men involved in this happening were Second Lieutenant James "Jimmy" Stuart of Water Valley, Miss. (1st Platoon leader), First Lieutenant Claude "Stan" Stanford of Mount Pulaski, Ill. (2nd Platoon leader) and a "Staff Sergeant Murphy" (1st Platoon senior enlisted) whose first name and hometown are not recorded in John's diary.

John reported that he and Stan learned by a phone call from company rear that Jimmy's promotion to first lieutenant had come thru and together they decided to deliver a bottle of whiskey (Jimmy's liquor allotment on account of his promotion) and some ammo by jeep to the 1st Platoon command post, where they intended to celebrate. "On his [Jimmy's] liquor," John noted.

The problem was that when John and Stan arrived at 1st Platoon they discovered to their dismay that neither of them had thought to pack the bottle. Not being an insurmountable situation, John phoned his command post, explained what had happened and ordered another jeep to bring up the bottle. In anticipation the four men huddled up and waited. "Sandbags and a tent roof," John described the platoon HQ. Then there was this:

> *Jerry started shelling. Several came near and one must have burst on or just above our shelter. Fragments came in wounding Murphy & Stan in the legs (not seriously). I felt something like powder burns on the arms but not enough to get the Purple Heart which Stan and Murphy will. Soon afterwards Hofmann brought the whiskey & we indulged quite a bit. Then I drove back — Stan, Murphy & I. I was feeling pretty good at that point. That sixth sense alone kept us on the road. Stan and Murphy went to medics to get sulfanil inside on wounds & sulfamethoxazole tablets to take and then we returned to the forward C. P. Quite an experience. Bon Nuit!*

> **19 Dec** — *What a night. Upon returning to C.P. we started drinking whiskey and beer. We drank the remaining half of Stan's quart and then my full quart, plus the beer. About 4:00 "B" Co was about to win the war by itself. At 5:00 we had reached the picture displaying stage and I was exhibiting Miss Sumner. Just a little later it was finis for me — I remember going to bed, with a little assist once, and that was all until 1 P.M. Stan stayed up drinking and @ about 0700 Murphy drove him down to battalion to have shrapnel removed from their legs. Stan was at that time pretty tight and the boys said they were afraid he'd fall out of the jeep, but he made it O.K. Fragments were removed from Murphy, but Stan's were pretty deep; so they were left in. What a hangover I had — ate nothing until late in the evening. That was probably the worse drunk I've ever been on — and quite unintentionally at that.*

That was the way it was for Company "B" 100th Chemical Mortar Battalion on the Italian front, December 18 and 19, 1944.

It turned out the Congressional Committee on Military Affairs did in fact see much of what Bill saw, and not from the air either. The nurses and doctors that Bill wrote about worked at the Eighth Evacuation Hospital at the front and one of a series of photographs published in *Life* magazine about the Congressional visit showed Representative Clare Boothe Luce standing in this hospital smiling sympathetically at a prone soldier on a cot with his head and left arm completely wrapped in bandages. The photojournalistic *Life* article, entitled "War Inspection: Congressional committee gets data firsthand on the European fronts," primarily showcased the publisher's wife.

Members of the committee, including Luce, wore standard winter issue G.I. attire for their trip into the Appenines: a fur cap with goofy-looking (dangling) dog-ear warmers, heavy full-length parka (reversible to change into camouflage white) and calf-high galoshes (undoubtedly the same issued to Bill). One photo of Luce wearing these boots showed smidgens of mud on her leggings, evidence of a long day's trek. Two pictures showed Luce in the company of women serving in uniform. The bond of feminism comes out unmistakably in these pictures, and there is no doubt Luce played to her political base, the first woman in U.S. politics to do so. In one photo Luce held up a sign posted outside the WAC's tent, "OFF LIMITS" while standing next to an officer identified as "Lieut. Vivian Randolph of Indianapolis." Neither woman smiled, conveying the intended impression that this is no joking matter.

Another showed Luce with three other females inside a WAC tent decorated for Christmas. Strung up letters spelled M-E-R-R-Y-C-H-R-I-S-T-M-A-S and two small Santa Clauses dangled from electrical wires. The overall impression was cold, but the concept of sisterhood was warmly conveyed. The WACs gave Luce holly branches arranged in a spent brass shell casing; Luce held and admired the seasonal offering as the camera shutter snapped. In World War II many photos were posed, as this one undoubtedly was; practically all of the news outlets practiced this and most certainly the government did it for "official" photographs.

The article accompanying the photo spread reported that the committee was not mollycoddled by the Army. At the first briefing near the war front, which was conducted by General Clark, the representatives were told that the tour would be rigorous, and it was. "Rising at 6:30 a.m. to inspect the Italian front," the storyline read, "… the Army cautiously kept them at least four miles back … but the going was tough enough." The article further reported that half the members had taken colds, with one, the chairman, being held back in France due to pneumonia. When the Military Affairs Committee returned home, *Life* reported that Luce "… stayed behind with a sinus infection." Additionally there was this:

> She [Luce] took up the G.I. gripe that Italy is the "short-changed theater" where the American soldier could do with "a whole lot more fellows like himself." With one group of soldiers she held an off-the-record political

discussion which Stars and Stripes, *the soldiers' newspaper, vainly insisted should be widely published.*[183]

Life also reported the acting chairman, a Democrat, offered a contrary opinion: "Morale is very high…" he was quoted as saying. He also indicated that the committee's preliminary conclusion was that there appeared to be no critical shortage of supplies.

After the Committee returned to the United States, Luce was treated to private tours of the battlefront. "The troops liked her," *Life* reported, and on one occasion they "kidded her by placing a tent they had thoughtfully erected for her as a battle-field powder room with the title of her first successful play." In the accompanying photo a very tired looking latrine-tent stands pitched seemingly on the moon. A massive barren mountain looms in the far distance; the only connection to earth apart from the tent is the presence in the foreground of two scrubby-looking trees devoid of leaves. A sign "THE WOMEN" is pinned on the canvas outhouse.

On these outings Luce got much closer to the front. Everywhere she went she was recognized and cheered, and her military officer entourage saluted. Laughter and applause abounded at an artillery company when she pulled a lanyard on the Krauts. On another occasion, an earlier inspection trip, a German 88 mm shell landed 1,000 yards distant. She had now given payback. In the distance, she actually saw German soldiers near a ridgeline frolic in the snow.[184]

Her sinus infection notwithstanding, Luce had never felt so alive. Her play was named *The Women*, but being with the men on the front was magical for her.

CHAPTER FIVE:

"I HAVE JUST READ AND RE-READ MY FIRST LETTER RECEIVED OVERSEAS!"

December 19–25, 1944

AS CHRISTMAS 1944 approached a full range of emotions from the ordinary men of this story would be released. There would be the joy of receiving that first letter from home, despair at not receiving any letter, a strong desire expressed to shoot down an enemy airplane, relief expressed that an attack had been postponed, thanks given to the Lord for blessings given, and lonely thoughts of **H**ome, family and what the Yuletide used to be like in better times.

Also, there was revulsion at the all-too human condition!

On December 19 in letter No. 41 to Dotty, Bill reported, "The plans for the Xmas party are going at a high rate. The Major and I got invited today. The Major said he did not intend to share in the expenses and I will follow his lead. It appears the C.O. (commanding officer) wants to impress his superiors by the lavish outlay."

In a letter written the following day, barely disguising his contempt, Bill detailed some of the elaborate preparations being made for the party: "Trees are being set up in several places, a bar has been constructed in one of the big halls by the stairway, some stoneworkers are repairing a doorway damaged by shellfire when this place changed hands and there is activity on all sides. The sign shop (road signs) has been making Christmas decorations for some time." There is no doubt that Bill (and likely Major Cowan too) believed these party efforts would have been better directed towards helping the men at the front. In another letter Bill wrote: "They expect 150 couples. It's a funny war."

On a side note, the day after the party Bill wrote Dotty: "Many of the men brought dates. There are a surprising number of women from the States here in all sorts of organizations. I guess I have much to learn how men with families at home can go out on a date… the men are about equally divided, some go and some don't."

Bill again complained about censorship: "We get practically no news from home at all here. The daily newssheet sometimes mentions Washington but only on some military affair." Bill was of the opinion that the Army Post Office intentionally delayed the delivery of hometown civilian newspapers so that any negative news they might contain would be stale-dated and less upsetting when received. Apparently Bill's view on this subject was shared by other theater G.I.s who griped to their representatives: "The Congressional Committee I believe got a pretty clear picture of the news isolation inflicted on us," Bill noted.

As the Christmas season approached John, like so many other G.I.s serving abroad, thought of home. He had been on the line now for going on two months and he thought of his parents who lived at 144 Tradd Street, Charleston. He loved the old homes and shade trees of this historic street. His parents lived in a charming white-painted wooden Greek revival style home, with screened-in side porches on two levels. Quite a number of the more substantial masonry homes in the area predated the American Revolution, with the two earliest dating back to 1718. John mentioned more than once in his diary about "… thinking of home and loved ones, of the gay debutant parties…" He also missed his church, the celebrated St Philips Episcopal built in 1836 with a steeple so high that it served as a lighthouse.

Despite the trappings of gentility represented by historic Charleston, John was aware that the Depression had been a difficult period for his parents, and that his father had lost a business and was not doing a whole lot now. On several occasions he wrote about receiving loving letters from his mother in which she (knowing his situation) invariably promised to "keep her chin up."[185] He also was mindful that, as an only child, if he were killed his parents would be devastated. John did not write about this subject and, no doubt being young and a military leader, put it out of mind. What good would it do to dwell on a subject like this? John intended to live! However, he did make one provision (and only one) in his diary: "If I should be killed and she be still single, I'd like for her to have my Citadel ring — Miss Jacqueline Sumner, 120 Hillside Ave, Rochester, NY."[186]

John thought of *The Citadel*, his alma mater. Money had been tight for his family. He needed and got a scholarship to see himself through. What he experienced there on the parade ground and obstacle course could not be compared to what he experienced now. His views at some point changed about making the military a career, but he wrote nothing negative about the army and remained proud of his military college. John had lost none of his patriotism but rather wrote about possibly going to medical school after the war.[187]

Bill wrote about the Battle of the Bulge that started in mid-December with a Nazi surprise panzer attack in Belgium. He opined: "I feel the Germans are making their last desperate stand on the western front now. They must know their jig is about up." Bill's assessment about Nazi defeatism was not entirely accurate. The Germans believed they could win this battle at its onset and fought incredibly hard. When this battle would finally end a month later, there would be 80,000 American casualties including 19,000 killed.[188]

On December 20 Bill wrote to Dotty and Davy: "I dreamed last night mail finally arrived, a whole bundle of letters." He told of the day's events: "I requested to spend the day with one of the truck companies. Mud, mud, mud everywhere. The men are in it continuously; repair the trucks in it; lose their tools in it and get used to it. It stands like soup over vast areas. Passing trucks throw it at bystanders. Children jump from rock to rock and most people just plod along slowly so as to not slip and fall." Bill told of army dump truck drivers unloading unfused artillery shells by dropping them directly on the wet ground. He didn't see a problem with this practice since no driver complained!

Bill wrote again about the Italian civilians: "In spite of the prevalent attitude of the soldiers toward the natives, I feel so sorry for them. They are so courteous and kindly when shown any friendliness. They will never have much of a chance living in a country where it is so difficult for the majority just to exist. I have seen them washing clothes in cold water, outdoors in freezing weather without soap. Of course the clothes get pretty gray, but it is the best they can do."

And he told about how the long-term veterans perceived him: "The men who have been here about two years are so bitter about talk of sending them to another theatre after this one is cleaned up. They regard me as a novice, having just arrived. Being away so long makes [them] quiet and reserved." For many of the soldiers in the U.S. Fifth Army the war began on November 8, 1942 with the landing in Morocco.[189] They had fought their way some 2,000 miles across scorching deserts, the island of Sicily and most of the way up the boot of Italy to arrive at the muddy and cold area described by Bill. These soldiers had no appetite to climb the heavily defended steep mountain slopes that needed to be ascended in order for the final North Appenines Campaign to have a chance to succeed.

At Caserta, Field Marshal Alexander was aware of the morale problem. With input from Truscott via Clark and administrative support from McNarney, he had a plan in the making to give the U.S. Fifth Army a needed combat boost. A certain combat infantry division, trained in the U.S. for a special kind of warfare and originally intended for use in Northern Europe, had suddenly been made available to serve in Italy and the MTO commanders grabbed at the chance to have it!

On December 21 Bill noted that he wrote "my first weekly report" and that "I made two recommendations that may do some good." He added: "Major Cowan was very nice and gave me some good advice. He is about fifty years old and has had a lot of experience. I enjoy his friendship." About the subject of rank in the U.S. Army Bill observed: "Majors and above are considered field officers, and captains and lieutenants are junior officers. We eat at different tables at mess and they are supposed to and usually do have better quarters. The Army sponsors the class system from top to bottom." Bill's report, when typed, would be mailed to AFHQ.

On 22 December Bill wrote to Dotty of, "a cold trip in an open jeep about forty miles from the big house" with "five of us plus all my stuff" (i.e., weapon, bedroll and borrowed cot) to see "where the freight is transferred from rail to trucks." He reported a flat tire and he and two other officers "practice shooting" their carbines in the afternoon. He also wrote that the favorite expression (or gripe) of the jostled U.S. Fifth Army was "Oh, my back!" "It is used so many places where it is hard to see where it applies," Bill wrote.

By the time Bill travelled near the front, the U.S. Army Corps of Engineers had done a stupendous job of removing most of the road landmines. A favorite technique of the Germans was to destroy a paved highway section by creating a large shell hole, or crater, in its middle. This would require a dirt bypass or side road on or near a shoulder, one that the Germans would agreeably build — laced with high explosives. QMC truck driving, particularly soon after an area had changed hands could be hazardous work akin to combat. Road shoulders were always suspect, but had to be used in traffic jam situations caused by breakdowns, accidents or whatever. Bypass dirt roads were everywhere and many washed out during periods of heavy rain. There was no end of things for the engineers to do. Before the war the Italians had been proud of their "Autostrada," a modern expressway that connected Florence and Lucca. The Germans made this road, and many other lesser roads, unusable.[190]

The army engineers were not the only specialists performing at pitch efficiency. The air war in Italy had been all but won. On December 22, the day Bill and his traveling companions did "practice shooting" the *USAAF Chronology* reported the following activity:

> *TACTICAL OPERATIONS (Twelfth Air Force): In Italy during the night of 21/22 Dec, A-20s hit scattered targets in the Po Valley; clearing weather during the day enables medium bombers to hit bridges at Torre Beretti, Pontetidone, and at Chiari; fighter-bombers concentrate on railway targets, destroying five bridges in N Italy and making numerous cuts in rail lines, several on the important Brenner Pass line; motor transport and guns N of the battle area are also successfully attacked.*

At this time frame Allied tactical bombing was done on a twenty-four-hour basis. "Lights… throughout the Po Valley" were bombed one USAAF report noted.[191] Presumably this was done to hit Nazi nighttime repair crews and vehicles that might be using headlights. The Po Valley extended some 400 miles east to west and encompassed 18,000 square miles. The large Po River that drained the entire valley into the Adriatic Sea was devoid of bridges due to the efforts of the USAAF. "All [German] supplies had to ferried," Truscott observed.[192] The General knew that in the upcoming battle this fact would inure to the benefit of his forces.

In later life Bill told of an enemy air incursion he experienced while in Northern Italy. "It turned out to be only reconnaissance," he said, "but it caught everybody's attention." Asked whether he saw the German airplane, he replied, smiling "Yes, it looked like a speck." This airplane presumably was *Bed Check Charlie*.

The fact that Bill reported seeing only a single enemy airplane during his period of a month near the front conforms to military history. The Germans were in a desperate situation as to fuel, including aviation gas, and to the extent that they used airplanes, with the limited exception of perhaps *Bed Check Charlie*, Luftwaffe flights were limited to strafing and tactical bombings sparingly done over the front only. The previous summer the Red Army had captured the oil fields at Ploesti, Romania, and this event denied the Nazis access to natural crude. Fuel had to be manufactured synthetically at coal plants inside Germany and a Luftwaffe in Italy was something the Germans could ill afford to adequately supply.

As an aside, John reported the previous month of seeing *Bed Check Charlie*, only he referred to airplane by a different name: "Just now @1855 ack-ack is firing at "Bedtime Charlie," John wrote. "Wish they'd give us back a couple of 40's [Ed: 40 mm anti-aircraft guns] in addition to our lovely 4.2's — we would like to get *Bedtime Charlie*. How bloodthirsty I must sound tonight."[193] On another occasion as the Yuletide approached, John observed: "This evening Jerry planes came down the road here. AA blazed away in great volume but we saw no hits — we all wished we had our old AA guns — that's good sport — no danger involved — just like shooting birds. Much better than shooting at an unseen enemy and having him return your greetings."[194] John's mindset at this time was that of military commander bent on victory. To him, peace and goodwill of the season meant *next* season! On December 21 he recorded: "Still no definite news of the 'push.'"

Late in the afternoon of December 22 Truscott was summoned to meet with General Clark in Florence. Clark had hoped to launch his Pianoro plan on Christmas day but something had come up that had caused him to re-think matters. G-2, U.S. Army Intelligence, had discovered substantial enemy forces massed north of Serchio Valley. Serchio Valley was the gateway to the vital Allied port city of Leghorn, approximately forty-five miles to the south. Looking at a map, the two generals were alarmed; they realized that the 92nd Infantry Division had no back-up. "No Army reserves were there," Truscott noted in his memoirs.[195] Most all of the combat divisions of Allied Fifteenth Army Group were positioned in central Italy, preparatory to the scheduled attack at Pianoro. Truscott was troubled by the identity of the German divisions amassing; he knew some of them were elite — the best that the Germans had.

In the U.S. Civil War there was a term for this — "in the air" — that meant being vulnerable to a surprise enemy attack. In 1863 General Stonewall Jackson pulled off such an attack at Chancellorsville and years later author Stephen Crane wrote a fictional work based on the event, *The Red Badge of Courage*. It is a story of a young Union soldier overwhelmed and traumatized. Had the 92nd Infantry Division been "left in the air"?

On December 22 Truscott saw a clear parallel to what was going on with the Battle of the Bulge in Belgium. Truscott commented dryly that it would not be pleasing "...to contemplate what might happen if German armor suddenly appeared in rear of the 92nd Infantry Division …" He noted that the two infantry regiments of the 92nd that would bear the brunt of the attack were the 370th and 366th, and was aware that the 366th (that had 100% African-American junior officers) had never experienced combat. "It had been an inactive front and was held by colored troops …" Truscott wrote.[196]

In the Belgium attack the Germans hoped to drive to Antwerp, splitting Allied forces. If the Nazi strategy succeeded there the war on the Western Front would be dramatically changed. In the MTO, the re-taking of Leghorn by the enemy, if it happened, would be a major setback. The enemy had heretofore not used panzers effectively in Italy. Was this about to change? What was going on?

Clark and Truscott agreed to put Pianoro on hold and ordered the nearest combat relief column in the vicinity, two brigades of the 8th Indian Division (then headed south to Lucca for "rest and refitting") to turn around and engage. Additional Allied troops — reserves assigned for the Pianoro assault — were ordered to proceed posthaste westerly to the coastal area.

What ensued would be known as the Battle of the Little Bulge. As Christmas approached the knowledge of what was about to happen at Serchio Valley was not widely disseminated; there is no mention of it to be found in any letters, journal entries or statements of the ordinary G.I.s quoted in this story.

December 24, 1944 Letter No. 12

Dear Folks,

I have just read and re-read my first letter received overseas! It was your letter No. 9 written the thirteenth. Eleven days and it was forwarded from AFHQ up here… Your letter makes this Christmas better than I had dared hope for…

… [I] have had several trips around the country and up in the mountains. We go in jeeps and trucks, some of them closed and some open. Sometimes I stay overnight in which case I take my cot, bedroll, blankets and heavy clothes… Sleeping with socks dries them out and keeps the feet warmer!

They had a big Christmas party here last night.… I wore my blouse for the first time overseas [Ed: dress "pinks" jacket with tie]. Several

high-ranking officers attended. Clare Boothe Luce, Rep[publican] repre-
sentative from Conn. was here and I had an interesting talk with her. She
remained after the Military Affairs Committee had gone back.... We had
a big turkey dinner and various kinds of entertainment. The big house
was cold in spite of fires in all the huge fireplaces.... The natives must
hate to see so much fuel consumed when they have so little to heat.

Per a well-researched and critically acclaimed biography written about Clare
Boothe Luce entitled *Price of Fame* by author Sylvia Jukes Morris, the Congressional Committee started back to the United States on December 18, but Luce
decided to stay an additional ten days. It may have been that the exhilaration of
being in a warzone proved to be a stimulant of sorts and she wanted more.

According to Morris, Luce told fellow committee members she was staying to
do additional fact-finding. After the committee departed for Naples from Florence preparatory to the long trip home she told a reporter she had stayed behind
because of an earache and fog.[197]

Bill continued his letter to his parents:

[The] night before last I stayed in an Italian house with some officers at
the installation I was visiting. Swarms of people seem to live in one house.
The rooms are small and dark with usually one window. I saw some older
people trying to keep warm by holding a small can of glowing charcoals
between their knees, wrapped up in shawls and bending over it. The sol-
diers in the foxholes full of mud and water are the ones who really suffer. I
often wonder how they manage to pull through.

... A strong wind has been blowing and there is some snow in the moun-
tain areas. The mountain roads are dangerous for vehicles when slippery
with snow and ice. There are many accidents.

I am getting the information that I was sent here after. I have come across
several situations that can be improved, and I have submitted my first
report... I feel I have a job to do. My training in the Ordnance Depart-
ment was perfect for this assignment...

I have just read your letter again. It is so much easier to write after
hearing from you. I am anxious to hear from Dotty. When I see the people
here, I am so thankful you folks have the food, fuel and shelter and live in
a country where there is enough for all. I took so much for granted before
coming here.

I have also observed that the closer men live to danger and suffering, the more grateful they are for things that ordinarily go unnoticed.

... The arrival of your letter and my thoughts of past Christmases and those yet to come when we will be together will make this one good also.

Love,
William

It is likely that Bill had a happier Christmas than Lieutenant Dick Stroud, the lucky guy who had thirty-two letters waiting for him when he arrived at the Naples repple-depple. Dick, then in Naples, wrote Sue: "... be assured sweet the worst thing that can happen here is for the mail from home to go awry." Stroud had not heard from his wife for a number of days and noted: "The last letter was dated December 9." That is how it went in the postal communications department for U.S. armed forces serving abroad in World War II; it was hit or miss, and a real emotional rollercoaster.

Jack King wrote nothing about Christmas (his diary entries skip from November 11 to December 31) and John Lesesne recorded: "Strange as it may seem this has been my happiest X mas in years — despite being far from home and at 'the front' — in plain view of Jerry." John had received a special present ("... the package from my folks was the long awaited scotch") and at his HQ asked for the blessing. "For dinner we set up a table, covered it with red and green tissue and sat down to eat in real style." That afternoon he visited the platoons, shook every hand and wished all a Merry Christmas. "And a white one at that," John described the special day.

First Lieutenant Wade McCree of the 92nd was with the British Army in central Italy when word came of the Pianoro attack scheduled for Christmas day had been postponed. McCree had no illusions about the strong German defenses. He recollected: "I personally felt a sense of relief because I knew we were going to lose a lot of men."

For most of the combat infantrymen at the front, Leon Weckstein, et al, even though the "push" had been delayed, the holiday season evidenced no morale improvement (he wrote of a "Chanukah unnoticed"). He lived in a shell-damaged hovel in Pianoro and there remained a constant need to patrol, to daily probe for the enemy so artillery, heavy mortars and tactical airpower might be called in for an attack. Eleven infantry divisions fell under U.S. Fifth Army command and control, and the daily routine for each encompassed much the same. A small patrol would be sent out here or there at nightfall carrying M-1s, Thompson sub-machine guns, a bazooka, hand grenades and ammo — all the weapons that men could physically carry.

Typically, two brave infantrymen would lead an approach to some objective, perhaps a farmhouse that had been under observation and thought unoccupied, or a ridgeline that might offer a new vantage point. These infantrymen crept forward in the darkness, faces blackened and used hand signals, hoping no one waited for them ahead. Platoon teammates covered their approach, weapons aimed at windows and other points where an enemy might pop out. If there was snow, the front men looked for tracks; if there was no snow they scanned the area as best they could, always thinking of what they might jump behind in case of ambush. A typical German ensnarement involved two or more burp guns firing causing the point leader (if he were not immediately hit) to dive on top of where a "Shu" or "Bouncing Betty" landmine had been planted. If the range were close enough, stick grenades would be thrown for the follow-up.

Night after night of this cat and mouse warfare, with little progress to show for it demoralized the men who had to fight it. In Northern Europe a major battle raged and someone was going to win decisively. Not so in the Italian campaign. Italy was slog, slog and more slog, and with little reported glory.

On Christmas Day U.S. Army Chief of Staff General Marshall wrote to an aide of President Roosevelt requesting that the President "include something positive" about the Italian campaign in his annual State of the Union address. Marshall had learned from MTOUSA, General McNarney, how U.S. Fifth Army morale suffered "… for lack of appropriate treatment of importance of the Italian campaign." McNarney's complaint was with the U.S. press: it no longer reported on what happened in Italy, but rather about military developments in France, B-29 raids in the Pacific and even what happened in the Balkans.[198] The problem was that parents of U.S. Fifth Army servicemen were writing letters to their sons stating that newspapers, newsreels and radio no longer covered the Italian front, the implication being that the small action stuff was not worth writing about.

Still, there was hope for the future. It was Christmas and Bill mailed home a simple poem that could have been penned by any of thousands of married-with-children G.I.s:

> "Heap on more wood, the wind is chill
> But let it whistle as it will
> We'll keep our Christmas, Merry still
> As long as I have you and Davy"

CHAPTER SIX:

ATTACK AT SERCHIO VALLEY

December 26–31, 1945

THE MEN OF THE 92nd had some sense that it was coming. Sergeant Charles Brown of the veteran 370th Infantry Regiment reported a recon patrol engaging in a forty-five-minute firefight on Christmas Eve. He wrote about it: "The fight had taken place in advance of Cascio in territory where Germans had not been seen recently." Per Brown, his white battalion commander refused to believe that the incident occurred when he and another black soldier reported it. The commander called Brown and the other soldier, a junior commissioned officer, "liars" to their faces. The next day, Christmas proved these men truthful. While singing carols and spirituals in the basement of a place called the big house, the report came in: "… a German patrol combat team was in the area."[199]

The German attack began early the next morning. Clark and Truscott had ordered reserves into the area on the 22nd but Truscott confided: "These movements got underway during the next two or three days, but they had not been completed when the enemy struck."[200] The Brazilian Expeditionary Force was in the area but Clark and Truscott made no mention of ordering it into action.

As an aside, the 25,000 man Brazilian force was the brainchild of President Roosevelt. The U.S. Fifth Army needed troops to replace those taken for *Operation Dragoon*, the invasion of Southern France, and Roosevelt persuaded the Brazilian strong-man government to supply them in the interest of hemispheric solidarity (an interest no doubt bolstered by Roosevelt's promise of continued economic cooperation). The combat effectiveness of the Brazilians was questionable, but due to the diplomacy of the situation and the fact that the press was largely controlled, not much was reported on this subject. This was by no means a rental of a mercenary army. Brazil had legitimately declared war on Germany in 1942 (as had *many* other countries in the Americas) over the issue of Nazi unrestricted submarine warfare. Brazil was the only South American country to send a division to Europe.

Truscott recorded: "…the Germans launched several limited-objective attacks in the Serchio Valley, with forces involving some five or six battalions, which struck the 1st Battalion 370th Infantry and the 2nd Battalion 366th Infantry, both of which 'melted away' — a term that was to be frequently used in describing action of colored troops."[201] Two battalions attacked by "five or six" means that for a short period the enemy at the place of attack had approximately a three-to-one manpower advantage. Truscott identified the known enemy forces in the region as elements of the 148th Grenadier Division and an "Italian division." He also reported U.S. Army Intelligence believed that the 16th SS Panzer Grenadier Division and the 157th Mountain Division "were moving up." Finally, he indicated that G-2 believed it possible that another two German divisions could be made available for the assault,[202] possibly *bringing the number to six enemy divisions* bearing down on the largely untested (and without backup) U.S. 92nd Infantry Division.

In their memoirs Clark and Truscott admit to no professional shortcomings in regard to what happened at Serchio Valley, but the fact is that neither saw the battle approaching and if they had, it might have been nipped in the bud. Kesselring, the master of *defensive* warfare was still on medical leave and he did not plan the details of this attack; he later complimented Wehrmacht General Kurt von Tippelskirch for doing this, noting the assault "… revealed the brittleness of the Allied secondary fronts."[203]

Serchio Valley represented something new and significant late in the Italian contest — aggressive Axis warfare designed to take the fight, albeit briefly and selectively, to the Americans. A majority of Axis troops engaged were Italian *fascisti* freshly trained and directed by the Germans.

It is arguable that Clark and Truscott, in view of what was then taking place in Belgium — a desperate no-holds-barred winner-take-all military struggle that started December 16 — should have anticipated something similar might happen Italy. They had the better part of a week to think about this.

No doubt that the German and Italian *fascisti* intelligence agencies read U.S. newspapers and were aware that an African-American division was going on the combat line and the political issues that existed behind this decision. Serchio Valley presented an opportunity for Axis forces to bolster their claim of racial superiority in a most publicized and homicidal way. It may be fair criticism to state that the Allied command all the way to the top — Eisenhower — might have anticipated this attack would come in Italy and for that reason.

In the early morning darkness of December 26, Austrian infantrymen from the elite Fourth Mountain Battalion, some dressed like partisans, infiltrated the small mountain village of Sommocolonia northeast of Serchio Valley and launched a take-no-prisoners assault.[204] Sommocolonia was lightly defended by two platoons of infantrymen from the 370th Regiment. Hopelessly outnumbered, these platoons (approximately seventy G.I.s total) fought heroically and delayed the Nazi spearhead a critical twenty hours. Only one U.S. junior officer and seventeen U.S. enlisted men managed to escape from Sommocolonia before the enemy captured the town. Approximately 100 Axis soldiers were killed in the assault, many by artillery strikes called in by Buffalo Soldiers on their own positions.

Other elements of the 92nd Division, some from the 370th (and by-in-large most members of the 366th) did not perform in a heroic manner that day, and what happened has been the subject of investigation, controversy, bitterness and ongoing recrimination. General Clark described: "The forward elements of the 92nd gave ground and some units later broke, falling back in a state of disorganization."[205] As stated, Truscott used the words "melted away" to repeat what had been reported in the press as a military debacle.[206] One history on this subject described the flight of the Buffalo Soldiers as follows: "The U.S. 92 Division retreated hurriedly in disorder..."[207] Still another history stated: "... the troops of the 92nd were driven back in confusion for five miles fleeing..."[208]

Depending on the authority one reads, the surrendered without-a-fight area was a six plus mile stretch across the valley. For a short period the Allied command was legitimately concerned that several enemy divisions might exploit this opening to recapture Leghorn, disrupting Allied supply lines.[209] Clark in his memoirs wrote: "This left a gap adjacent to the [Serchio] river and made a more general withdrawal necessary."

The Italian fascist Monte Rosa Division supported by the 16 SS Panzer Grenadiers succeeded in briefly recapturing the town of Barga, and the road was open to to the town of Lucca.[210] The Buffalo Soldiers sustained approximately 1,000 casualties while fleeing, most were killed; 300 were taken POW.

Truscott directed three combat divisions to stop the Axis forces: the Indian 8th (an infantry division famous for its ferocity — the "fighting Gurkhas" [211]) the U.S. 1st Armored and U.S. 34th Infantry (the division John's 100th Chemical Mortar Battalion Company "B" supported).

On December 27, the day after the German attack, Bill was on the road. Not identifying his location or the military units that he saw, he described the miserable conditions that the Allied relief columns had to endure:

> ... I saw traffic at its worst — miles and miles of roads filled. Ice and snow makes it pretty dangerous. I also saw the big winch in operation... ... I was dressed warmly... but one just gradually gets colder and colder.

John's Company "B" did not move with the 34th but rather stayed in the central battle line, rejoining the 91st Division. His diary entry of that day indicates that the circumstance of the enemy attack in the west caused his unit to temporarily act as infantry:

> **27 Dec** — I got a call from Colonel Boyle, the Chemical Warfare Service officer 91st Division. He intimated we would soon be with 91st again. I went down to get the dope — we'll be with the 363 Regiment — a good outfit. After seeing Colonel Boyle I went to company rear to get .50 caliber machine guns, bazookas, and rifle grenades for the platoons. Maj. Mac advised this as the infantry is spread thin [Ed: "spread thin" as a consequence of the redeployment of the 34th to Serchio Valley] and we may need them for local security. I made a quick reconnaissance with Key, and found some pretty good positions, about one-half mile forward...

The official U.S. Army history of the battle indicates that the enemy began a planned withdrawal from Barga on that same day, December 27. The enemy knew that if it continued its advance beyond Barga it would be cut to pieces by fighter-bombers and also advancing U.S. armor. Having inflicted considerable casualties on the Americans, the Axis forces withdrew to the safety of the Gothic Line and most lived to fight another day. Despite atrocious weather that continued, the U.S. Twelfth Army Air Force was able to provide many tactical sorties over the four-day enemy withdrawal[212] (at this point in the war the fighter-bombers had moved off the island of Corsica into Italy proper).

The India 8th Division accomplished the relief of the 92nd with hardly firing a shot. The sarcasm started up on the day contact was made, an exemplar being this report that got out from a Gurkha officer: "On our first patrol we captured two Brazilians, one German, two Italians and three Negroes."[213]

Following the military debacle at Serchio Valley, the U.S. Army public relations establishment turned on the 92nd. General Mark Clark called the Buffalo Division, "the worst in Europe"[214] and the press hyped how the coloreds "melted away" — those two hurtful words appeared in print everywhere. The aftermath quickly turned into an exercise in blame-shifting: African-American soldiers, mortified, sensed that the fault was being unfairly placed on black junior officers, mostly from the 366th Infantry Regiment, and believed it rightly belonged on General Almond and his all-white senior officer cadre.

A poisonous environment set-in for the 92nd. Black soldiers felt they had been offered up as cannon fodder and then showcased as "inferior" to the press. They did not understand why Almond was not sacked for incompetency. Allegations of racism went rampant, even so far that some blacks raised the question: who was the *real* enemy?

For its part, the U.S. Fifth Army believed it had been fair in its treatment of colored troops — that is, white infantry in the battle line were dealt with in an equal fashion; also that the question of dereliction of duty needed to be investigated in the 92nd and if found, acted upon. Lieutenant Wade McCree of the 92nd while serving alongside international forces in central Italy acknowledged that the consequences of a finding of cowardice in the universal military could be severe. He recollected a hard case, one where a unit, "... hanged one of their boys for desertion under fire."[215]

Draconian individual punishments would not happen in the U.S. Fifth Army but there would be consequences for the events that took place on December 26 and 27. Approximately 10% of the U.S. fighting force had been ineffective in the field, and the command structure would not acknowledge even partial responsibility for this result.

Captured German officers offered this assessment to Allied authorities:

> *The front line troops of the 92nd were vigilant and in readiness for defense, but the German command considered the division, whose combat efficiency and training it judged inferior to the other American divisions, to have made poor use of terrain, to have irresolute command, and to lack tenacity.*[216]

What happened at the "Battle of the Little Bulge" and also what occurred later with the 92nd in Italy would be reviewed in depth by President Truman following the war with an eye in mind of preventing a reoccurrence.

On December 28, a month and a half after leaving the United States (Bill counted forty-four days),[217] he finally received a letter from Dotty. It was *her letter #41* written and mailed only ten days earlier. Bill wrote back to her in the vernacular of Jimmy Stewart: "Gosh, it's wonderful to hear from you!" In the same letter Bill made a political observation about the battle then raging in Belgium: "Events at the fronts are not good now. Isn't it a good thing for the republic that Dewey was not elected? If he were in, this would be blamed on the administration or pending change." The political firestorm that Clare Boothe Luce ignited the previous summer with her convention speech over the conduct of the war still simmered.

At year end Bill alluded to what had happened in Italy: "The enemy made some thrusts on this front, but I think they were just intended to keep us off balance."[218]

The aftermath of Serchio Valley fit into the design plans of the new commanding general of the U.S. Fifth Army, Lucien Truscott. When the battle commenced on December 26 it temporarily put the Allies on the defensive and forestalled the launch of the Pianoro Plan.[219] The battle also expended some ammunition, and this caught Truscott's attention.

Towards the close of 1944 an important decision had to be made by the Supreme Allied Commander Field Marshal Alexander, and he received conflicting advice from Clark and Truscott. General Truscott wrote that General Clark "was still bent on carrying out the Pianoro attack" in the face of worsening snow and ice conditions in the mountains. Truscott argued strongly against Pianoro by throwing into the equation factual information that he had recently garnered:

> *An examination of our ammunition reserve during the latter part of December showed there was only enough to support fifteen days of offensive operations, and no more would be available until the end of January.*[220]

Truscott pointed out what his superior overlooked in his zeal to launch an attack: to sustain a major offensive such as contemplated a minimum of thirty days of ammunition was needed. Truscott, who knew the importance of being assertive, would remain a rooster over this issue.

—ᴍ—

At the time when Bill saw traffic at its worst he also witnessed other things. On the ground he observed that the behavior of American soldiers did not motivate Italian civilians to embrace the Allied cause. He wrote: "... I came into the city this morning and spent the day observing the operations of a Truck Battalion. This one is bivouacked right in the town. They have some of the streets fenced off and set up their service, repair and administration facilities in the most convenient places." Bill focused on the American behavior: "Army personnel just move right into the civilian homes and take over the places. Usually there are extra rooms and the civilians are moved to some remote upstairs corner. Many of them object but to no avail. This is the nicer section of town and the buildings are well constructed and from two to five stories high..."[221]

Before the year was out Bill would embellish: "... It is difficult for me to understand the attitude of the American soldier towards the Italian people. They regard them as no good and stupid and push them around.... The [Italian] men do more work than necessary and the women [also] appear to work hard. Some of the American drivers blow their horns at them and practically run them down on the road." Bill added: "Perhaps it is hard for our men to forget that they were enemies not so long ago. When our men read of the good treatment of Italian prisoners of war at home, they boil over.[222] [Ed: up until April 4, 1945 U.S. policy was to ship Italian and German POWs to detention camps in the United States]

By this late juncture in the war many of the longest-serving U.S. Fifth Army G.I.s were exasperated to the point that they needed a scapegoat — someone to blame for their unhappy circumstances, and no doubt Italian civilians made for a convenient whipping boy. Bill observed: "One gets the impression that things are dragging because the men [here] are weary of it all and want to go home."

Bill's description of Italians being mistreated by the army calls attention to what Lieutenant Wade McCree reported:

> I soon became aware of two interesting phenomena. First, that the
> Italian people had suffered a great deal and second, that our troops

[African-Americans] had a great deal of empathy for them. The Italian
people recognized this and they immediately developed a wonderful
rapport which apparently did not exist in the same intensity between the
Italians and our white troops.[223]

The excitement generated by Serchio Valley quickly faded. On December 29
Bill wrote to his parents about making more open jeep trips to Army installations
and what it was like to take a shower at the big house:

There is snow in the mountains and chains are sometimes required on all
four wheels.... Some truck outfits abuse their trucks and others are very
careful of them.... Often I go out and stay overnight with a unit in which
case I take my cot, bedroll and knapsack with toilet articles, etc. Lots of
days I eat each meal with a different group. The army is eating well and
all the units have plenty for a few unexpected guests. Some of them are
clean and orderly and some are not.

... Took a shower this evening when I returned to the big house where
I stay most of the time. The shower is in a swimming pool... a tent on
the floor with hot and cold water piped in. It's a real experience! Besides
being about freezing, the shower spray is very hot on one side and ice cold
on the other.... the pipes back up above and hot and cold drops some-
times make one jump. A shower of any kind is a luxury here though.

I think I'm going to gain weight. I feel fine and have a terrific
*appetite...*224

For John Lesesne December 29 was not routine. He recorded that a sergeant
from battalion "C" Company had died. "That leaves us the only company with
no men killed...," John wrote. "It's nothing but the grace of God."

The move of Company "B" to the sector controlled by the 363rd Infantry
Regiment was completed on the last day of the year and John was pleased with
the sites he had selected. He was also glad to again to be working in support of
the 91st. He wrote:

Here we are off to ourselves, with the guns behind a high hill. Good posi-
tions tactically — close to front, but safe — I hope! The company C.P. is
in a big house, while the platoons occupy a barn to rear, two small caves
and dugouts. We have no traffic in or out during day as it is suspected
that Jerry can observe the road. We are quite comfortable and I like our
position very much.

John's boys no longer had to sleep in foxholes with nothing overhead but shelter halves. Farmers had cut the dugouts John referred to into soft limestone, and these along with the natural caves offered excellent protection from shelling. All manmade structures were drab in appearance — unwashed and unpainted farmhouses and unkempt (due to the war) out buildings, but they were structures nevertheless!

John's new observation post was a church in the small town of Scascoli. He recorded: "The steeple provides an excellent O.P. Just in front the hills slope down to a riverbed and on the opposing hills are Jerry positions."[225]

For John and his men, the enemy was closer.

Before she left for home in time to celebrate New Year's Eve with her husband in New York City, Congresswoman Clare Boothe Luce granted that interview with the "vainly" insistent *Stars and Stripes* newspaper reporter. She talked about an idea she had come up with to improve the sagging morale of the war-weary U.S. Fifth Army. The USAAF rotated its strategic bomber-crews home on furlough after completing thirty-five combat missions, so why shouldn't the U.S. Fifth Army do something analogous for its longest serving foot soldiers? To appear in print in early January she elucidated: "A certain division in Italy has had 400 days of actual combat, casualties have been heavy and eventually the men get into a frame of mind in which the only future they see is death."[226] Troop replacements were needed for Italy, she argued.

No doubt her statement when published would play well with the long term U.S. Fifth Army rank and file and concerned parents back home but at the time she gave this newspaper interview the larger U.S. Army was still engaged in the massive Battle of the Bulge and General Eisenhower was not about to order replacement troops to a stalemated (and arguably less critical) secondary front such as Italy. The political issue Luce pressed, i.e., Roosevelt's competence as a wartime leader, would remain however, and be taken up on the floor of the House when Luce got home.

Jack King recorded in his diary how he and some of his army buddies hailed the advent of 1945. "Arrived at Villanova [Ed: today known as Luciana] this afternoon," he wrote. "Set up in a small house for the time being. We'll have our New Year's Eve celebration tonight." Jack had to have been in a mild shock, however, over his new quarters. "We are sleeping in two C.P. [Command Post] tents outside the office," he recorded. Despite the cold and damp Jack and his HQ buddies had no trouble sleeping, at least that first night anyway. "What a celebration," Jack continued, "cognac, champagne and wine! Wow! We all went to bed about 11:15 — guess we started to celebrate a little too early." For entertainment Jack and his Army friends had watched *Tom and Jerry* cartoons — popular animated slapstick movies about Tom the housecat hopelessly trying to catch the infinitely smarter Jerry the mouse. For inspiration that night Jack could turn to his diary quotation, but most likely he did not: "Resistance to tyrants is obedience to God" — *Thomas Jefferson.*

Bill spent a quiet New Year's Eve at the big house at Signa and received wonderful news from Dotty, to which he responded: "Your letter that arrived today answers one of the uppermost questions in my mind for the past seven weeks. It will be the best thing that could happen for all of us — the ideal family in spite of the obstacles." Henceforth Bill's letters **H**ome, some of them anyway, would be addressed "Dear Dotty, Davy and Little X."

Bill reported that dry weather had set in: "… the mud has turned into dust. You should see how dirty and dusty the men driving tanks and trucks get. Sometime I wonder how they can breathe." He continued: "The C.O. invited Major Cowan and I to his room along with several other guests and members of his staff to start the New Year's celebration. He served some French rum and Coke, which didn't taste as if there was much Coke in it. The cheese, pickle and meat hors d'oeuvres were swell."

John enjoyed New Year's Eve viewing a fireworks display from his new command post near Scascoli. On the other side of the small river "Jerry shot flares and quite a bit of ack-ack at midnight," he wrote. Company "B" was about to settle in for the winter, but this was hardly a relaxing undertaking. John would reasonably soon report snow two feet deep ("… makes it hard to track equipment…") but the cold weather he liked for a specific reason: "As long as the ground remains frozen our mortars will hold up much better."[227] Like Bill and so many other soldiers (undoubtedly on both sides) John had had his fill of Italian mud! John and Jack were about twenty miles distant from each other at this time; Bill approximately another twenty miles farther south, closer to Florence.

—⚌—

As 1945 approached Allen Dulles was happy in the knowledge that his wife Clover would be coming to Berne the following month. His professional life, however, was more stressed than ever. In mid-December Mussolini made a public appearance in Milan's Liric Theater before a huge crowd of die-hard fascists.[228] In his harangue Il Duce "… threatened the Milanese with the wrath of the Germans," and Dulles was very concerned about this.[229] Dulles viewed the propaganda newsreel of this event, and found it discouraging indeed that so many Italians would scream encouragements to such a false leader — their exuberance was irrational and loyalty misplaced, he appreciated. This would be Mussolini's last public speech but Dulles had no way of knowing it. The OSS Berne spy chief truly feared for the destruction of major Italian industrial and economic centers — he felt it might really happen.

Dulles was aware that the Italian government in the south was heating up politically. The leftists now controlled the cabinet after twenty-three years of hard fascist rule, and they demanded the purge of all who worked for Mussolini and the establishment of a socialist government that entailed agrarian and industrial reforms. A "High Commissioner for Sanctions Against Fascists" had been appointed and one of the items on the commissioner's "to-do" list was the prosecution of Marshal Badoglio. Prime Minister Bonomi had to balance his powers with the powers of the cabinet and also the powers of the Allied Military Government. Additionally, the crown that had appointed him had to be respected like it or not — the Italian constitution still provided for a monarchy, even one with most of its powers transferred to less-disliked Prince Umberto. Finally, Bonomi had to at least try to accommodate the other factions of government, namely the Liberals, Actionists and Communists.[230] His was a thankless job.

Italy was unstable and Dulles knew it. He also knew that the British would take an active interest in what was going on, as they hoped to preserve what they could of a Mediterranean empire. What role he might play in this evolving situation, if any, was not clear to him, but he resolved to trust his instincts.

—ɯ—

John spent New Years Day "registering" Lampkin and Lippy on the opposite side of the river where the hill-town was. "Got quite a few hits on houses probably occupied but could observe no Jerries," he recorded. The U.S. Army history for the 100th Chemical Mortar Battalion states: "Throughout the winter months most firing was of the harassing type."

Bill celebrated New Year's Day in a special manner: "This afternoon I went with some other officers to a football game between two Army teams in the neighboring city. It seemed strange watching football so near the front lines. They nicknamed the field the "Spaghetti Bowl" and an Army team and an Air Corps team were the opponents. I would estimate fifteen thousand soldiers attended. The game was good and an easy win for the ground forces."

Wild cheering for a favorite team generated not all the racket Bill took in that afternoon. Bill and the others watched the game under what Bill indicated was an umbrella of protective air cover. "Many planes [flew] overhead on the lookout for Jerry," he wrote. "Some planes were so high we could only see the trail of white vapor. Others flew so low you could almost hit them with a baseball." The Germans had not used massive air power in Italy for an appreciable period, but the Allies could ill-afford to take a chance, especially with thousands of G.I.s lined up like clay pigeons at an open-air sporting event. The absence of a Luftwaffe did not mean one no longer existed. Indeed, hours earlier on that same holiday the Luftwaffe made an 800 airplane attack in the ETO[231]

The U.S. Fifth Army "Mudders" crushed the U.S. Twelfth Air Force "Bridge-busters" by a score of 20-0 at a large sports arena located in Florence. "There were three bands… and the Red Cross provided doughnuts and coffee…" Bill wrote. Bill underestimated the number attending: there were 25,000 spectators.[232]

Many of Bill's letters mentioned the American Red Cross, and the beneficial things it did for the troops, from providing canteens for evening ice cream to putting on dances and other special events for G.I.s. For Dick Stroud it was more basic: "Another nice hot shower at the Red Cross and of all things, a Dallas newspaper in the reading room."[233]

Among Bill's files is a perfectly typed letter addressed to him in Detroit dated April 4, 1944, from an "E.F.S. Wright, Field Director, A.R.C., 463rd Bombardment Group." Stationed in Foggia, Director Wright had a sense of humor. After complaining about "tents and sloshing thru mud" he relates an improved situation: "We have now moved, and although we are still living, and will continue to live, in tents, there is a suggestion of grass in front of the tents."

Wright next describes an airbase in an idyllic setting: nestled in a wide valley "between two ridges of snow capped mountains ..." "We hear and see planes of all kinds, sizes and descriptions from morning to night and from night to morning."

A grim note in Wright's next paragraph, however, appears: "Yesterday I had to notify boys of death, in one case of a mother and the other of a father." In World War II, both in Europe and the Pacific, there was no such thing as military emergency home leave.

On January 2, 1945 Bill wrote his parents that he was scheduled to spend three days along the highway at a traffic control post and would be making some trips with truck convoys. He added: "We have been getting lignite for fuel. It is a poor grade of coal but heats very well ... Dotty writes that Davy finds a pail and wants to, 'milk the cow.'"

> *Jan 3, 1945 10:10 p.m.*
> *Letter No. 58*
>
> *Dearest Hon. and Davy:*
>
> *I am writing this note in an Italian house where the troops live who operate a Traffic Control Post. Coming out here has been quite an experience. One officer (a Lt. Scott from Atlanta) and several enlisted men operate the post. We just came in from the shack, a little building by the side of the road where the convoys of trucks are checked. They also have wrecker service and operate a snow station a few miles up the road. The wrecker had a very busy evening. There are so many accidents, usually due to carelessness. It's hard to make the men drive slowly and be careful even [when] their own lives are at stake.*
>
> *Lt. Scott has two small rooms, each with the usual small window. Part of the glass is missing in these and after dark the [windows] are blacked out... [There is] a pocket size battery radio. It plays with lots of rattles, static and hoarseness but it plays and that is a lot.*
>
> *These houses are extremely dirty and dusty. There appears no way to settle the dust from the stone floors and crumbling plaster walls and ceilings. Most of the roofs are tile and patched and piled up with broken pieces until the water just gives up and quits trying to break through.*
>
> *In one room I found a tall clock reaching clear to the ceiling. It was not running and I did not investigate it due to the possibility of booby traps.*

A person must be on alert at all times to be careful where you step, what you touch and to curb one's curiosity. I guess the house must have about twenty rooms in two stories, most of them small and sordid.

... The stars are very bright tonight. We were out on the road a while in the jeep to look at the wreaked equipment and see that all personnel had been removed.... It's nice to have the radio on even [if] the programs are a re-broadcast and the news is nil.

Bill's observation about booby traps was on point — German soldiers were adept at removing the four to five second "delay train" from their stick grenades so that when the arming pin was pulled out the bomb would explode immediately. A tripwire was a simple method of triggering an explosion. Pulling out a cabinet drawer, opening a door or even straightening a crooked picture on a wall might well spell one's last activity on earth.[234] The Germans routinely booby-trapped buildings, and in the outdoors they were masters at planting foot activated landmines.

John Lesesne's diary makes no mention of booby-traps but in one entry he wrote, "Lippy's platoon is well forward, in front of the 81's, nothing on his left but a minefield."[235] John did not indicate who laid this minefield, but if enemy, the U.S. Army Engineers would be called in for the removal process. The first thing the engineers would try to do would be to determine the extent of the field by using metal detectors, probes and specialized equipment; yellow tape would then be used to denote borders and safe corridors.

The Germans had a unique mine contraption that struck terror into the hearts of all Allied infantrymen on patrol. Known by the nickname, "Bouncing Betty," the buried device when stepped upon released a spring that triggered a first charge that blew the bomb approximately six feet into the air. When it exploded its shrapnel could wound or kill all in the vicinity, not just the unfortunate soldier who happened to step on it. Safety while on patrol called for being spread out, but for rookies in the field sometimes this did not happen.

The Germans in Italy used mine warfare extensively for its multiplier effect. One of the reasons the U.S. Army put out regular nighttime patrols even during periods of lull was to harass the Germans and preclude them from doing this kind of deadly work.

The drab and dirty house interior as described by Bill undoubtedly was like inside the "big house" that John used as his second command post — limestone plaster dust everywhere.

———∽———

Not everything Bill wrote during this period when he was near the front was negative. In one late December letter to Dotty he mentioned an endearing custom adopted by some of the married men: "Every day's passing brings our reunion one day closer. I am going to write a few extra letters in a few days until our letter numbers equal the number of days we have been apart. Today makes fifty-one days so I have three extra letters to write. One officer here has been doing that and at present his number is over seven hundred. Surely ours will not go that high." First Lieutenant Dick Stroud wrote home practically every day but if he missed one he would make up the following day sometimes with up to four short letters.

The prince and the pauper

Copyright by Bill Mauldin (1944). Courtesy of the Bill Mauldin Estate LLC.

CHAPTER SEVEN:

"EVERY LAST PIECE OF CHARCOAL, BOARD AND NAIL"

January 4–13, 1945

IN THE FILE OF LETTERS Bill saved written to him by his mother is the following dated January 4, 1945: "Dear William: We thought you were in England and now know Italy!" Such a statement would not likely be made today by the parent of a soldier serving in a regular U.S. military unit abroad.

Not everything Bill observed in Northern Italy was in ruins and some places were hardly damaged. It all depended on where the combatants had clashed and what targets the USAAF attacked. Bill wrote about one trip: "I was out on the road today and visited, among other places, the walled city of Lucca. A high, elaborately constructed wall surrounds the entire old section of this town. Fortunately, the town escaped the fate of many other cities when the Germans were driven out. It was a beautiful day here and most of the population was out in their Sunday best…"

Unfortunately for Bill his outing did not include a sampling of food from a region fabled for its cookery. "We had lunch at a Traffic Control Post in Pistoia. I can see why the men all say they will never eat Spam after they get out of the Army…" Bill wrote. John wrote about his boys subsisting on packaged food known as "10 in 1s" — a field ration designed to provide one meal to ten men. "The platoons have eaten them for a month straight," he observed, not criticizing this unavoidable regimen but rather suggesting its awfulness.[236] John often delivered these and other types of rations when he drove out to visit the platoons.

On the day Bill's mother wrote about him being in England, January 4, with the ammunition deficiency still critical Alexander had no choice but to cancel Pianoro. The four commanders, Alexander, Clark, Truscott and McCreery agreed among themselves that the Allies would stay in "defensive positions and build up ammunition reserves for a spring offensive with a target date of April 1st."[237] While MTOUSA worked at delivering the needed ammunition and other supplies to the front, Truscott started planning a new series of attacks that he hoped might take the Germans by surprise.

For his part, General Clark in his memoirs made no mention of the Pianoro Plan by name but rather alluded to, "… the fifteen-day attack now planned for December," noting: "This plan was later dropped." On a preceding page Clark reported an ammunition allotment in mid-November for the U.S. Fifth Army of only "… *fifteen rounds a day (emphasis added)* per gun for 105 mm howitzers…" and similar low numbers for other, larger caliber guns.[238] The reader will recall what John wrote in his diary (on more than one occasion) about his shortages of mortar ammo during this period. 4.2" would be considered large caliber.

Truscott published his memoirs in 1954 (with the benefit of having presumably read Clark's which came out four years earlier) and while he did not accuse Clark of misfeasance, a fair reading of both books together would cause one to conclude that Clark *had to have known* that the ammunition build-up was not sufficient to sustain his planned December offensive, and even probably known this *before* the Battle of Serchio Valley. Per Truscott, Clark nevertheless argued hard for a late December launch. The likelihood is that Truscott had done what Churchill and Alexander had hoped all along that he would do — stand up to Clark and stop him from being foolhardy. John's comment of December 21 ("Still no definite news of the 'push' ") suggests that on that date at least he, John, contemplated an attack might yet happen.

Lieutenant Wade McCree offered this as the reason given for the cancellation of Pianoro: "Our attack was cancelled because of the breakthrough in the Ardennes Forest, better known as the Battle of the Bulge, in Northern Europe. A large part of our aircraft in Italy was flown north to help stop this threat."[239]

The *USAAF Chronology* does not support McCree's statement. G.I.s awaiting battle at the front like McCree had to be told *something*, and it would not do for them to learn (or the enemy for that matter) that the "push" had been cancelled due to the lack of ammunition!

Truscott undoubtedly saved many Allied lives by doing his homework. Clark's plan of attack had been up a roadbed with the enemy fortified and holding the high ground; Truscott wanted none of this. Truscott would now have the opportunity to do what he did best — figure a way to slip behind the German line. Truscott eschewed using the phrase in press releases "Truscott's Fifth Army" but for all intents and purposes from this point forward the U.S. Fifth Army *was his to command.*

The Anglo-American decision to remain in defensive positions in Italy would become viewed with suspicion by Joseph Stalin. A commentator reported that on January 12, 1945: "... 5.3 million Russians are engaged on the Eastern Front in 527 infantry divisions..."[240] The Red Army fought along its entire front (including in mountainous areas) winter-be-damned and Stalin had to be asking himself why were the Americans and British in Italy not doing the same?

Over a year earlier, specifically October 1943, a British POW "escaper" heading south passed through the same area in Northern Italy described by Bill; he said this about his experience: "... fresh wholesome food; the recurrent halts for wine; a sense of peace and goodwill inspired by the peasant people."[241]

What had happened during the fifteen-month period?

By early 1945, over 100,000 Italian civilians would be dead in addition to an estimated 300,000 Italian military.[242] Cities and villages would be in ruins throughout the country. American and British tactical air attacks had indiscriminately killed many noncombatants, including women and children.[243] The major Northern Italian cities of Milan, Turin and others were spared from wholesale heavy strategic bombing because Italy was an "ally," but the tactical bombing and strafing near those cities was relentless. The fact was that not even bicycle travel was safe if in the range of prowling fighter-bombers.

In Naples one U.S. soldier was getting to know the natives in a better light and this proved a positive experience for him. Lieutenant Dick Stroud wrote home:

> *The family that I live with, Momma (forty-two), Pappa (fifty-six), Victorrio (nineteen), Francesca (nine) and a servant woman are merchants of the first class and prosperous on the comparative scale. They have been extremely pleasant and have been teaching me the language — a very happy situation.*[244]

Getting up in the morning in a private residence and walking to work had to be almost blessedly civilian-like for Dick. As an aside, Dick, who disliked ascending and descending the many stairs of Italy, was rewarded a few days later when his new family moved from the fifth to the first floor. "Wonderful!" Dick exclaimed, but then added: "I hope some Lt. Col. does not find out."[245] In a subsequent letter Dick identified the family as the Buonannos.[246]

—⚏—

Luce's comment given to that *Stars and Stripes* reporter before she left Italy was published on January 4 and it caused the American press to rejuvenate a theme that had been reported on and off since D-Day, an accusation that General McNarney and the War Department had worked assiduously to rebut: that Italy was a *forgotten front*. Upon reading the press reports of this latest Luce interview, General Marshall bemoaned "[they]…hit morale a dreadful blow… a really dreadful blow…"[247] As a consequence of this renewed negative reporting, Marshall toured the Italian front the following month after attending the Yalta conference. He was photographed pinning medals on G.I.s for consumption by hometown newspapers.

On the other side of the political aisle, war news from the recent Congressional front tour was reported favorably. A few days after the Luce proposal became public, Congressman John M. Costello, Democrat from California and Chairman of the Military Affairs Committee was quoted in a magazine, presumably speaking for all the European battlefronts that the committee had visited: "The men are doing an exceptionally fine job." With no direct tie into Italy Costello added there was, "no critical shortage of supplies," noting specifically that commanders, "naturally would like to have more of everything."[248]

The political battle-line remained drawn.

—⚏—

On January 7 John had a frightening experience:

> *The infantry is blasting 60 mm mortar pits back at company rear. That is definitely not good. Would hate for Jerry to trap the rest of my company up here. On returning to my command post I had a .50 caliber machine gun set-up. I fired a few bursts to test it. Infantry boys going for water*

reported a sniper firing at them and search parties were sent out. Only when two doughboys came here did I realize the trouble I'd caused…

I am planning to have more vehicles brought up to enable us to get away quickly, and… [will] prepare positions a little further back. We'll pull out from here, go back several hundred yards and set-up while Jimmy covers us, and then he'll pull out while we cover him.

John knew the instant he heard the sound of mortars firing to his rear that the 363rd Infantry Regiment was attempting to repulse a German incursion of sorts. Two U.S. infantrymen typically operated a 60 mm mortar from inside a "pit" — a small sandbag encirclement — and the sound of a .60 was unmistakable to his trained ear. He also was aware, as he stated, that if company rear were to be overrun then the rest of Company "B" at the line might be next.

John recorded later that day that he received a report that a sniper had pinned down two communications men about 200 yards from his C.P. "That's getting rather close," he observed. Anticipating a fight, he again reacted: "I have now got a system set up by which we expect to deliver defensive fires less than two minutes after they are called for." The 4.2" packed four times the wallop of a 60 mm infantry mortar and could make a huge difference if enemy troops were still in the area.

The incident apparently passed; his diary makes no further mention of it.

January 8, 1945

Dear Dotty and Davy:

One new [road] stretch today took me high up in the Apennine Mountains. [It is] the most beautiful country I have seen over here. The road winds up and up. [There are] many beautiful large villas clinging to the mountainside and small terraces up the sides, on such steep slopes it hardly seems possible to climb them. The Germans did a through job of destroying the many railroad tunnels and bridges. It was snowing hard when we reached the summit and the plows were working. It seemed like New York State to see so much snow.

Dotty, would you mind sending me a box of ABDOL pills with Vitamin C? They build up a resistance to colds. You will probably have to show the postmaster my request.

The page of Bill's letter (not its envelope) with his request for vitamins bears a round purple postal stamp reading: "DETROIT, MICH. JEFFERSON STA JAN 24 1945." When Dotty mailed Bill his pills, the local post office stamped this page to prevent its possible reuse at other post offices for black market trade.

Bill's missives from the big house during the period January 9-14 are largely uneventful (i.e., sitting in on meetings, participating in an inspection "… of a number of exceptional enlisted men…", attending movies in a cold theatre and looking forward to finding bundles of mail when he returned to Caserta). On January 12, however, Bill reported a decisive engineering victory: "At last I solved the problem with the shower which sprays hot on one side and cold on the other. I tied a sock over the spray that mixed all the water in a solid stream of one temperature. It worked fine and I had a most enjoyable shower." He also alluded to an invention brewing in his mind: "I spent some time drawing pictures of a new truck for the Army" (more to follow).

John's personal shower history was different than Bill's (and likely Jack's and Dick's also). On November 20 John wrote: "The Army has a pretty good system — you get a shower, turn in the dirty clothes and get clean ones in exchange — no paperwork." An Army mobile shower unit (van) made the circuit of the front, John explained. The van next showed up on December 11, but that day proved inconvenient. "Boys afraid to leave their holes to get showers," John noted. The following day the goal was accomplished. "Took about three hours of waiting and then the water was cold, but I was determined," John noted. As commander, he let his men go first.

John was able to take one more shower over a five-month period and that happened on February 12: "I had a water mark around my neck," he wrote. Thinking of this, that is, about being clean only from the neck up for months at a time makes one appreciate what war at its most basic element is really like. John's diary indicates that Company "B" was pulled off the line for a week starting April 3 to prepare for the final battle, and presumably he and his boys also showered then.

—ɯ—

At the beginning of 1945 the East/West military alliance against the fascist powers seemed to be working. Indeed, Stalin had launched a massive winter offensive on January 15, 1945 and he cabled an important, supportive military message to his counterpart across the Atlantic detailing the Soviet contribution to the Battle of the Bulge:

PERSONAL AND MOST SECRET FROM PREMIER J. V. STALIN TO THE PRESIDENT, Mr F. ROOSEVELT

After four days of offensive operations on the Soviet-German front I am now in a position to inform you that our offensive is making satisfactory progress despite unfavourable weather. The entire Central Front — from the Carpathians to the Baltic Sea — is moving westwards. The Germans, though resisting desperately, are retreating. I feel sure that they will have to disperse their reserves between the two fronts and, as a result, relinquish the offensive on the Western Front. I am glad that this circumstance will ease the position of the Allied troops in the West and expedite preparations for the offensive planned by General Eisenhower.[249]

On the international political front, however, a major difference of opinion had developed between the United States and Great Britain on one hand and the Soviet Union on the other involving the governance of Poland. It was hoped by the Western leaders that the issues involving that "liberated" country could be diplomatically resolved.

The previous August had been an eye-opener for Roosevelt and Churchill. When the Red Army approached the outskirts of Warsaw the Polish resistance inside the city rose up to fight the Nazi occupiers, anticipating military assistance from Stalin. Instead of helping, the Soviet dictator had his forces hunker down for a period of sixty-three days giving the Germans the time to re-group and wipe out the resistance. This came on top of an unsettling allegation made by the Nazi government the previous year that it had located fresh mass graves of Poles hidden in a forest named Katyn, part of an area formerly occupied by the Soviet Union. The Nazis claimed that these dead Poles had been mostly officers in the Polish Army or polish policemen, and that the Soviets had murdered them. The Soviet Union vehemently denied the killings and accused the Nazis of the mass murder. The photographic and other evidence coming out, however, pointed to Soviet culpability. An estimated 20,000 had been shot Russian style in the back of the head. Had the Soviet secret police, the NKVD done this?

Although Stalin's January 15, 1945 "personal" military message to Roosevelt was positive and reassuring on its face, Roosevelt and his advisers were not dupes.

Extremely troubling to them was the pattern of the Soviet approach to defeat Nazi Germany. Rather than send one or two military spearheads directly at the heart of the Third Reich and finish off the war quickly, Stalin unquestionably was taking his time and methodically advancing a huge front. The Red Army gobbled up vast amounts of territory extending from the Baltic Sea in the north to Adriatic Sea to the south. Was this a Soviet war of territorial conquest? Did the Red Army intend to occupy these countries until such time as communist governments could be installed?

A pro-Soviet puppet government had been set-up in Poland.

Was this Stalin's intention for Northern Italy?

From the macro to the micro, from high diplomacy to the daily life of soldiers everywhere, time marched on.

In mid January something important occurred for Company "B". John Lesesne wrote proudly in his diary: "DeLallo was finally awarded the Bronze Star, thereby becoming the first man in the battalion to be decorated for gallantry in action." Whether John had been slightly disappointed that the Silver Star that he recommended had been downgraded, he did not record, but the answer is most likely no. A fair reading of the four corners of John's diary if nothing else reveals that the most driving component of his nature is manifested in his usage of the word "first." John was a competitor at everything, and he undoubtedly wanted the letter "B" (as in Company "B") to stand for *best* in battalion.

Back in the United States Representative Luce scheduled January 18 as the date for her to report to Congress about what she learned during her "official" trip as a committee member and also matters that she additionally learned during her ten-day personal extension. This was an uneasy period for her, however, a despondent one, as two matters weighed heavily: while in Italy she had fallen in love and her lover was now an ocean away and also, she had suffered through a dreadful anniversary.

Luce's extended visit to the Italian winter front resulted in an unsustainable romance with a charismatic, if not dashing, combat leader. Her lover and battleground tour guide had been none other than U.S. Fifth Army commanding general Lucien Truscott.[250] Luce and her husband Harry had an uneasy tolerance for serial spousal infidelity (he had his peccadillos too). In Truscott's case, what happened may have been out of character. Per Luce's biographer, the affair started the evening she wore the black silk dress.

A year earlier, on January 11, 1944, Luce's only child Ann Clare Brokaw, age nineteen, an honors student at Stanford University had been killed in an automobile accident. Luce's response to this personal tragedy was to throw herself with abandon even deeper into the political arena; she was now, however, getting strong pushback for being so assertive.

The affair with Truscott was revealed only in recent times and Bill never knew of it; his observation, however, "They expect 150 couples. It's a funny war," had been valid all the way to the top. The Greatest Generation lived up to its name, yes, but the press at the time did not report on the subject of adultery involving public figures. Today the conflict of interest issue — a member of Congress on an inspection trip and a commanding general of the army *being inspected* would generate headlines and disciplinary action. If word had somehow gotten out about the Luce-Truscott affair it would have been a public relations calamity for Marshall. Parents of G.I.s would have been mortified, and rightfully so. Having observed this, one should let the rest of the story of Luce and Truscott play out; there would be more personal recklessness to follow coupled with great irony.

The Battle of Serchio Valley had a strange afterglow for the leader of one of the forces that participated in it. For the first time since the Armistice an Italian fascist division had acquitted itself with high bravery in the face of overwhelming military odds. One author who fought with Royal Italian Army from 1943 to 1945 related that *Il Duce* was so encouraged by the new spirit of Italian fascist aggressiveness that he willingly submitted himself to the harsh winter conditions near the front.

> *... Mussolini was so heartened by the news of the partial success of his troops that in January 1945 he went to visit the Italia Division in the mountains between Pontremoli and Aula. Although the weather on Lake Garda was spring-like, [Ed: Mussolini's government was seated at Salo on beautiful Lake Garda] the Cisa Pass over the Apennines was deep in snow. Mussolini trudged cheerfully through the snow while his entourage,*

*including the German doctor Zachariae, had to push the cars through
one drift after another in a freezing wind. Aula was derelict and abandoned but Mussolini, ignoring the snowstorms, pushed on to Pontremoli,
where he slept soundly on a camp bed under two horse blankets, happy to
be with his Italian soldiers.*[251]

The sixty-one-year-old puppet dictator's euphoria would be short-lived.

The U.S. Fifth Army Transportation Section was well supported by staff personnel, but not all of the support was apparently welcomed by all of the men. Bill
reported: "This is quite a complete organization. They have a dentist stationed
here [and] expect to get a doctor. Yesterday a chaplain arrived. Many of the men
deride the chaplain and his part in the war… we have a lot of training to do to
fortify [Davy] against the [Army] influences he will meet."

As an aside, there were soldiers who did not deride the Chaplain Corps. Jack
King reported that he regularly attended weekly worship services and specifically
remembered a Catholic priest, a Father Hickey who did a road circuit for the U.S.
Fifth Army. "He was all over the place with a driver," Jack remarked, "conducting
universal worship services." Jack savored the memory; it happened he ended-up
married to a Hickey (no relation). Dick and John also regularly attended worship
services, as did Bill.

That serviceman's diary that Jack owned quoted the Bible on a number
of its pages in a patriotic (war-serving) context, e.g., "Righteous exalteth a
nation" — *Proverbs XIV: 34*, "Fear not" — *Genesis XLII: 23*, "He went forth conquering and to conquer" — *Revelation VI: 2*, "Man ought always to pray, and not
to faint" — *Luke XVIII: 1*, are a few examples.

Jack's diary appears to be commercially produced and not a publication of
the Chaplain's Corps, suggesting that American values in 1945 were different
than today — that it was OK then to routinely and selectively parade-out Judeo-
Christian scripture in support of the U.S. government and its military establishment. A desperate struggle had to be won, after all, and Nazism was an abrogation
of the laws of God and teachings of Christ. Why not use all the arrows in one's
quiver, the leaders may have thought at the time, including the justly spiritual?

As the end of his assignment in the north approached, Bill observed: "To
my surprise, today was also spent out on the road. I am getting to know every
bump in the roads and there are many of them." Borrowing words from Al Capp's

cartoon strip *Li'l Abner*, Bill observed: "The back seats of these jeeps, "ain't fit for hoomins." He seemed to be having a good day, however. "I enjoy being out though, and see more of the country and people."[252]

"Yesterday evening in town some of the soldiers were eating as we stopped by an outfit. A bunch of children were waiting around the tubs of water where they washed their mess kits. The kids had containers and were grateful for scraps left over on the soldier's plates. Older folks stood back a few paces and they too looked hungry."

"Last night one of the little buildings set up along the road to check traffic by the Army caught on fire and burned down. Today the civilians cleaned up every last piece of charcoal, board & nail and even swept the ground for little bits which would burn. You have no idea how scarce fuel is. People carry little pots and kettles around with them that contain a few coals, especially the older people. Women wash clothes in streams with snow on the ground. Tiny children with bare legs squat down on their heels, drape their coat around their knees and fold their arms tight to try to keep warm. Their little hands look swollen and purple and some of them [are] quite dirty. The little tots are cute, even in such adverse conditions and you should see their smile for a piece of chocolate. I doubt we could endure living under the conditions here. The population of Italy is about one-third that of the whole United States and the country has so many mountains [that] much of it cannot be farmed."

Bill closed his letter with his usual warmth: "... Each passing day brings us one day nearer to each other. If it took a thousand years, it would be worth waiting for..."

John Lesesne, Jack King and Dick Stroud did not travel to the extent that Bill did and hence could not observe the civilian population like he did.

On January 13, at 4 p.m. the *USS West Point* pulled into the Port of Naples after an almost record nine-day passage, one of three ships carrying the U.S. 10th Mountain Division, an elite combat unit that had been specially trained at 9,200-foot-high Camp Hale, Colorado.[253] Upon disembarking and experiencing Neapolitan hawkers-of-everything and viewing for the first time actual urban battle damage (Naples had been hit hard the previous year by both sides) these fresh infantrymen went by rail and boat to staging areas south of the German-occupied city of Bologna. There they faced the steep slopes of a number of key objectives, an Apennine ridge named Riva, a peak named Mount Belvedere and others.[254] The high grounds of each were blanketed with snow and enemy troops who had successfully repulsed several U.S. Fifth Army assaults. The 10th brought with it equipment specially suited for mountain warfare — a portable tramway, for instance, that could be installed in less than a day and could evacuate wounded from an elevation some 1,600 feet high. The ride down lasted four minutes as opposed to the six to ten hours it would take if litter bearers had to be used.[255] Additionally the division had a supply of M-29 Weasels, a tracked vehicle with armored siding built by Studebaker especially for use over snow. The 10th had not trained specifically for the Italian campaign but when Marshall offered the division to the U.S. Fifth Army, General Clark immediately accepted.[256]

The use of the 10th Mountain Division in Italy had been carefully scripted in advance of the division's arrival on the scene. At this late juncture in the war, Allied commanders appreciated that much of the combat effectiveness had been sapped from the veteran U.S. Fifth Army (an observation the reader will recall also made by Bill).[257] The 10th was the surprise for the Germans envisioned by Field Marshal Alexander and company. The arrival of the 10th was not a replacement action envisioned by Congresswoman Clare Boothe Luce; no soldiers would be furloughed home, but rather a much-needed booster shot given into the arm of the tired U.S. Fifth Army.

MTOUSA had requisitioned sure-footed friends to assist the 10th: 7,120 American mules had been imported on mule ships and these ships were busy bringing replacement animals at the rate of 500 a month, as well as copious amounts of American grain and hay.[258] Every detail for the 10th had been being attended to.

The men of the 10th Mountain Division were young and athletic and many were from the best eastern colleges;[259] they had learned to ski and rock climb at privileged New England clubs. Well trained by the Army in mountaineering and infantry tactics, these young lions, the last combat division to enter the European fray, undoubtedly were eager to make a reputation for themselves. They may have also initially believed, albeit with the naïve bravado of youth, that the Germans holding the high ground would fold at the mere sight of the awesome firepower they would deliver.

The 10th received a brutal awakening upon arriving at its staging area south of Bologna. Per one commentator, at "... a rail line running along the border of the 86th Regiment's training area," seven men of the 10th died by mine explosions, including a Catholic chaplain who had hastened to perform last rites.[260] The enemy had struck first and by stealth, and had lived up to the words of a propaganda flier it had previously strewn: "This is not Camp Hale where you had 15,000 men skiing at the foot of Tennessee Pass."[261]

In Italy it had again become more dangerous to be a combat soldier.

Naples, January 1945
— *Sarah Stroud Ollison photo collection*

CHAPTER EIGHT:

BILL RETURNS TO CASERTA

BILL FLEW BACK to Caserta on January 14 in perfect weather and wrote about his flight to his parents the next day: "I saw many battle marks on the country below. Some villages had been wiped right off the face of the earth. The bomb craters around the bridge sites look like pockmarks."

Waiting for him at AFHQ, to his joy, were thirty-nine letters. After making a "beeline" to collect them, he made an interesting comment to Dotty about his presence in Italy: "Don't ever wonder why I came over, Hon. I felt that eventually I would have to come and this seemed the best opportunity in view of the nature of the work and of accomplishment." Bill also offered a blunt critique on the command at Leghorn, the U.S. Fifth Army Transportation Section. He told Dotty of "brazen" adultery by two senior officers and stated that "socially minded" leadership there had "permeated the entire outfit." Telling her of a drunken brawl in which "a man got badly hurt" he then opined, "I have never seen so many incompetent and undeserving officers. They get promotions by glad-handing... and the officers who go straight get sent to the outposts." Bill explained that he could not communicate this to Dotty while he was in the North for fear the local censors would turn him in to the officers who misbehaved.

Dick Stroud apparently agreed that promotions were based upon a good ol' boy network: "Promoting each other all over North Africa," his daughter recollected him telling a nephew.[262]

Fear of having one's letters opened and read and the contents disclosed to the command authority was a real concern for servicemen serving in World War II. Dick complained to Sue about it. "Does it get monotonous having my letters all the time restricted to our personal affairs?" he asked.[263] Evidently Dick yearned to tell his wife everything that he observed and felt, but sensed it would be unwise for him to do so.

Among Bill's news clippings is an article from *Time Magazine* published shortly after the European war ended, that, among other things, suggested that the sorry situation Bill described may have been endemic to the entire U.S. military in Italy. The article is about the comic genius, Bill Mauldin:

> Up Front *[Ed: a book by Mauldin] which is like a long letter home, sets forth some of Mauldin's favorite gripes, which are the gripes of all infantrymen. Among them: revulsion at "spit & polish" in the field; envy of rear-echelon men who take over the towns after the infantrymen have captured them, occupy all the best spots and drink all the liquor; disdain for brass hats full of arrogance and stuffing.*[264]

One of the stories Bill often repeated (with glee) was how Mauldin found a way to "stick it" to Patton by creating a cartoon character named "General Blugget" (a contraction of "Blood and Guts"). In 1943 Patton had alienated himself from the U.S. Army over an incident in Sicily when he slapped a battle-fatigued soldier in a hospital.

To the soldiers who served in Italy, one of the proudest memories that they brought back, and never forgot, was that of Bill Mauldin. "He was ours," Bill used to exclaim. "He was made from Italian mud. He was our spirit." And that spirit was Willie and Joe. Per the *Time Magazine* article:

> *Willie was born full-grown during the Italian campaign.*

> *He needed a shave and his clothes hung in weary folds on his weary frame. Even on the day of his creation, his thick fingers were curved, as though from grasping a pick handle or an M-1 rifle. He did not smile and he has never smiled since.*

> *Willie was born into the 45th Infantry Division, where his creator, Private Bill Mauldin, also served. Willie had a sidekick, Joe. Together Willie and Joe slogged from Italy to Germany.*

> *Willie and Joe were citizen soldiers.*

Mauldin celebrated the combat infantrymen, the men Bill saw on his trips to the front; the men who struggled to live in winter conditions and who knew come spring the shooting would start up again: the dogface soldier trying hopelessly to heat his tin coffee mug with a pack of matches; bearded privates looking blankly at the newly reported ninety-day-wonder baby-faced lieutenant; a master distiller making grappa with a buddy; a G.I. in a tent with a skinny, begging, wet dog outside: "Let 'im in," the G.I. says to his tent-mate. "I wanna see a critter I kin feel sorry fer;" Willie looking down at an Italian waif looking up holding a pail — the unmistakable image of child hunger.

Of all the literary-media-giant war correspondents to cover the European war, i.e., Ernie Pyle, John Steinbeck, Margaret Bourke-White, Robert Capa, and yes, Clare Boothe Luce, et al, Mauldin was most powerful, in Bill's mind. In the *Time* article Mauldin is quoted as confessing to being sometimes "seditious." Mauldin had plenty of company, no doubt, including Bill. A delightful letter written by Bill near the end of his tour attests to this; it was written at a time when Bill had had his fill of rank-pulling pompous, strutting militarists and wanted only to go home and get on with his life.

"Rumor has it that the romantic Lt. Col. is moving from the office at the service area to one here in the palace," Bill started. "The men over there are highly pleased to get rid of him as he runs a close second to a character named K----. I hope he will not get in our hair and [I] will try to stay clear of him. He will be in the same office with his friend so probably will put on his best front. This is one case where I have not been one of the agitators. To me it has been rather funny." Bill concludes by mentioning the dream of all oppressed G.I.s: "Some of the men are even reported to be on the lookout for him after he becomes a civilian."[265]

And consider that Bill saved this favorite:

Undated

SING A SONG OF OFFICERS

I have a lieutenant of twenty and one,
A ninety-day wonder in pinks,
"Take over," he'll tell me, "I must sleep it off,
That liquor in town really stinks!"
… Salute 'em.

My captain goes haywire when up at the front,
Forgets to give orders and hides,
But back in the rear he comes out of his hole
And orders resound from all sides.
… Salute 'em.

My major lives up to the leaf he just earned,
In manner befitting his class,
With waiters salaaming, an opulent mess,
He plays to the rank and the brass.
... Salute 'em.

My colonel drives off in a Packard Sedan
Shined up by a detail of ten;
"My motto," he says to the nurse at his side,
"Is everything just for the men."
... Salute 'em.

Oh sing to the bars, the spit and polish
In the manner you know will suit 'em;
Since you cannot ignore the fact we're at war,
Repress your desire to boot 'em — Hell!
... Salute 'em!

Attributed to Sylvia H. Simons, ARC

John's diary entries suggest that he was respectful of those who outranked him, for the most part, anyway, but on one occasion he wrote: "Yesterday we were honored by a visit from Maj. D — [Ed: name deleted], who as usual, brought something about which to bother me, and then held forth in his habitual long-winded manner — the subject is immaterial — he always has something to say."[266] On another occasion John was more direct; he wrote about meeting the operations officer of a regiment belonging to the 34th Infantry Division (he would have been a major): "At first glance he seems to be an arrogant son-of-a-bitch."[267] There is no mention in his diary of a second glance.

On January 17th Bill reported that his trip north had been a success: "Some of the recommendations I made are receiving plenty of action... I believe my C.O. was pleased... and he gave me my next assignment. It may take a couple of weeks and involves no travel.... [I am] to set up certain operations as they should be done... It covers a lot of ground... I am thrilled."

—⟋⟍—

Luce's biographer Sylvia Jukes Morris wrote this about Luce's forty-five-minute speech to Congress on January 18, 1945:

In more than two and a half years, she [Luce] said, American forces had
suffered a colossal 98,366 casualties, 90 percent of those being infantry-
men. Citing the four hundred consecutive days Truscott's Thirty-fourth
Division had spent in wretched conditions, holding down a far larger
enemy, she urged yet again that combat ground troops be allotted the
same recuperative leave that airmen enjoyed... "[268]

Democrats viewed Luce as an irritant and not many attended her speech. Vice President Truman criticized her for overstepping her bounds as a representative lawmaker. Truman had to be circumspect in how he treated Luce however — the Associated Press editors had a few days earlier named her Woman of the Year.[269] For his part, General Clark thanked Luce for giving her speech in Congress. "Her interest and efforts gave all of us a real lift and helped to clarify the Italian war in the minds of the people back home," Clark wrote, oozing discretely.[270] From within the Republican Party, however, Luce was beginning to lose support. The presidential election of 1944 had been decided, a number of fellow Republicans pointed out to Luce. The war was being won. Why continue to press this issue?

The *Stars and Stripes* interview and her Congressional report notwithstanding, Clare Boothe Luce herself began to realize that heaping political criticism on the conduct of the "overlooked war" was not the right thing to do for the G.I.s who had to fight it. Also, her lover in Italy, Lucien Truscott did not agree with her on the subject of rotating U.S. troops home en masse. He would write after the war that if all those serving in combat commands for more than two years had been furloughed to the U.S. the number would be near 70,000, and this would not have been a prudent thing to do with the final battle looming.

For Clare Boothe Luce's part, and not unlike Bill, she learned firsthand the strong aversion G.I.'s had developed to almost all things Italian. Luce was concerned about this, no doubt, and she cared about the suffering G.I.s and also the Italian civilians caught in the crossfire. She had no way of knowing it at the time but she would years later successfully seek out and become U.S. Ambassador to Italy. It was during this earlier wartime period, however, that she learned firsthand of the problems confronting this foreign country; she would later put her knowledge to good use. Something else happened to Luce during this period — she developed an affinity for Roman Catholicism.

—ɯ—

Duty at Allied Forces Headquarters, hundreds of miles from the front, was less arduous than temporary duty in Leghorn and vicinity. On January 19, 1945, Bill wrote Dotty letter No. 71 at 7:10 p.m. from the Palace. "I am writing this in our favorite room," he states. "When I say 'our' I mean yours and mine because I think it is the one you would like best. It is smaller than many of the others but is bright and cheerful." In a subsequent sentence he adds, "The orchestra is playing in the next room."

A typical day's excitement at the palace was described as follows: "One of the officers received a box from Home with a large loaf of bread in it. The bread was dried up and moldy and we all wondered about it until he opened the two halves of the loaf and discovered a bottle."

The Transportation Section of MOTUSA was a big operation, Bill learned. Its organization chart reflected a chain of command, top to bottom, consisting of five levels. At the top there was the Chief of Transportation, and under him an executive officer. The chain then branched off into "administration" and "operations" sides, each headed by an "assistant executive" who was in-charge of six groups. Bill worked on the operations side in the "Highway Group" that was responsible for the movement of freight and passengers by vehicles. The other operational groups were water, air, rail, floating equipment and "movements" (that booked and scheduled water bids). On the administrative side, there was control (inspections), planning, supply, "troop" (training), office administration and (perhaps quaint by today's vernacular standards) "personal baggage." This last group dealt with items belonging to deceased, missing, missing-in-action, captured or interned personnel.[271]

Hundreds of MTOUSA army officers reported to the transportation chief and Bill was relieved to be at the bottom of this feeding chain, that is, to be only a field operative reporting to Major Renick. As group head, in Bill's opinion, Renick had the un-envious task of navigating through the layers of bureaucracy in order to get things done.

As regards management (either in the military or civilian-corporate) Bill decided early on after graduating from college that he had little interest in it. He did not wish to supervise and evaluate others but rather relished inventing things. He wanted projects that he could perform while acting alone. He would chair meetings if called on to do so both in the Army and in later life at automobile companies, but that was usually not his first choice. Professionally he was and always would remain a lobo — a lone wolf. He wanted to be either at a drafting board or in the shop, with his hands touching metal.

Free time at Caserta was taken up by games of chess, checkers and movie watching. "I finally have the rats banished on the outside," Bill noted for his assigned accommodation in that single "clammy" former hospital room. "Did I tell you that a few nights when I first arrived, they ate my candy bars and soap?" It turned out the rats were not completely gone; Bill later wrote: "I still hear them running through the partitions once in a while." Additionally, there was air pollution to contend with during the winter months: "We have had frost the last three nights and it has been quite cold," Bill indicated. "It was very smoky out tonight. There is practically no wind and the little stoves burning soft coal here in the army area make quite a bit of smudge."[272]

On January 21 Bill made known what he felt Germany deserved: "I hope the Russians are the ones to reach Berlin first," he wrote, "because they will use their own way of preventing future German aggression." This is the only comment directly critical of Germany to be found among Bill's surviving letters.

Jack King enjoyed Villanova. On that same day as Bill wrote about Russians punishing the Germans, Jack recorded that the 91st Headquarters Company moved into a large building there that Jack referred to as The Castle or alternatively he used that ubiquitous term Big House. "What a beautiful place," Jack wrote. "It's on top of a mountain that overlooks a wide valley. There isn't too much snow here. It's close to Florence. All the walls are hand-painted and it is supposed to have fifty rooms." By "painted," Jack undoubtedly meant frescoes, an art technique in which the Italians had been experts for ages.

Living there left good memories for Jack. Things became quiet and routine and sometimes he and some of his buddies got leave to do tourist-type things. "We got into Florence," Jack related, "and along the Arno River there was a very nice little pensione [boarding house] that we got acquainted with where we would bring in coffee, sugar, flour and things of that sort and the Italian operator would furnish bacon, ham and things that we couldn't get." This happened more than once, Jack explained: "Every time we got a leave," he remembered. "We stayed right on the bank of the Arno River, near the Ponte Vecchio." Jack told of five or so guys going together and renting several rooms. "It was a bed and breakfast." They spent the evenings at local bars and tavernas.

"Ponte Vecchio was the only bridge the Germans left standing," Jack added and he opined that the enemy had not done this out of respect for historic preservation. "It was so narrow with its shops that the big trucks and tanks could not use it," he explained. It was visits like these — staying near a famous landmark in a beautiful medieval city in a gorgeous countryside and friendly people that caused Jack King to become lifetime-enchanted with Italy. After the war he married and brought his wife Eileen over several times for vacation. He also shared with her his war diary and even pictures of his various Italian girlfriends, which they laughed about together. Eileen encouraged Jack to keep these images as memorabilia. Eileen knew that her husband had not been a masher, and when interviewed, Jack proclaimed so himself: "I was always a gentleman!" he proclaimed laughing hard at the memory.

This delightful story from Jack's diary comes from the Villanova period.

> "Had a date with Ann today. We met at our first… dance in Florence. She goes to the University of Florence and is studying math. Seems to be a swell girl and although she speaks very little English we have a lot of fun. I usually try to get my day passes on the days there is a dance [scheduled] at the rest center and she is usually there. She won't tell me her last name or address but we will be moving on so it doesn't matter. She's afraid that some of the Italian boys will see her out with an American soldier and cut her hair off. They are very jealous. She cut her last class to meet me at the movie theater. I was ten minutes early so as to be sure and not miss her. When she showed up she had a girlfriend with her. We went into the show and I bought the tickets. It was dark inside and somehow her friend got between us. What a deal!"

When the final Allied offensive in Italy was on and Jack and his company drove northwards, Jack would make another observation about Italian girls and their relationship with Italian men.

On January 24 Dick Stroud was pleased to send home his first snapshots taken with a "very nice" borrowed camera. He explained to Sue that the pictures of "… the streets, people, buildings, etc., show up much better than they really are…" Dick embellished that these pictures might remind him when he got home "…

of many instances and perhaps some things about which I cannot write just now." He explained: "We cannot photograph damaged places."

During this time frame Clare Boothe Luce worked on a major editorial that would be published in *The Woman* column of *Life* magazine towards the end of the month. *Life* was going to put forward a controversial recommendation, one without attribution as to authorship. "Since the manpower need is so tough, why not draft women?" the editorial started. Luce undoubtedly had a hand in either writing or approving what followed:

> ... the objections of labor will be mild indeed alongside the shocked objections of self-appointed defenders of American womanhood. These objectors will be men, not women. Public-opinion polls show that women are much more willing to be drafted than men are to draft them. To intelligent women a draft is not a move to enslave them. On the contrary, it would be a milestone in an age-long process: their emancipation.[273]

Clover Dulles joined her husband in Berne after a warzone adventure of her own. Her passage to Lisbon had been approved by the State Department and from there she had been given temporary government employment as a "relief driver" in a column of U.S. vehicles to be delivered to Paris. From Paris she had been fortunate to obtain a ride from a French Army officer who had been scheduled to drive to Lyons, less than 200 miles from Berne. On this leg of her journey the driver-officer got lost and wandered perilously close to a bypassed pocket of holdout Wehrmacht soldiers! One Dulles biographer noted, "... there may have even been some gunfire but no harm was done."[274]

Reunited with her husband at 23 Herrengasse in late January, one of the first persons Allen introduced was Mary Bancroft and by all accounts (including Mary's exposé memoir) the two women took an immediate liking to each other and remained friends for life. Having experienced Allen's infidelities so many times in their marriage, Clover (again according to Bancroft) had no illusions about the relationship existing between Mary and Allen. "In fact, the second or third time we [Clover and Mary] were alone together," Mary revealed, "she [Clover] said, 'I want you to know I can see how much you and Allen care for each other — and I approve!' "[275] Allen Dulles characterized his wife as "an angel" and she was for putting up with his indiscretions.

Martha Clover Todd Dulles and Clare Boothe Luce were different kinds of women. One submitted and the other believed what was good for the goose was the *right* of the gander, but with a caveat — there were to be no gigolos (with the further caveat that no historian has located any yet).

In a letter Bill wrote to Dotty dated January 28, 1945, he complained about a pair of his dress shoes being stolen the day before. Stating they would fetch up to $50 on the black market, Bill wailed, "[They] were Nunn-Bush and my favorites." In the following paragraph Bill described an aftermath of the incident. If there any document showing Bill as a sensitive, caring human being, this is it: "The little Italian boy who polices our barracks was heartbroken today because he was afraid I would blame him for taking my shoes. I have been giving him candy every day or so under rationing. I enjoy giving it to him because he is always so grateful and looks so hungry. I think he has grown to like me. He told some of the men how good I had been to him. I always make my own bed and he is always scrubbing the floor, cleaning my overshoes, polishing my work shoes and trying to help. I finally got him to understand that I did not suspect him and he managed to stop crying."

As it turned out, Bill was not the only American serviceman to forge foreign friendships. On the same day Dick Stroud wrote home that his host family "… invited me to dinner again, but I am not up to it, the volume for one thing, and the food is pretty hard to get for another, but they are very nice to me." Dick reported giving them "some wine."[276] In the children's department Dick had a victory that day also. He wrote proudly of his intent to respond to his first dictated letter received from Pumpkin, age two. "He writes quite well," Dick observed, then quoted his son: "When *don't* him come home." Dick promised: "I will at the very first chance."

For his part, Sergeant Jack King received some company on that date, January 28. "The forward unit came back and joined us," Jack recorded in his diary, confirming that the 91st had been taken off the line for rest and relaxation, and that an element of it would temporarily join up in the HQ building where he worked. Concurrent with this happening Jack assumed that the chain of command within his company would be reshuffled, but in this regard he ended-up pleasantly surprised. "I thought that Sergeant Batt would be put in charge of our orders section but he was not and I was left as section leader," Jack wrote. "I am now sweating out a six-day pass to Rome," he offered. "Several fellows ahead of me though. It will probably be my turn to go forward soon."

Amid the beautiful trappings at the Royal Palace, Bill observed disturbing things. "There are so many evidences of poverty here," he wrote in a letter to Dotty dated January 31, 1945. "An Italian just came by collecting cigarette stubs from the ashtrays in the office." He further added, "You never see a stub on the street. The natives regard them very highly. At entrances to movies, they stand in line to recover the discarded butts as the soldiers enter."

Around this time the water at Caserta was lost for several days. There were no showers and emergency drinking water was dispensed in "Lister bags." On February 5 he wrote his parents: "We finally got our water back again on Saturday. [It] must be terrible in those cities without water for long periods after air raids."

In Northern Italy John Lesesne's gaming luck, after more than two months of unabashed success changed abruptly as he dolefully noted in his diary:

> Played poker & won about $7.00 but on each of 1 succeeding nights lost about $40.00. Lost on draw, nothing wild, with four of a kind — that was typical of my luck — all of it bad.[277]

In mid-February, Bill took on a new job that involved daily trips to the Naples rail yards. On February 7 he wrote to Dotty as he had earlier about the abject poverty and included this: "And yet some of them sing beautiful Italian songs. They put their souls into their singing." Apropos of nothing, he added (in characteristic engineer-like Bill fashion): "I am working on an automatic rocket launcher design in my spare time."

In a letter written two days later Bill reported, "I saw many strange sights in town today [including] swarms of people. I did a little window-shopping. Such prices I never dreamed of — three or four hundred dollars for silver trays. 15,000 lira or $150 for a manicure set on the black market. Cigarettes are selling at $2.05 per pack and a truckload of them is pure gold. I still can't figure out how anyone buys anything. People approach you on the street trying to interest you in their special wares… Many of the children have sores on their arms and legs covered with filth. I never knew people were so close to animals."

There is no doubt that World War II Naples was unlike anything Bill and Dick had ever experienced in their lives. One historian described it this way: "In Naples it was estimated that one-third the food landed from ships was stolen and put on the black market. In addition, there was much drunkenness among the Allied troops, and prostitution rose to enormous proportions as mothers and sisters found it the only way that they could procure Allied rations to feed their starving families."[278] Allied forces did provide some food for the starving Neapolitans but one thing the natives refused to eat, as a matter of pride, was corn. The difference between field corn for livestock, and sweet corn for human consumption, escaped them.[279]

Bill described the worst that he ever saw: "On good [weather] days, lots of unfortunate people are placed out on the sidewalks against the walls where they beg. The most pathetic sight I have ever seen though are small children five or six years old, sitting along the street holding a small baby in their arms trying to keep the half naked baby warm. Their clothing is so ragged and their bodies are dirty beyond description." Bill placed a partial criticism for this crisis that went beyond simply blaming the war: "One wonders why a ruler in a land as crowded would encourage large families. The population of Italy is about one-third that of the whole United States."[280] In yet another February letter he wrote about the children in Naples being afflicted with "open sores."

For his part, Dick Stroud wrote: "Wealth, if there is any here, is in the hands of the few — the rest have to beg, steal or what have you."[281] He described seeing street people with "no shoes, feet swollen and blue." "It was cold," he continued. "One wonders where they sleep and if they eat. The women and children suffer just as much." In his next sentence Dick made a comparison: "The church is wealthy."[282]

For Dick, as with everyone else the war was a wearing, tedious experience. He wrote about having lots to do workwise but little to do on the off hours. "We get pretty tired of shows which is about the only amusement," he wrote. Dick described a trick G.I.s played on the natives who they taught a few words of English. With regard to the servant girl at his residence, Dick recounted, "When some of my friends come to the house, she meets them at the door, smiles a nice welcome and quotes, 'Come in you ugly bastards.'" Dick observed: "This is mild in comparison with some of the greetings one gets. The natives of course use these phrases proudly…" Dick explained the phenomenon: "Anything to break the monotony," he observed.[283] The practice fit into the surreal environment that was wartime Naples, Italy.

Two months later[284] the situation in Naples had not improved.

Bill wrote: "Honestly, Hon., I don't know how they can live... Often people will be helping an animal pull a cart." Out of "squalor" (Bill's word) however, the Neapolitans did produce pageantry. "I saw an elaborate funeral procession today in Naples," Bill noted. "About thirty or forty men in costume, looked like the church, lodge or such a body, walked ahead of a huge, ornately covered carriage pulled by two teams of horses. This was followed by about 100 men marching in a group with heads uncovered and followed by two more carriages covered with flowers. This was the most elaborate one I have seen."

The prolific British writer, Norman Lewis, wrote *Naples '44* based on a journal that he maintained as an intelligence officer while in the city. Lewis observed that, "Neapolitan funerals are obsessed with face," and then told a delightful story about an aristocratic-looking, dapperly dressed man who acted the part — for a price — of the sophisticated "uncle from Rome." His thespian role was to convince Neapolitan mourners that the dearly departed ("a near-pauper all his life" Lewis noted) was in fact from a well-to-do, even gentrified Roman family. Unfortunately for this imposter-for-hire, World War II temporarily put him out of business. The "uncle" actually did live in Italy's culture capital (and had the rich voice to prove it) but until Rome liberation day he lacked the ability to travel to and from Naples.

The Lewis book is one of the strongest written about the occupation and it contains far more tragedy than humor. One month after the Allied invasion, Lewis recounted seeing, "hundreds, possibly thousands" of starving Neapolitans scouring outside for anything that might be eaten including dandelions.[285]

Bill described the public transportation beyond the horse drawn carts. Naples did have electricity. "The street cars have so many people riding on top of them hanging from sides and ends and bulging out the windows that they look like a swarm of bees on a hive." As for motorized vehicles, he observed: "You should see these old Italian trucks. Some of them must be twenty or twenty-five years old and still running. Everything is so old and just pieced together."

Pulitzer prize winning *Life* magazine photo-journalist Margaret Bourke-White was so moved by the starvation and utter scarcity that she witnessed in Naples and upset at the mismanagement of the "AMG" [Ed: Allied Military Government] there that she wrote the following as the closing paragraph to her description of the situation in the city: "We Americans, moving on as a victorious army, have an opportunity to mold the world — an occasion almost unprecedented in history.

Our soldiers buy that opportunity with the dearest possession they have." She concluded powerfully: "We have no right to ask them to lay down their lives unless we administer what they have gained with the full intelligence that their sacrifice deserves."[286] The book in which Bourke-White wrote the above was published in 1944 and titled *They Called It, "Purple Heart Valley."* Bill owned this book and kept it with his files on World War II Italy.

For his part, Bill Mauldin, who left Italy to cover the invasion of Southern France, was judgmental of the Neapolitans noting that the same Americans who caroused irresponsibly in the city "behaved pretty well" when they later participated in the liberation of towns in France "where they were welcomed openly and sincerely." "We are swindled unmercifully everywhere we go," Mauldin observed, and he opined this after he singled out Naples for special reproach.[287]

Panorama of Italy [continued]

A hill-top village; a walled in land,
Grimy old hags, all twisted in pain;
Beautiful image, most blessed of mothers;
Scalped monks and alm-eating brothers.

Stately cathedrals, with rich-toned bells;
Ricoverb shelters, with horrible smells;
Moldering catacombs, a place for the dead;
Noisy civilians, clamoring for bread.

Palatial villas, with palm trees tall;
A stinking hovel, mere holes in a wall;
Tree-fringed lawns, swept by the breeze;
Goats wading in filth, up to their knees.

Revealing statues, all details complete;
A sensual lass, with sores on her feet;
Big-busted damsels, but never a bra;
Bumping against you, there should be a law.

Sweeping boulevards, a spangled-team;
Alleys that wind, like a dope fiend's dream;
Flowers blooming, on the side of a hill;
A sidewalk latrine, with privacy nil.

Girls with shoe soles, two inches thick;
Unwashed peddlers, whose wares make you sick;
Grapes, lemons, postcards and nuts;
Dolce and vino, to torture your guts

During the winter lull at the front Captain John Lesesne experienced what was becoming a pattern with the nine enlisted men that he lived with. "Lost at poker again last night," he wrote. "At one time I was down $65.00 but came back a little to make it $50.00 (total of $130.00 for the *week*). Today I won back another $15.00; as I'm now out about $110.00."[288]

On February 12, 1945, Bill wrote this about his immediate superior: "Major Renick is a grand person. He has two sons in the service and was in the last war. He does not seem old enough." Bill reported to Dotty that Renick had received 530 letters from his wife and that his "… youngest [son] is being equipped for tropical duty. The Major is quite worried and would like to go Home before his son leaves."

A sure sign that the Allies were winning appeared in a same-dated letter from Dick Stroud. "We get five days every two months," Dick wrote Sue, referring to the accumulation of leave time. "I think my first trip will be to Rome." German soldiers, harassed continuously from the air surely were not granted leave for rest and relaxation. Dick mentioned that he could "easily get anywhere" and that he hoped to also see Pisa and Florence. Another sure sign was the bulletin that Dick mailed home for the performance of the *Mediterranean Symphony Orchestra*, T/Sgt. Joseph Wincenc, Guest Conductor. The program called for works to be performed composed by Sibelius, Tchaikovsky, Schubert and others. The lead performance, however, perhaps a poke of subtle humor, was the Prelude to Act III of the opera *Lohengrin* by Richard Wagner — one of Hitler's favorites. Concerts were performed weekly and conducted by USAAF Special Services enlisted men.[289]

On February 13 Jack diarized: "The Division [91st] is going back on the line."

—∞—

The mid-February visit to the Italian front by General Marshall was mostly for morale boosting. Undoubtedly exhausted from attending a stressful conference at Yalta, Marshall wanted little fanfare, only numerous photographs taken of him pinning decorations on heroes. Marshall instructed General Clark, who was at the time at his command post near Florence: "Do not meet me at the airport. I will come to your headquarters. No honors." General McNarney accompanied Marshall on the visit, and when the two flag officers deplaned at Pisa, as instructed, only a car and driver awaited them.

It was a different situation, however, when the generals arrived at Clark's command post. Clark had lined up, in his own words, "not a small guard of honor, but a really big one," and Marshall was at first frosted at the sight of it. Clark explained in his memoirs, *Calculated Risk*, his motivation behind doing this: "... I devoted considerable time to trying to explain our problems to the War Department and that, finally, I took a calculated risk and deliberately disobeyed a direct order from General Marshall in an effort to get our story across."

Clark, who now commanded the U.S. Fifth Army and the British Eighth Army plus the foreign and auxiliary units that supplemented these forces, intended to make a visual representation to Marshall of the challenges he confronted in leading what he termed a "polyglot" army. It is honest to state that Clark was in less than a charitable mood when Marshall and McNarney arrived, and part of this may have been caused by a crisis brewing at the Italian front due to a decision made at Yalta.

As "honors" Clark lined-up soldiers to be reviewed by Marshall, not the elite of the Fifteenth Army Group, but rather exemplars of those who he, Clark, perceived as dregs. Clark caustically explained in his memoirs:

> "The First Battalion, 135th Infantry, 34th Division," I said as Marshall
> paused before one of the few squads that were familiar to him. I didn't
> need to explain anything to him about the 34th's grand performance; nor
> did I need to add anything when I stood before the next squad of rigidly
> erect Negro soldiers from the 92nd Infantry Division. But from then on he
> [Marshall] was on comparatively unfamiliar ground.[290]

Continuing, Clark used anecdotes and stereotypes to describe the "comparatively unfamiliar" soldiers that he had lined-up for the General of the U.S. Army to inspect. First up were the 1st Division, Brazilian Expeditionary Force who had made for extra work for the Americans: "We had to scramble to find Portuguese interpreters...", Clark complained about them. Next up were the 1st Argyll and Sutherland Highlanders: "[They] would stop in the middle of a battle for their afternoon tea," he chided. Then it was the 3/8 Punjabs, 19th Infantry Brigade, 8th Indian Division that, "... had to maintain a herd of goats... [as] their religion prohibited them from eating pork," Clark observed suggesting that this practice was somehow either wrong or unreasonable. Clark closed with a jab at the "Springboks," the 6th South African Armored Division: "[They] left their tanks and fought on foot," he despaired. The Welsh, Canadian, Polish, New Zealand and a few other nationalities escaped his criticism, and General Clark did pass out a compliment here and there but not many. Most of his praise went to Army nurses or British female auxiliaries, "the girls."

This chapter from Clark's memoirs does not reflect well on him as a leader. A special stress was building on him at this time however, and perhaps this contributed to his complaining about his job and even disobeying a direct order from the top general in the U.S. Army. He concluded by stating: "General Marshall ended his inspection in much better humor than he had started. He said he was glad I had ignored his instructions." If true, perhaps this reveals something about Marshall?

Jack recorded in his diary that day: "General George Marshall, chief of staff to the president visited us today. He inspected the 361st on the line... Some of the boys saw him pass the C.P."[291]

Rumors swirled at this time about the treatment of Poland at the Yalta conference, and General Waldyslaw Anders the commander of the hard-fighting Polish Corps (who reported to McCreery) had occasion to talk extensively with Marshall over a dinner held by Clark. Marshall telescoped to Anders that all was not well in regard to the Polish question and Anders appreciated that Marshall could not disclose to him what had been agreed upon at Yalta in advance of the formal announcement.[292]

When General Anders subsequently learned that the Big Three had contracted that all of Poland be turned into a Russian communist buffer zone (under a new lackey Polish Provisional Government of National Unity) against future German invasions, and that the Soviet Union would have unending sovereignty over "the area East of the Curzon Line" (the approximate size of Missouri) effectively resetting a boundary line that had been accepted by treaty in 1923, he became shocked and angry. Meeting with Clark, Anders was in tears. He threatened to resign his commission and withdraw the Polish Corps from the Gothic Line. He even asked that Clark take his men as POWs.[293]

The military emergency was averted a few days later when the Polish government-in-exile in London instructed Anders to keep on fighting, but the incident undoubtedly left Clark feeling more like a besieged diplomat than a commanding general. To his credit Clark made every rational and emotional argument that he could to the devastated Polish Corps leader in order to hold the fighting alliance in Italy together.

Many issues were resolved at Yalta, but a really big one involving Italy was left open for further discussion. The signed document had this provision:

IX. ITALO-YOGOSLAV FRONTIER — ITALO-AUSTRIAN FRONTIER

Notes on these subjects were put in by the British delegation and the American and Soviet delegations agreed to consider them and give their views later.

The Yalta Agreement contained a "Declaration of Liberated Europe" that most pleased Roosevelt and Churchill. Stalin had agreed to embrace the principle enunciated in 1941 with the Atlantic Charter: "... liberated peoples..." would be allowed, "... to create democratic institutions of their own choice." Specifically the Yalta document guaranteed: "The right of all people to choose the form of government under which they will live — the restoration of sovereign rights and self-government to those peoples who have been forcibly deprived of them by the aggressor nations."[294] The problem was, to Stalin's thinking this meant the unrestricted right to choose a Soviet-aligned politburo.

The goodwill generated between the Allies at Yalta quickly evaporated into a land grab between West and East with Northern Italy up for the taking. Allen Dulles in his book explained it thusly:

... while zones of Allied and Soviet occupation in Germany, including Berlin, and in Austria had been fixed by earlier agreement between the Allies and the Soviet government, this was not so in Northern Italy, since Italy was treated as an ally, thus, prior occupation of this area by Communist-dominated forces might well determine the zones of postwar influence or even occupation.[295]

On February 15 Bill complained vehemently to Dotty: "Of all things now I have a historical summary to write! The higher the headquarters, the more elaborate the procedure and this HQ is plenty high." In a subsequent missive he quipped: "It takes a lot of words to fight a war."

Little of military significance was happening in Italy at this time but on other fronts reports were positive for the Allies. Dick wrote Sue: "The war news is some better and of course it leads us to thoughts of home ..." As a relatively new arrival Dick reflected about the long-term veterans the same as Bill: "It seems so long to me, even now, how must those who have had years of this feel?"[296] Dick reported on liking a circumstance that undoubtedly was unhealthy for him: "There is one good thing about our diet," he wrote, "no salads — not one have I seen!" He had also been pleased to learn from his wife that "Pumpkin" now was a big boy and wanted to go by the name Richard or Dickie. "I shall respect his wishes," the proud father declared.[297]

At his command post in the big house near Scascoli John wailed into his diary: "Because I lost all my money playing poker I've not been on pass ..."[298] John now cogitated on a method different than gambling to raise money for a trip to Florence.

On Sunday, February 25, Allen W. Dulles received an urgent message to meet with Max Waibel of the Swiss military intelligence in Lucerne that evening. Dulles had entertained several "peace feelers" in the past few months from Catholic clergy and prominent Italian businessmen; both purported to have contacts with the enemy, but nothing panned out. Both the Church and the industrialists were mortified over the prospect of the Germans implementing a scorched earth policy in Northern Italy, such as was then happening in Eastern Europe.

Dulles routinely supplied information to G-2 (U.S. Military Intelligence Corps) and in Italy he regularly worked with representatives of the Italian partisans, arranging for weapons and money deliveries and strategizing with them (when they would cooperate that is). It was Dulles' job to know what was going on behind enemy lines and he did this by running a spy network. The American intelligence community had suffered a shock when the Germans launched the Battle of the Bulge on December 16, 1944, and Dulles was keenly aware that his tradecraft was as much an art as an objective science. Some informants acted for altruistic reasons and others for lucre; Dulles's job was to determine the reliability of their information and pass it on through proper channels if he believed it to be credible. If money was needed to secure information this did not present a problem. "I have *millions* at my disposal," Dulles once boasted to a confidant.[299]

Waibel, who requested this meeting — to be held over dinner at a favorite trout restaurant — was, in addition to being competent, a credible source to Dulles. The Swiss, neutral as they were, were aware of which countries were going to win the war and they very much wanted the conflict over quickly and without Northern Italy being completely destroyed. The Swiss and others were cognizant that the joy of Rome and Paris being liberated intact the previous summer might not be replicated with Milan and Turin. Another practical reason for the Swiss to tacitly help the Allies was the fact that their country was simply not in a position to absorb more war refugees.

Dulles was keenly aware that while Hitler lived the roadblocks to peace were almost insurmountable; still he would try — he had to try — if this war, or even a portion of it, could be cut short for even a single day by a signed piece of paper, lives would be saved on both sides and property preserved. Dulles appreciated that his only chance for success would be to maintain absolute secrecy. How could the Gestapo be fooled?

Dulles had been working in Hegenheim, France, when the urgent message to meet with Waibel was delivered to him from his office. He and Gaevernitz made the two-hour drive to Lucerne together and they were not disappointed for having made the trip. Waibel introduced the two intelligence agents to an Italian businessman and a Swiss professor-schoolmaster who had been in contact with an important subordinate of the leader of half the German combat units in Northern Italy. If what these men declared was true, it was mind-boggling "useful" spy-craft information. Dulles later wrote about it: *"It was the SS, not the German Army, that was capable of some independent thought and action."*[300]

Dulles and Gaevernitz stared incredulously at each other as they digested this proposition along with their half-eaten meals. Both had the same thought in mind: what terms should be set for a face-to-face meeting with the enemy?

On the final day of February John copied into his diary a song that 3rd Platoon members wrote to be sung to the melody of *Dear Mom*. It started:

> *We're called Lippy's Raiders, we're all on the ball,*
> *If Lippy gets ammo, Bologna will fall,*
> *We'll kill all the Guineas, Tedeschis, and all,*
> *And we'll love it, Dear Sarge,*

The song complains about certain officers overeating, overdrinking and leaving the battle area (e.g.: *"There came a shell, it was coming my way, and if we know colonels he sure didn't stay"*) and the fact that John recorded its six stanzas in his diary is perhaps telling about his relaxed (tolerant) relationship with his men.

"Tedeschis" is Italian slang for Germans, and no compliment.

John felt good about himself when he copied out this funny song and he had reason to feel good. Earlier in the week he had met with his commanding officer Russell McMurray who now went by the nickname "Colonel Mac" having been recently promoted to lieutenant colonel. John showed McMurray his design plan for a new 4.2" baseplate, one that (in John's words) "… would afford 360° traverse and some shock-absorber action." McMurray had been so impressed about prospects for the invention that he ordered John (as John recorded it) "…[to] go to see Cmd O., 5th Army…" [Ed: Commanding Officer U.S. Fifth Army — General Truscott].

John complied immediately and subsequently noted: "He [Cmd. O, 5th Army] told me to come back in ten days… [when a]… section would have a shop set up to make one." As stated, John had written the names of many senior officers in his diary book but he did not *dare* record the name "Truscott"! Nor did he reveal the name of the place where this meeting took place, but rather he wrote: "… I went back to _____ where I talked with him." John likely met Truscott at his headquarters at Futa Pass.

Temporary duty orders were issued to John and he stayed at "the Rest Camp in Florence." With his money gone John had finagled a way to finance his trip to Florence!

John wrote about his invention:

> If it works it will increase by many times the amount of fire we can place on any one point at one time. Also, it will allow sustained fire for a much longer period without digging out baseplates. These have been the two biggest faults with the present mortar.[301]

Bill, who started his Army reserve career as an ordnance officer, would have been intrigued. John's first two sentences read like patent claims.

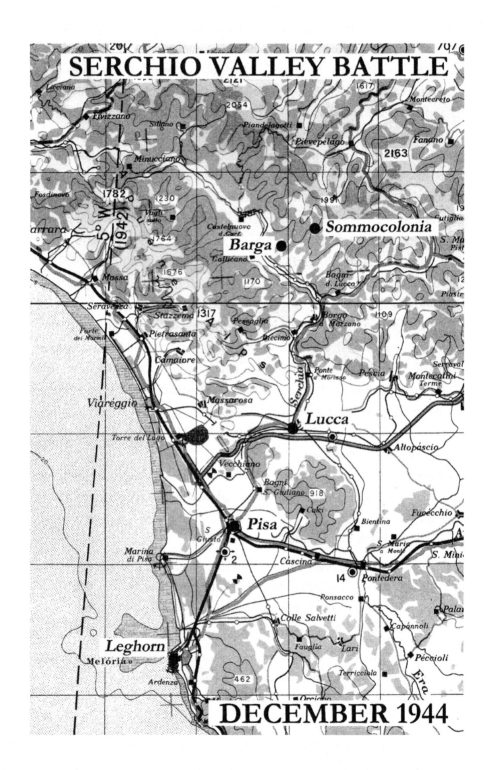

Previous page:

The battle at Serchio Valley started during the early morning hours of December 26, 1944 when Axis forces launched a surprise attack in strength against the village of Sommocolonia. A small number of U.S. soldiers from the 92nd Infantry Division — the African-American "Buffalo Soldiers" — put up a stubborn resistance but when they were finally overwhelmed, a division-wide 92nd disorganized retreat set in. Italian fascist and German forces advanced approximately 8 miles over a two-day period (driving 5 miles into the valley to the town of Barga) and then abruptly executed a planned withdrawal. The battle had little strategic significance but its outcome emboldened Mussolini and heartened his German allies. It also created troubling questions for the U.S. Fifth Army — why had the 92nd not been warned that the attack was coming? Why was no reserve in place? Had the road to the vital port city of Leghorn been left vulnerable to possible panzer attack? Approximately 1,000 casualties resulted in the 92nd. The white leadership of the 92nd and its black junior officers and enlisted men failed to work together in a productive manner and animosity between the races resulted. The racial ramifications of this battle to the U.S. military and the events that followed would eventually become the subject of a government review process following the war which resulted in President Truman desegregating the armed forces by executive order in 1948. The map area west of Barga shows Serchio Valley running parallel to the coastline.

Map source: FIRENZE (FLORENCE) N.E. 42/10 British War Office 1944 Geographical Section General Staff, No. 4072 with the names of major locations enhanced by the author.

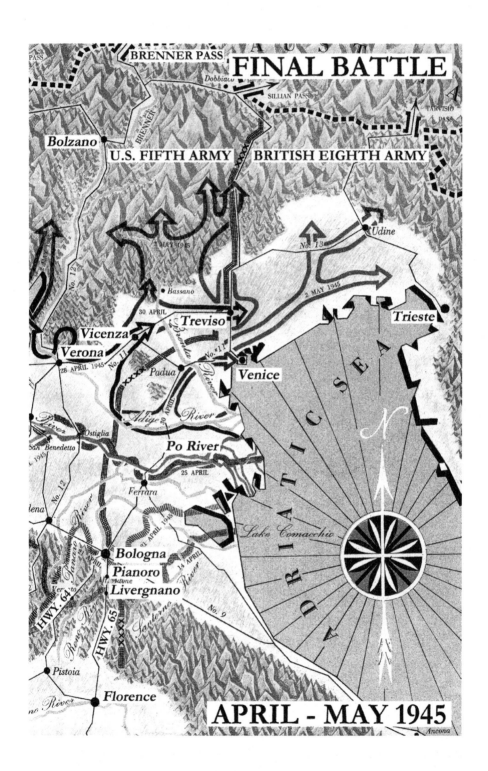

Previous page:
Battle map showing the final campaign in northeastern Italy.
Approximately 300,000 American and British soldiers moved northwards
in the final attack. This map shows conquests made by the military units
depicted in this story. The U.S. 10th Mountain Division, the spearhead
of the U.S. Fifth Army pierced the Gothic Line April 14 west of Highway
64. The 91st Infantry Division (with 100th Chemical Mortar Battalion
attached) then pushed upwards from Pianoro, passed through Bologna
April 21 and engaged in heavy combat at the Po River. Thereafter the
100th detached from the 91st to enter Vicenza; the 91st continued to
Treviso where the remnants of the German 14th Army were "trapped" and
destroyed. On May 2, the day of the German surrender the 91st entered
the British sector to assist in the occupation of the Trieste area; the 10th
Mountain Division prepared to assault Nazi Headquarters at Bolzano.
"Phase I" and "Phase II" battle lines planned by Truscott are shown; also
the meandering north-south demarcation line for American and British
forces (identified by "xxxx").

Map source: 19 Days, from the Apennines to the Alps, *a 1945 publication of
the U.S. Fifth Army (names of major locations enhanced by author)*

At war's end Dick Stroud became critically ill and had to endure two major
operations before eventually being returned to the U.S. aboard a hospital
ship. Compared to today, communications were primitive in World War II.
Dick's loved ones received only telegrams and a form letter that yielded
little medical information. A phone call was not an option. — *Sarah Stroud
Ollison photo collection*

What U.S. General Mark Clark termed "a polyglot army" Naples, Italy,
January 1945 — *Sarah Stroud Ollison photo collection*

Now a war trophy on display in Aberdeen, Maryland, this rail gun named Leopold
was one of two such weapons used by the Germans to shell the stalled Allied
invasion force at Anzio. It took 150 artillerymen to service this behemoth. The
gun was moved by a diesel electric motor and had its own portable turntable.
Following the war Bill calculated bridgehead strengths for removal of Leopold
to Port of Naples. Nicknamed "Anzio Annie" by those on the receiving end, the
scream of its large incoming projectiles (564 lb.) fired 30 or more miles away was
terrifying. The fact that the Germans were able use this World War I technology
at Anzio is a testament to the botched Allied invasion there: dugouts and a siege
resulted from the failure to advance on Rome when the opportunity briefly
presented itself after the initial landing.
— *Richard Allison photo collection*

Captain Bill Allison, Naples 1945. The likeness of this street artist portrait is remarkable. The collar insignia is that of the U.S. Army Transportation Corps, an army specialty that fit in well with Bill's automobile engineering background. — *Richard Allison collection*

The officer looking at the child is Lt. Dick Stroud. This photojournalistic shot was taken in Naples during January, 1945; the bar's name epitomizes Americanization. No doubt Dick disapproved of the child being there, as would have Bill. Vice fueled by extreme wartime poverty was rampant at these establishments. Dick wrote sarcastically to his wife, "The women have a profession too, a *respected* one, if you can imagine." Dick worked with young adults all of his professional life, and following the war went from teaching chemistry to become a high school principal.

— *Sarah Stroud Ollison photo collection*

"You're in the Army now…" Publicity shot of Private Jack King holding his
new staff of office, a mop, taken May 30, 1943 at Fort Benjamin Harrison,
IN. Tall and affable, Jack was then a two-week recruit. No photos of Jack
survive from Italy. Following the war Jack pursued a career in law. — *John
L. King photo collection.*

A common street scene in World War II Naples. Bill wrote about using larger carts and work animals: "Most civilian transportation is by high two-wheeled carts... they balance the load over the single axle and sometimes it looks like the loads would almost lift the horse!"
— *Sarah Stroud Ollison photo collection.*

Infantry Staff Sergeant Leon Weckstein attended this Jewish ritual feast,
the yearly retelling of the liberation of the Hebrew peoples from Egyptian
bondage, which was held in the train station at Florence on March 29,
1945. Weckstein wrote about it: "Several thousands of G.I.s of my faith,
all from the Allied forces, had congregated ... to participate in a massive
Seder and delicious repast of typical holiday fare." Two months earlier
Auschwitz concentration camp had been liberated with the international
press reporting the discovery of huge SS gassing facilities used for the
mass murder of Jews and others. The attendees at this special religious
observance, hosted by the U.S. Army Chaplain Corps knew that a final
reckoning with fascism approached and that they would be part of it. The
cover design of this worship bulletin cleverly shows symbols of the three
Abrahamic religions, Judaism, Christianity and Islam. Can the reader
spot each? The shoulder patch of the U.S. Fifth Army is located center
high. — *Image credit: United States Holocaust Memorial Museum, courtesy of
Gerald (Gerd) Schwab.*

Close to actual size, these pages from Captain John Lesesne's unauthorized pocket diary describe the aftermath of a friendly fire incident where 1st Platoon, Company "B" 100th Chemical Mortar Battalion killed a G.I. infantryman from the 361st Regiment of the 91st Infantry Division on the night of November 17, 1944. On a preceding page John wrote: "I checked with Jimmy and he said he'd been firing at Canovetta and had gotten a short round of W.P." [white phosphorous]. In 2016 the diary was gifted by the Lesesne family to The Citadel Archives and Museum. — *Ann Lesesne collection.*

While serving in Italy bachelor and combat commander John
Lesesne received letters from friends, including *nine* girlfriends!
An ordained minister wrote him and urged that he re-enroll in
Episcopal seminary following the war. John recorded in his diary:
"Wish I could whole-heartedly do so, but am afraid I can't." The
1941 honors graduate from The Citadel instead pursued a career in
medicine. — *Ann Lesesne photo collection.*

Naples, January, 1945 — *Sarah Stroud Ollison photo collection.*

USAAF 18th Depot Supply Squadron of the Air Service Command, Naples.
Requisition forms were completed at the center tables. The officer reading
is Lt. Dick Stroud. — *Sarah Stroud Ollison photo collection.*

Company "B" 100th Chemical Mortar Battalion members duck
away from a 4.2" round just fired at night on the Italian Front in the
Apennine Mountains. Company commander John Lesesne recorded
witnessing this event in his journal. —*Photo by Margaret Bourke-
White/The Life Picture Collection/Getty Images*

A machine gunner and two riflemen of Co K, 87th Mountain Infantry,
10th Mountain Division, cover an assault squad routing Germans out of
a building in the background. This image shows the treacherous terrain
the Allies encountered at the Gothic Line. *Sassomolare Area, Italy. Porretta
Moderna Highway. 4 March 1945.*

CHAPTER NINE:

BRITS, YANKS, ITALIANS AND A SS-OBERGRUPPENFÜHRER

February–March 7, 1945

AND THEN THERE was Bill's relationship with the British. In a February letter to Dotty he complained: "The British greatly outnumber our forces here [and] in general pass out higher ranks than our forces enjoy."

As regards the British, Bill would write a month later: "You remember one time, Hon., I remarked I would like to be invited to tea by the British? Well, we are now on the tea delivery list! One of their officer personnel comes in twice a day, morning and afternoon, counts heads in the office and a few minutes later pops back with a tray of tea for all. This morning he also brought cakes. The trouble is, now that it has started, we don't know how to get out of it gracefully… It's very nice of them and I appreciate the courtesy but these British have a way with you."[302]

For the British, being in charge at Caserta meant more than just having a commissioned officer politely pressure Americans to consume their national beverage. Bill's statement, "these British have a way with you" had deeper meaning. It undoubtedly irritated the British that the Supreme Allied Commander in the war, Eisenhower, was American, and that their empire in the Mediterranean had been challenged. The British still dominated in the area however — they continued to hold Gibraltar, Malta and the Suez Canal. The loyal subjects of King George VI were not about to let their American "guests" at the Royal Palace of Caserta forget this fact! It was no accident that General Clark learned from Churchill (and not the U.S Army) that General Truscott had been selected to lead the U.S. Fifth Army in its final battle in Italy. The British wanted Clark, who was known to be strong-headed and not particularly cooperative with the British, to appreciate that His Majesty's Government was in charge, and that Field Marshal Alexander had the backing he needed — and from both sides of the Atlantic.

It was undoubtedly beneficial for the Italians that the Supreme Allied Commander of the Mediterranean Theater of Operations was a British field marshal rather than an American general. In 1944-45, the British had a soft spot for the Italians that the Americans lacked. Bill reported that many veterans of the U.S. Fifth Army after two years of war, simply wanted to pack up and go home. To many British, however Italy already *was* a second home.

Great Britain and Italy shared a historic friendship going back to the Napoleonic era. In the mid-19th century English volunteers assisted Garibaldi in the unification of Italy, and Queen Victoria so enjoyed the beauty of the Italian Lake District that she let her subjects know it. Lake Maggiore was her favorite, and where the British Monarch went, British royalty followed. It was not long before upper class Britons embedded themselves in a culture with a rich ancient past and a historic renaissance that re-spawned the Western world. For natural beauty Italy was unsurpassed, and the British loved its outdoors and mountaineering, consuming good Italian food and wines, and, of course, owning posh villas. They genuinely liked the Italian people too. The two countries fought as allies against the Austrians in World War I to mixed reviews, yes, but the point is they fought together.

In the martial arts, modern Italian soldiers never matched the ferociousness of the Roman legionnaires but this did not bother the British, other than perhaps Winston Churchill who famously quipped at a dinner party to the Nazi Ribbentrop (who bragged that Italy would be allied with Germany in the next war): "That's only fair — we had them last time." The subsequent mid-World War II publicity photos showing thousands of Italian POWs being guarded at bayonet point in North Africa by a single British Tommy served to bolster Churchill's sarcasm. The British laughed about this — but not with the rancor they reserved for the hated Huns.

Then there were the jokes:

"Did you hear about the latest Italian tank model?"

"No."

"One gear forward and five in reverse."

The British viewed Mussolini as an aberration, a leader out of character for the Italian temperament, someone bound to eventually disappear along with his mean-spirited ideology. But even Mussolini, as bad as he was, resisted the systematic murder of Jews. His campaign against them had always been "largely verbal"[303] to please Hitler; it was only after the Italian armistice when the SS flooded south in force into Italy that a manhunt for Jews began. The British were keenly aware of this.

A British historian who fought with the Eighth Army described the way he and undoubtedly his brothers in arms viewed the situation: "… it was the Italian people themselves who saved the majority of the Italian Jews from death at the hands of the Nazis, risking their own lives to help them hide and flee."[304] And the Italian people had good reason to fear: after their 1943 switching of sides they witnessed 600,000 Italian soldiers disarmed by the Nazis and "… shipped off to slave labor camps in Germany."[305] Hitler did not take half measures.

The British appreciated something else that was less of a concern for Americans. It was essential that the British maintain good relations with the Italians, particularly as the end of the war approached. Many of the Italian partisans fighting the *Fascisti* were die-hard communists. Italy was geographically a long way away from the United States but not that far distant from Great Britain. The political heart and soul of Southern Europe would be challenged in Italy and other countries nearby, and the communists had a reputation for advancing their cause without the application of fairness standards. While the war advanced the anti-Fascist political parties, including the communists, worked together through an organization called the Committee for the Liberation of Northern Italy (CLNAL) which was formally recognized by the Allies; everyone sensed however, especially the British, that when the war ended democratic cooperation between the Italian political factions would be difficult to achieve.

On a side note about the partisans, Allen Dulles, who dealt with this committee, observed:

> *The Italian partisans were in a difficult spot. The long German stand at Monte Cassino and the stubborn attempts of the Germans to hold every foot of ground as they retreated after Cassino meant that the Partisans in the North throughout two difficult winters (1943-44 and 1944-45) could not act in conjunction with Allied armies that still had not reached the areas where the partisans were entrenched. Anything beyond sporadic*

*raids against the German occupiers would have been tantamount to
suicide.*[306]

Kesselring, who had returned to his headquarters at Recoaro in mid-January
after the better part of three months' medical leave, agreed with Dulles. The field
marshal observed that partisan activity increased as the war progressed: "…
the number of special incidents rising to five or six a day," he wrote. Kesselring
viewed these attacks as a matter of nuisance: "They [the partisans] were only a
vital menace where they were directly coordinated with military operations."[307]
Blowing up rails and supply dumps behind the lines during the winter stalemate
helped the Allied cause, yes, but was not that important in the overall scheme.

Dulles' observation about anything beyond sporadic raids being suicide for
the partisans was correct. The previous September 26 a number of partisan bands
had grown so unwisely bold as to declare a large area north of Lake Maggiore as
the "Republic of Domdossola." Kesselring called upon his ranking SS General to
put on his Polizeiführer hat and restore German military government. According
to British author James Holland, Karl Wolff, the peace-talking Papal audience
attendee of the preceding May, made quick work of his assignment, killing 1,539
partisans in a matter of days.[308] Another commentator noted how SS police units
under Wolff late in the war "… gained a reputation in northern Italy for burning
villages, inhabitants included …"[309]

The British equivalent of the OSS, the SOE — Special Operations Execu-
tive — operating out of Bari helped the partisans in Northern Italy as best it could.
Limited quantities of food, fuel and weapons were air-dropped into remote areas
starting in May 1944[310] and by summer agents and liaison officers were flown in.
Likewise, the OSS contributed. Towards war's end, Italian-speaking uniformed
U.S. Army commando teams were sent in on C-47 transport planes flying out of
Siena.[311] A day would come, the western Allies hoped, when 200,000 partisans
hiding in cellars in the cities and camps in the woods would rise up in unison
and join free nations in the liberation of Italy. Supporting those who fought out
of uniform was a mission appropriate for the undercover SOE and OSS. For
the British especially winning the support of the Italian people was of critical
importance for the upcoming doctrinal struggle.

It was the way the Italians treated escaped British POWs in the fall of 1943,
however, previously alluded to, that really started to ease the intolerable situation

that existed when Italy and Great Britain waged war on each other. The British historian noted: "… the succor given by Italians of all classes to escaping British POWs after 8 September 1943 is evidence of a love of Britain still alive in the hearts of most Italians."[312] Kindness and support was showered upon thousands of British escapers hoping to pass into neutral Switzerland or (to the far Italian south) join the British Eighth Army. Much favorable press was generated about this, and some of it no doubt was propaganda to convince the British people at home that there really had been a rapprochement between the two former enemy nations.

Italians were equally supportive of escaped Americans as they were to the British. There exists a remarkable account of American Army Ranger/POW Lieutenant William Newnan, alluded to earlier who in February 1944, escaped in enemy territory some 270 kilometers north of the Italian battle line (the Germans had trucked him north and he escaped while waiting rail transit to a stalag POW camp inside Germany). Alone and on a foot trip south to rejoin the U.S. Fifth Army, Italian natives at extreme danger to themselves gave Newnan food, shelter, civilian clothes, a dictionary of useful Italian words and phrases, a map and advice on how best to avoid enemy contact. Safe houses were known as "grottos" and assisting Italians, "Padrones." Newnan made it safely into Rome and was put up in a seminary to await (along with sixty Jews and handful of other Allied escapers) the city liberation. A risk taker, Newnan enjoyed dining at fine restaurants frequented by the SS; he paid for some of his meals with Italian lira that he obtained from banks by cashing checks drawn on a checking account held joint with his father — at Wabeek State Bank, Detroit no less! Newnan laughed about this: "There is no better way to inform the family every month that you are all right." He wrote the word "Rome" on the memo section of the checks so his loved ones would know where he was.[313]

Newnan had indeed been fortunate to escape involvement with the likes of the *Oberbefehishaber des Sicherheitspolizie und SD, SS Obersturmbahnführer* Herbert Kappler, the head of the German police and security services in Rome, who arranged for the Ardeatine massacre at a time when he, Newnan was hiding out not far away. Newnan alludes to this event in his book and is critical of both the Communists and Nazis.

And what was the difference between Newnan, an American escaper and the British escapers? The British 1943 escaper phenomenon got hugely reported as it involved thousands of POWs.

Per a RAF report the Italians handed out civilian clothes, food, railway tickets, money and "lavish friendship."[314] Other accounts confirm special Italian guides for the overland trek of 1,000 British to the Swiss frontier and the use of safe houses and other thought-out evasion schemes.

The Americans had no real stake in the escaper situation, but this much-publicized episode helps explain the British-Italian "reset" of 1943. Mussolini, with his Mare Nostrum policy ("our sea") had challenged the British Empire. The British government did not want this to happen again. Royal Italian Army officers at Caserta no doubt would also be encouraged to consume tea and cakes — and lots of both, more than the Americans for sure!

Shortly after the war ended in Europe Bill attended a formal British garden party at the Royal Palace. He described it as follows: "It was quite an affair — lots of beverages, little sandwiches, cakes, roasted nuts, cherries and guests. All branches and types of uniforms were there… and there was an orchestra." Bill embellished the setting: "The *Tower and Garden* is the place in the palace grounds built for the Queen — a sort of love nest or something surrounded by a moat and entered by a little bridge." Bill told of the imbibing: "Many got pretty high. I know the effect it has on me so I went light. One of the British officers tried to climb a palm tree on a wager afterwards but did not make it. I am sure the Major and George are going to have headaches tomorrow."[315] Most of all, Bill let his wife know that he wished she were there with him: "You would have enjoyed the party," he wrote, along with his customary closing endearments.

For his part, cartoonist Bill Mauldin poked some fun at the fastidious British. In his book *Up Front* Mauldin noted that many Brits were piqued that the American army was so wealthy it could afford to squander valuable material knowing that abundant replacement supplies were readily available. The British did not share in this luxury. A cartoon that Mauldin generated while covering the Anzio beachhead showed a British Tommy addressing two passerby G.I.'s, stating, "You blokes leave an awfully messy battlefield," referencing that British soldiers were required to pick-up everything off the ground that might be useable.

Mauldin reported that the British soldiers at Anzio seemed to like his cartoon but that "… the British at Naples [Caserta] made a complaint. They didn't understand the picture but they were certain it was anti-British." Ordered by his American superiors to leave the British alone, the twenty-three year old satirist bemoaned: "Their brass hats are very stuffy, like a lot of ours, and I think it would have been a pleasure to work on them."[316] Mauldin noted the British thought the Americans were "overdecorated" which could offset, one might suppose, Bill's observation that the British were overpromoted. In a letter to Dotty, Bill observed: "By the way, I have decided that the British term 'Bloke' is about equivalent to our 'Jerk.'"

Technical Sergeant Jack King, behind the Gothic Line in central Italy had no recollection of seeing the British. First Lieutenant Dick Stroud's letters make no mention of them, but he had to have run into them as the RAF ran air operations from the same areas as the Americans. Captain John Lesesne worked in training two British officers and ten non-coms on how to operate the 4.2" mortar. "They are very nice fellows," John wrote. "We enjoyed having them."[317] It turned out that a British mortar crew participated with Company "B" in one of its final firing missions before the big spring offensive.

Bill respected the British but was proud to be American. On July 3 he wrote Dotty: "Tomorrow is July 4th. I think I will whistle 'Yankee Doodle' when I walk by the British offices." In 1750 Bill's ancestors, originally midland Scots, fled the English-induced strife in Northern Ireland and ended-up later fighting as Pennsylvania militiamen for American independence. It was in Bill's genes, no doubt, to whistle *Yankee Doodle Dandy*.

On February 12 John mused about the dichotomy of using a church steeple as a tool for armed conflict. The former seminarian wrote:

> *The O.P. at Scascoli always gives me a strange feeling — I feel that I'm trespassing. We go there before daylight, open the main doors and drive the jeep in. The church itself is very pretty and a bit ornate. There are several holes in the ceiling and the beautiful curtains and draperies, wet as they are, are a sad sight. It seems strange to use the House of God as an aid to killing men — this is war.*
>
> *At the O.P. day before yesterday an infantry observer near me saw a Kraut move within a small circle of rocks — probably, judging by its position, a machine gun nest. We opened fire on it. After getting an over, with the next round, same data, we got a hit on the outside of the pile of rocks. The next round went directly in — the inside of the circle was not*

more than two yards in diameter. It was Jimmy's platoon firing with the panoramic sight, which they have just begun to use, and it was the prettiest firing I've seen yet.

When John wrote this he also observed that the onset of better weather had created a new set of problems for Company "B": "The weather has been warm lately," he wrote, "and with the consequential melting of snow, the ground has become muddy, and we've had difficulty in keeping baseplates from sinking. Last night we hauled in two truckloads of fine sand — this will help considerably."[318]

In mid-February the *New York Times* reported that the Germans again had beat-up on the 92nd Division in an article entitled, "Americans Lose Ground in Italy:"[319]

After a four-day fight in which they suffered relatively high casualties and losses of armor, regiments of the American Ninety-second Division — in which all the enlisted men are Negroes — have been forced back to their original positions just south of Strettoia, it was officially announced today.

After giving the specifics of the pullback, the article continued:

In view of the exceptional detail and candor of material supplied on the setback suffered by the Ninety-second Division, something should be noted now that has been troubling headquarters for some time: how to handle the division's public relations in view of the super-sensitivity of some Negro papers at home, which have unquestionably tended to over-emphasize the division's accomplishments, and the inevitable racial aspects of the situation.

The *Times* article then accused the *Pittsburg Courier* of "irresponsible" editing and also the misquoting of General Almond, stating that the words attributed to him "... had actually been spoken by a colonel on his staff." The *Times* commended the U.S. Army command for, "... taking no chances on the distortion or false play of the story..." and its, "... praise of individual accomplishments by members of the division..."

The *New York Times* support for the U.S. military establishment over the "Negro press" is a cause for one to reflect on how much America has changed since World War II.

For his part, General Truscott remained steadfast in criticizing the 92nd. Truscott pointed out in his memoirs that for over a month following the attack at Serchio Valley, the 92nd was re-trained, physically conditioned and refitted for combat, "… with superior support by artillery and air." His final assessment of the division was, however, following the second engagement "… the infantry [92nd] was devoid of the emotional and mental stability necessary for combat."[320]

He also wrote this: "I would integrate colored personnel into units according to the ratio of colored population to white."[321]

In a V-mail Bill wrote to Dotty on February 17 he noted: "How discouraging it would be if the Russians were not making such progress." The day before Russian forces had encircled the city of Breslau, a little over 100 kilometers from the heart of Germany.[322] The same thought was with Joseph Stalin and he would soon raise it with President Roosevelt.

In the same V-mail Bill alluded to how "extremely restless" the men at AFHQ had become. "It's like trying to hold your breath for a long time," Bill wrote, "waiting for the big news to come." The writings of Dick, Jack and John all mirror similar sentiments; anticipation was in the air.

In Bill's case, while duty at AFHQ was undeniably one of the best officer assignments to be pulled anywhere in World War II Italy, it was not without stress brought on by the acute awareness of what the result might be if all details were not attended to properly. The stakes were as high as they could possibly be. In more than one letter Bill reported working to 11 p.m. the night before.[323] The Transportation Section was charged with getting the men and supplies in place for the next big (and hopefully final) push but nothing was assured.

In Switzerland Allen Dulles conveyed his terms for a meeting with the SS: he, Dulles would meet face-to-face with the SS leader himself and not the subordinate; the meeting would be held in neutral Switzerland at a place Dulles would select, and finally, as proof of good faith and also high authority to act, the SS would turn over in secrecy, prior to the meeting, two internationally known Italian partisan prisoners named by Dulles (one of whom — Ferruccio Parri — would become Prime Minister of Italy following the war).

It was agreed that Swiss intelligence officer Max Waibel would arrange for a secret border crossing for the SS leader and that the two intermediaries — the Italian businessman and Swiss professor-schoolmaster — would convey these terms immediately.

The following day Dulles, who spoke passable German, assigned a codename for the project: *Operation Sunrise.*

On the night of February 18 the 10th Mountain Division made a 1,500-foot ascent up Riva Ridge (thought unassailable by the Germans) and captured it.[324] From there they continued with an assault on Mount Belvedere.[325] Beyond were the road to Bologna and the entrance to the Po Valley. The U.S. Army Transportation Corps had done a good job for the 10th. An author who wrote a history of the 10th Mountain Division reported the following occurring on February 19th.

> *Hugh Evans in C Company had his spirits briefly bolstered by a trip back to a near supply route, where he picked up a load of white phosphorous grenades. Field after field along the entire two-mile route was filled with ammunition — the clearest sign yet that the 10th's assault would get the support it needed. The massive arms cache also brought home to Evans the fact about which he and his comrades were proudest — and most scared: At this stage in the Italian campaign, they were the sharp point of this American spear.*[326]

The 10th captured Mount Belvedere that date in a daring nighttime bayonet charge, achieving the element of surprise by foregoing the usual telltale pre-attack artillery barrage. Deliberately, the forward 10th elements made their assault with empty rifle-clips! The thought was that engaging in a firefight on the slopes would stop upwards momentum. Utilizing the darkness, the orders were, "Keep going no matter what," i.e., infiltrate and bypass all German positions and proceed to the summit. On the way up, the 10th was to defend itself only with hand grenades that were to be thrown at German muzzle flashes. In the race upward through the darkness the 10th charged through minefields, artillery barrages, enemy machine gun and small arms fire.

Perched on the top well before dawn, the men of the 10th loaded their weapons and killed those Germans who did not immediately surrender. Resupplied by the pack animals, the Division then successfully defended the summit, withstanding seven German counterattacks over a two-day period. When the battle was finally over, the slopes of Mount Belvedere and adjacent Mount della Torraccia ridge looked like slaughterhouses. The 10th had suffered 926 casualties, including 195 KIA.[327] They held 1,000 prisoners, however, and what's more, the U.S Army was now in position to sweep down and capture the highway system heading north. The truck companies that Bill had worked with would soon surge forward; the stage was set for a general coordinated advance of U.S. Fifth and British Eighth Armies. One of the planners of this event, Truscott would later record in his memoirs: "The performance of this 10th Mountain Division in its first battle was impressive; they performed like veterans. The operation aroused the admiration of the whole Army." The commanding general of the U.S. Fifth Army was getting what he wanted: "Better still we had set the stage for a main effort in the spring offensive west of Highway 64."[328]

Truscott had been cagy in his use of the 10th Mountain Division in this limited engagement: he called it to halt leaving 25% of the ridge overlooking Highway 64 in enemy control "… to avoid focusing too much enemy attention on this part of the line," a battle history noted.[329] Kesselring failed to foresee what Truscott was beginning to contemplate; the Field Marshal kept in place, astride Highway 65, his strongest defenses. Truscott looked at the map: the distance up Highway 65 to Bologna remained twelve miles; the distance up lesser defended Highway 64 was now reduced to twenty miles.[330] He then scoured photos of the terrain and the concrete poured defensive system that had been constructed so carefully over a period of a year and in multiple places by the German Todt organization. Slave labor had been used, tens of thousands.

Where was the easiest place to blow past it?

The aftermath of the very successful action by the 10th was a sad event. Bodies littered the mountain slopes after the wounded had been evacuated. A year earlier war correspondent Ernie Pyle described what it had been like when no tramway was available. In Italy at the time, an emoted Pyle wrote a column about the tragedy of war. Undoubtedly pack animals were also used for this purpose in 1945. Pyle's newspaper article is entitled *The Death of Captain Waskow*.

Dead men had been coming down the mountain all evening, lashed
onto the backs of mules. They came lying belly-down across the wooden
pack-saddles, their heads hanging down on the left side of the mule, their
stiffened legs sticking out awkwardly from the other side, bobbing up and
down as the mule walked.

Twice in his diary John Lesesne mentions the Germans using mule carts to remove bodies following a mortar attack by one of his platoons; presumably a white flag of truce was out when this happened, but John made no mention of it.[331]

In charging up a mountainside with empty rifles in the face of a strong enemy defense, these young men from Camp Hale, Colorado, these latecomers to the war, these Ivy Leaguers had accomplished what they vowed to do. They displayed incredible physical courage, and they won, totally.[332]

In Washington, D.C., Clare Boothe Luce, always the hard-working and successful journalist, prepared a feature article about the Fifteenth Army Group for publication. It was to be a favorable piece based upon her inspection trip; she would comment on the need for this multi-national Army corps to press on with the fight in Italy, the special challenges confronting it and extol the soundness of its leadership. These things Luce had fervently come to believe. The rest of the truth may have been, however, that Luce very much wanted to return to Italy and viewed her article as a possible lead-in on a plausible cover for her to do so. The final drive had yet to start, which meant there might be time yet for her to see someone special to her.

On February 23 Bill wrote his parents: "We have been so busy in our little department... I am having a lot of new kinds of problems to work out." He added: "War news continues to be good. Everyone expects big events soon. They cannot come too soon for me."

It was during this period that Truscott began to solidify in his mind how the Germans might be fooled as to where the Allies would attack. If they could be made to believe that the Allied main assault would come up Highway 65, this could preclude a significant number of Allied casualties. Truscott pondered this prospect and eventually came up with a notion that he dare not share: Mark Clark had *trained* Kesselring to anticipate a frontal attack into strength! Had this not happened time and time again in the battles at Cassino and most notably there, the Rapido River fiasco? Now that Clark commanded both the American and

British armies, Truscott sensed that the German commander could reasonably anticipate that the main Allied attack would come at Pianoro.

The opposing armies were roughly the same in numerical strength, Truscott knew, and he was also painfully aware that the Germans in Italy had never been routed; this enemy had not tasted defeat, as had repeatedly happened to other Nazi armies on the Eastern and Western fronts. The Krauts, as he referred to them, in Italy were not in a frantic, hopeless situation. Moreover, G-2, Army intelligence had opined that the Germans had "fourteen days of supplies of all classes"[333] which was more than enough to wreak defensive havoc on any battlefield.

Truscott asked himself: what advantages do I have? He immediately appreciated the biggest one — what he termed "limited enemy air activity" over the Gothic Line — the Germans did not frequently send out photo reconnaissance planes and this afforded the opportunity for deception. [Ed: Kesselring agreed noting the "… diminution of effectiveness in depth," of German aircraft ground-reconnaissance].[334]

Truscott came up with a name for his new plan: "Modified Pianoro." The name would mollify General Clark, he knew. The hoax he contemplated for the Germans he codenamed "Big Game" (more to follow).

As for Bill, despite the increased workload in anticipation of the final assault, not every day was spent in the office. As section leader, Major Renick allowed some Sundays off. On the sunny Sunday afternoon of February 25, 1945, Bill took a long and pleasurable hike "… up the Palace grounds and cascades and then to the top of a fairly high hill overlooking the whole countryside." There he and his three companions, including Renick, viewed Mt. Vesuvius. The following evening Bill would dress up in his "blouse and pinks for the second time overseas" to attend a reception for a colonel who was departing. Bill complained about the $5 cost. "I guess some of the boys will get their money's worth in liquid form," he wrote to Dotty.

At month's end Company "B" received a special guest. John had been notified a few days earlier that she was coming and joked about it in his diary: "Everybody will get up early tomorrow and police the area."

When she did arrive John and others from 1st Platoon were waiting for her. "About dark, Margaret Bourke-White *Life* photographer came in and wanted to photograph our guns in action; so Section 4 fired about fifteen rounds with her taking pictures each time," John wrote. John's diary does not indicate whether

Purple Heart holders/Platoon Leader First Lieutenant James "Jimmy" Stuart and Platoon Staff Sergeant Murphy were in attendance, but chances are they were.

The *Life Magazine* photo article came out April 16, the same date that the 100th Chemical Mortar Battalion moved its headquarters from Filigare to points north to press the attack. The photo selected by Bourke-White for the mortar section of the article is a dramatic nighttime flash picture taken at the precise moment of firing; the large mortar barrel is flamed and a smoke cone is frozen in time, while a crew of five is turned away, bending downwards in an attempt to lessen the blast impact. The photo caption included: "Men have mouths open to lessen the concussion on their eardrums."

Other pictures show phosphorous artillery shells landing, panoramic views of a rugged mountain terrain, and day-to-day G.I.s trying their best just to cope — living in tents, caves and stone homes. The image of the combat infantrymen comes though the most powerful — the men who patrolled frequently, faces blackened, on a missions to capture prisoners or gather information on "enemy defensive fire points." "The Italian front is a foot soldier's war," the *Life* article declares, contrasting the slow-moving mountainous Italian front to fast-moving events taking place on the fully mechanized and largely flat Western Front.

Indeed, infantry staff sergeant Leon Weckstein reported what combat infantry patrols in Italy were like with the 363rd Regiment in his book *Through My Eyes*. Separated from his men during an enemy howitzer barrage in the vicinity of Pianoro, he wrote: "I began digging like crazy, figuring I'd join them later after dark, as was my practice. I wasn't aware of it at the time — and it may sound incredible — but at that moment I happened to be the lead man of the entire Fifth Army! Not one American or Allied soldier was closer to the enemy positions than I was at that moment, and the German gunners wasted no time in letting me know that they knew it." Weckstein managed to dig a small slit trench in which he "… acted out the role of a scared snail for the next two hours." His biggest fear was the enemy switching to "overhead fragmentation bursts" which did not happen.[335]

That was the way it was on patrol with the combat infantry in Italy. No conquest to claim while always wet, cold and terrified. Infrequently there was a sympathetic story such as appeared in *Life*.

—ʍ—

It was early March 1945 on the world stage that the relationship between East-West, represented by the Soviet Union on one side and the Americans and British on the other, began to cool. In mid February Roosevelt sent Stalin a nicely worded thank you telegraph for hosting the Yalta Conference and two weeks later followed up with a message extending "... my heartiest congratulations to you as Supreme Commander on this, the twenty-seventh anniversary of the founding of the Red Army..." and wishing "...the speedy attainment of our common goal — a peaceful world based upon mutual understanding and cooperation." On March 4, however, Roosevelt sent a communication to Stalin that included this: "It is urgently requested that instructions be issued authorizing ten American aircraft with American crews to operate between Poltava and places in Poland, where American ex-prisoners of war and stranded airmen may be located."

Stalin promptly replied that there was no need for U.S. planes to fly to the area as the Americans, approximately 1,200 of them, had been removed to an assembly point in Odessa where they would be cared for by the Red Army. Roosevelt replied the same day: "I cannot, in all frankness, understand your reluctance to permit American contact officers... to assist their own people..." [336]

This incident tipped off the Roosevelt administration of a significant Soviet policy in the making. Shortly after Nazi Germany invaded the Soviet Union in 1940, a massive number of Red Army soldiers defected to join the Germans in the fight against Stalin. By refusing to hand over 1,200 Americans in March 1945 as requested, Stalin signaled his intention to hold these men and other Anglo-Americans hostage pending a massive prisoner swap immediately following the war. The upshot was approximately 2.6 million Slavs (i.e., Soviet citizen defectors) being forcefully repatriated to Stalin's control in May 1945 in exchange for Stalin's release of over a 100,000 British and American former POWs that ended up in Red Army custody.[337] Stalin liquidated most of his returned countrymen either directly by firing squads or indirectly in the work camp-gulags of Siberia.[338]

On March 8, Clare Boothe Luce boarded a British plane bound for Italy, her expenses paid by a foreign government. Her biographer wrote:

> *In return for Alexander's generosity she knew he expected her to publicize the achievements of the British Eighth Army, just as she had Mark Clark's 15th Army Group. She had accordingly contracted to write a series of syndicated articles for the New York World Telegram.*[339]

Luce's second visit to Italy sparked political controversy. The invitation from Alexander to Luce caused consternation on the part of General Marshall. The War Department had denied Everett Dirksen, an influential Republican Representative from Illinois, permission to visit the Italian front. The Republican controlled leadership of the House demanded an explanation from Marshall as to why Luce got to go and not Dirksen. All that Marshall could do was point to the British invitation to Luce and the U.S. Joint Chiefs of Staff denial of the Dirksen application. Marshall's response was looked upon as lame in the halls of Congress. The brouhaha settled, but not before the second Luce trip garnered critical attention from members of her own political party.[340]

On the same day Luce arrived in Italy, March 8, *SS-Obergruppenführer and General of the Military SS, Highest SS and Police Leader and Military Plenipotentiary of the German Armed Forces in Italy*, Karl Wolff, the third highest ranking officer in the SS, met one on one with Allen Dulles.[341] Dulles had arranged for the meeting to take place in the library of a nondescript apartment the OSS maintained in Zurich.

Dressed in civilian attire and accompanied by three SS aides, the Italian businessman and Swiss professor-schoolmaster, Wolff passed through the border unnoticed (and unquestioned by customs) riding in the last car of a passenger train that had its doors and window curtains closed. As a precaution, the Swiss arranged for the last two cars of the train to be reserved with a security man in the forward car, so that no one could walk in on the party by surprise. As an additional measure, a cover story had been arranged by Waibel: the Germans traveled as part of a German-Italian commission headed to discuss with the Swiss government the use of the port facility of Genoa. Reaching Zurich in the mid to late afternoon, all in the party except Wolff enjoyed the hospitality afforded at an apartment maintained by the professor-schoolmaster and his wife. Wolff was driven through a darkening sky to where Dulles waited.

Earlier in the day Dulles had met with Ferruccio Parri, one of the two political prisoners the SS had brought to the border and released to Swiss control as part of the meeting agreement. Parri told Dulles that when the SS had taken him out of his jail cell in Verona that he expected to be either shot or sent to Nazi Germany.[342]

Operation Sunrise had commenced and Wolff was a big player; he commanded approximately 150,000 Waffen-SS combat troops in Italy and he reported operationally to Kesselring. Per the Dulles book, through intermediaries, including of course Gaevernitz, Wolff and Dulles had agreed earlier that this meeting would be for the exclusive purpose of discussing the ways and means by which the whole German army in Italy might surrender unconditionally and that there would be no discussion of political issues. Dulles had prepared for all contingencies; nearby OSS assassins were at the ready. He recounted: "If Wolff was trying to trick me, the consequences could be unpleasant."[343] Wolff had come on his own volition, making assurances, per Dulles, "that he was acting without the knowledge of Hitler or Himmler."[344]

Before a crackling fire with "scotch offered" the two enemies discussed the daunting, almost impossible task that lay ahead. In his remarkable albeit perhaps selective recall book, *The Secret Surrender*, Dulles outlines the almost insurmountable "roadblocks" to be overcome.[345] The biggest hurdle was the irony that Hitler at this closing stage of a losing, calamitous war was more powerful than ever in Nazi circles. The failed assassination plot of July 20, 1944 had played into his hands. It enabled him to execute eight high-ranking German military officers amid much publicity and compel another, Rommel, to quietly commit suicide to protect his family.[346] Afterwards, Hitler ruled by pure terror much like a mad Roman emperor, with the fanatical SS acting as his Pretorian guard.

Another obstacle to overcome for peace was the Allied policy agreed upon in 1943 at Casablanca: unconditional surrender. The basis for this policy — to compel the German people to finally accept that they had been militarily vanquished and not "stabbed in the back" as they had fervently and willingly been led to believe after World War I — was sound, but, as stated, it removed *any* room for negotiation! In this regard Wolff, in a personal sense impressed Dulles: "Neither at this meeting nor later did Wolff suggest that this action would be contingent upon any promise of immunity for himself," the future leader of the CIA wrote. Wolff had not come to negotiate on his personal behalf (he had however previously furnished Dulles with a document that listed "the present Pope" as someone who might give "information" about him suggesting he viewed the Pontiff as a character reference).[347]

What Dulles did not write is whether immunity was nevertheless offered.

Additional "roadblocks" to peace were the several wishful and unrealistic German "hopes upon hopes": the unfounded belief that last minute "miracle weapons" like the V-1s and V-2s and others would turn the war-tide at any moment in the Reich's favor; that the British and Americans would suddenly come to their senses and wage war against the Soviet Union, and additionally — critical to the Italian front — that a so-called "Alpine redoubt" would enable die-hard Nazis to hold out for months and maybe even years. In regard to this final pipe dream, while Dulles was certain that such a redoubt would not succeed (how does one eat when surrounded on a mountain top) he was not unmindful (nor displeased) that the man sitting before him commanded the troops that controlled the Brenner Pass.

Lastly, there was another intangible that could not be downplayed as a possible roadblock to peace. Dulles and Wolff, strange partners that they had become, had to contend with the German militaristic mind. Members of both the Wehrmacht and SS had sworn personal loyalty oaths to Adolf Hitler (often stating "even at the peril of my life" or words to that effect) and done so in every situation invoking the name of God. A commanding general or even a field marshal ordering soldiers to lay down their weapons without Hitler's approval risked being disobeyed and possibly a great deal more. Wolff told Dulles he needed Kesselring's support to succeed with the surrender of Germans forces in Italy and that he thought he could get it; Dulles instructed the SS "uber leader" to immediately go to Kesselring and obtain whatever assurances were needed.

Per the Bancroft account, Wolff, fresh from his secret meeting with Dulles was animated — happy — on his return trip. He was pleased over how well the meeting had gone and purportedly blurted, "Why — why — didn't anyone ever tell me there were Americans like Dulles?"[348] A fair reading of the Dulles book suggests that Dulles and Wolff took an instant liking to each other.

Dulles recounted in his memoirs that he subsequently learned that both the American and British governments informed the Soviets of his secret meeting with Wolff within three days after it took place (this would be March 11) and that while the Soviets had no objection to discussions pertaining to a Nazi surrender in Italy taking place it (the Soviet Union) wanted three Red Army officers to sit in on any future parleys. The U.S. turned down this Soviet request giving as a reason that the Soviets had never allowed reciprocal participation in the surrenders of German armies on the Eastern Front.[349]

With this action — the denial by U.S. authorities of Soviet participation in Dulles-generated surrender talks with an enemy leader — the Americans had planted a seed of distrust. The "fly in the ointment" such as there may have been one, had gotten "stuck" a month after the Yalta Conference.

Yalta left open the question of the status of postwar Northern Italy.

As it would play out, not only did Stalin have an interest in joining forces with the Italian communist partisans, so did the fast emerging-in-prominence communist leader Marshal Tito of Yugoslavia, who particularly desired to occupy and annex, if obtainable as a spoil of war, the Italian northern Adriatic port city of Trieste.

Dulles in *The Secret Surrender* makes the statement: "It wasn't until well after the end of the war, of course, that I learned the full details of this disagreement between Russia and the Allies, which, as we will see later, became such a serious threat at a crucial stage of *Operation Sunrise*."[350] This is an understatement to say the least; the "disagreement" as we will see, readers, threatened the establishment of the United Nations itself.

Anecdotal to his first critical meeting with Wolff on March 8, Dulles in his book relates how Wolff almost got compromised on his railroad trip into Zurich. An avalanche that day temporarily blocked Gotthard Pass requiring all passengers, including Wolff, to leave the train and walk a distance along the tracks to embark upon another awaiting train. Wolff spotted some Italians that he knew in the distance. Dulles wrote, "… only by considerable ducking and stalling…" did the SS high general avoid being spotted by these people. If he had been recognized in Switzerland and word got out about it, *Operation Sunrise* might have, probably would have been over before it started.[351]

What the Dulles book does not recount is that Wolff *was* spotted upon his arrival in Zurich. Nosy Mary Bancroft, super sleuth that she had become, reported in her spy memoir that as she walked home from work that evening she spotted Gaevernitz (who she regarded as "extremely attractive") emerging from the Banhhof Enge railroad station. "Gero did not see me," she noted, "for I quickly stepped into a small shop… so I could take a closer look at the men accompanying him." Nosy as always, Bancroft thought she recognized Wolff from the pictures she had seen of him in newspapers. Bancroft claims to have pestered a denying Dulles until he "… finally confessed that it had been General Wolff whom I had seen…"[352]

Apart from being believable and perhaps a tad humorous — i.e., the mental image of sex-obsessed Mary Bancroft taking cover to get a "closer look at *the men*" (Wolff was strikingly handsome) this reported incident also reflects upon the make-up of a controlled and equally sex-obsessed Allen Dulles. Bancroft does not say *when* Dulles fessed up to her, his lover, leaving a reader to speculate, perhaps after the war?[353] Dulles over his many years of top-secret government service had trained himself to compartmentalize, no doubt. Several of his biographers relate how when he was director of the CIA his best friends (including females batting eyes and effervescing) could not get *anything* out of him, not even over dinner in his home when the wine flowed and Clover was in the kitchen. Dulles would stonewall gracefully and withhold completely; he had the ability to lightly re-direct a conversation into one of a plethora of other compelling subjects, and to do so laughingly. His winks, nods and friendly gestures conveyed *no meaning*.

An unanticipated change in circumstances confronted Wolff upon his return to Italy: to his dismay he learned that Kesselring was no longer his commanding officer and was in fact at that time hundreds of miles away. The Luftwaffe field marshal had been summoned to the Wolf's Lair in East Prussia and placed in command by Hitler of the Western Front.

To make matters even more challenging for Wolff, his immediate boss in the SS, the number two under Himmler, a brute named Ernst Kaltenbrunner, learned that Wolff had spent the day in Switzerland. Why had Wolff done this? Kaltenbrunner, who regarded Wolff as a rival, eventually learned through informants of Wolff's unauthorized meeting with the enemy. Kaltenbrunner reported this happening — arguably an act of treason — to Himmler and the two plotted and schemed how Wolff might be portrayed in the worst light possible to the Führer.

Himmler had a problem, however. A year or so earlier he had denied Wolff permission to remarry following a divorce; Wolff did not hesitate to go over Himmler's head and he obtained permission directly from Hitler. To ordinary people this might appear as an inconsequential matter, a tempest in a teapot so to speak, but in the strange world of the SS this was not so. Himmler constantly reassessed his power in relation to those nearest to his Führer, and modified his behavior towards these people accordingly. Wolff was away in Italy. What harm could he do to Himmler from there? Himmler instinctively knew that extreme caution on his part was required, however, in his future dealings concerning Wolff.

Not knowing who would be selected to replace Kesselring in Italy Wolff sent a message to Dulles via an intermediary approximately a week after the meeting stating that he, Wolff was prepared to act alone if it came to that. The envelope that contained the message also contained a small gift for Dulles, a souvenir of sorts. Wolff's car had been attacked by a fighter-bomber from the American 12th

Air Force east of Milan; as a keepsake from this event, the uninjured-but-nearly-killed SS General delivered to Dulles a small piece of his burned uniform with the request that the USAAF consider giving leeway for single automobiles.[354]

The two men shared the bond of humor, no doubt.

Dulles subsequently learned from Wolff the German thinking behind maintaining such a large military force in Northern Italy, a question that perplexed Allied military commanders by reason of Germany's obvious need for additional troops to hold off Allied advances elsewhere. Wolff explained that a plan had been made to shift nine divisions out of Northern Italy in September 1944. Hitler did not implement this plan owing to the belief that the Gothic Line would hold for some time and that Northern Italy provided "... a great deal of food and commodities."[355] Additionally, and perhaps not so compelling an argument considering what was already going on in the European air war, the assessment was made by Hitler that Allied air bases in Northern Italy would increase the danger for Germany. In the end however, per the Dulles narrative (attributing Wolff as his source) it was Hitler's fear of withdrawal — his mental paralysis — that kept him from ordering German troops out of Italy. Hitler would not willingly withdraw troops from any occupied country, not even far away Norway.

As regards trying to hold the Po Valley for its food stocks, Hitler might not have been off base. Indeed, in a commemorative history put out by the U.S. Fifth Army written soon after the war ended entitled: *19 Days from the Apennines to the Alps* (approved by Lucien Truscott and hereinafter referred to as *19 Days*) the following is noted about the region:

> *These German forces were virtually self-sustaining in the rich valley of the Po. What our troops had come to call The Promised Land was indeed a "land of milk and honey" — to say nothing of wheat and rice and fruit and livestock. While Southern Italy lived on semi-starvation rations... the Po Valley residents... [and] the Krauts had all they could eat...* [356]

On a side note personal to Truscott, if he had been pleased or displeased to learn that Hitler had ordered Kesselring to duty away from Italy, he did not make any indication of it in his memoirs (Kesselring is hardly mentioned). Perhaps telling about Truscott's attitude, he wrote: "I never had any wish to exchange civilities with any of the numerous enemy generals who passed through my headquarters..."[357] To Truscott, the war was never about *him* defeating a famous

German general, or *him* liberating an important city, or *him* being photographed accepting a surrender. He did wear that silk scarf and leather jacket, yes, but he never thought of himself as Caesar draped in red single-handedly lording it over a defeated Vercingetorix. And for this, his men loved him.

But he was human and his special someone close to him had returned to Italy.

The first order of business for Clare Boothe Luce upon arriving was a courtesy call on Field Marshal Alexander at the Royal Palace of Caserta, where she was suitably impressed with his Excellency's mess, a massive glassed-in tropical garden. She was less impressed with the office sectionals of the Caserta palace where Bill worked, noting it was an "Italian Pentagon, a bewildering labyrinth of incomparable galleries and rooms."[358] If Bill ran into Luce on this visit, or even knew she was back in Italy, he never indicated. In a 1983 interview Luce commented about the British drinking tea at their end of the building with the windows wide open and the Americans drinking coffee at the other end with their windows tightly shut.

Luce visited both British and American units, including the 10th Mountain Division. She stayed in Italy for approximately a month and during that time had a friend and colleague in Congress extend an olive branch to that august body. There were people in high places in Washington D.C. who seethed about her second trip to Italy, and no doubt for *all* the reasons under the sun including, but only whispered, one of the Ten Commandments. The press would not cover what was going on, no that was not how it was done in 1945, but surely many knew the real reason for Luce's second trip to Italy. In making a political peace offering to Congress, Luce did not apologize for anything she had done but rather softened a political stance, a position that no longer served the interest of the Republican Party or the nation. She would remain unapologetic and feisty the rest of her life, both in and out of public service and live her life on her terms as it suited her.

For General Marshall's part he knew what was going on (per Luce's biographer) and was very concerned. If a photograph might surface of Luce and Truscott together, or something about their illicit relationship, perish the thought, *be made public*, Marshall appreciated that the U.S. Army would have a public relations disaster on its hands. Too many parents and congressmen had received complaining letters from members of the U.S. Fifth Army about the spartan conditions of wintertime Northern Italy. To have it disclosed that the commanding general and the Congresswoman were partying and trysting at villas in Florence and Rome[359] while the G.I's suffered simply would not do. Aghast at this self-centered and reckless behavior, straight-laced Marshall knew there was little he could do to stop it. In this regard he was not unmindful that it was Churchill and Alexander who had requested that Truscott return to Italy, and now it had been Alexander who had invited Luce back!

While Luce and Truscott cavorted, John Lesesne grieved. He received news that one of his best friends, Captain "Hut" Martin had been killed in France. "We both had appointments to West Point and planned to room together," John wrote, "but my eyes left me out. He went on and finished in Jan '43 and was assigned to engineers." On the same day that this bad news arrived something unrelated but positive happened for John:

> We have just gotten a fine letter of commendation from Col Broedlow, C.O., 361st Inf., for good work in supporting his regiment last Nov. and Dec. I'm more proud of this than any other honors I've ever had. A compliment from the infantry, that branch which has the toughest job in war is really something.[360]

Not everything was good for John, however. His baseplate project had developed a case of the slows: "I went to Leghorn twice in connection with my baseplate plan," he reported, "and one is being made, but the PBS takes its time, can't work on Sunday. I'll probably get it in a couple of weeks."[361]

At this stage of the Italian war, getting ammo for the mortar men did not seem to be a problem. On March 7 John wrote: "We fired about 420 rounds @ $30.00 per round" [Ed: $12,600]. The Transportation Section, mud notwithstanding, delivered.

As of March 12, Jack was still comfortably ensconced at Villanova. "Work has slacked off considerably," he diarized. "We now have a volleyball team and play between the officers and enlisted men." The rear echelon had it good Jack always admitted.

The following day Bill assured his parents, "I am gaining weight… I have never felt better (am knocking on wood) and have an excellent appetite. I have eaten cauliflower all winter… grown locally and prepared in a number of different ways…"

Later Bill would again write about Italian produce: "We are getting fresh vegetables now from the country. Many of them do not taste at all like they do at home. Onions are quite flat and carrots are so woody that it's no pleasure to eat them. They have a plant called fennel. It looks like celery and tastes like medicine. Not many of the men like it."[362]

On March 16 John mentioned for the last time his baseplate project. Discouraged, he wrote: "Today I went to Leghorn to see about the baseplate — nothing had been done — I have to try to improvise one myself." On one of his last missions a few days later before taking ten days personal leave to Rome and afterwards putting Company "B" through special training for the final push in Italy, John's boys fired some 700 smoke rounds in support of an infantry attack that failed to take Mt. Adone. John recorded "… our mission was a success [Ed: referring to the smoke laid down]…" but that "… we broke two baseplates…" Time simply ran out for John's baseplate invention. The war in Europe would be over before it could be produced.

On St. Patrick's Day, Bill told Dotty how nice she looked in green ("… or any other color for that matter") and then told her about a nifty sports car he had seen in the vicinity. That Bill liked working at the Royal Palace of Caserta, with its warm library, courtyards, wheeled toys, love-moat and orchestra, there is no doubt. As an additional attraction, the palace was surrounded by a countryside at pastoral peace. On another long and pleasurable hike near Caserta Bill walked into what could have been a scene from ancient times:

> I saw a herd of sheep and also one of goats. The sheep were fenced in by a rope net suspended on stakes stuck in the ground. Every few hours the shepherd moves the net enclosure to fresh grass. The shepherd has a little cone shaped grass hut that he moves around with his portable pasture for protection from the weather.[363]

In a letter written to Dotty he noted: "It was a beautiful sunshiny day. We left our big window open and needed no fire. It was on the cool side but not bad. Our big window is a huge double door that opens right out into space at the story level. An iron railing serves as a balcony. It gives a feeling of being quite high when looking down from the doorway. The Italians are great for balconies."[364] In another March letter he elaborated: "Our fifth floor is about as high as seven normal stories due to the extra high ceilings…" He also told of a chair placed in front of the open window-doors so one could sit and sun in "our reading room."[365] There was no elevator in the Palace Bill explained. "I like the exercise."[366]

It seemed the Americans as well as the British enjoyed open windows.

Overlooking an athletic field and swimming pool not yet in use,[367] one Sunday that month Bill wrote the following to his mother from his office-in-the-sky: "Our windows face west. I can see the sun just setting in a ball of fire. It is one o'clock there and if it is a clear day the same sun will be shining down on you… I get awful lonesome at times but realize I am no better than the rest and that I have been here such a short time by comparison." Dick Stroud wrote the same about the sun shining down on Sue.

CHAPTER TEN:

THE NORTH APENNINES CAMPAIGN COMMENCES

March 1945–April 15, 1945

THE PLANNING FOR the final Allied offensive in Italy was completed in late March when the Fifteenth Army Group issued Operations Instruction No. 4. The attack was to proceed in three phases with the British Eighth Army going it alone for the first two days of Phase I. D-Day, as Truscott referred to it was set for April 9. Phase I of the joint plan called for the British to break through the defenses at Santerno River and "... clear the plain east of Bologna." The two-day planned delay for the American advance would (hopefully) cause the enemy to start reinforcing defenses to the east (in the middle of the boot area) near Pianoro. The largest attack would then come from Americans pouring down from the mountains to the west of Pianoro — "debouching" as Truscott referred to it — fanning out into a wider area. The spearhead of U.S. Fifth Army would be up the western side of Highway 64. The goal of phase I was to capture or isolate Bologna, with the British on the east and the Americans on the west of the city.

Truscott's "Modified Pianaro" plan had *nothing* to do with Pianaro other than to draw German soldiers there so they would become useless.

Subsequently the joint plan called for:

> *Phase II contemplated a breakthrough by either or both armies to encircle the enemy forces south of the Po [River], while Phase III called for the actual crossing of the river and the capture of Verona which guarded the gateway to the Brenner.*[368]

Color "phase lines" were on a map of Northern Italy to show where the Allied armies were supposed to be located at the end of each phase. A "green line" showed the border of Phase I, and this line indicated modest distance gain (most of the fighting would take place during this phase causing a slow rate of advance). When both the British and American armies reached the "green line," however, the Gothic line would be a thing of the past and the speed of the Allied armies was anticipated to increase considerably. Significantly, the "green line" did not show the city of Bologna fallen, but rather surrounded on three sides. The intent was to keep on moving.

A "brown line" denoted Phase II and it encompassed a much larger geographic area, one that breached the Po River in several locations. The intent of Phase II was to trap as many Germans as possible south of the river.

The final "black line" represented an east-west tour of Northern Italy and into the Alps.

In boxing terms the Fifteenth Army Group would lead with its right, land a haymaker with its left, open up a flurry of wide enveloping body blows and end it with a head-on fan charge to both sides of the other end of the ring. The only things needed for victory were more supplies laid in, mechanized vehicles positioned and a period of good weather to dry things out.

If one believes that it is inappropriate to compare warfare to the sport of boxing, then one should read *19 Days*. The chapter describing the Gothic Line assault is entitled, "The bell and opening rounds." Cheating was permitted in this prize match, particularly shots taken "below the belt," the belt being the Po River. The plan called for the Germans to be backed up against this major waterway where they could surrender or die. There is little if any respect expressed for the Germans in this free-flowing history; they are often referred to as "the Boche" or simply "Krauts".

As D-Day approached Truscott followed the progress of his planned soldierly trickery. II Corps and IV Corps of the U.S. Fifth Army were positioned abreast of each other on the line facing the enemy. II Corps stood to the west, closest to the Ligurian Sea. As alluded to "Big Game" was designed to give the impression to the Germans that the 85th and 88th Divisions from II Corps had moved behind the lines from west to east. Truscott intended the enemy to believe that approximately 25% of the American fighting force had repositioned itself with the British Eighth Army in central Italy preparatory to a massive attack on Pianoro.

The truth was that none of the elements of II Corps moved very much.

The ruse was accomplished over time by the establishment of phony command posts and supply dumps, issuing fake radio traffic ("for real" messages went by wire), holding a fictitious change-of-command ceremony and "artillery support reduced and then gradually built up again,"[369] intended to cause those on the receiving end to believe pieces had been repositioned. No doubt Bill and the U.S. Fifth Army Transportation Section were involved in setting up and stocking the phony supply dumps near the front so German patrols could spot them. Without regular aerial photoreconnaissance the Germans were at a distinct disadvantage. *19 Days* summed up what the Transportation Corps was able to accomplish as D-Day approached:

> *All winter long the war correspondents had written dolefully about "the Forgotten Front." All winter long the artillery observers up front had cursed at their inability to register on the choice targets visible through their binoculars, because the big guns had been pulled out of Italy. [Ed: sent to Southern France] But in the coming spring equipment began to move up Highway 64 and Highway 65. Huge supply dumps were created; vast stocks of ammunition piled up; heart-warming convoys of tanks, tank destroyers and artillery rolled steadily up the roads. Officers and enlisted men broke into spontaneous cheers when they again saw 8-inch howitzers rumbling by. The time had come to move down out of the mountains.*[370]

Not wanting the Germans to know that heavy guns were in place, Truscott did not permit their use in the artillery build-up that took place during the days preceding D-Day. Only on D-Day itself would the Germans learn what awesome shell firepower that they were up against.

As D-Day approached a debate ensued over whether a final battle in Italy needed to be waged. Germany itself was on the verge of collapse. "Why attack now?" some asked. In weighing in on this issue, Truscott was not unmindful of the fact that the travel time from Bologna to Brenner Pass in peacetime was conservatively a day or less (today it takes three and one-half hours by vehicle). The U.S. Twelfth Air Force had done a splendid job in chewing up the rails, roads and bridgeheads leading to the pass but this did not mean that the damage it inflicted could not be repaired or patched, and that certain waterways could not somehow be crossed. The enemy was resourceful, Truscott knew, and if it made a concerted effort to get to the Fatherland a good number of them probably would make it.

Truscott wrote at the time:

> "It is largely a question of where the lives are to be saved. It will require just so much effort to destroy the German will to fight. The attack of this army against the German's sole remaining army may be the very factor, if launched now in coordination with attacks on the eastern and western fronts in northern Europe, that will cause the final German collapse; I think there is a great possibility that that may prove to be the case.

He additionally propounded for, "... destroying the Boche here... [so] he will be unable to withdraw to the Alps" and pointed to the need to "... quickly complete the liberation of all of Italy."[371] Clark and Alexander agreed. What no American or British general could (or would) discuss at the time was that the liberation *of part of* "all of Italy" might end-up being done by communist allies. There existed an unspoken reason to wage this final battle: if D-Day were put into play the city of Trieste and points west might not fall into the hands of the advancing Red Army or Yugoslav Army; Italy might yet be saved from a fate as bad or worse than the Nazi occupation.

As earlier stated Dulles realized for Northern Italy: "... Communist-dominated forces might well determine the zones of postwar influence, or even occupation."[372] Of interest is that in certain places in *The Secret Surrender* Dulles refers to the Americans and British as "the Allies" without including the Soviet Union.

During this period Truscott and Luce saw as much of each other as often as they could arrange and a true love affair resulted, with Luce sending him edelweiss and Truscott writing romantic poetry.[373] Theirs was a star-crossed passion, however. Both knew it would not, could not, last and that neither in the end would be willing to leave a spouse. Whatever one might assess of the morality of their situation there was rich irony here. Truscott, supported and no doubt counseled by Luce, who was always assertive, was at his absolute most brilliant as a commanding general. Lincoln reportedly wanted to send his generals the brand of whiskey favored by Grant; if Roosevelt had known about the Luce and Truscott affair, what might he have done to inspire his other generals?

It was Luce's wit, as much as her good looks that made her a magnet to successful men, men who had much to lose if discovered. In one telling anecdote,

Luce's biographer, Sylvia Jukes Morris has Luce wearing an unknown medal on her lapel and a G.I. in Italy asking her what it represented. "Order of Chastity Second Class," she quipped laughing, to the roar of approval of all soldiers in earshot — exactly the response that she unabashedly intended.[374]

Luce was simply fun to be around, and a winner in her own right. She was to Truscott the reverse of what Delilah had been to Samson. No doubt Truscott shared with his lover his thoughts and ideas at this critical, exciting time in history, and for her part, Luce had to have been thrilled to be part of what was going on. The fun was in the chase, as it had been with Bernard Baruch, Conde Nast, Joe Kennedy and others, including Randolph Churchill the son of the Prime Minister.

During this period Truscott fooled everyone as to his military intentions including members of his own army. He had soldiers of the 85th and 88th divisions, well inland, practice amphibious landings. Word got out (as Truscott expected it would) and Truscott knew he had achieved the level of deception desired when a reporter for the *Stars and Stripes* newspaper "protested vigorously" at being denied permission to accompany the 85th on the "landing" that he assumed would be made.[375] The need for secrecy was given as the reason for the request denial and if a correspondent could not be "embedded" (using today's terminology) then for certain the rumor *had* to be true! This reporter had stumbled onto a good story and intended to follow up on it!

On the diplomatic front, the first indication of trouble from the Soviet government over *Operation Sunrise* came in the form of a sharply worded classified letter dated March 16 from the People's Commissar for Foreign Affairs of the USSR to the U.S. Ambassador. In his letter Vyacheslav Molotov acknowledged that he had been told about the first meeting with Wolff. He then wrote this:

> On the same day, March 12, I informed you that the Soviet Government had no objections to negotiations with General Wolff at Berne, provided Soviet officers representing the Soviet Military Command took part. In giving this reply, the Soviet Government had no doubt that the United States Government would react positively to its proposal for the participation of Soviet officers in the negotiations with the German General Wolff at Berne, and there and then named its representatives.

*Today, March 16, I am in receipt of a letter from you which shows that
the United States Government is barring the Soviet representatives from
the Berne negotiations. The U.S. Government's refusal to admit Soviet
representatives to the Berne negotiations came as a complete surprise
to the Soviet Government and is inexplicable in terms of the relations
of alliance existing between our two countries. In view of this the Soviet
Government finds it impossible to assent to discussions at Berne between
representatives of Britain and the United States, on the one hand, and
of the German commander, on the other, and insists on the discussions
already begun at Berne being discontinued.*

*The Soviet Government insists, furthermore, that henceforward separate
negotiations by one or two of the Allied Powers with German representatives without the participation of the third Allied Power be precluded."[376]*

On March 19 SS General Karl Wolff was back in Switzerland, this time as a
visitor at the lakeside villa at Ascona available to Gaevernitz. Alexander had sent
two general officers from Caserta to meet personally with Wolff. Dulles wrote
about this: "The Allied generals were to remain at their villa on the hill during
the morning while we [Ed: Dulles and Gaevernitz] prepared the ground with
Wolff."[377] The Dulles version of this event does not explain what "ground" needed
to be prepared.

The meeting with Wolff had been allowed to proceed despite the strong protest
of Molotov and presumably as a consequence of this event, Molotov subsequently
informed the U.S. State Department through Ambassador Gromyko that his
duties in the USSR would preclude him from attending the San Francisco conference.[378] This conference was scheduled to start April 25 and was viewed by the
Roosevelt administration as a keystone of its foreign policy; it was to formalize
the framework and future workings of the United Nations.

Per the Dulles account, at the March 19 meeting Wolff informed Gaevernitz and
him that Kesselring's successor in Italy would be Wehrmacht General Heinrich
von Vietinghoff, most recently of the Latvian front and a retread to Italy having
previously commanded at Cassino and at a higher level during a period when
Kesselring recovered from his injuries. Vietinghoff was to return to Italy that day,
Wolff told Dulles.[379]

Asked by Dulles what kind of man Vietinghoff was, Wolff was blunt in explaining that although his past relations with Vietinghoff had been "close and friendly"

the general was a non-political aristocrat and old-school militarist, implying that he was a professional soldier who would view obeying a sworn personal loyalty oath as a matter of honor.[380] Per Dulles, Wolff explained that he never had the opportunity to discuss the subject of surrender with Vietinghoff, but intimated he would try to reason with him now. Wolff also stated that buy-in from additional German generals would be essential and reiterated that he intended to person-ally attempt to enlist the support of Kesselring who would be influential with Vietinghoff. Wolff then asked for a week or so but no promise was made to him that an Allied attack would be forestalled. It was agreed that any surrender would take place at Caserta and that the Allies would fly in the German representative or representatives from neutral Switzerland. Additionally, Wolff agreed that Dulles could place a wireless operator in SS headquarters so that future communications between the enemies could be direct and immediate.[381]

The morning session completed, Dulles wrote that he and Gaevernitz briefed the two generals from AFHQ, Briton Terence S. Airey and American Lyman L. Lemnitzer, on what had transpired at lunch[382] (both worked for Alexander). In the afternoon session without mentioning names, Dulles introduced Wolff to these two Allied officers. In a telling anecdote about Wolff, in his book Dulles related how Airey vowed not to shake the hand of the SS general. Wolff, being the irrepressible extrovert that he was, made short shrift of this resolve. The Allied generals and Wolff entered their meeting room by separate doors to find a large table separating them (as previously planned by Dulles). Dulles wrote, "Wolff stepped briskly around the table, squeezing his large body through the narrow gap…" Airey, reflexively, accepted the SS "uber" leader's outstretched hand as did the surprised Lemnitzer. [383]

Lemnitzer knew when he looked Wolff in the eye that he looked at the Waffen-SS general who commanded all of the forces that faced off against the U.S. Fifth Army. This had to have been a peculiar moment for both men, but especially Lemnitzer, as Wolff had no idea who he was other than a "military adviser" to Dulles (Lemnitzer then served as American Deputy Chief of Staff under Alex-ander and was senior to Airey who was an Assistant Chief of Staff).[384] Dulles pointed out in his book the uniqueness of this situation — no truce had been called yet enemy military leaders dressed as civilians were meeting on neutral ground to talk peace. Lemnitzer spoke English and Gaevernitz translated. It was agreed by all that Germany was defeated and that the responsibility fell upon

Wolff to insure "… in collaboration with the appropriate military commanders to produce the specific plans to achieve the desired end of unconditional surrender" and additionally that no political issues were to be discussed. For his part Wolff explained that if he was successful two German representatives would be coming to Switzerland for transportation to Caserta, one representing the Wehrmacht and the other the SS. Lemnitzer and Airey agreed that Wolfe should seek out Kesselring and Vietinghoff for approval and return to Ascona for another meeting as soon as possible.[385]

While the Dulles anecdotal account of the March 19 meeting makes for an enjoyable, even compelling read, and a researcher later noted, "Two hours of talks between Wolff and Dulles were recorded in detail," (footnoting where this detail is to be found in the National Archives and summarizing it)[386] apparently no verbatim (word for word) transcript of what was said at either meeting was made, nor was a recording done. One thing seems reasonably certain: while the war was being waged Generals Lemnitzer and Airey would not likely discuss with Wolff the possibility of his arranging for German forces in Italy to move in a tactical manner favorable to Allied forces. Such a discussion would violate a military code of honor, strange as that may seem today. Two civilian spies however, meeting with Wolff alone, might not be bound by such a code. What actually transpired at Ascona that March 19 may remain the subject of moot speculation, as a month later the Germans fought as hard they could.

A week later on March 25 Roosevelt waded into what he would later label as the "Berne incident." The president sent two cables to Stalin on that date, the gist of the first being a plea: "If his [Molotov's] pressing and heavy responsibilities in the Soviet Union make it impossible for him to stay for the entire conference, I hope very much that you will find it possible to let him come at least for the vital opening sessions…"[387] The second presidential cable pertained to *Operation Sunrise*:

> *Unconfirmed information was received some days ago in Switzerland that some German officers were considering the possibility of arranging for the surrender of German troops that are opposed to Field Marshal Alexander's British-American Armies in Italy. Upon the receipt of this information in Washington, Field Marshal Alexander was authorized to send to Switzerland an officer or officers of his staff to ascertain the accuracy of the report and if it appeared to be of sufficient promise to arrange*

*with any competent German officers for a conference to discuss details
of the surrender with Field Marshal Alexander at his headquarters in
Italy. If such a meeting could be arranged Soviet representatives would, of
course, be welcome.*

In 1997 writer L. James Binder completed a biography entitled *Lemnitzer, a Soldier for his Time*, and in it he made this curious observation about Lemnitzer's wartime diary:

*But as the winter wore on into March [1945], there began to appear
references to something he [Lemnitzer] called "the Switzerland project."
On March 13 he cut his entry short with "Situation on front moving fast.
10th Mt. Div. is across Po." — the latter sentence crossed out. There are
no more entries until April 5, seemingly a strange omission, for Lemnitzer
was faithful about detailing every day's activities, no matter how busy he
was.*[388]

On March 13, 1945 the situation on the front was *not* "moving fast" and the 10th Mountain Division had neither entered the Po Valley nor crossed the Po River, begging the questions: was Lemnitzer thinking ahead to the military future when he penned this diary entry, and was what he wrote (and then crossed out) connected to "the Switzerland project"? Why did Lemnitzer write what he did?

Following the March 19 meeting Lemnitzer and Airey obtained approval from Alexander to remain in Ascona in the hope that another meeting would come about. Theirs would be a long wait, as Wolff's automobile journey across war-ravaged central Europe to locate Field Marshal Kesselring proved to be an odyssey of sorts, with him being shot at again from the air. No mention of what was going on was made public. If anything were to be reported, it would be the "news" announcement of the surrender itself. Until this event occurred maintaining secrecy about negotiations was critically important.

In preparation for that big day when hopefully the doings at Ascona would be revealed to the world through a joyful international press release, General Airey while waiting in Switzerland purchased a clever present for his boss at Caserta. The General bought an adorable dachshund puppy for Alexander, the probable intent being so the Field Marshal could have a four-legged Hun on a leash. After the German surrender in the South was a fait accompli, this story did get reported and the press had a field day with it as the public loved it.

With the final assault looming, on March 28, 1944 Headquarters, U.S. Fifth Army issued General Order No. 32 deactivating the 366th Regiment of the 92nd Infantry Division as a combat unit. Word that this was coming was passed to members of the 366th a couple of weeks earlier, and one Buffalo Soldier affected wrote in his memoirs: "A more devastating blow could not have been dealt ..."[389] Without weighing the military merits or demerits of this action, which Truscott implemented, one can reasonably infer that what happened here was hurtful for African-Americans and whites alike. Friendship and tolerance across the races is a must if any joint endeavor is to succeed. Soldiers do not always fight for patriotic reasons; they will often risk their lives, however, and fight tenaciously to save the life of a "buddy." This identification of amity between the American races was absent in World War II Italy.

On March 29 Stalin cabled Roosevelt and explained why he believed that Soviet representatives should be immediately part of any surrender process in Italy. "I must tell you for your information that the Germans have already taken advantage of the talks with the Allied Command to move three divisions from Northern Italy to the Soviet front," Stalin complained. In a following paragraph the Premier rebutted a point previously made by the President:

> "As a military man," you write to me, "you will understand the necessity for prompt action to avoid losing an opportunity. The sending of a flag of truce to your General at Konigsberg or Danzig would be in the same category." I am afraid the analogy does not fit the case. The German troops at Danzig and at Konigsberg are encircled. If they surrender they will do so to escape extermination, but they cannot open the front to Soviet troops because the front has shifted as far west as the Oder. The German troops in Northern Italy are in an entirely different position. They are not encircled and are not faced with extermination.[390]

Stalin was flummoxed because the Red Army was fighting and dying massively for every increment of new territory it captured. He feared that Alexander was formulating a clandestine bargained-for-exchange with the enemy to receive territory without the same sacrifice on the part of Anglo-American soldiers.

—〰—

During this time frame Dick Stroud performed a short stint of temporary duty in Bari, Italy on the Adriatic side of the boot. Dick was frustrated there and found a clever way to reveal his feelings to Sue without naming names. "Our staff consists of a brigadier general," Dick balefully wrote, "one colonel, five lieutenant colonels, thirteen majors, twelve captains, five first lieutenants and one second. My situation is absolutely hopeless."[391] A few days later Dick was happy to report: "I have located Virgil's tomb," signifying he had returned to Naples.

On Easter Sunday, April 1 Bill and three other named MTOUSA officers, one from the Transportation Corps and two from the Air Corps, flew to Leghorn under travel orders, "for the purpose of performing an assigned mission."[392] Whether these men were part of the same team is unknown. On April 3 Bill V-mailed his parents, reassuring them: "We flew up and had nice weather," and informed them that he had checked into an Army-run hotel. "There are five in our group and I wish I could tell you about our assignment," he wrote. His V-mail to Dotty the same day reported, "We had our big conference this morning. It lasted about two and a quarter hours. I was chairman and I think it went over OK. A lot of rank attended. Our mission is rather important and a good experience. I have seen a lot of people I've met in other places over here." Bill added, "Our group is taking tomorrow to rest up, clean up details and get ready for eight days of intensive activity…" The U.S. Fifth Army was preparing to launch its final offensive and undoubtedly its Transportation Section supplemented by PBS was planning how and where its vehicles would be used. The fact that Bill mentioned "eight days of intensive activity" in a letter dated April 1 suggests that he probably knew D-Day was scheduled for April 9.

On that Easter morning Wolff contemplated his upcoming return to Ascona scheduled for the following day. As stated, his trip to see Kesselring had been dangerous and time-consuming but also productive. Wolff expected to have Vietinghoff and possibly even the Nazi ambassador to Italy with him when he returned to Ascona. Wolff had already communicated to Dulles that Kesselring had "consented" to his plan, and that he was very encouraged about achieving a prompt peace. Wolff was encouraged, that is, up until the moment when his phone rang and he heard the voice of Heinrich Himmler. The SS Reichsführer informed Wolff that his wife and children had been removed from Italy to Austria and were now under SS "protection."[393] Shaken, Wolff canceled the Ascona meeting and two days later Airey and Lemnitzer returned to Caserta.

Roosevelt also was having a challenging Easter Sunday only of a different nature. The President had decided to "widen the political front" so to speak, and he approved a long message to go out under his name to Stalin expressing his concern over the failure of the Soviet government to live up to the terms of the Yalta agreement with respect to the governance of Poland, pointing to the fact "...the Commission which we [Ed: the Big Three] set up has made no progress." While his complaint went on and on about Poland, Roosevelt also threw in this:

> "... I must make a brief mention of our agreement embodied in the Declaration on Liberated Europe. I frankly cannot understand why the recent developments in Romania should be regarded as not falling within the terms of that Agreement. I hope you will find time personally to examine the correspondence between our Governments on this subject."[394]

A historian later recorded: "Liberated countries such as Romania and Yugoslavia had suddenly been taken over in internal power grabs by groups of declared Communist parties."[395] There was little Roosevelt could do about this phenomenon other than protest, which he did.

In a separate message to Stalin sent the same day Roosevelt tried to put the Berne matter to rest:

> There is no question of negotiating with the Germans in any way which would permit them to transfer elsewhere forces from the Italian front. Negotiations, if any are conducted, will be on the basis of unconditional surrender. With regard to the lack of Allied offensive operations in Italy, this condition has in no way resulted from any expectation of an agreement with the Germans. As a matter of fact, recent interruption of offensive operations in Italy has been due primarily to the recent transfer of Allied forces, British and Canadian divisions, from that front to France. Preparations are now made for an offensive on the Italian front about April 10, but while we hope for success, the operation will be of limited power due to the lack of forces now available to Alexander. He has seventeen dependable divisions and is opposed by twenty-four German divisions. We intend to do everything within the capacity of our available resources to prevent any withdrawal of the German forces now in Italy.

> I feel that your information about the time of the movements of German troops from Italy is in error. Our best information is that three German

*divisions have left Italy since the first of the year, two of which have gone
to the Eastern Front. The last division of the three started moving about
February 25, more than two weeks before anybody heard of any possibility of a surrender. It is therefore clearly evident that the approach made of
German agents in Berne occurred after the last movement of troops began
and could not possibly have had any effect on the movement.*[396]

—⚭—

The following day in Washington D.C. the Republican gentlewoman from
Massachusetts, Mrs. Rogers, asked the speaker pro tempore of the U.S. House
of Representatives for unanimous consent to address the House for 1 minute to
speak on the subject of General Mark Clark and the U.S. Fifth Army in Italy. Edith
Nourse Rogers, one of two children born to a wealthy textile plant industrialist
was sixty-four years old and a member of Congress for some twenty years when
she made this request, first winning her seat in a 1925 special election to replace
her late husband who had died of cancer after himself serving in Congress since
1913. Dignified and brassy ("I am a Republican by inheritance and by conviction."
"I hope that everyone will forget that I am a woman as soon as possible.") she
was especially beloved by veterans for her steadfast advocacy of special rights
for them and for frequently pitching in, starting in World War I, as an American
Red Cross volunteer.[397]

The Congresswoman from Massachusetts, who had become known by that
time as the "Angel of Walter Reed Hospital," was unanimously granted her request
to be heard:

> *Mr. Speaker, a few days ago the gentlewoman from Connecticut [Clare
> Boothe Luce] wrote a very interesting and illuminating article in appre-
> ciation of General Mark Clark in Italy. I visited Italy in October and saw
> there the work of Gen. Mark Clark and his officers and men, the G.I.'s
> who are living down in the fox holes doing the fighting. I saw then the
> tremendous handicap under which these men are fighting: the weather,
> the snow, the ice, the mud and the high mountains they have to surmount,
> and the disheartening lack of replacements. But whether lying wounded
> in hospitals or at the actual fighting front, I witnessed their courage and
> tremendously fine morale in spite of their hardships and difficulties.
> They then were engaging twenty-eight German divisions. Their work has*

*had a lot to do with enabling the other armies to go forward to Berlin.
General Clark's forces were made up of soldiers of different nationalities
which made his work much more difficult. He has accomplished much
in making the Allies more united. He and his gallant army deserve our
undying praise and thanksgiving.*[398]

Clare Boothe Luce could not have picked a better spokesperson to endorse the favorable article she had written about the U.S. Fifth Army. The "disheartening lack of replacements" was put on record, yes, but the hot rhetoric over the administration's misconduct of the war had been eliminated.

As an aside Luce decided not to run for a third term in Congress in 1946, having apparently become disenchanted with the politics of holding public office. She would later go on to serve her country with distinction as U.S. Ambassador to Italy. Luce held some progressive ideas for a conservative, including this one as an extraordinary wartime measure: "Those who can afford it," she said, "the well–to–do and the rich, must be taxed almost to the constitutional point of confiscation."[399] She recommended no exemption for her husband, Henry Luce.

If Roosevelt thought he had put the "Berne matter" behind him with his Easter message to Stalin, he was mistaken. On April 3, the Premier fired back stating flatly among other things: "As regards my military colleagues, they, on the basis of information in their possession, are sure that negotiations did take place and that they ended in an agreement with the Germans."[400] Two days later Roosevelt issued point-by-point denials and even brought Alexander's boss into the message exchange for the first time:

*I have complete confidence in General Eisenhower and know that he
certainly would inform me before entering into any agreement with
the Germans. He is instructed to demand and will demand unconditional surrender of enemy troops that may be defeated on his front. Our
advances on the Western Front are due to military action. Their speed has
been attributable mainly to the terrific impact of our air power...* [401]

To which an emotional Stalin replied in part:

*It is hard to agree that the absence of German resistance on the Western
Front is due solely to the fact that they have been beaten. The Germans
have 147 divisions on the Eastern Front. They could safely withdraw from
fifteen to twenty divisions from the Eastern Front to aid their forces on*

*the Western Front. Yet they have not done so, nor are they doing so. They
are fighting desperately against the Russians for Zemlenice, an obscure
station in Czechoslovakia, which they need just as much as a dead man
needs a poultice, but they surrender without any resistance such important towns in the heart of Germany as Osnabruck, Mannheim and
Kassel.*[402]

Amidst this diplomatic crisis General Truscott would launch *Operation Craftsman.*

The Stalin/Roosevelt message exchanges are indeed remarkable — one subject not broached in these communications likely explains why the Germans fought so hard on the Eastern Front: the Red Army waged a war of revenge and German soldiers harbored no illusions about what would be done to their womenfolk if they ended-up in the custody of the Russians. The vastly outnumbered and out-gunned German military fought furiously to buy time so their loved ones might escape to the relative humanity and shelter of the approaching Western powers. Indeed, the historian Rick Atkinson wrote this about the Red Army conduct at time the Yalta conference convened (no participants raised this as an issue to be discussed):

> *Soviet atrocities were now rampant in the east; they included the burning
> of villages, wanton murder and mass rape in East Prussia, Silesia, and
> elsewhere. By late 1945, an estimated two million German women would
> be sexually assaulted by Red Army assailants… In Königsberg, nurses
> would be dragged from operating tables to be gang raped. "Our men shoot
> the ones who try to save their children," a Soviet officer said. German
> fathers executed their daughters to spare them from further defilement.*

Atkinson estimated a "… migration of 7.5 million Germans to the west over the next few months."[403] He also stated, "The Soviets currently possessed a seven-to-one superiority over the Germans in tanks, eleven-to-one in infantry, twenty-to-one in artillery."[404]

From Stalin's perspective — and there are circumstances that at least explain the horror inflicted by the Red Army but do not justify it — his country had been viciously attacked without provocation and much of it destroyed. And the Nazi policy in retreat was scorched earth. Looking at the staggering casualty figures for his country the Soviet leader had to have been angry to the point of apoplectic.

He did not have reliable figures at this juncture for British and American loses, but most certainly he knew that the number of his casualties was astronomical compared to theirs. Indeed, it is known today that the total military deaths of World War II were: Soviet Union: approximately 13,600,000,[405] the United States 405,000,[406] Great Britain and Commonwealth, 452,000.[407] Estimates of Soviet civilian deaths vary widely, but often quoted in the range of ten to twelve million. Stalin had to have been incensed that Eisenhower was able to reap so much conquest for so little comparative sacrifice — in his top secret cable to Roosevelt, Stalin had named "Osnabruck, Mannheim and Kassel," by way of example, but he also knew there would be more cities that would quickly surrender to the Americans and British. At this late stage in the war all the average German civilian wanted to do was find a way to slip though western front lines carrying a white flag and talk about his favorite uncle in Milwaukee.

From Eisenhower's perspective, he had to have been painfully aware that the U.S. Army order of battle was far different than the Red Army's and he had to have been concerned about this. As stated earlier, of the sixteen million Americans who served in uniform throughout the world during World War II fewer than a million were engaged regularly in combat. A commentator noted: "The [U.S.] infantry represented just 14% of the troops overseas."[408] This number along with the British manpower contribution was sufficient to defeat the Nazis in western Germany but it would not deter the Red Army from additional aggression if Stalin chose to wage it.

This analysis on Eisenhower's part likely led to another reason for Stalin's perturbation with Roosevelt. On the night of February 13 and the following day British and American heavy bomber forces laid waste to the City of Dresden, a good-sized city previously untouched, and afterwards put out a press release having the audacity to claim:

> "Both the Eighth Air Force and RAF attacks on Dresden were in support of one offensive of Marshal Koniev's forces, smashing toward the city in a bid to cut the Reich in two... "

Some thirteen square miles of city had burned to the ground and untold scores of thousands of Germans killed. While it is doubtful that Stalin had sympathy for the victims incinerated, this event clearly demonstrated the incredible destructive power of the British and U.S. air armadas (which is no doubt what

Eisenhower wanted the Soviets to see). And no doubt, Koniev, after capturing the smoldering ruins of Dresden, did see it and reported what he saw to Stalin. The Soviet military juggernaut was powerful, yes, but did not contain in its arsenal the 4,000 heavy bombers that Great Britain and America possessed. When the Swedish press ran the story of a terror bombing Stalin had his propagandists join in the worldwide condemnation, claiming that this act had not been done at the request of the Soviet Union.

Stalin also had to be aware of the breakneck industrial production going on particularly in the United States. In Detroit, for instance, the Ford Motor Company was turning out B-24 heavy bombers at a rate of one an hour and this was being matched by Boeing with other models in other areas of the country. Having accomplished so much for mother Russia Stalin may have thought, why press his luck?

On April 4 Bill wrote Dotty that his next day would be spent in the country. He also told her of his walking through Leghorn proper but did not mention the name of the city: "I hope it never comes to America," he wrote. "I am not permitted to describe conditions but one has to see it to believe." On the 7th he penned her a brief note: "Missed writing you yesterday... worked last night until after eleven o'clock. I am not too satisfied with results but we are doing all we can," followed by, "I visited two more units today... I have waited for a long time to visit all of the truck companies in the area." Bill's task was large. Records show that for the final American offensive in Italy, the U.S. Fifth Army had five heavy QMC truck companies (with ten-ton semi-trailers) and twenty-six light QMC truck companies that drove the workhorse of the truck fleet, the Deuce and A Half.[409] Also there were the many PBS QMC truck companies to incorporate into the mix for the final assault. Bill had done a lot of traveling.

With the end of the European war in sight, Dick posed a carefully thought out question to Sue:

> *There is a strong possibility that those of us who do not have a lot of over-seas service will have to stay here quite some time and may never have to go to CBI. Which would you prefer that I do — assuming of course I have a choice?[410]*

"CBI" stands for "China, Burma, India Theater of Operations," a geographically defined area of war. A concern of G.I.s serving in Italy was that after V-E Day they would be promptly shipped through the Suez Canal to this theater to join in the fight against Imperial Japan. Dick had to know that the U.S. military would not give him a choice in this matter; like so many scores of thousands of husbands serving in Europe, Dick did not want to unduly upset his wife over what he knew would be coming so he created a fiction of hope to breach the subject matter with her and also to make her feel that she was participatory. His kind sentiment to his wife makes for an endearing family record. As will be seen, USAAF units were the first to be redeployed after V-E Day; the supply officers for these units, perhaps not immediately in every case, would surely quickly follow. This would be an easy vote for Sue to cast — stay in peacetime Italy for as long as possible! Apart from war, CBI had disease to offer.

On a side note, G.I.s around the world had taken to jokingly referring to "CBI" as standing for "Confusion Beyond Imagination." John Lesesne noted in his diary: "We all pray for leave in the States before going to CBI."[411] John had no doubt read Luce's prognostications in the *Stars and Stripes* and somehow wished, hope upon hope, that America would send those who had never served overseas to CBI first.

As D-Day approached, General Truscott prepared for the attack. G-2, Army Intelligence, informed him that eight German Divisions and one Italian division opposed the U.S. Fifth Army where it would attack and that there were two additional German divisions held in reserve south of the Po River. All in all, the U.S. Fifth Army faced 789 enemy guns, made up of light artillery, antitank and self-propelled guns. Included in this figure were forty-seven tanks "employed as artillery."[412] Earlier, U.S. observers had witnessed situations where the Germans used one truck to pull two other trucks and also oxen to place artillery pieces. What was unknown however, was how much fuel reserve they had conserved for use in battle. Was the fourteen-day prediction from G-2 accurate? Would the German tanks back out of their dugouts and maneuver? There was going to be a major shoot out, no doubt. The good news for Truscott was there was no indication of an enemy build-up west of Highway 64.

In the middle of this springtime arrived. "Grass is almost knee high," Bill wrote, and he noted that the Italians south of the Gothic Line were attempting to rebuild. "If only the people [Ed: the Italians] had more to work with," Bill empathized in his usual fashion. "They remove the rubble of destroyed buildings and place the pieces back on each other starting to build the endless walls. They expect and get so little of the material things we enjoy. In the hurry and hustle of operations one grows so calloused toward their state. So many of them are very skilled workmen, especially in stone, wood, etc. If only they had more resources to work with."

The Allied spring offensive actually started four days before D-Day on the Ligurian coastal plain south of Massa during the early morning hours of April 5, when the Japanese-Americans of the 442nd Regimental Combat Team followed by another U.S. regiment from the 92nd Infantry Division, the 370th moved out. From Truscott's perspective, this first military operation was small in scope, but he knew the enemy could not be sure of this. He was pleased that Eisenhower had agreed to return the 442nd from Southern France, for he knew this highly-decorated regiment would provide just the shock value needed to get the German's attention. War was nothing more than intimidation on a mass scale, Truscott appreciated, and the quickest way to end it was to wage it in an absolutely brutal fashion. These Japanese-Americans (no doubt to prove their loyalty to country) fought fanatically. The use of the 442nd in front of the 92nd Division "Buffalo Soldiers" may have been intended by the U.S. Army as a means to demonstrate how aggressive warfare should optimally be waged, and at the same time (for lack of a softer word) ... humiliate the 92nd? Appreciating the terrible state of race relations in Jim Crow America at this time, yes, this claim may be historically accurate. One can reasonably envision numbers of white soldiers laughing mean-spiritedly and jokingly about this. The 366th, the unit that got into the most trouble at Serchio Valley became a service unit — doing everything but fighting.

World War II was largely a racial war. In Europe there was the Master Race against the Slavs and the Jews and in the Pacific there was enough ethnic and cultural hatred to fuel a take-no-prisoners mind-set for all combatants. And *within* the American armed forces? As stated, there were many African-American G.I.s who viewed they were fighting two enemies, the second being the U.S. Army.

The U.S. Army negative racial experience in World War II Italy undoubtedly weighed in on President Truman's decision to integrate the U.S. armed forces by executive order in 1948. This act on Truman's part put into play (in progressive circles for sure) the validity of the long-standing "separate but equal" constitutional doctrine. Arguably Truman's act contributed to the birth of the U.S. Civil Rights movement.

—∿—

Captain John Lesesne noted: "On the night of the 3rd [April] we moved out of the line into bivouac for re-equipment and physical conditioning … we hiked, played football, softball etc." John wrote church services were "well attended" which was understandable, his "boys" sensing that the time had arrived to pray. John wrote of he and others attending strategy sessions with members of the 361st and 363rd Infantry Regiments. John was proud to be able to finish the war supporting elements of the 91st Infantry Division. Leon Weckstein wrote earlier about calling in for mortar fire. Did he request fire from Company "B"?

For Clare Boothe Luce the time had arrived for her to pack up and depart Italy — which she did for Paris on April 7. Before she returned to the United States Luce would experience something that would haunt her for the rest of her life — she made an inspection trip to the Buchenwald concentration camp, liberated April 11 by Patton's Third Army. This, and other recent events in her life — the tragic loss of her only child, the harsh political environment — that she had fostered on herself — adulterous relationships with high-powered men, intense, exciting but not permanent, had changed Luce, no doubt. She would soon seek out mental and spiritual help, and adapt to remain the remarkable person that she was (her serial lovers would continue however).

On the same day that Luce left Italy Dick arrived in Rome for his much antici-pated few days of vacation leave. Staying at Hotel Savoy he wrote to his wife that he needed the rest, indicating that he had been "… run around the past few weeks." Dick connected what he saw with home: "The Tiber is like the Trinity [River in Texas] …" he wrote. "It is the Tiber that reminds me darling of our blessings." He commented on the Vatican Guard with their funny uniforms, "knee britches, capes and quaint hats," but most of his long letter pertained to family matters. Dick enjoyed touring Rome, yes, and before he became deathly ill, also Pisa and Florence. He would rather have been in Texas, however. Like Bill, his loneliness comes out in all of the letters.

In Berne, Allen Dulles appreciated that his job as a peace seeker was about to become considerably more difficult. When the fighting started up, which he was now sure it would, disengaging the armies would present a real challenge. There was nothing Dulles could do about this circumstance, however, other than wait and see what opportunities might develop. It was good for him to have both Clover and Mary with him and each enjoying the other's company.

In the north Bill had worked himself into a frazzle and was about to pay a price for it. He had seen the suffering this war had caused and he had written home about it. More than anything else and like everyone else, he simply wanted the war over *and now*.

John moved his boys up on the 10th, the date he stopped writing a diary. The 91st was so close to the front line he reported three German soldiers ("Krauts" as called them) being captured 200 to 300 yards ahead. John saw these POWs and recorded this: "Three kids, ill-clothed, ragged, and dirty." The killing in Italy en masse was about to re-commence; the U.S. Army history for the 100th Chemical Mortar Battalion will tell the rest of John's and Company "B"'s story. Indeed, Company "B" fought.

The U.S. Fifth Army history written immediately after the war portrayed American soldiers as "... straining at the leash..."[413] for the final assault to commence, but Staff Sergeant Leon Weckstein who had been in the thick of it since Rome with the 363rd Infantry Regiment (that had experienced considerable combat since the previous summer) was honest in admitting that he dreaded what he knew was coming. Writing it was "wishful thinking" to believe the Germans might give up, he observed: "... those defenders of the black swastika acted like a rattlesnake that refuses to die after decapitation."

Weckstein had a strong personal reason to kill Germans. His war biography tells of a remarkable event that happened on March 29, 1945 as the date approached for the North Apennines Campaign to commence:

> I had just returned from Florence where I attended the largest Passover service ever held in Italy and maybe the world. Several thousands of G.I.s of my faith, all from the Allied forces, had congregated at the unusable train station downtown to participate in a massive Seder and delicious repast of typical holiday fare. Apparently, back home our rabbis had managed to persuade the producers of matzos and kosher wines to subsidize the auspicious event.[414]

Military chaplains had planned this religious event. One can imagine the emotion of the Jewish attendees upon hearing the story of the liberation of their people from Egyptian bondage. Thinking about this event today one has to ask: in our progressive secular run country would military chaplains be permitted to do this? The cover of the program for this event bears the symbol of the U.S.

Fifth Army and can be located on the website of the United States Holocaust Memorial Museum.[415]

Bill's angst built up as the date approached; it would manifest itself in a special letter he wrote to Dotty a couple of days later. On the morning of April 9, D-Day, the day the British Eighth Army was to launch its major offensive, Bill wrote Dotty a V-mail stating he "had experienced chills all day" and that he suffered a fever the previous night.

D-Day commenced with a massive aerial bombardment. "Nothing like it had been seen before in Italy," the U.S. Fifth Army history recorded. Five hundred heavy bombers belonging to the U.S. Fifteenth Air Force, four engine B-17s and B-24s, each capable of carrying between 5,000 to 6,000 lbs. of high explosive bombs, took off in waves from Foggia and headed towards the Gothic Line. These bombers had heretofore been used primarily against industrial targets outside of Italy. This day they aimed at enemy transportation and marshaling yards in no fewer than eleven areas at or near where the Eighth Army advance was to occur.[416] The U.S. Twelfth Air Force also joined the fray, as did the RAF; additionally there was a huge artillery barrage. *19 Days* described:

> *Then finally a fresh wave of heavies went over — but dropped no bombs. By now the Boche had become practiced in ducking, and as he ducked, the Eighth Army took off.*[417]

The British 5th Corps and Polish 2nd Corps led the charge, crossed the Senio River and advanced steadily. At 6:45 p.m. that evening, Bill wrote Dotty an airmail letter: "This morning I wrote that I was not feeling so well yesterday. If this arrives first I just want to say I am all OK now."

Bill white-lied.

His letter continued: "My Colonel called today from my home station to see how we were getting along. [He] will be glad when this project is completed and hopes the results will be satisfactory. The two other members of my team are good men and carry a fair share of the load." He added that his Colonel was "very nice." Bill had to have been upset however, or at least anxious in the extreme. On top of this, he was becoming ill.

What had Bill and the others been arranging? These transportation specialists were tasked with pulling off a one-day performance so the surprise planned by Trustcott would succeed. Timing was everything and the responsibility was awesome. *19 Days* recorded:

> To support the action in the IV Corps sector it was necessary to establish
> dumps up the valley along Highway 64. The sites for these were spotted
> but not stocked until the last night before the attacks but then every truck
> that could be found was sent up; by evening of D-Day regular issues were
> being made from the new dumps.[418]

On April 10 at 5:39 p.m. Bill wrote his parents and complained about "fighting a light cold for a couple of days," undoubtedly the same malady that he wrote about twice to his wife the day before. He informed his parents that he had seen the leaning tower and added that in a few days he expected "… to return… to complete the second half of the job."

On the date he wrote this Bill and the others were making preparations for what would become known in U.S. Army history as the North Apennines Campaign. "They say April is a rainy month but it has not been one so far this year," he indicated, making no reference to how important this dry weather had been for what he and many others were doing. In point of fact the weather had been so dry that army engineers poured water and oil on dirt roads in a half-successful attempt to inhibit telltale dust from rising.

On the same day approximately two hours later, perhaps influenced by fever, or simply so fatigued that his emotions poured easily onto paper, Bill wrote an impassioned letter to Dotty about his world view for America. He had seen the U.S. soldiers waiting at the front, many half his age, and he had little doubt that these men would win, but win what and at what price? Bill wanted their contribution to count for something. His comments were precipitated by a reported incident at home involving his son. Bill responded to a letter Dotty had written earlier, relating how some older boys had spoken sharply to Davy.

> So the kids told him, "Pipe down, pee-wee?" How representative of
> Detroit. It must have been funny. How does he respond to such treatment?
> Does he have lots of comeback or feel hurt? I hope he will be a politician,
> yet know when to defend his rights.
>
> I have been thinking a lot about the future of our country, Hon. The
> present is so important, while we still have bargaining power — and yet
> we seem to make so little of our opportunities. People debate whether we

*should hold our bases, which have cost us so much in lives and equipment.
I could write so many things if it were not against regulations. Other
countries have their plans far in the future. We alone have no apparent ax
to grind over here and yet we carry the load, at least in the west. Soldiers
of other countries are so worldly-minded. At **H**ome in normal times we
have such an abundance of things lacking here. Our chief desire is to get
Home and enjoy the luxury of it all. If the rest of the world knew, and
I am sure that powers against us will see that they do, they can be led
against us so easily. Now is the time for us to occupy the important place
in dictating the peace that the world is ready to offer us and expects us
to assume. Instead, it looks like we would become a puppet at the peace
conference, bowing and scraping, and glad-handing all the latecomers — afraid to offend and cautious to our own subjugation.*

*Well, enough of that for now. I just had to blow off some steam. There is
little you or I can do about it as citizens but as heads of a family, perhaps
we can start Davy and our little X so that they may be able to do something in the right direction.*

*I would like Davy to be a leader of men, not by force but by superior rea-
soning and honest confidence. The prime requisite is personality combined
with honesty, clear thinking, a keen mind and faith that he has a job to
do and nothing will stop him. When boys of twelve say, "Pipe down, pee-
wee," to a boy of three, or not even three, it may indicate the beginning of
a great career.*

*I guess I can't get off the pedestal, Hon., but I will try anyway. It isn't
often I feel like going strong.*

The news had broken about the difficulties with the upcoming United Nations
San Francisco Conference and it had obviously been upsetting to Bill. One can
only imagine how Bill might have reacted if he had been privy to the top-secret
correspondence between Stalin and Roosevelt. These cables were only declassified five decades after the war. As much as a monster as Stalin was, he had reason
to be upset with the Americans and British over what he knew was secretly taking
place in Switzerland.

Not mentioned in Bill's letters is the reason behind his expressed opinion
that the United States had become "*... a puppet at the peace conference, bowing*

and scraping... " Perhaps Bill's reaction was in part due to him reading an article in the *Stars and Stripes* three days earlier that accused Stalin of keeping his top man, Foreign Commissar Molotov, at home due to his displeasure over how the Americans were making such a protest over Poland. The *Stars and Stripes* published what in today's parlance would be labeled as "spin"[419] (as an aside Molotov did end-up going to San Francisco).

The following day Bill typed a one-page memo entitled "Sand Fly Fever, 4-ll April 1945, Leghorn" that described the symptoms that he experienced that went along with the "chills" mentioned to Dotty: "Angry red bites on the legs above knees, extremely itchy... severe headache... back and leg muscles lame, felt miserable... urine very dark, bowels loose... perspired... fever... muscles hurt when rolling eyes... excessive discharge of solid formations from nasal passages, eyes watery." An article written by three military doctors after the war[420] noted that Sand Fly Fever was so serious a problem in the Mediterranean Theatre that "... it was considered a likely threat to manpower in the Battle of Sicily."[421]

In Berne, Allen Dulles was excited to learn though an Italian intermediary that General Wolff was re-engaged in risk-taking activities to bring about a German surrender. Ten days had elapsed since Himmler made his phone call and Vietinghoff was Wolff's stumbling block now. In the face of military annihilation, the Wehrmacht general was bone-headed; Vietinghoff wanted certain "points of honor" met before any surrender could take place. AFHQ Caserta was not buying into this. Vietinghoff insisted on a "military surrender" with his men standing at attention, and, per Dulles, "... the Germans... returned to Germany still in possession of their belts and bayonets as evidence that they had made an orderly surrender."[422] Without these concessions Vietinghoff feared being vilified in German history as a traitor. How Wolff had handled Himmler and protected his family, Dulles did not know, but this was not his concern. One problem that was his, however, and he surely knew it, was that the word "Berne" had been used in diplomatic channels.

On April 12, 1945, as scheduled, General Truscott initiated *Operation Craftsman*[423] but U.S. troops did not really go anywhere. Bad weather had set in and Truscott was reticent about committing ground troops to an assault without heavy bomber support. Truscott was a cautious general and his men appreciated it.

The American attack started on April 15 (or late April 14 depending on the source). Eleven U.S. infantry divisions were involved in the assault, including the 10th Mountain Division[424] "... spearheading the Fifth Army drive." The 10th blasted through the remaining German defenses to gain the downslope of Mount Belvedere. "The fighting was fierce with the loss of 553 mountain infantryman killed, wounded, or missing in the first day."[425]

The U.S. Army history for the 100th Chemical Mortar Battalion shows it moving out on April 16.

Front wide, coast-to-coast, the winter respite from combat had enabled twenty-four Nazi and five Italian *Fascisti* divisions[426] facing the Allies to construct or bolster three lines of defense.[427] The first line of course was the Gothic Line that was designed to deny access to Bologna and also an east-west entry into the Po Valley[428] The second line was the Po River that was located some fifty miles to the north of the mountain range and flowed in an easterly direction toward the Adriatic Sea (the river varies from 130 to 500 yards in width). The Germans hoped to use the Po to their advantage the opposite of the way the Americans and British hoped to use it; they intended to shoot across the river from entrenched positions. The last defense, named the Adige Line, was a system of WW I-style trenches in the Alpine foothills intended as cover for a possible general withdrawal of all German forces into Austria. The Germans still had significant manpower in Italy at this final stage of the war (as stated — 300,000) but they lacked air support, equipment and supplies. Their morale had to have been horrible. What the Germans lacked in material, the Americans had plenty of — thanks to the efforts of Bill and Dick and many people like them.

Bill indicated in later life that it took a huge amount (in terms of tonnage) of supplies a day to sustain an infantry division on the move, and on April 9 all the supplies needed by the U.S. Fifth Army were at the front, courtesy of the U.S. Army Transportation Corps. "Three B's were there," Bill said: "Bread, bullets and bandages."

Shortly after *Operation Craftsman* was initiated, Bill was ordered back to Head-quarters to complete "the second half of the job," whatever that job might have been. Before he left he wrote Dotty: "Today we completed our touring around the units here ... Things are happening fast."

Sunday, April 15, 1945
Letter No. 36 8:10 a.m.

Dear Folks,

In an hour we start for the airport to return to our home station. Our mission here is finished and we now have about two weeks of the same kind of work near my regular station. It has been quite a tiresome job and one that might not be so pleasant. I believe, however, that the results will be satisfactory. I'm glad it's half over...

Sue, Dick and Pumpkin

CHAPTER ELEVEN:

THE END OF THE WAR IN EUROPE

April–May 1945

IN MID APRIL President Franklin D. Roosevelt died unexpectedly of a cerebral hemorrhage. Bill wrote about it: "… It was quite a surprise to hear of the President's death … Now we are forced to change horses. I hope our country is never again so nearly dominated by one man. The new President will have a very difficult job."

Bill's comment about President Roosevelt "dominating" the country may have been motivated more over concern for Roosevelt's unprecedented four terms than concern for his leadership. Bill often voted Republican, yes, but not in every instance. Indeed, on August 8, 1945 Bill wrote Dotty about the Detroit mayoral race: "The American system calls for changes and frequent change prevents politicians from getting too well entrenched." In that election Bill favored the labor candidate, Frankenstein.

On a side note, as for voting Republican, for 150 years Bill's ancestors lived in the foothills of Pennsylvania's Allegany Mountains where voting for the Grand Old Party of Abraham Lincoln was simply the norm, much in the same way, but opposite, as the Dixie South always voted solid Democrat.

Jack's reaction to the president's death was different than Bill's. "No man is indispensable," Jack wrote, "but it would certainly be better if he were here." Jack also offered this: "Our new president, President Truman, was sworn in immediately and said that the San Francisco conference would not be postponed. I think this was a very smart move. He has come into office at a very crucial time. The whole world will be watching him. I pray that things will work out."

Dick's comment about Roosevelt's passing was simply, "very regrettable."[429]

Roosevelt's last message to Stalin, written on the day of his death contained this: "Thank you for your frank explanation of the Soviet point of view on the Berne incident which it now appears has faded into the past without having accomplished any useful purpose."[430]

The day following Roosevelt's death Allen Dulles was summoned to Paris to meet with his boss General Donovan who wanted to discuss *Operation Sunrise*. Dulles took Gaevernitz with him and it was at this meeting (per the Dulles account) that the detail in the diplomatic exchanges between Roosevelt and Stalin were fully revealed. Dulles wrote, "Donovan's news surprised and disturbed me." "As I thought of the Soviet attitude, I began to see what was probably troubling the Soviet leaders. If we were successful in getting a quick German surrender, Allied troops would be the first to occupy Trieste…" Dulles explained that the communists might occupy Trieste by the Red Army coming in from Hungary or "Tito's followers reaching up from Yugoslavia."[431] A fair reading of the Dulles book and other histories causes one to believe that the real surprise for Dulles was that the Soviet spy network was so efficient.

On the night of April 15, after an intensive air bombardment, the U.S. Fifth Army launched an all-out attack over mountain tops and through passes in the direction of Bologna; the casualties were heavy on both sides and the fighting was described as "… fierce small unit actions that moved from ridgeline to ridge-line."[432] The British continued their advance in the east, and ended-up assisting the Americans when the U.S. Fifth Army drive temporarily stalled. Units of all nature and description were thrown into the fray.

As much as he detested living in the hovel of a bombed out Pianoro home for months on end, Staff Sergeant Leon Weckstein dreaded the prospect of hearing the words: "Be ready to move out." Weckstein wrote about what happened to him:

> Sergeant Brown answered the crank-up field phone and handed it over to Colonel Woods, who paced nearby. In his quietly official way, the colonel responded only with a minute or so of "Uh huhs," then finally ended with a firm "Wilco, out." He sighed profoundly before relating his news to us in the command group.

> "That was the general. Another regiment will be relieving us and going through our forward positions in about two hours. We're supposed to sit tight and hold this location until they tell us what sector they want us to cover."

The enormous consequences of this unexpected news didn't hit me imme-diately. It hadn't quite sunk in to my fatigued brain that my fighting days were almost at an end. Then it finally dawned on me that I'd probably live at least another day and maybe a lot longer... [433]

While Weckstein and his regiment received a reprieve, other units in the 91st did not. Nor did the 100th Chemical Mortar Battalion. Per its history: " 'D: Day' for the 100th Chemical Mortar came on Monday, 16 April 1945..." Battalion Headquarters started out operating jointly with Headquarters Company 91st Infantry Division.

Company "B" moved out on the 16th and advanced at a rapid rate, again per the history. It followed the infantry in jeeps and the progress was stop and go but satisfactory. The "push" that John referred to months earlier had finally arrived. John had undoubtedly been ordered not to take along anything extraneous on his person, and as for his diary he was aware that if captured while possessing it, the result might be a nasty interrogation in addition to losing something he wanted to keep. The diary he left behind along with other unneeded personal items.

Bill's flight to Naples had been delayed two days. On April 17th he mailed a short note to his parents announcing his safe arrival. "I have a busy day coming," he wrote.

The following day Jack King witnessed an aerial attack. "Our forward unit moved out of Lorino," he recorded, "and we moved in." "The 155th and 240th [Ed: antiaircraft battalions] set up all around us [with] the ack-ack up on the hill. Boy it will be noisy tonight."

It turned out Jack was prophetic. The Luftwaffe, long largely dormant on the Italian front, came out in force to attack the area. The following day he wrote: "Boy it *was* noisy last night! Jerry came over about 11:30 p.m. I could see his tracers and those from the ack-ack. What a sight." Jack had been in bed when the attack started.

The battle history *19 Days* described the start of the North Apennines Cam-paign as follows:

"... As the enemy line crumbled under the weight of our attack, the pace of the battle stepped up. Battle groups moved forward less cautiously, then faster, and soon were up on tanks, trucks and jeeps, pressing forward at all possible speed.

The same officers who yesterday would not order the advance without the mortars, artillery, and the air to pave the way now threw caution to the winds, and were possessed with a mad desire to get ahead and in a hurry. It may have looked like confusion and disorganization, but the scent of victory was in the air. The battle was changing from the heavy attack on an enemy in an organized defensive position to the pursuit of a not yet beaten but retreating foe."[434]

Jack recorded in his diary for April 20: "Only three Jerries came over last night. The boys [Ed: the spearhead of the 91st Infantry Division] are going great guns and are in the [Po] Valley." "We will be in Bologna by Sunday," he forecast, signifying April 22. At this point, there was little that the Germans could do militarily to forestall what was happening. Due to the speed of the Allied advance many Germans ended-up with their backs to the Po River.

19 Days described the rout:

Germans were ordered to make for the Po and get across by any means they could devise. Said one divisional order captured by the Fifth Army: "We will cross the river as individuals as best we can. Motorized vehicles will be left behind and destroyed if possible. Horse-drawn vehicles will be taken across if possible, with the horses swimming. Heavy weapons will be discarded and we will defend ourselves with rifles and machine pistols."[435]

It happened that many Germans became trapped on the southern bank of the Po River and refusing to surrender, were dealt with accordingly.

In the international diplomatic arena, the only message President Truman received from Premier Stalin during his first week in office was an appropriately-worded cable expressing condolences over the death of President Roosevelt. From the extensive fighting taking place in Italy, Stalin was aware that the Germans had not "opened up" the front as he feared might happen.

With Italy fully engaged the Third Reich was in grave trouble. All fronts, east, west and south pressed forward for the kill. In Italy, since the borders had not been agreed upon at Yalta, it was simply a question of who occupied what territory first.

The "Berne incident" seemingly was over. As stated, Dulles, however, per *The Secret Surrender* believed the diplomatic brouhaha raised by Stalin signaled something. Following his April 13 meeting with Donovan, Dulles cabled a "theory" that he had come up with to Lemnitzer: "They [Stalin et al] desired to get their hands on Trieste," Dulles wrote, "and North Italy before the Allies could occupy the area."[436]

Dulles knew European history as well as current events. Over two hundred years earlier Peter the Great became great by opening a Baltic seaport for Russia through the means of warfare against then powerful Sweden. Dulles had to have thought: Was Joseph Stalin about to do the same for Russia with the Adriatic Sea?

Trieste was a major port city, annexed to Italy following World War I, and before that historically part of the Habsburg Empire. Italy had no clear claim to the city other than having it awarded as the result of being on a winning side in the previous world war. Looking at a map, Dulles had to have appreciated the strategic military advantage the Soviet Union would achieve if it gained the port city of Trieste. The Soviet Navy would gain a second entry point into the Mediterranean.

Dulles also had to have asked himself: Did the Red Army or its surrogates — Tito for instance — hope to link-up with Italian communist partisans who would be holding parts or perhaps all of certain major cities in Northern Italy? Marshal Tito had recently emerged as the clear leader in Yugoslavia, and was having considerable military success; the British and Americans viewed him as a minion to Stalin (at this time frame there was no reason not to).

Surely Dulles had to be thinking along these lines in mid-April 1945. It is not an exaggeration to say that Dulles detested the Hammer and Sickle as much as the Swastika, and that he viewed communism as a monolithic force of oppression bent on world domination through a form of state-dictated economic slavery. And had not Stalin purged his own country from 1935 to 1937 in order to stay in power? The Red Army had gotten the worst of this reign of terror but also government officials, intellectuals, priests and even peasants died, and how many hundreds of thousands or even millions all told? And before that had he not liquidated a huge number of Ukrainians? Bolshevism, well intentioned at its beginning perhaps, had become a monstrosity in the decades leading up to World War II.

Being true to history the argument can be made that Truman, Marshall, Eisenhower, and Alexander all shared the same view about the Soviet Union as did Allen Dulles. At the tactical command mission level — Clark and Truscott — political decisions were seldom made or even discussed. At the military theater level and above, however — Alexander and up — that was not the case.

Looking back and pondering on the information that Donovan had provided to him on April 13, Dulles had to have felt that Stalin had nothing to lose by protesting so vigorously *Operation Sunrise*. The fact that Stalin may have had a spy ring at work did not really matter; in the end it would be a mechanized race between the East and West, nothing more, nothing less and all the pre-war area of Northern Italy would be the prize.

As regards Northern Italy Dulles now, on April 20, appreciated something exciting and important. What Stalin wanted could be prevented if proper actions were quickly taken. The Gothic Line had been breached! The Yugoslav Army was better situated than Stalin's Red Army to take the city of Trieste, but it was perhaps a week away, and maybe longer. Dulles had to have sensed that what was to become known in western Europe as "the American Century" was doable. Italy could be "liberated" as a whole nation along with practically all of central and western Europe!

Dulles had to have been thinking: if there was still a way to get the Germans to lay down their arms in Italy the process of British and American expansion into contested areas could go forward all the faster. The Germans were de facto defeated but not yet surrendered.

At Caserta General Lemnitzer also thought ahead: what U.S. infantry division might end-up best positioned to carry out a show of force if it came to that? If a face-off were to develop, any antagonist could be stared down with a proper use of force.

A seminal quote attributed to Allen Dulles later in life justified, in his mind, his plotting with an enemy general to the exclusion of an ally. Many political writers today take strong exception to what Dulles did, but at the time he did it the leadership of America and Great Britain did not. During the Cold War years Dulles explained why he did what he did:

> One of our greatest assets is that all men aspire to be equal and free. This fact haunts the rulers of the Kremlin today for even they cannot change this law of nature and they know it. It is up to us, not only by example but by positive acts, to make the most of this driving force within mankind.

The Berne incident was supposedly a thing of the past, but it still needed to be put to rest for the official record. Dulles arrived at his office on Saturday,

April 21 to find a cable waiting for him that had been sent the previous day from Washington, D.C.:

> BY LETTER TODAY JCS DIRECT THAT OSS BREAK OFF ALL CONTACT
> WITH GERMAN EMISSARIES AT ONCE. DULLES IS THEREFORE
> INSTRUCTED TO DISCONTINUE IMMEDIATELY ALL SUCH TACTS.

The telegram continued stating that the Combined Chiefs of Staff (this would be the Americans and British) determined "... it is clear... that German commander-in-chief Italy does not intend to surrender his forces at this time on acceptable terms... accordingly, especially in view of complications which have arisen with Russians, the U.S. and British governments have decided OSS should break off contacts... that whole matter is to be regarded as closed and that the Russians be informed..."[437]

The fact that the U.S. and British highest commands had collaborated on a message that mentioned Dulles specifically by name is perhaps the clearest indication of just how important a player Dulles had become in the MTO. This communication would later beg historians to ask the question: did the Combined Chiefs really mean what they "instructed"? Or was their cable a ruse — a wink and a nod — to obfuscate a cloak-and-dagger bargaining situation with a most nefarious, criminal enemy that was still ongoing?

It turned out that Jack King had been a little off on his forecast for the liberation of Bologna; the city fell on Saturday and not Sunday as he had predicted. "We entered Bologna today at 1:15 a.m.," Jack wrote on April 21. "The Fifth and the Eighth Army were said to have entered simultaneously but I think we were the first," he embellished proudly. Jack's daily diary inspiration when he wrote this was: "Nothing is impossible to a valiant heart." — *motto of Henry IV.*

Jack was miffed, however, that a reporter from the *Stars and Stripes* failed to laud the 91st for its lead in taking the city. He complained bitterly to his diary: "The papers always keep mentioning the 10th Mountain Division... but the spearhead, that was us! I can't understand why they can't say who we are! Should give the boys credit!"

Bologna had fallen to the Allies only six days after *Operation Craftsman* had launched.

The history for the 100th Chemical Mortar Battalion reports, "For the period from 16 April to 22 April the Headquarters and Headquarters Company were attached to the 91st Infantry Division." The 100th would act independently on a need/request basis from April 23 until the end of the war. Again, from the battalion history:

> So rapidly did the advance go that by 23 April battalion rear moved from Filigare and set up at Casalecchio. The following day Companies A and B fired in support of crossings over the Po. A continued advance brought a further displacement of Battalion Rear to Miradola.

Within a week, headquarters of the 100th had travelled twenty-three miles up Highway 65 and was ten miles north of the town of Pianoro. Given the fact that Highway 65 was the most heavily defended area of the Gothic Line at Pianoro, how did these American G.I.s accomplish advancing at the average rate of five plus miles per day, a good distance through an intensely fortified area?

If John had kept a diary it would have reported he pursued a fleeing enemy. To the west of Highway 64, II Corps had gone up, over and debouched, just as Truscott had planned. This American spearhead was then in a position to strike in any direction; the German command had no choice but to abandon their fortified positions at Pianoro and make a run for it. If they stayed in their bunkers the Americans would have surrounded them. Truscott pulled it off — he fooled the Germans as to where the attack would take place.

In 1952 while in prison, writing secretly from memory, former Luftwaffe Field-Marshal Albert Kesselring wrote:

> From the middle of October the situation south of Bologna gave matter for grave concern. If one or another sector in the Po plain between Bologna and the Adriatic were lost it might be of secondary importance, but if the front south of Bologna could not be held then all our positions in the Po plain east of Bologna were automatically gone — in which event they must be evacuated in good time so at least to save the troops and material. Therefore all our strongest divisions must be fed to this part of the Apennines.[438]

In a subsequent chapter in his memoirs he described the result: "C.-in-C. South-West (Army Group C, Italy) had suffered such serious losses in the fighting south of the Po that retirement was difficult and a stand in the well-constructed

Southern Alps Line jeopardized."*439* Finally, looking back at "Northern Italy after the Apennine Battles," Kesselring simply wrote, "Allied strategy showed a remarkable improvement."*440*

Combat ended for the 100th Chemical Mortar Battalion at month's end with its headquarters located at Vicenza. This mortar battalion tally for the Northern Apennines and Po Valley Campaigns was impressive:

> *During April and the offensive the battalion fired 637 missions, silenced five enemy MG positions, hit thirteen German dugouts, took 243 prisoners of war, and fired fifty-six special smoke missions. Ammunition expenditure reached a high of 22,159 rounds of which 13,271 were HE and the rest WP.*441

Dick celebrated the good news of Bologna falling and the general advance at a nighttime poker party in Naples. Sue had mailed him smoked cheese and crackers to which "… three cans of American beer, the first we've had over here," were added. He wrote: "It was fun and I won $3.00. Oh, boy."*442*

On Monday morning April 23 Bill completed a project in Rome as part of a three-officer team, and had some time for sightseeing. He wrote Dotty about touring St. Peters, and conveyed to her the surest sign yet that the war was winding down: "I saw a U.S. citizen here today with his wife and little girl. Some are coming to live here for years and bringing their families." He added: "Surely it can't last much longer." Bill stayed in a hotel and liked it: "… first bed springs since home."

On that same Monday, Allen Dulles received a phone call from the Italian intermediary who was one of the men responsible for bringing Wolff into Switzerland on March 8. Per Dulles, Wolff at that time was last known to have "disappeared into Hitler's bunker" *443* where (it was learned subsequently) he had been summoned to answer accusations made against him by Himmler and Kaltenbrunner. When he received the call Dulles did not know whether Wolff was captive or otherwise disposed. Dulles used the word "astounding" to describe the news he received: Wolff and two lower ranking German military officers, each with full powers to sign surrender documents were coming to Switzerland to surrender the German Army in Italy and Austria. The upshot of this was Dulles reporting the news to Donovan and Alexander, and subsequently being ordered by the CCS in Washington to do nothing that "... could be construed as a continuation of *Sunrise*."[444]

Dulles had been removed. His very name had been associated with the "Berne incident" and *Operation Sunrise* and his actions in meeting secretly with an SS general had offended the leader of the Soviet Union, the West's most important ally in the war against Nazi Germany.

Dulles was out.

The CCS communicated additionally, however, that it was acceptable *for the Swiss government* to meet independently with the German emissaries to ascertain if they acted on their own volition (i.e., free of promises that may have been made by *Operation Sunrise*) and had proper credentials — signing authority. If yes-yes to both questions, then the Swiss government had permission of the CCS to communicate directly with AFHQ Caserta.

Dulles does not indicate in his account whether he and Waibel laughed over this, but chances are they did.

In the week to come there would be additional exasperating delays in the surrender process and considerable gnashing of teeth on all sides, but yes, the proverbial "ship" had left the dock. Perhaps it is gratuitous to add but the Swiss government undoubtedly felt it needed a Russian led communist government across its border as much as a dead man needed a wound dressing.

On April 25 Bill wrote Dotty: "This afternoon a considerable load was eased on my mind. Our project is all but completed. The final report is being written and in process of being typed. It was a good experience but I am glad it is over... The Army in Italy is finally breaking loose."

And winning the Allies were. On the same day Jack recorded in his diary: "The boys are having a picnic, have taken Jerry trucks to try and keep up with them. Truckloads of Jerries are coming back — kids thirteen and fourteen years old, old men about forty-five. One of the boys brought in a luger." Although a rout was taking place, the war was not over. Jack added: "Forward C.P. shelled and one killed."

Losing badly, some of the enemy still was not yet ready to give up. "About this time [April 25] both the German Military and the SS staffs were in the process of moving to Bolzano in the South Tyrol," Allen Dulles noted.[445] The SS headquarters in Bolzano was the Palace of the Duke of Pistoia, and commanded by General Wolff; in this edifice there was a secret hideout where "Little Wally," a Czech radio operator, worked for Dulles. Bolzano was 138 miles north of Bologna, and the retreat there bought the Nazis a little time. Wolff or his representatives could not come to Switzerland as easily as had been hoped; Hitler still lived, the Gestapo remained, and German generals vacillated.

The following day Bill had a compliment for Mussolini (who would be captured and executed two days later) and the resilience of the Italian people: "If Mussolini had just kept on the ball, he could have done great things for this country," Bill wrote. "Before the war they were planning for a world's fair here and many of the buildings were being constructed just outside of Rome. They certainly are beautiful. On the Appian Way, south of Rome, it runs for miles thru the Pontine marshes. There, he built good houses and laid out farms, pumped the water out of the marshes and established a homesteading project. The Victor Emmanuel Memorial in Rome is huge, in white marble and so elaborate they call it a wedding cake. It also was built by Mussolini. The Italian people feel he went "crazy in the head." [Ed: Bill was incorrect about Mussolini building the Victor Emmanuel II monument. The huge shinny-white "Altar of the Nation" was dedicated in 1911 in honor of the unification of Italy fifty years earlier].

Relieved that his military mission would no longer be a matter involving possible life or death for American soldiers if he failed to do competent work, Bill concluded: "I have determined not to take my job so seriously as in the past…"

In the meantime, southern Italy continued to wear on all American servicemen. Lieutenant Dick Stroud wrote home in reference to the Naples area: "I've never seen an Italian take a drink of water," noting further that: "Diseases of all sorts are prevalent."[446] Dick wrote this not knowing that in his personal case his observation about diseases would soon prove prophetic. Three days later Dick wrote Sue: "I, long ago, thought the Europeans would be highly educated, highly cultured… they are, about 2% of them…"[447]

In a letter to Dotty dated April 27, Bill discussed a R.O.T.C. classmate at the University of Michigan who had activated in the Army prior to Pearl Harbor and progressed quickly up the ranks to "full-bird" colonel. "I am amused at Ray's desire to get out of the Army. When it comes to applying for a discharge, I'll wager he will not be anxious. I don't believe his civilian job paid nearly as well… I'm afraid he will be disappointed if he expects rank in the Army to establish him in civilian brackets."

Reflecting back on R.O.T.C., his twelve-year career as an army reservist and his friend Ray's desire to leave the active duty army, Bill now weighed whether he wanted to continue to hold his reserve commission after the war. His overriding goal was to be with his family and to do the engineering work that he wanted to do. Was the promise of a military pension worth the risk of being recalled for yet another war?

Dick Stroud didn't have twelve years invested in the military reserve, but he viewed the issue largely as Bill did: "Almost ten years of habits were broken suddenly when I went into the army… that is a shock," he wrote Sue at the end of April. "My chief desire now is that this separation from my family be ended and as quickly as possible."

For John Lesesne's part he did not care to see his friends in the service at home experience deployment. On this subject in November he wrote: "Got a letter from Jack S — expects to come over soon — he won't come if he can possibly get out of it — guess he's wise at that."[448]

In a similar vein, in the same letter to Dotty, Bill discussed a married couple back home that had been good to her during her pregnancy. The husband, Bill later related, had enrolled in a seminary school with no intention of becoming ordained in order to bolster his claim of conscientious objector status. In his letter Bill wrote about this man: "I suppose I should resent Rich's not being in service but I am a pacifist myself and have wished many times that I had never taken R.O.T.C."

As of April 28 Jack King, 19, was of a somewhat different mindset. Things had gone so swimmingly with the assault that he wanted to be nearer to the action! Jack complained that HQ Company was "… still in Lorino," and the tenor of his additional comments show that he was not pleased about this circumstance. "Even PBS is passing us by," he bemoaned, a clear reference that rear echelon MTOUSA was more into the fight than he! "Our first lines are supposed to be 130 miles away."

By April 29 both the 91st and the 100th were in the vicinity of Vicenza but their headquarters were detached — the 91st no longer needed heavy mortar support.

—⚉—

The final Allied assault, planned by General's Truscott, McCreery and Clark and approved by Field Marshal Alexander, was as successful as any military plan could possibly be. *19 Days* dedicates a chapter towards its end paying tribute to our "Our informal allies" — the partisans. As stated, one of the big concerns was that the major Italian industrial cities would be destroyed, either intentionally by order of Hitler, or inadvertently by the vicissitudes of war. *19 Days* reported:

> *The Po Valley campaign was unique in that not one important city needed to be besieged; not one put up a protracted, determined resistance. Most were "occupied" rather than "captured" some with virtually no fighting, others after sharp conflict with enemy rearguard troops.*[449]

The reason for this was twofold: first, the juggernauts put on by the American and British armies bypassed most cities "… rendering [them] incapable of being held by any normal military standards," and second, the partisans "… who made the cities so hot for the Germans that even a suicide defense was out of the question."[450] Recognizing that many partisans were communist and others not, the U.S. Fifth Army decided to thank all partisans for saving American lives. Special kudos were awarded to these civilian warriors for the liberation of "Milan, cradle of Italian fascism …":

> *When the first Americans entered Milan they found the partisan headquarters in a prominent building, boldly labeled and with the Italian colors draped across the street. Streetcars were running, electric lights were burning, and the water supply was intact. The customary sabotage by the enemy when he was driven out of a city was nowhere to be seen.*[451]

On April 28 at approximately 2:00 p.m. two German military representatives dressed in civilian attire, one a Wehrmacht officer and the other Waffen-SS, arrived at Allied Forces Headquarters, Caserta, under a confidential safe-conduct.[452] Each carried a short letter written by his commanding general stating the bearer "is authorized to make binding commitments."[453] Accompanying the German envoys as interpreter at the request of Field Marshal Alexander was Gero von Schultz Gaevernitz[454] (the persona non grata Dulles was nowhere to be seen).

It had been agreed beforehand that introductions were to be made with head nods only; that there would be no handshaking. The enemy officers were driven to a barbed wire fenced compound on top of the hill behind the palace and above its cascades — the same hill that Bill had hiked earlier for the beautiful view of the

Bay of Naples and Mt. Vesuvius. There was no view for the Germans, however. As a security precaution the entire compound had been wrapped in canvas; no one could see in or out. After drinking tea, the Germans were given copies of voluminous surrender documents and left to examine them in the company of Gaevernitz. It would be this and the following day that the right hand man of Allen Dulles would put the cap on that special medal to be awarded him personally by Harry Truman. The SS Major had for the most part been ordered by Wolff to sign whatever was put in front of him and bring a copy back to German headquarters at Bolzano post haste. The other German officer, a Lieutenant Colonel Schweinitz was a bag of nerves. He believed that his commander, Wehrmacht General Heinrich von Vietinghoff, the old-school career militarist, had sent him south with the discretion to negotiate "points of honor." Gaevernitz acted in a capacity far more than just an interpreter — he served as Schweinitz's father confessor, hand-holder and best friend.

At 9:00 p.m. a second meeting was held and this time a Russian general and his interpreter attended. The Germans were asked if they had questions. Haggling over minor points ensued; German officers in the field were to be permitted to *temporarily* retain their side arms pending the final surrender (to maintain order) and the Germans were to be allowed to use their military transports for the delivery of food (only) to their units. The surrendering German representatives and most particularly Schweinitz wanted a guarantee that their units would be demobilized in Italy and promptly returned to Germany, as they had been allowed to do in World War I; he did not receive it.[455]

The following day, April 29 at 2 p.m., the German envoys signed an "Instrument of Local Surrender of German and Other Forces Under the Command and Control of the German Commander-in-Chief Southwest." At the time of the signing German forces in Italy were so scattered it was necessary to make the cease-fire effective at 1200 hours on 2 May so the German high command could have time to locate their soldiers and "get the word out."[456] This was to become the only negotiated surrender of a German Army during World War II.[457] Dulles and company had pulled off *Operation Sunrise*. At the time the German surrender took effect the U.S. Fifth Army had taken more than 80,000 prisoners[458] and the British had taken a high number also. The military struggle continued, however. Indeed, *19 Days* detailed a military contribution specific to the 91st Infantry Division a day after the document had been signed:

The Army boundary was now shifted to a north-south line through
Treviso, to relieve heavy pressure on the Eighth Army. Immediately the
91st, advancing east south of Highway 53, passed Vicenza, crossed the
Brenta River, and drove on to take Treviso, only twelve miles due north of
Venice, before it halted and began mopping-up operations. It was at this
point that the remnants of the German 14th Army, which had been delay-
ing the Eighth along the Po, were frantically attempting to escape through
a narrowing gap between Treviso and the sea. On 30 April elements of the
91st and the South Africans linked up with the British 6th Armored Divi-
sion just east of Treviso and closed the trap.[459]

The document of surrender (that contains three appendixes, one each for the
German land, naval and air forces) placed many duties on the "German Authority" and promised nothing significant in return — other than perhaps the implied
promise of no annihilation.

The complete text of the surrender document can be found on the Yale Law
School web site *The Avalon Project.*[460] One might think at first blush that such a
lengthy "Instrument of Local Surrender" would make for boring reading, but it
does not. This document formed the basis for disengaging hundreds of thousands
of armed men involved in full-scale combat. Was there an advantage to the Allies
in having such a detailed document?

The advantage was huge. The German high command was obligated to issue
simple and understandable orders to their forces as to exactly what they could not
do and what they must do. On the "could not" side, the Germans could not leave
their present positions, requisition or purchase "supplies from local sources" and
remove, destroy or damage any property (defined to include "all" documents).
On the "must do" side, the Germans were required to completely disarm, inform
the Allies of their numbers, locations and dispositions, identify and render safe
all minefields and booby-traps and release all prisoners.

The surrender document is well drafted, obviously the work of knowledgeable
commanders undoubtedly assisted by skilled judge advocates. Upon reading it,
notable is a section that directed the Germans to immediately stop persecuting
the Jews. The document did not mention the word "Jew"; rather it extended
Geneva Convention status "to persons who are confined, interned or otherwise
under restraint... originating from discrimination on grounds of nationality, race,
color, creed or political belief[461] (more will follow on this subject).

As stated, the German officers who signed the surrender document were of low rank: a lieutenant colonel from the General Staff and an SS-Sturmbannführer major. A lieutenant general signed for the Supreme Allied Commander of the Mediterranean Theater of Operations, Field Marshal Alexander.

Per author Richard Lamb, *Italy at War 1943-45, A Brutal Story*, the Wehrmacht lieutenant colonel tried very hard at the last minute to negotiate, "… for assurances that all surrendering Germans would be treated as POWs and kept in Italy" (presumably over fear of being delivered to the Russians). The surrender document that Schweinitz signed, however, again, contained no such assurances.[462] Gaevernitz with his people skills and sincere liking for the German people — his people despite the error of their ways — found a way to make this German feel good about himself in the honor department. For that, Gaevernitz performed a real service in the interest of peace. Two years after the war William Donovan recognized in tribute Gaevernitz's "… decisive part in the negotiations which lead to the capitulation of all German forces in Italy."[463]

In addition to surrendering German troops in Italy, German forces in the western area of Austria also surrendered, causing the *Stars and Stripes* to gloat on May 3: "This means that vital cities like Innsbruck and Salzburg are ours without a fight…" The newspaper also extolled the fact that the U.S. Fifth and British Eighth Armies "… need not begin the heart-breaking task of conquering the mountains that lead to the Brenner Pass and into Austria." An additional benefit, and a big one, was that the Italian surrender document provided a format to be considered and used in the final German surrenders taken on May 8 and May 9 — the surrenders that ultimately ended World War II in Europe.

The fact that the surrender took place at the Royal Palace in a ballroom raised the question whether Bill, then present there, had perhaps heard a rumor or otherwise sensed that maybe something important was afoot? Bill's letter to Dotty, written at 8:20 p.m. on the date of the signing, April 29, suggests not: "The war is moving pretty fast now. Everyone wonders what will happen next." The negotiations (to the extent there were discussions) had been conducted in secrecy. War correspondents were allowed to witness and photograph the short signing ceremony but the press release was delayed. Hitler was still alive, and would remain so for another nineteen hours. The Allies did not want the German commanders in Italy assassinated by the Gestapo before they issued and promulgated the agreed upon surrender order to their troops

In the early afternoon of May 2, the day the surrender was to take effect, Staff Sergeant Jack King was en route by HQ Company truck convoy to finally join up with his division. It was a lengthy and tiring trip, from Lorino to Treviso, a city north of Venice, but also fortunately, an uneventful one. Jack and his fellow soldiers did not know yet about the surrender. He wrote: "We were about the first American troops the people had seen. Some gave us wine and flowers."

At noon the following day a C-47 air dropped the *Stars and Stripes* edition that announced the German surrender in Italy. "Wonder how soon before the rest will fold up?" Jack asked in his diary. He also commented on debris remaining from the recent battle: "Quite a bit of Jerry equipment lying around," he wrote. "We walked up town where it was supposed to be off limits but it didn't make any difference. Boy, did our air force work it over. They heard that Hitler and Mussolini were here and tried to get them."

Jack observed the aftermath of the last major battle fought in Italy when the 91st linked up with the South Africans and British and received a huge contribution from the Allied air forces. This was the "narrowing gap between Treviso and the sea" mentioned in *19 Days*. The Germans had been caught in the open fleeing and had no chance.

Arriving at the same location only earlier than Jack, battle-hardened combat infantryman Leon Weckstein from the 363rd Regiment described what he saw:

> We were tongue-tied, shaken by the sight of hundreds of mauled bodies,
> Tiger and Panzer Tanks smoking or aflame, and vehicles and equipment
> of every type smashed and shattered haphazardly as far as the eye could
> see along the once scenic valley's field and river ditches. It appeared to
> us like a ghostly graveyard of immolation solemnly dedicated to Hitler's
> madness, the last dark act of a modern-day tragedy.[464]

The war in Italy was over. *19 Days* discloses U.S. Fifth Army casualties for this final battle over two separate time periods, and perhaps surprising is the high number of non-battle injured:

> In the nine days from 5 April, when the preliminary attacks on the west
> coast began, through 13 April, the eve of the all-out attack, the losses
> totaled 4,495. These included 195 killed, 999 wounded, forty-five missing
> in action, with 3,256 non-battle casualties from all causes. From 14 April
> through 2 May the losses were 12,059, which included 1,394 killed, 5,009
> wounded, seventy-four missing, with 5,582 casualties from non-battle
> causes.[465]

All totaled, 19,475 Americans died in Italy during World War II, an average of thirty-two a day.[466] For the final North Apennines and Po Valley Campaigns, the *19 Days*, the average was eighty-four a day.

In fairness it should be mentioned that other American divisions besides the 10th Mountain and the 91st Infantry were in the vanguard of the conquest of Northern Italy. The much-maligned 34th Division that had participated in the relief movement towards Serchio Valley, suffered 16,401 casualties during a twenty-month period, the highest total number for a U.S. division in the Italian war. The 88th Division, in fourteen months, suffered 13,111 casualties for a higher monthly rate. Yet other divisions took part, and on eastern Italian coast the British had sobering statistics too.

The 10th Mountain Division had been in Italy for only 114 days before the surrender. It suffered 975 killed (later adjusted to 998) and 3,849 wounded, for the highest per-month casualty rate in the Italian war: 1,209 a month.[467] The war in Italy did not fade away. It ended in a bloody spasm.

As an aside, the Dulles book reported on a meeting between two opposing commanders immediately following the cessation of hostilities: "Generals Clark and Senger, two opponents who had faced each other across the battle line all the way up Italy, talked over tactics and strategy of the war… When Clark asked Senger why the Germans stayed south of the Po to be smashed to bits instead of retreating into the mountains where they could have held out intact for a considerable period, Senger answered with one word and a shrug of the shoulders. 'Hitler.'"[468]

Regarding his trip to Rome, Bill related years later that some kind of communications center, what today might be termed a command and control, had been established there. Beyond that, there are no additional details of Bill's military activities in Rome; they were likely connected to the last battle, but this cannot be known for certain. It may be that the command in Rome communicated with the Transportation Section in the Pentagon, but that is speculation. Bill's letters state that he was not completely satisfied with the results of this project. It was no longer critical, however, as the war was on its way to being won.

What needed to be transported by Bill's section had been. In terms of material, "Naples and its satellite ports had discharged 5,711,417 long tons of general cargo."[469] By comparison, Leghorn, which had been open less than half as long, had unloaded 1,375,205 long tons of cargo.[470] On the Air Forces side (Dick Stroud et al) the job also got done — the supplies got through. MTOUSA had succeeded.

Two days after the Italian surrender was accomplished, on Friday, May 4, 1945, at approximately 11:00 a.m., U.S. Army soldiers supported by MTOUSA and ETOUSA (representing the U.S. Fifth and U.S. Seventh Armies) advanced upwards towards each other without fear of being shot at and "crossed the Brenner Pass to clasp hands."[471]

Bill was in Naples when this happened and it was still a depressing place.

Panorama of Italy [continued]

Two-by-four shops, with shelving all bare;
Gesturing merchants, arms flailing the air;
Narrow-gauge sidewalks, more like a shelf;
Butt-puffing youngster, scratching himself.

Lumbering carts, hogging the road;
Nondescript trucks, frequently towed;
Diminutive donkeys, loaded for bear;
Horse-drawn taxis, seeking a fare.

Determined pedestrians, courting disaster;
Walking the street, where movement is faster;
Italian drivers, all accident bound;
Weaving and twisting, to cover the ground.

Homemade brooms, weeds tied to a stick;
Used on the streets, to clean off the brick;
Bicycles and pushcarts, blocking your path;
Street corner politics, needing a bath.

A crowded train, with fares in the cab;
More on the cow-catcher, breeding a cab;
Miserable buses, which move with a grind;
Packed to the roof, more left behind.

Arrogant wretches, picking up snipes;
Miniature Fiats, various types;
Young street singer, hand organ tune;
Shoeless boys, a sidewalk saloon.

Garbage strewn gutters, reeking with stench;
Weatherbeaten beggar, a God-awful wench;
A boy on the corner, yelling, "Gior-nal-e";
A half-dressed urchin, fly-covered belly.

Barbers galore, with manners quite mild;
Prolific women, all heavy, with child;
Duce's secret weapon, kids by the score;
Caused by this bonus, which isn't any more.

No birth control, in this fair land;
One child in Army, two by the hand;
Page Margaret Sanger, just turn her loose;
Her gospel is needed, put it to use.

A beauteous maiden, a smile on her face;
With a breath of garlic, fouling the place;
Listless housewife, no shoes on her feet;
Washing and cooking, right out in the street.

CHAPTER TWELVE:

AFTERMATH

May 1945

THE WAR WAS OVER in Italy but there was little time for the 91st to celebrate. Tito's forces, regular and partisan, had pushed into Trieste and environs. The British and New Zealanders wasted no time deploying to the contested area and U.S. forces followed. *The 91st Infantry Division in World War II* history reported:

> *The day peace came to Italy General Livesay announced to the 91st Division that it had been selected by General Truscott for a mission of the utmost importance and delicacy: the occupation of the western part of the province of Venezia Giulia, including Trieste — a region claimed by Marshal Tito for Yugoslavia.* [472]

The first U.S. contingent to arrive on scene was the 361st Regimental Combat Team and the division history records it did so "with colors and guidons flying." The opposing forces stared each other down but fortunately there were no shooting incidents. By the evening of May 5 Americans were dug in with still more on the way. Sergeant Leon Weckstein from the 363rd probably spoke for the average dogface when he wrote:

> *With the imminent defeat of the Germans, he [Tito] and his National Liberation Army assumed for some ungodly reason that they were entitled to gobble up those fringe territories for Yugoslavia, that is until the Allies swooped into this disputed territory en masse, virtually overwhelming his forces and permanently putting an end to his willful aggression.* [473]

The reality however, was more complicated than Weckstein depicted. The 91st Division history explained the problem existing immediately after World War II:

*Although in February 1944 Field Marshal Alexander and Marshal Tito
had reached an agreement that Venezia Giulia should be administered
jointly by the British and American military governments, the area
had been conquered by Tito's forces, and a government controlled by
him announced its intention of administering it by right of conquest. In
support of our view that unilateral action should not be taken in an effort
to present the world with a* fait accompli, *the 91st Division in connection with the British Eighth Army was ordered to the area to take up
positions.*[474]

As stated, the Yalta conference in February 1945 had failed to agree upon
what power or powers would administer the region. The Yalta protocol read: "…
delegations agreed to consider them [Ed: "them" being the Italo-Yugoslav and
Italo-Austrian frontier issues] and give their views later." Tito viewed this Yalta
wording as rescinding what he had agreed to the previous year with Alexander.
Tito's position was arguable.

The war in Europe ended with two surrenders by the Germans — one taken on
May 8 at American and British headquarters at Reims and the other the following day in Berlin by the Red Army. Bill wrote of how he learned the capitulation
was coming.

May 7, 1945
Letter No. 183
3:30 p.m.

Dear Dotty and Davy:

*The news just came. It was reported that the war in Europe is over. There
was much blowing of whistles for about five minutes and then they all
stopped suddenly. Everyone was wondering if it is official or a false alarm.
At any rate Hon., I can think of no better way of celebrating than by
writing a note to you.*

*Somehow the cost of the war in lives, material and suffering leaves me so
empty I don't feel like celebrating. Those of us who are left can be thankful. I wish I had faith that we can build a future without war but I am
sure we cannot. I know of only one way and men drift further from that
every generation. Well anyway, we can at least hope — and build a bomb
cellar at the same time.*

At about the same time, Bill wrote to his parents, "We all wonder how soon it [i.e., V-E Day] will affect us and where we will go next. I dare not think there is a possibility of my going in that direction."[475] Bill would not pen such a comment to Dotty for concern over upsetting her.

On May 9, Jack traveled with Headquarters Company from Traviso to the town of Soleschiano, near Gorizia, in the province of Venezia Giulia. He noted in his diary that the trip took four hours. "We rode in a German bus," he recorded. "Was it nice."

On that day word was passed that negotiations were taking place "… to determine the boundaries and spheres of influence between Allied troops and Yugoslav troops." This was good news undoubtedly for both sides; no survivor of the German war was anxious to have fighting erupt again. The 91st Infantry Division was directed on how to behave: "Information must be collected unobtrusively and friendly relations maintained …"[476]

Headquarters Company situated itself in the centrally located municipality of Cormons, with satellite regimental command posts spread out in forward areas to the east. The region, a flat coastal plane, had historically been a gateway for the invasion of Italy. As recently as World War I the Austrians and Italians waged war for this province.

Without an international accord no nation had a clear title to Trieste.

Duty in 91st Division sector quickly became routine. Organized athletics, dances and other garrison activities served to make life pleasant for the G.I.s, and there were no serious incidents with communist forces. "While we had a presence in the area we didn't assume a combative attitude — just be alert," Jack recollected. "They had no airplanes. I don't recall ever feeling threatened."

Alexander came north to settle this matter with Tito in person, and everyone assumed progress was being made when on May 19 the announcement came out that negotiations had broken down. Alexander declared: "We are now waiting to hear whether Marshal Tito is prepared to cooperate in accepting a peaceful settlement of his territorial claims or whether he will establish them by force."[477]

The offshoot of this was the arrival of more American troops and the "… guarding all bridge, road, ammunition, and supply-point positions …". Also:

> At 2000, 20 May, Field Order no. 52 was issued, recapitulating previous
> verbal orders for certain moves and ordering further deployment of the

Division. Elements of the 361st Infantry were directed to move eastward in
the Division zone, and set up roadblocks at pointes leading into Tarnova
from the east. The southern half of the Division sector was taken over by
[Ed: unit identifications deleted]. All individuals and units were warned
not to fire on any Yugoslav or partisan troops unless first fired upon.

The tenseness of the situation may be judged from the fact that, in
addition to the ground observation posts, from 20 May until the end of
the month the Division Artillery air observation post flew observation
patrols every two hours during daylight. All artillery batteries were laid
and ready to fire in support of the infantrymen, should they be attacked
in force. All members of the division were ordered to carry individual
weapons whenever they left their company or battery areas. Lastly, radio
communication systems were set up for use in the event that ground wires
were cut.[478]

While this was going on, the 100th Chemical Mortar Battalion moved temporarily into the town of Feltre and subsequently on to Cortina, where it guarded
German hospital installations. The 100th stood 125 miles west of Trieste and was
not called upon to participate in the face-off.

For a few days the Trieste standoff ensued and senior officers from both sides
parlayed. The Yugoslav commanders reportedly issued oral threats and the American commanders responded indicating they had no offensive intentions but also
had received orders not to withdraw. The largest concern for Tito likely was Allied
airpower. Tito knew that the heavy bombers at Foggia could be brought into the
situation quickly; also that he could not match the tactical air arm of the Allies,
the fighter-bombers.

On May 24 at 1100 the crisis abruptly ended: word was passed that a diplomatic
agreement had been reached dividing the disputed region. What followed that
evening was the sound of the Yugoslav Army firing into the night sky in a face-
saving celebration of Tito's upcoming birthday. The next day a parade-ground
review of Yugoslav troops by U.S. commanders was held with honors rendered.
An evening banquet ensued given by the Yugoslavs in Trieste "where good will
was exhibited by all parties concerned."[479]

Ultimately a border was agreed upon (called the "Morgan Line" named after
a general on Alexander's staff) that ran for about seventy miles in a north south
direction from Trieste. Zones "A" and "B" were created by this line and troops

redeployed accordingly with the British and Americans going into "Zone A" to the west. Most of the city of Trieste ended-up in Zone B, but the split in the harbor made the city useless for a Soviet naval base. The Dulles objective had been achieved.

As an aside, the issue of Russia having naval access to the Mediterranean remains today. A recent news article linked "Russian Aggression" to its new ties with a debt-ridden EU member: "Greece is the only part of the Balkans accessible on several seaboards to the Mediterranean," the article stated, "and thus is a crucial gateway to and from the West.[480]

In Italy, 1945 played out as well as it possibly could for the Western alliance. Because of his covert dealings with a ranking Nazi SS officer, Dulles today is a controversial figure in history, and while the extent of his contribution to the final victory in Italy will be the subject of continuing academic debate, one thing is certain — Truman and Eisenhower regarded him as a results-based hero. Truman would lavish praise on Dulles and award him the Presidential Medal of Freedom; Eisenhower later as president would appoint him director of the CIA.

And what were the 1945 results? The infrastructure of Northern Italy had been preserved, the communist partisans within the bypassed cities such as Milan and Turin had been disarmed with "thank you" commendation ceremonies (indeed the 91st Infantry Division participated in one such event before it left Traviso when it, "… accepted the arms of twelve partisan brigades …"[481]) an Allied assault on Bolzano (planned to include the 10th Mountain Division) proved unnecessary thereby saving lives and Italy remained intact as a country with a chance that a democracy might re-emerge.

And as for the Swiss?

This nation was ecstatic. The refugees were to be repatriated and their bank vaults remained out of reach. The distance from Berne to Trieste is 475 miles.

In the middle of all this Staff Sergeant Jack King ordered roses for his mother. Life was getting back to normal.

—◊◊◊—

Current academic thinking holds that Allen Dulles' 1964 compelling read *The Secret Surrender* is accurate regarding the part of the story it tells (only part) and misleading in a number of respects. In 2013 Cambridge University Press published a book authored by Kerstin von Lingen that contained this as its introductory paragraph:

> "Conspiracy" generally means the secretly arranged agreement between two parties to the detriment of a third. This definition certainly applies to the negotiations held in Switzerland starting in March 1945 between Allen Dulles from the U.S. intelligence service in Europe and Karl Wolff, the highest ranking SS and police leader in Italy, on a separate surrender of the German Army Group C in northern Italy. These negotiations, known under the code name Operation Sunrise, were conducted and an agreement reached between the German Wehrmacht and the Western Allies to the exclusion of their Soviet ally. The agreement gave the Anglo-American troops military, political and strategic advantages in the region around Trieste, and enabled them to bypass the feared German Alpine Fortress and to advance directly into southern Germany without any major troop losses. Therefore, Operation Sunrise was a decisive factor in the strategy of the Western Allies to establish their dominance over Central Europe and thereby shape the political postwar order."[482]

Does von Lingen make her case? No and yes. *Sunrise* no doubt brought about the early May 2 surrender but it is strongly arguable that the same military result would have happened without *Sunrise*. The "feared German Alpine Fortress" did not really exist (recall Kesselring's comment about the "jeopardized" German Southern Alps Line) and the German armed forces were in no condition at the time *Sunrise* took effect to even slow the advance of British and American forces upon the Trieste area (recall that the "trap" sprung at Treviso that destroyed the remnants of the German 14th Army).

In regard to the shelter from prosecution provided to Wolff after the war, it would appear that Dulles *did* negotiate secretly with the enemy for surrender with terms given (i.e., de facto immunity given to Wolff) in violation of the agreement announced at Casablanca.

Did the western Allies establish, "… dominance over central Europe and thereby shape the political postwar order"?

One might reasonably argue that it was a good thing that the western Allies did what they did in being heavy handed with Stalin. It is respectfully submitted that an excerpt from historian Rick Atkinson's *The Guns at Last Light* should be considered in pondering how to wrap one's arms around the merits of the issue.

Atkinson described the last day of the Yalta Conference, a grand banquet held during the evening of February 8, 1945.

> *Roosevelt, who had tossed down two cocktails before dinner, toasted Stalin as the "chief forger of the instruments which had led to the mobilization of the world against Hitler"; "the atmosphere of this dinner," he added. "[is] that of a family." Guests hopped around the table clinking glasses; only the foolish had failed to heed Russian advice to coat their stomachs with butter and oily salmon before the first sip of vodka. A huge man in a black alpaca jacket stood behind Stalin's chair, advising the marshal on what to eat and drink. When Roosevelt asked the identity of a pudgy Soviet guest sporting a pince-nez, Stalin replied, "Ah, that one. That's our Himmler." It was Lavrenty P. Beria, sadistic murderer and rapist who served as chief of the secret police."[483]*

That Stalin would joke about "our Himmler" eleven days after his Red Army liberated Auschwitz Concentration Camp and his troops reported finding an SS-managed gas chamber there that could accommodate 6,000 people,[484] speaks volumes for the kind of human being and leader Stalin was and explains the real need for the West to stop his advance. In virtually every country "liberated" by the Red Army a National Liberation Army sprung up that stifled democratic opposition by the use or threat of force.

—*m*—

Was there a "conspiracy"? A "... secretly arranged agreement between two parties to the detriment of a third?"

The circumstances certainly point to one, yes. Although Wolff had not asked for immunity (per the Dulles account) if the western Allies had not taken steps to protect the former SS general from prosecution, at his trial, Wolff might well have revealed information on the witness stand that would have been highly embarrassing to the U.S. and British governments.

Allied prosecutors shortly after the war had in their possession documentary evidence linking Wolff to the mass murder of Jews in 1942 at the infamous Treblinka death camp. A book published in 1953 by author Gerald Reitlinger entitled *The Final Solution: The Attempt to Exterminate the Jews of Europe 1939-1945* tells of a personal letter written by Wolff on August 13, 1942 thanking the Nazi Minister of Transport for his assistance in delivering trainloads of the "Chosen People" (Wolff's words) from the Warsaw ghetto to Treblinka where the SS had constructed a gassing installation. Reitlinger scathingly wrote:

> *As a witness at the trial of Oswald Pohl [Ed: an SS officer executed for genocide] on June 5th, 1947, Karl Wolff had 'not the slightest recollection' why he had taken such a close interest in those trains. He was not unduly pressed on the subject. Karl Wolff was a 'good German.' He had gone as Kesselring's peace envoy to Berne in March, 1945, and in May he had signed the capitulation of the army in Italy, as a consequence of which he was allowed to wear his general's insignia in court at Nuremberg. The sight was apparently so impressive that no one thought of asking him what he thought happened to 70,000 people, who were moved in the course of a fortnight to a single improvised camp, from which there was no transport to take them any further. Nor was Karl Wolff asked under what conditions of hygiene he supposed that 5,000 old people and children could travel in a single goods train.*[485]

Yes, the circumstances suggest that Wolff had secretly arranged to help Dulles with an early surrender and that this was done with the intent to disadvantage Stalin.

As regards the subject of conspiracy however, a "secretly arranged agreement between two parties to the detriment of a third," as pertains to disadvantaged Stalin, one might do well to look to the most monstrous wickedness Stalin ever did and then reflect upon the question of comparative morality.

A bombshell of a document implicating Stalin was uncovered after the war:

> *The Reich Foreign Minister to the German Foreign Office*
> *Telegram*
>
> *VERY URGENT*
> *Moscow, August 23, 1939-8:05 p. m.*
> *No. 204 of August 23*
>
> *Please advise the FÃ¼hrer [Führer] at once that the first three-hour conference with Stalin and Molotov has just ended.... The signing of a secret protocol on delimitation of mutual spheres of influence in the whole eastern area is contemplated...*
>
> *RIBBENTROP*[486]

Poland, an innocent third party, was about to suffer severe detriment, indeed, as the consequence of a secretly arranged agreement between Nazi Germany and the Soviet Union. After the Germans started World War II by invading Poland on September 1, 1939 (causing France and Great Britain to declare war) the Soviets waited until September 17 to announce the nonexistence of a Polish government. Stalin then had his Red Army ruthlessly occupy eastern Poland as previously agreed upon with Hitler.

In the relative morals department Dulles comes off advantaged when compared to Stalin. Stalin and Hitler had clandestinely agreed to start an aggressive military chain of-events in 1939 that escalated wildly and ultimately resulted in the deaths of scores of millions of people. Of course Dulles did not know of this infamous 1939 secret pact when he dealt improperly with Wolff in the spring of 1945, but his every instinct about Soviet Union perfidy proved to be correct. Von Lingen limits her analysis to one side of the equation, and in fairness to her so states in her book.

—◊—

Italian Jews

In 2009 author Elizabeth Bettina wrote a powerful book entitled *It Happened in Italy: Untold Stories of How the People in Italy Defied the Horrors of the Holocaust.* In the *Introduction* to her book Bettina tells of an exhibit at the Museum of Jewish Heritage in New York City:

> *"… a large plasma television that displays a scrolling map of Europe. It depicts Europe before and after World War II. Each country's map shows two sets of numbers: one set reveals the number of Jews in that country before the war, and another, the number murdered during the war. What numbers appear for Italy? There are no numbers at all."* [487]

Bettina explains that Italian Jews had in fact been interned by Italy during the war prior to the 1943 armistice, but the treatment of these Jews had been humane when compared to Nazi run concentration facilities. Food, shelter, clothing and the other necessities of life were provided. Jewish children were schooled at these camps, and no Jew suffered the holocaust at the hands of an Italian.

As the Germans moved to occupy Italy in 1943, many Italians rushed to the rescue the interned Jews, but not all could be saved from the SS. In the aftermath of the war, only one Italian leader would be judged harshly by history. A commentator summed up what the Pontiff failed to do:

> Hitler ordered Rome's 12,000 Jews rounded up and sent to the extermination camps. Pope Pius XII, who would not protest the slaughter of German Jews, stood by silently while twelve hundred Jews were arrested in Rome and held in a building a block from the Vatican before they were sent to Auschwitz, where most of them were gassed. But many priests, nuns, and Catholic laity opened the doors of convents, monasteries, and homes to Italian Jews, saving thousands. Almost 80 percent of Italy's 32,000 Jews survived the war.[488]

The Italians who sheltered Jews did so at serious personal risk to themselves. As stated, Hitler did not take half-measures, and those who defied his dictates paid a price if apprehended.

Bill never mentioned the subject of Jewish concentration camps in Italy. He may not have been aware that there ever had been any. Bettina states: "Next to Denmark, Italy had the highest survival rate [of Jews] of any Nazi-occupied country in Europe."[489] When one thinks on this, and also the fact that Italy had been under the iron fist rule of the fascist dictator Benito Mussolini for such a long period, the Italian people come out favorably.

On Friday evening May 11, 1945 Bill wrote letter No. 44 to his parents:

> ...Under the army point system, I will be a long time getting home. I have about fifty-two points to my credit and over eighty-five are required to be in line to complete one's army work. It will be many months before most of us get moved out and then there is no telling in what direction...

"Points" referred to by Bill meant that a soldier in the theatre was to be given an "Adjusted Service Rating Score" as of 12 May 1945 based on a "credit point" for each month of active service since 16 September 1940, a point for each month overseas, twelve points per each child under eighteen years of age (up to a limit of three children) and five points for each combat decoration and battle participation award received.[490]

Bill's estimated point count seems correct. He then had slightly less than three-years active duty with five months overseas. This service would account for forty points. Add twelve points for Davy and the number fifty-two is obtained. The fact that Dotty was pregnant did not count.

Dick Stroud's point count, with only one child and arriving in Italy at approximately the same time as Bill arrived, would have been similar to Bill's. And for Jack King? John Lesesne?

The point system could be a challenge for the typical U.S. soldier, even one *who served the entire 602-day Italian campaign.* Such a G.I. had little chance of going home unless he happened to have two minor children:

Est. 24 mos. active service + 20 mos. overseas + 20 combat/battle = 64 points.

Jack's point count would have been approximately forty-nine and John's, fifty-seven — a long ways away from the eighty-five needed for a trip home [Ed: see endnote [491] for calculations]. Infantry veteran Leon Weckstein would only have five more points than Jack as he had been awarded the Legion of Merit award.

Still, the Army had devised a methodology where its longest serving soldiers in the Western hemisphere could avoid being shipped off immediately to fight against Japan. Those who had served longest — from the invasion of North Africa in November 1942 — depending on additional prior active duty and battle decorations might qualify for a furlough home. Whether the incessant political nagging of Clare Boothe Luce to return home those serving the longest had a hand in the development of this point system is unknown.

On a side note, a furlough to the United States did not mean a discharge from further military duty. Among Bill's files is a letter from his mother telling about hometown hero-pilot Robert Wingert who completed his "tour" of combat missions over Germany — in his case at a time when the requirement was thirty missions. The USAAF returned Wingert stateside per its policy. "He [Wingert] will likely have six months in the States then the Pacific," Bill's mother wrote. "His family is bitter about this, feeling he has done enough."

On May 15, 1945, U.S. Patent Application #2,446,205 was filed for a "MULTI-AXLE VEHICLE" with "INVENTORS" listed as Marshall E. Wickersham and William D. Allison. The thoughts that Bill had for a new truck trailer design for the Army while he served at the big house the previous January would materialize in the form of a U.S. Patent granted for 10 claims. The patent preamble permitted free usage "for governmental purposes," and the application was for the "... transporting of extremely heavy equipment, such as disabled combat tanks and the like." The invention distributed the weight over twenty-four wheels, each on an axle enabling it to move up and down over rough terrain. Wickersham worked at the Tank Command in Detroit. That Bill was concerned about being ordered to the Pacific there is no doubt. He did not raise this prospect with Dotty but on May 16 he wrote his parents: "There is no indication as to what happens next ... I have my fingers crossed on the prospect of going to the Pacific. That would be hard to take but in points of overseas service, I do not rate so high. The ones with the least service would be most apt to go if needed."

Bill's concern about possibly going to the Pacific Theatre, undoubtedly shared by many other Allied soldiers in Europe, is understandable. Earlier, on April 1, 1945 what would become an eighty-two-day battle for Okinawa had begun and the fighting there was raging when MTOUSA reviewed its troop strength for redeployment purposes. At the battle of Okinawa's conclusion, 107,000 Japanese soldiers would be dead and 7,500 would be POWs — representing an unprecedented kill ratio of 93%. The U.S. would suffer 12,000 killed or missing and another 37,000 wounded.[492] With the notable exceptions of the Battle of Stalingrad and the Jewish Holocaust, the war in Europe had never witnessed a kill ratio like Okinawa.

No doubt the battle casualties of Okinawa were suppressed at the time but with the reports of mass Kamikaze attacks and the never-surrender Bushido code in play on the ground, Bill and his comrades-in-arms in Italy had to have been keenly aware of the horror unfolding in the Pacific. Bill and others surely asked the simple question: If the Japanese would fight this hard for an island territorial possession, how hard would they fight to defend their home islands?

And who would one suppose were the first U.S. servicemen to leave Italy for that other conflict? There was no surprise here. U.S. airmen had indispensable warfare skills; they would be the first to join the fray on the other side of the world. Per the official history of the U.S. Army Transportation Corps: "During May 1945 the bulk of the redeployed military personnel leaving Italy belonged to the Air Forces." The four-engine heavy "strategic" bombers, the B-17s and B-24s stationed at Foggia with the Fifteenth Air Force would fly ferry routes across the oceans and lands; the smaller, tactical aircraft, P-47s, A-20s and the like of the

Twelfth Air Force would be crated-up and stowed for a very long ocean voyage. Dick Stroud did not immediately go because there was clean-up work to do in Italy. Airplane parts in supply depot bins across the country had to be inventoried, packed and trucked to seaports — Leghorn and Naples — for loading and shipment to CBI or the Pacific Theater, and this process would take some time.

On May 22, 1945, Captain John M. Lesesne braced to attention, eyes fixed forward. "For meritorious service in support of combat operations..." the adjutant started reading loudly as the Bronze Star medal was pinned on John's blouse by his commanding officer, Lieutenant Colonel Russell E. McMurray.

> *... during the period November 1, 1944, to May 2, 1945, in Italy. Captain Lesesne led his company in close support of infantry operations delivering effective fire on enemy installations throughout the winter campaign and the race across the Po river valley. During 183 consecutive days of combat, he maintained his company command post with the forward gun positions to insure complete and effective control of all operations. His courage, initiative and constant attention to the comfort and well-being of his men during the long months on the winter line were instrumental in keeping morale and fighting spirit at a high level. He repeatedly exposed himself to enemy fire while on daylight reconnaissance for gun positions. On many occasions he was far in advance of the infantry heavy weapons and seized every opportunity to displace forward in order to render more effective support. The initiative and self-sacrifice displayed by Captain Lesesne reflect great credit upon himself and the military service.*[493]

On Monday, May 28 after returning from a vacation trip to Florence and Pisa, Dick Stroud was stricken with excruciating stomach pains. A friend drove Dick to the U.S. Army hospital at Caserta and forty-five minutes later an emergency procedure was performed on him to remove a gastric ulcer. The following day Dick dictated a letter to a Red Cross worker explaining what happened to Sue. In his letter Dick did not mince words: "It means I shall very soon come back to the United States." He told his wife to expect a period of convalescent leave in a stateside hospital and that a U.S. Army medical board "will recommend a medical discharge ..."

Dick added a positive note: "The fact that this operation became necessary should leave me in an even better state of health." While Dick's medical record is unavailable, chances are that while touring in Northern Italy Dick ingested H. Pylori — a bacteria known to cause ulcers. Dick reassured Sue: "I'm feeling almost normal and there is no reason for anxiety on your part."

A few weeks after V-E Day Bill wrote to Dotty: "My best bet to get **H**ome quickest is to be useful here,"[494] and he set out doing just that. At the end of May he performed a week's temporary duty in the north of Italy inspecting roads, bridges and tunnels formerly maintained by the German Army.[495] His travels took him through Verona (where he stayed in a villa he adored) to within fifty miles of Austria and Switzerland. On May 29 he wrote his parents: "Rode 275 miles in a jeep so [I] had a busy day. On one road we passed through sixty-five to seventy tunnels. The Germans had installed an airplane engine plant in the tunnels, leaving one lane open for traffic. [I] saw many mountains, some snow capped and the country is beautiful ..." What he did not report was that he had experienced a head-on collision in one of those tunnels. Fortunately Bill had been thrown clear but others had to be evacuated by ambulance. "We hit a car full of German officers heading south to surrender," Bill explained years later. "They got the worst of it."

The tunnels that the Germans used for manufacturing were located on the western shore of Lake Garda and they were packed with "... large numbers of drill presses, lathes and other machine tools." The Nazis hoped to retain these tunnels to manufacture weapons for Hitler's "National Redoubt."[496]

Bill's concern about being shipped to the Pacific had a real basis to it. The official Army history contained this about post-war Italy: "The tempo of redeployment began picking up during June [1945]. In that month twenty units under Transportation Corps control were redeployed from the theater, including five port companies and six Quartermaster truck companies destined for the Southwest Pacific."[497] These embarked personnel headed towards the Panama Canal and not home leave. Bill was on a general's staff and not part of a company; if whole units were going over, however, at some point members of a flag command would be going also.

The seaports of Leghorn and Naples were discombobulated by the outbreak of peace in Europe. Not only did troops and equipment need to be shipped out, vessels that had recently arrived "… were reloaded with ammunition, pierced steel planking, vehicles and heavy weapons, and then rerouted to the Pacific." "Sixteen vessels arriving in convoys … were returned to the United States undischarged."[498]

On June 2 life for the Stroud family forever changed and the manner in which Sue learned of it is emblematic of the challenges members of the Greatest Generation had no choice but to accept, and did accept. On that date Dick had to undergo another emergency surgery. He survived it and afterwards directed a telegraph be sent to his wife: "Operation over. Condition Satisfactory. Wait instructions in my letter. Hope to see you soon. Richard E. Stroud." On the same day an Army hospital chaplain wrote a letter to Sue. Both the telegram and the letter went to the street address in Longview, Texas where Dick's sister, Nell, resided. The letter read:

> *My Dear Mrs. Stroud,*
>
> *The Hospital Commander regrets to inform you that your husband 1st Lt. Richard E. Stroud is now considered to be seriously ill. The diagnosis which has been made is a perforated gastric ulcer, and it has been necessary to perform two major operations which your husband withstood very well. Although his condition is serious, we are quite hopeful of his recovery. Rest assured that he is being given the very best of medical treatment and attention; this hospital is modern and well equipped and our medical officers are experienced, expertly qualified American doctors.*
>
> *Please do not write the Commanding Officer of this hospital in response to this letter since it contains all information available at this time. Due to the great number of patients treated at this hospital, the task of answering such letters on each patient would be a difficult one if we did not receive your cooperation in this request.*
>
> *You will receive further letters at fifteen-day intervals as long as your husband's condition is considered serious. When you receive a postal card with the notation "Final Report," you will know that your husband's condition has improved to the point where no further reports are warranted. Your husband's correspondence address is now, "2628 Hospital Section, APO #698 c/o Postmaster, New York, N.Y."*

I hope that it will be of comfort to you to know that I will administer to
your husband's spiritual needs while he is in this hospital and I assure you
that I will take a deep personal interest in his case.

Yours very truly,
IRWIN W. KRAEMER
Chaplain (Major)

One can imagine what it must have been like on that 125-mile drive from Longview to Garland, Texas, to deliver a letter such as this. "Condition satisfactory" by Dick's telegram had been turned into "seriously ill" by the government via its slow moving Army mail delivery system. Also imagine the ensuing wait for additional news.

It happened that an "official" telegraph was sent to Sue on June 9 and this time it was addressed to her at her parent's Garland address. The telegram started, "The Secretary of War desires me to express his deep regret that your husband 1st Lt Stroud Richard E has been seriously ill …"; it confirmed the same hospital mailing address for Dick, the one conveyed by Chaplain Kraemer and contained no new or additional information about Dick's medical condition, presumably because the telegram was not a "fifteen-day interval" letter. No doubt Sue had to have been terrified when she received and opened this telegram. Quickly scanning the top of the first sentence for an instant did she suppose her that her husband was dead?

Like so many desperate loved ones in similar situations in World War II, Sue Stroud (probably with the help of her parents and sister and brother-in-law) found a way to work around, or outside of, U.S. Army red tape. Contact was made with one of Dick's army friends in the Naples area, perhaps by telephone (this could be arranged but was rare) who visited Dick in the hospital and sent Sue his own telegram: "Have done as you asked. Operation over. Condition satisfactory. Anxiety unnecessary. James M. Bryan."

Joyously for everyone Dick lived and the war was over for him — he would not be shipped to CBI after all. The cause of his second attack was the surgeon going on leave and in his absence food being improperly fed to Dick. His stiches burst and peritonitis set in, very nearly causing death. A hospital ship remarkable for its cleanliness brought Dick back to the States for a period of recuperation, and eventually he made it back to his beloved Sue and Dickie — formerly known as "Pumpkin." He would have stomach problems the rest of his life, however.

As an aside, Dick's daughter wrote about this incident: "My father told me with some disgust, that if he hadn't been an officer, he would have died. His roommates on the ward kept yelling for a nurse after Dad's stiches burst. Being even a junior officer had its compensations — in this case his life."[499]

For those who routinely enjoy iPhones and iPads today and are perhaps not completely cognizant of what their grandparents and great-grandparents endured to preserve their freedoms and create the conditions for their prosperity — know this personal history of Dick Stroud and the others as well — and think about the subject of war on every Memorial Day and Veteran's Day. War is about more than just shooting. It is also about a father becoming deathly ill, a young son sending roses to a concerned mother, warriors living under terrible conditions in stress while trying to kill people who otherwise might be friends and, in another case, a father seeing suffering children beg for chocolates and not being able to do much about it. With respect to World War II in particular, know that it was Nazi Germany that declared war on America. Hitler did so on December 11, 1941 in a speech before screaming, stiff arm-saluting maniacal members of the Reichstag.

In early June Bill discovered why his workspace was on the top floor with unoccupied floors below. Writing from the "old building" nearby (where Bill stood watch on the first floor as duty officer) he observed: "The Colonel is in here swatting flies… We are lucky to be up on the fifth floor of the palace. They are not bad up there. I guess they get tired before they fly up so high."[500]

On June 6, 1945, Bill wrote his parents, "Promotions have been frozen now so I cannot hope for anything in that direction." Also in early June the Army ordered Bill to attend a seven-day course entitled "Work Simplification" with the idea he would become an instructor on the subject. Bill complained bitterly in the same letter to his parents, "I have no choice and my work piles up deeper and deeper." He took the course with a forced smile, however, and ended-up receiving a special letter of commendation from MTOUSA (i.e., the commanding general himself and not a form letter either) for a study he published on how to calculate relative work efficiencies of truck companies.[501]

Bill used to laugh when he talked about his version of Army "red tape," and there is no doubt that he had to bite his tongue during "Work Simplification." One of his favorite stories was how he had been ordered to submit some kind of a report, and he knew, with absolute certainty, that whatever he submitted up the chain of command would be returned to him for revision. "So I typed two reports," Bill said, "a long one and a short one. I submitted the short one, and when it came back to me with a note on it that they wanted more detail, I waited a day and then submitted the long one. They loved it, especially thinking I had worked through the night to please them."

On June 12, Bill learned of the birth on June 4 of his second son, "Dick," who was named after his late uncle. Two telegrams sent to Bill from Dotty's parents in Detroit announcing the birth were late to arrive and Dotty experienced complications following delivery. She ended up having surgery and was in the hospital for 19 days with her newborn while her parents took care of Davy. Dick was born premature and held for a period in an incubator. Bill experienced a stressful waiting period somewhat like the Stroud family. Such was routine for World War II.

Bill on watch

While Bill thought of his family, in Charlottesville, VA, General Truscott enjoyed a well-deserved eight-day home leave with his wife Sarah and children, Lucien, III (recently out of West Point), daughter Mary and son Jamie. The General was exhausted after making a six-stop flight from Italy to his home state of Texas where he had been feted with gun salutes, a car parade and a ceremonial barge trip down the San Antonio River to a Mexican floorshow and party at La Vieta. On his return trip east he was invited to the White House along with Generals Gavin and Patch, and, after a meeting with President Truman, photos were taken outside. In between these activities, Truscott informed the War Department of his preference to serve in the Pacific war if a position should become available (as an aside the war ended as he was being considered for a command in China). After home leave and prior to returning to Italy, Truscott again visited Washington D.C. where he had cocktails and dinner with his "wartime friend" Clare Boothe Luce at the Wardman Park Hotel. The next day he met with Speaker of the House Sam Rayburn, the Texas delegation and general officers at the Pentagon.[502]

In late June Bill reported participating in the shipment of the German railway gun "Leopold" (nicknamed "Anzio Annie" by the Americans) to the Port of Naples where (according to a *Stars and Stripes* news article Bill saved)[503] it was to be "... crated, hauled, hoisted in the belly of an ocean going freighter" destined for the United States. The gun and its carriage were ninety-six feet long and weighed 462,000 lbs. It could shoot 564-pound shells[504] a distance of thirty-six miles, and is thought to have killed (at least) three Americans at the Anzio beachhead. Bill's job was to arrange for the rail line and to confirm by both inspection and calculation that the bridges en route could sustain the enormous weight. Today this war prize is on display outside the Army Aberdeen Proving Grounds Museum, Maryland. During later years Bill occasionally mentioned this episode. From an engineering standpoint he was proud that the bridgeheads held — as he had predicted they would.

In early July the Fifteenth Army Group disbanded and General Clark moved to Austria to take command of U.S. forces there. Italy, since its government had switched sides in 1943, was to have a more favorable status after the war than the other Axis countries that fought to the bitter end. Clark entered Austria as an occupier.

Allen Dulles also moved during this period to Wiesbaden, Germany to assume his new appointment as OSS director for that country. This represented a promotion for Dulles, who, in government circles, was being lauded as a major contributor to the successful end of the war in Europe.

Back home "Wild Bill" Donovan had fallen out of favor with a number of important government people for a number of reasons. The OSS had developed under Donovan a Gestapo-like reputation and many politicians were concerned with this intelligence agency continuing to operate in peacetime. There had been an investigative report prepared by Roosevelt military aide Colonel Richard Parks, Jr. (a G-2 Army intelligence officer and competitor of the OSS) offering examples of OSS amateurism, incompetence, nepotism, waste, lack of training, corruption, drunkenness and even orgies. In addition to this there had been negative input about Donovan from the FBI Director J. Edgar Hoover.[505] Lastly, it was a known fact that U.S. Army and Navy commanders in the Pacific had banned the OSS.

The biggest strike against Donovan, however, may have been personal. When Truman had been vice president Donovan largely ignored him. Truman would not forget.

Dulles had been wise to stay out of this, and being posted in far away Europe helped. Near the end of his government career, Donovan did Dulles a big favor. He encouraged Dulles to tell the story of *Operation Sunrise*, and Dulles did so in a riveting article published in the *Saturday Evening Post* in September 1945, the effect of which was to make Dulles a national figure.[506]

In early July the Military Rail Service of the United States completed its repair of an important rail line. For the first time since February 1943 northern and southern Italy were again connected by rail; "line sixty-nine running from Bologna through Verona to the Brenner Pass," was open.[507] Italian artisans and masons, a stone at a time repaired bridges. This would take years but it would be done.

On July 10 Bill wrote: "Anxious as I am to get home, the possibility of the Pacific makes it easier to stay here."

Following V-E Day Bill was involved in the redeployment of POW's to their native lands. He arranged for their transportation home by both truck and rail, and he also looked out for their best interests. On July 19, 1945 he wrote his parents: "One of the officers in the next room just decorated me with the 'Adolph Hitler Medal.' He bent up some wires in the shape of a swastika and hung them on me," Bill continued. "I'd been working all day getting some guards lined up to protect twenty-one carloads of captured German mail. No one knows what to do with it except the Italians, who would like to steal it." When he wrote this Bill was undoubtedly cognizant that Germany was largely a country of displaced persons and also what this mail might accomplish in the way of reuniting families if delivered. Bill concluded: "I guess I made a lot of phone calls and he felt I was working for the Germans — in fun of course" [Ed: from a poem appearing in a subsequent chapter Bill had revenge on his mocker].

German POWs were put to work in trucking operations both by PBS and the U.S. Fifth Army, with upwards of 6,000 serving at railheads or driving trucks. The POWs were also employed as guards of U.S. Army trucks to prevent pilferage, which was a real problem, particularly with the natives as Bill wrote. Jack King experienced a camera being stolen during company redeployment. "It was stolen by some of the truck drivers," Jack noted in his diary. When interviewed about this, Jack confirmed the drivers had been Italian. Bill wrote that sometimes it was more than petty theft: "Once in a while an Army truckload or two gets sold or hijacked and just at this time a truckload of sugar is worth about twelve thousand dollars. It's an awful temptation to hold in front of the drivers." The irony of a former enemy being a reliable protector of Allied property did not escape Bill. "The Germans were good soldiers," he said, "who wanted to work."

Things for the U.S. Fifth Army relaxed greatly. At Cormons a USO troop put on a show for the 91st Infantry Division. "I got my picture taken with Jinx Falkenberg!" a smiling Jack happily remembered. Jack was correct to be enthusiastic (all one needs to do is go on Google). This buxom beauty, a Hollywood bombshell had an audience with the Pope on July 19 along with the USO troop.

On July 22 one of the officers Bill worked with, a Captain Quinn, died unexpectedly of a heart attack. Bill wrote: "He was about my age and has a wife and little girls in Texas. He was a swell fellow and was Texas state champion rifle shot. His funeral was yesterday in Naples and most of the section attended. It was a regular military funeral. I thought how much it would mean to his family if they could know just what took place but they will learn so little through the regular channels. The American military cemetery in Naples is on top of a high hill and is very well kept. It will be an awful blow to his family; he appeared in perfect health." Bill's comment about the family learning so little through regular channels brings to mind that infantryman from the 361st Regiment, 91st Infantry Division that was burned to death the night of November 17, 1944 by a defective chemical mortar shell fired by one John's platoons. Perhaps Colonel Broedlow or a buddy wrote the parents the truth, but it is a certainty that the telegram from the War Department was a form message. One cannot help but contrast this to the situation in the U.S. Army today. When a U.S. soldier dies overseas now, a full obituary appears the next day in his or her hometown newspaper, often with details of how the death occurred.

By this date Jack had still not seen Venice, and he was exasperated to the point that he determined to exercise self-help. On July 24 he wrote: "Clarence Epling, David Ethim and I decided to go to Lido Beach, Venice for four days tomorrow. That's what's nice about being in Division Headquarters. You can cut your own orders and no one will know the difference."

The distance one way was eighty-four miles and they hitchhiked.

Bill celebrated his 37th birthday on August 4 and when he wrote to his parents, he expressed increased frustration with his situation: "Of all my birthdays this has been the most lonesome. Ever since Dotty and I were married, our lives have been influenced and almost controlled by the war and military." He followed up five days later with another letter after two climatic world events had taken place: "So much has happened around the world these last few days. Everyone is waiting for more news. We usually get a paper at breakfast but it has not come yet this morning. We heard last night that Russia is declaring war on Japan today and that another atomic bomb has been dropped. So many stories are circulating about the power of the bombs one doesn't know what to believe. If even a small part of the stories are true, man had better go easy."

Having studied physics and chemistry, Bill was anxious to learn all he could about atomic energy. Among his memorabilia are *Time* and *Newsweek* magazine articles entitled "The Birth of a New Era" and "Fat Boy Hits Nagasaki." Bill typed a full-page report entitled, "NOTES ON THE ATOM BOMB" in which he summarized, among other observations, one of his fears: "If abundant elements such as water, silicon and oxygen are subject to atomic breakdown, the entire earth might be destroyed or disintegrated by atomic fire or explosion." A *Newsweek* article that he clipped, dated September 17, 1945 contained a very accurate prediction:

> *Without exception, every government, civil and military official having direct knowledge of atomic power warns in the gravest terms that this leadership is only "temporary" — that the United States may be presumed to have not more than five years in which to make its decisions, probably less.*

On August 14, Bill announced the big event in a matter-of-fact manner: "The news this noon sounds like the war is over. Now when I get Home I should be able to stay." With the nightmare of possible Pacific duty over, Bill's feelings about not remaining in the service after he returned stateside crystallized. On August

18 he wrote: "I for one have had my fill of the Army... and I hope we can guide our little fellows into other fields of work." Soon after, he revealed his intention to resign his commission at the earliest possible moment, ending a twelve-year career as a drilling reservist. Considering Bill's expertise in shipping supplies by truck over mountains during wintertime and how the Korean peninsula was rugged and not unlike Italy in regard to weather, it was indeed fortunate for Bill and his family that he made the decision to do what he did.

Bill was always proud that he had served in Italy and did not become anti-military during the 1960s and 70s. Nor did he embrace anti-hippy flag-waving, as some World War II veterans tended to do during that politically polarized era. In regard to his personal choice though, it was his decision to get completely out of the service.

And how did the protagonists of this story relate to the womenfolk in their lives?

A recurring theme in Bill's letters to Dotty is guilt over enjoyable travel. Indeed, in the late summer of 1945 he would write to her: "Many of the men are taking tours thru Switzerland. They say it is wonderful. I have not applied to go because I want to see that with you."[508] Still, Bill had the opportunity to take in the sights of places like Pisa, Florence and Verona, and he happily did so.

Before he took ill, Dick Stroud also saw Pisa and Florence and other places and experienced an occasional pang of guilt not unlike Bill. On one occasion he tried to make Sue feel OK about an excursion that he took to a popular spot by writing this: "I'm very glad you cannot be with me here at a time like this," he wrote to his wife, "under normal circumstances we might enjoy it but now, gosh, no!" Dick then perhaps overdid it somewhat: "Any normal person who could have a choice would prefer White Rock Lake to Capri."[509]

And so it was for the married men. Their sentences in many instances could be interchanged without the ability to discern who wrote what.

John's and Jack's writings had a distinctly different flavor. John described meeting an Army nurse in Florence:

> *Mary Ellen... was in Florence too; so I asked her to have dinner with*
> *me at the hotel the next nite. After dinner she suggested that we go to her*

apartment to drink her whiskey ration — a qt. of Bourbon — she had
"cokes" too; so we had some fine drinks. Drank from 8:30 to 1:15, and then
I went home feeling fine. Next day I went to see Maggie again… [510]

On another occasion he wrote: "During these last ten days I've spent a while in Rome. There, I'm ashamed to say, I cut up quite a bit. Met a lovely little blonde Yugoslav named Marushka — what a gal!"

In addition to Mary Ellen, Maggie, Marushka and the other women he met in Italy, quite a number of young ladies mailed John letters from the United States, the Canal Zone and North Africa. Nine, to be exact, with all the names diarized! Bachelor John had that rare male knack of moving on with ladies still feeling good about him.

With the European war over, Jack and some buddies were granted eight days leave which they took on the Italian Riviera at the resort town of Alassio near Genoa.[511] Jack's part time companion and tour guide during there was Ines Grande and Jack has fond memories of her to this day. "Walked around town early this afternoon with the boys," Jack wrote, "went in a picture shop, saw this girl working there so I asked her to go swimming with me. [She] said she would tomorrow at 12:00; has off from 12:00 to 2:00 as is customary over here." Jack noted that Ines spoke "pretty good English" and two days after they met he recorded: "Now I have a steady swimming date with Ines. She had most of Sunday off so we spent practically all of it on the beach."

"She is president of the young people's organization," Jack noted, "and I think a little communistic." Ines Grande was special. About their last night together, Jack wrote: "Met Ines at the Fannia Club, stayed until midnight then walked her downtown — couldn't take her home — oh, me!" Jack met Ines the following day at the shop and she gave him a pair of silk hose and a painting for his mother and peaches for him to eat on the long drive back (which would take him through Milan where he saw its magnificent cathedral). Telling about this story is something that Jack wrote in passing about another girl, this one unnamed, the following month: "First time I kissed a girl since coming overseas." Ines likely had not let Jack escort her home that night for concern that they might end-up smooching and someone would notice.

—〰—

The precipitous and unexpected surrender of Japan in mid-August 1945 really got things moving at the Transportation Section of MOTUSA. Almost in the blink of an eye there was no need for redeployment planning to the Pacific; practically everyone would be going home! Of the 92,000 seaborne passengers to depart Italy in August, approximately 84,000 "were destined to the United States."[512] The problem was a shortage of ships:

> *All available shipping was employed to move U.S. personnel from the theater, including the regular troopships, hospital ships, converted Italian liners, and many fitted Liberty and Victory ships.*[513]

The slow moving Liberty and Victory ships were overloaded with passengers by as much as 30% but no one getting a berth on one of these cramped, non-luxurious, poor riding vessels complained. And as it should have been, the longest serving soldiers — those who landed in North Africa in November 1942 — received priority. The goal was for the entire U.S. Fifth Army to be shipped out by mid-September — for these combat veterans the point system was put aside. Bill would have to wait his turn; his repatriation would take some months longer and he would experience hiccups along the way. In August 1945 a theater record was set when the converted troopship *Wakefield* embarked 8,227 passengers.[514]

Captain John Lesesne embarked for the United States with his battalion aboard the liberty ship *Alexander Graham Bell* on August 27, 1945. Seventeen chemical mortar battalions served in Europe during World War II and seven in the Pacific. John had served in the Canal Zone for nineteen months, North Africa for six months and Italy thirteen months. He finished out his Army career as the battalion operations officer. All told the 100th fired 62,679 rounds in Italy — but this number may not include the 350 rounds that John fired "off the record" for the 34th Infantry Division! The 100th deactivated October 13, 1945 at Camp Miles Standish, MA.

Jack King and the unit that he served with embarked on the troopship *SS Mt. Vernon (AP-22)* at 11:15 a.m. September 1. This converted liner (known as the *SS Washington* before the war) would provide for a smooth and fast trip home. "There is going to be a ceremony with all the brass making an inspection at 3:00 p.m.," Jack wrote as he waited to get underway. In preparation for long hours in a cramped berthing area, Jack sold two cartons of cigarettes for $40. "Wanted to have some money to play poker with," he wrote. The Army being the army would not tell Jack and the others in advance when the plan was to get underway (even in peacetime!) but when it stopped issuing passes to Naples and started paying wages in U.S. currency, Jack knew that the special day was close. When interviewed about his recollections from World War II Jack was very forthright about how fortunate he had been to always be in a safer rear echelon assignment. He jokingly added only one regret about his Apennines experience: "I did not get on skis."

Jack wrote this about coming home:

At sea — September 10, 1945

Got my first look at the good old USA at exactly 10:26 a.m. today. It was just a peninsula at Hampton Roads but knowing it was America made it look awful good. Everyone is walking around with a big smile on his face. We are supposed to dock at 2:00 p.m. You can't imagine what real houses look like after months of nothing but dirty stone buildings. We passed some naval station on the way in. There was a big American flag to greet us. The buildings were of red brick and the trees and grass were a deep rich green. It looked just like a picture postcard; even the air smelled better. People passed in launches and we waved and shouted at them. What a day! What a day!

Jack's diary inspiration when he wrote the above was, "America means opportunity, freedom, power." — *Emerson.*

On September 20 General Truscott saw the last of his deactivated U.S. Fifth Army off from the Port of Leghorn; he then travelled to Germany by automobile. Truscott did not know it at the time but he would soon replace George Patton as Third Army commander. Patton had gotten himself into hot duck soup again, this time for not going along with the de-nazification program and ineptly putting his foot into his mouth about it and in public no less. At a press conference Patton likened, "… the German political scene to the struggle between the Democrats and Republicans."[515] On the same date, President Truman signed an executive order disbanding the OSS, determining it would be easier to start over with a new agency under a new name than to attempt to change the OSS culture from within.[516]

On September 25, 1945, Bill wrote Dotty: "Last night just as I was leaving the office I got a call to set up trains to handle 7,000 German PWs (Prisoners of War). I had them all arranged this morning when the Colonel came in at 8:30 a.m."

With this Bill had arranged for the last shipment of German POWs out of Italy. MTOUSA deactivated its POW command at 12:00 noon that date, having accounted for 324,642 POWs.[517] 7,984 of these prisoners were "repatriated Russians,"[518] who had defected from the USSR early in the war and now faced an uncertain future.

Things were winding down fast by this date. Orders effective 1 October 1945 identify only nineteen officers working at the Headquarters, MTOUSA Transportation Section, with Bill being one of them. It is curious to glance at the last names of these officers, if for no other reason than to think about ethnic diversity in America today. The Order is signed, "BY COMMAND OF GENERAL McNARNEY."

TRANSPORTATION SECTION

COL KENNETH D McKENZIE
COL JOHN T DANAHER
LT COL HUGH M BROOKS
LT COL EDWARD P KETCHAM, JR
LT COL JOSEPH J MUCKERMAN
LT COL SAMUAL E. SAX
LT COL JAMES H. WHITMAN
MAJ WALTER E ADAMS
MAJ JULIUS B GARETT, JR
MAJ FRANCIS X QUINN
CAPT WILLIAM D ALLISON
CAPT FRED H BURGHARDT
CAPT LELAND P CHRISTENSEN
CAPT BURTON E O'BRIEN
CAPT JAMES A ROBINSON, JR
CAPT GEORGE T SIMPSON, JR.
2ND LT JOSEPH P BOCK
WOJG CHANDLER C. JORDAN

The Order is eighteen pages in length with almost 1,000 officer's names listed, comprising thirty-seven divisions and sections. Jack King wrote about typing up such orders for the 91st Division. Shortly before he shipped out for home Jack recorded: "Had to get out two General Orders last night. Really knocked them out. One was thirteen pages and the other nine."[519] This was tedious and time-consuming work and the army insisted on uniformity — set margins, spacing and (of course) error free typing. This paperwork moved Americans home.

With the specter of military service in the Pacific Theatre removed, Bill had but one goal in mind, an objective articulated in an unattributed poem to be found amid his documents. The poem is typed, not mimeographed and Bill may have written it, probably did. Bill had no desire to stay and help build an American empire in Europe.

To the tune of *Lily Marlene*

*Oh, Mr. Truman, won't you send us **Home***
We have conquered Naples, now we've conquered Rome.

We have subdued the Master Race;
There must be lots of shipping space.
*Oh, please send us **Home**;*
*Let those at **Home** see Rome.*

We met the Seventh Army in the Brenner Pass;
We all had hepatitis and shrapnel up our — .
Oh, why don't you pick some other guy?
Don't send us out to CBI.

*Oh, please send us **Home**;*
Let those at Home see Rome.

Undated

CHAPTER THIRTEEN:

CAR GUYS AND RE-EMPLOYMENT

ONE TIME WHILE the war was still on at Caserta Bill wrote these upbeat words: "I saw a nifty European touring car today with the top down. Leather bucket seats, low to the road, pale blue and three stars on the bumper (a Lt. General)."[520] In a similar letter, Bill, like a kid describing a favorite toy, wrote: "It was an Alfa-Romeo built in Milan. Beautiful job, low to the ground, long, independent suspension all around (torsion bars on rear) and aluminum body, wire wheels, deep red upholstery and a nice motor. I have mental notes on all its features. I must have looked funny there in the palace courtyard, sprawled out there on a mat looking underneath at the suspension... The Italians display marked ability..."[521]

On another occasion while near the front with the war on Bill lamented what he missed most in his professional life: "I drove a captured German car today. It was about the size of our jeep. I enjoyed the experience. I can scarcely wait to get back to spring suspensions and car design... I am convinced more than ever that car design, also trucks, has only really started."[522]

Among the several newspaper and magazine articles that Bill clipped and pasted is a short piece upon which he had notated by hand, *Time, August 6, 1945.* The story was entitled, *Autos — Joe & Henry,* and it described the agreement between two industrialists to manufacture automobiles in California and Michigan:

> *From the west coast summer home on Lake Tahoe, Shipbuilder Henry J. Kaiser last week long-distanced an old friend, Joseph Washington Frazer, president of Detroit's Graham-Paige Motors Corp. As reporters listened in, Shipbuilder Kaiser rumbled: "Congratulations, Joe." To which Joe replied: "Thanks for the flowers, Henry."*

*In this cozy fashion, Joe & Henry let out the best-kept financial secret of
the year. They had formed a new company, jointly owned by Kaiser interests and Graham-Paige, to invade the dog-eat-dog auto business. With
Kaiser as board chairman and Joe Frazer as president, the Kaiser-Frazer
Corp. will build two cars, the Kaiser and the Frazer.*

The article stated that, "The Powerful Field" of established manufacturers
would counter this new competition by introducing their own new models. One
can imagine how Bill reacted upon reading this *Time* article: The race for new
automotive technology was on again and soon he would be in the thick of it!

The only nonfamily personal correspondence that Bill kept in his World War II
memorabilia file is an onionskin typed copy of a letter that he sent to his former
boss, Richard J. Scanlan, at the Hudson Motor Car Company. The candid, highly
personal response Bill received is remarkable. In his letter to Scanlan Bill hints he
wants his old job back and elicits an offer from his former employer to rehire him.

September 10, 1945

Dear Dick,

*According to the September third issue of Time Magazine Hudson cars
are again rolling off the line. Of all the big news items of recent months,
that is one of the best I have seen… [Ed: Bill then describes his military
duties in the Army Transportation Section, which is omitted]*

*During the last three months we have placed in operation nearly two
thousand captured enemy vehicles with German drivers and mechanics.
I have had an opportunity to go over their equipment in some detail, also
to drive several of their cars. The Germans used a wide variety of trucks
including Italian, French, Belgian, Austrian and other models. Some of
their designs are pretty elaborate including independent suspensions all
around on trucks of six or eight-ton capacity.*

*There is a possibility that in a couple of months I can be declared surplus
and then with luck I may be returned home. I have requested release
from active duty at the earliest possible date. My military career is almost
"Finito" — I hope.*

*Have come across a number of interesting suspension designs. There is a
much greater variety of suspensions here than at home. Independent rear
suspensions as well as front are quite popular. As yet, I have seen none*

that approach our "Auto-Glide" principle or involve load compensation.
There is a great need for better suspensions over here because the cars are
lighter and the roads are rough.

Bill concluded: "I hope your sons and the others in service came thru safely...
My own estimate calls for Christmas, and I hope to see you by that time."

Whereas Bill had written essentially a business letter (i.e., a letter likely to
end up in his company personnel file), Scanlan chose to reply in a very different
fashion. Scanlan wrote in longhand, not on company stationery, and in a casual,
even rambling fashion. From both the tenor and substance of his response it is
apparent that Scanlan did not intend for a copy of his response to be in the possession of Hudson Motor Car Company. Scanlan's letter to Bill not only speaks
volumes for their friendship and mutual trust, but also outlines what Detroit
had to overcome to retool after being the World War II "Arsenal of Democracy."

October 3, 1945

Dear Bill:

Thanks for a pleasant surprise with your letter of 10 Sept which arrived
at my desk in the last Lori. Needless to say it was good to know you are
OK and on the job as usual. I had been inquiring about you here and
there but could learn nothing. We've burned up the little old wires at that
Harding address [Ed: the Detroit apartment Dotty and Bill maintained]
but to no avail — we figured the little lady and the children had gone to
your parents or some thing for the duration. [Ed: the author also chides
Bill for also being unreachable through his lawyer, Elmer Jamison Gray.]
So you see William we had been interested all this time even though you
hadn't received any mail.

It was my intention to inquire about your plans "after." I told Baits and
Northrup you'd surely visit us when you arrived in Detroit and I'd see
what the possibilities were of you taking up where you left off. This was
several months ago and we've been expecting a call or a letter ever since.
Their interests are selfish naturally and mine too. But my selfishness is in
a slightly different direction. I think you should shop around a bit and
keep your mind open for a while. It's a big industry and we are only a
small part of it. There is an internal situation at [a] level that may move
in varied directions before you return or in early summer. There was a
battle for control at the last annual meeting and anything can happen

at the next one. This is strictly confidential of course — no word to Gray or others — please. The uncertainty of the matter suggests that you weigh the facts carefully before planning your future in uncertain hands. When you get here you can have all the dope. In the meantime you can rest assured we'll be operating when you arrive and your old job will be waiting for you if you want it.

As I write a loudspeaker (UAW-CIO) is blasting across the street to instruct two picket lines (clock and c-clock) in front of the building. The foremen walked out on or about Sept 1st protesting a cut from forty-eight hours per week to forty. [Ed: Scanlon then devotes a half-page describing the foremen's "phobia" that a 20% "base rate" cut might be increased by management to 30%] We tried to operate without them [Ed: the foremen] but after four hours of crap games, penny pitching and the normal shall we say "reluctance" to work, we sent 6,000 people home. The clock line represents the foremen, the c-clock the hourly workers in protest of the "lockout." Of course the nucleus of the whole foreman picture is recognition — and Ford having recognized their position has put the industry on the spot. Packard is carrying their case to the Supreme Court and we'll probably be in a turmoil until the thing is settled.

Add to this the oil and gas strike and you have the whole picture. Detroit gas stations are closed — dry. A few have been "authorized" for emergency purposes by the CIO boys. Men in uniform can get gas but there are so many now and they have been filling family and friend's cars, so the clamps are down on all but the serviceman's own car at the moment.

Scanlan tried to end his letter on an upbeat note, stating the World Series would start in a couple of hours with the Tigers playing the Cubs, and further stating, "Michigan has won all but one of its games so far (they played two)." In the final paragraph, however, he again referred to the labor strife racking our nation: "Ford is down too — Chrysler and GM are threatened... The gas strike has crippled twelve states and promises to permeate the country." On the last line he simply ran out of space and closed abruptly: "Fine war — great life — write when you can and come on HOME!!! DICK."

Having received the assurance he sought, on October 11, 1945, Bill wrote Dotty an upbeat letter that recapped Scanlon's assessment of the situation and concluded: "It [Scanlon's letter] gave my morale another great boost. I feel as independent as Thomas Jefferson." The following day Bill would be more reflective:

*The letter from Mr. Scanlan yesterday was good reading. Even if I may
not go back to Hudson, it is nice to know the job is there and waiting.
I had such a difficult time getting a job when I got out of school [Ed:
Bill graduated from the University of Michigan in 1933 when the Great
Depression was in full tilt]. I have always been afraid to let go of the life
raft and start swimming. The next month or two may make conditions
very favorable for a change. I would not want to take any step that would
risk the material security of my Family and the Boys future. Going back
to Hudson indicates security. Going on our own is a bid for more than
security.*

Ultimately Bill did take back his job at Hudson, and when he left a few years
later to promote his torsion-level ride suspension to Packard, it was a friendly
employee/employer parting.

Others of his age and circumstances shared the professional stress Bill confronted — the concern about being able to earn a living following the war. Dick
Stroud mused in a touching letter to his wife about the subject:

*This time darling no more travel for me… I get rather a funny feeling
sometimes but it is because of the fact that we wonder how we will fit back
into the groove we left. We want to, we know that. We want, so we wonder
just what will we do? We think of Crit, Joe, Charles, Cotton, Neil and
others we know like them who have jobs and homes and don't have to
start over. It scares us!*[523]

In World War II there were no veteran's reemployment rights. Of course Bill
and Dick were worried. In Dick's case, like Bill's, starting over happened. After
he regained his health, Dick Stroud went on to become principal of one of the
largest high schools in Texas — a job quite different from teaching a class in high
school chemistry. No doubt the organizational skills the Army Air Forces fine-
tuned in him as a supply officer paid dividends in his later professional life. The
flawless typing undoubtedly helped too.

Jack and John didn't have to worry about reemployment. They determined
to continue on in higher education and Congress provided; the G.I. Bill would
assist them financially.

Copyright by Bill Mauldin (1944). Courtesy of the Bill Mauldin Estate LLC.

CHAPTER FOURTEEN:

BILL COMES HOME

September–November 1945

ON SEPTEMBER 14, 1945 Bill reported to Dotty: "Our operations will be closed out about the end of September and transferred to PBS (Peninsular Base Section) at Leghorn and Naples." When this was accomplished, Bill indicated that those "declared surplus" with the highest points would rotate home first.

The mass redeployment of staff personnel started on September 26, 1945: "The *Vulcania* sailed yesterday after several delays," Bill noted. "I knew so many on board. There was Major Beck, Capt. Grey, Col. Ketchem of our Section and a number of WAC's who worked in Trans., etc. I think a big reception is being planned for them when they arrive in New York. My turn will eventually come."

The reduction in force was planned in increments: "The schedule for our Section calls for twenty officers on duty October 1st, fifteen on November 1st and twelve on December 1st," Bill wrote. "I feel my chances are good for November."

At this juncture Bill had an "Adjusted Service Rating Score" of seventy-seven points, reflecting a considerable improvement over the fifty-two points he anguished over during mid-May. He had been awarded eight points for the months of June, July, August and September and five points for the European-African-Middle Eastern Campaign Medal with the North Apennines battle participation award (a star worn on the medal). It was the birth of a second child however, that really helped in the points department — twelve points in June! "They announced the critical score as of October 1st would be seventy-five," Bill gleefully wrote home.

Bill was ecstatic: "That likely means that I will not be considered for assignment in Penbase and stand a good chance of being declared surplus some time next month — I hope. It's wonderful and I still can't believe it. The men in the office were kidding me about going home with only one stripe on my sleeve. One stripe is worn for each six months overseas. One is plenty for me if I can get [home] before November 12."[524] [Ed: the one-year anniversary of his departure from Hampton Roads] "I don't think there is any chance of getting there so soon but here's hoping! [Ed: Army vernacular referred to the stripe as a "hash mark" — to be worn at the bottom of the left blouse sleeve]

On September 28 Bill mailed Dotty a three-page sketch of a house that he was planning that is remarkably close to the one he and Dotty built in 1947 in Grosse Pointe Farms, Michigan, and lived in for fifty-two years — 39 Radnor Circle. "The other bedroom will have a section of outside balcony or porch without a roof at the second floor level where the evening sun may be enjoyed. That idea is very popular over here and I think you would like it."

On October 5, Bill wrote to Dotty: "I wonder how Davy will remember me. When I see Davy first I want it to be in the daytime and for him to know I'm coming so he will understand I'm returning from a trip and not be surprised at finding me there some morning."

Every serviceman with a young child or children regardless of the country one served grappled with this issue. Two months before Dick Stroud was stricken and returned to the States, he wrote Sue: "I shall have a lot of catching up to do when I get home, not to mention getting our son to accept me as a member of the family." Dick added: "What fun that will be!"[525]

Bill also complained vehemently about certain officers who used influence to get head-of-line trips home: "I did not mean to blow off steam but we are all getting pretty resentful seeing a system set up and then pushed aside as convenient for those with connections." The following day he added: "… It was eleven months last night since we said goodbye in Olean. I remember how excited Davy was when we took him to Franklinville to see Ruth [Ed: the widow of Bill's brother Dick] off on the train earlier in the evening. When I put him in bed, he said, 'No, no, say prayers' and chewed on his blanket. Does he still chew his blanket?"

In his letter of October 6, Bill added, "It has further been disclosed that promotions are not to be offered as a reward for volunteering to remain here. I wish I had known that a few days ago when I was approached on the subject." Bill later recounted that his Section — with or without Army authority — had offered to promote him to the rank of Major if he agreed to extend until 1946. Bill turned the offer down.

Several days later Bill noted: "A lot of our communications are started out by some officer who is just leaving and by the time the information is collected, no one is interested or knows what to do with it." Two days after that he complained, "When will my fate be out of some Army officer's hands?" Bill stewed over the latest rumor that he, George and many of the others had been "offered" to Penbase. He also noted that the British were faring worse than the Americans in the going-home-department: "… they [the British] are being held on duty an additional four months," he wrote. Bill pointed out that the British had a geographic advantage, however: "They have a leave service set up by which they go by train from here to the English Channel and then home for a month. Most of those staying the extra four months will have a month at home."[526]

By this time frame Luce, Clark, Dulles and Truscott had all left the area and only Luce would return to Italy at a future date in a long term official capacity. The reputations of these Americans would be forever intertwined, to one degree or another, however, with the war in Italy. The Allies had won this conflict decisively and *finally* the "old-timer" veterans of the Africa and Sicily campaigns had been shipped home! Political, espionage and military biographers would write about these four well-known people; they would also cover the pantheon of British participants in the Italian war.

MTOUSA, General McNarney, remained in Italy for the time being as there was still closing up work to do. On October 8, 1945 a trial that he convened began at the Royal Palace of Caserta, and it made the international news. The Americans prosecuted German General Anton Dostler for ordering the summary execution of fifteen American commando sappers a year and one-half earlier in what turned out to be that failed attempt to blow up the train tunnel near La Spezia. Bill did not write or ever talk about this trial, but he had to be aware that it was taking place because it was a big deal at the time. This was the first trial of an enemy general officer for a capital offense, a war crime. There was not much Dostler could do to contest the facts alleged — he had ordered the executions by telegraph and the testimony of his subordinates (who carried out his order under protest) was consistent. Still the law over collateral issues would be argued — had the Commission that tried him been properly convened? Did it have jurisdiction over the accused? Had the American commandos been "saboteurs" subject to prompt death penalty under international law? This trial was to be a precursor to the Nuremberg Trials and the world press covered it. The photos of a squat looking Dostler sitting next to his interpreter in an elaborately furnished, Roman decorated, high-ceilinged palace of justice, scowling and wearing his jack-booted leg-striped general's pants and matching military blouse with insignia of rank displayed (something denied Nuremberg military defendants) made for good copy. The General physically appeared like a stereotypical Teutonic militarist; Allied prosecutors had made a good choice in selecting him to be first up in a long docket of cases the world would judge.

It was a foregone conclusion what the verdict and sentence would be.

Bill passed the time writing a long Army history ("Those who can't make it write it") ordered by a lieutenant colonel who instructed him precisely what to write and praised him for what he wrote. A full bird-colonel then ordered Bill to re-do it as "it was all wrong."[527] The person Bill was most frustrated with was himself: on this occasion he failed to anticipate how the chain of command would react.

If Bill had a sense of accomplishment over defeating the Nazis, it is not evident in his letters. On October 16, 1945 he observed caustically: "I suppose years from now highly-paid historians will be perusing thru the [records] we save and then trying to write new texts and manuals for the war which so many people would like to see come in the next generation."

In the third week of October, Bill learned he and the others would not be reassigned to Penbase and his spirits soared. People he knew and had worked closely with were now leaving in droves. "You can see how fast the place is finally breaking up and also how little there is to do," he wrote. As it turned out for him, this statement proved only partly true. Dotty and her boys visited New York State when Bill penned this:

> *Friday Oct. 19, 1945*
> *Letter No. 349*
>
> *Dear Dotty, Folks & Boys:*
>
> *I could write a page on what happened today. The Political Advisor's office in Belgrade wanted a thousand tons of coal and would I please make arrangements including getting the coal and delivering it? The only way we have been supplying them is by air so it presented a problem. Besides passing through British and Russian controlled territory, no trial run with our supplies has been made over the rail lines in question. The*

British won't unload a ship in Trieste unless there is proof that the coal can be hauled by rail and there are not enough cars in Italy which can be spared — we'd have to get them from Austria which comes under the U.S. occupation forces, etc. I tell you this so you will understand why my hair is thinning and also why I want to become a civilian. I wouldn't mind the work if I could accomplish anything.

Saturday Nov. 3, 1945

Dearest Dotty, Folks and Sons:

I worked for a couple of days setting up rail transportation for about 30,000 tons of flour from Italy to Austria and the day after I get it all set, a bridge over the Po river is declared unsafe for traffic. We will not know for a couple of days whether the move can come off. Sitting down here, it is so hard to accomplish anything. The country is a mess. Shipping from one country to another presents a lot of problems such as guards, authority for the move, who will furnish equipment, who will load and unload, are the lines open, landslides, floods, poorly reconstructed lines and a thousand other things. I'll be happy to work on simple gadgets like suspensions.

Ed: Bill's sense of frustration was heightened by the fact that he had not received mail in a couple of days and he had learned that he would not be ordered to the depot by November 9 as he had expected. His last paragraph began with, "This has been a very bum letter." He enclosed the following article from the *Stars and Stripes Mediterranean* dated November 1st:

HERE'S HOW IT'S DONE MATES

The lights in the Pentagon Building are burning long and late these nights, as Washington labors to speed up redeployment and get our boys back home. But, lo and behold, officials over there in the capital have only to turn to our readers for a practical solution to all of their problems.

For example, T-4 Russell R. Ross: "Admit Italy to the Union as the 49th State, then the boys would already be back." This solution has outstanding possibilities.

A helpful hint from Pvt. J.K. Wearne, and proposed by many others, reads, "I think I will go back on the Italian immigration quota."

*The next... solve[s] the shipping problem back to the States in an
extremely efficient manner.*

*Nicholas McGillicutty writes: "If they would release us from this depot, I
think we could get home much quicker by furnishing our own transportation. An Italian fisherman told me that he would carry twelve of us to
New York in his shrimp boat, for twenty cartons of cigarettes, one American civilian suit, one pair of G.I. shoes, ten pounds of sugar, ten pounds of
coffee and two boxes of chocolates for his bambino. This is cheap at half
the price."*

Panorama of Italy *[conclusion]*

*The family wash, of tattletale gray;
Hung from a balcony, blocking the way;
Native coffee, God, what a mixture;
Tile bathrooms, with one extra fixture.*

*Families dining, from one common bowl;
Next to a fish store, a terrible hole;
Italian zoot-suiters, flashily dressed,
Bare-footed beggars, looking oppressed.*

*Mud-smeared children, clustered about;
Filling their jugs, at a community spout;
Dutiful Dotty, with look of despair;
Picking lice from a small daughter's hair.*

*Capable craftsmen, skilled in their art;
Decrepit old shacks, falling apart;
Intricate needlework, out on display;
Surrounded by filth, rot and decay.*

*Elegant caskets, carved out by hand;
Odorous factories where leather is tanned;
A shoemaker's shop: a black market store;
Crawling with vermin, no screen on the door.*

*No sense of shame has this itching boy;
Unfortunate children, with nary a toy;
Pathetic monstrosity, the hunch back dwarf;
Oil strewn shore, craft rotting at wharf.*

I've tried to describe the things I have seen;
A panorama of Italy, the brown and the green;
I've neglected the war scars, visible yet;
But these are the things we want to forget.

I'm glad I came, but damn anxious to go;
Give it back to the natives, hell, I'm ready to blow.

Sometime towards the end of October or early November Bill received a letter dated 11 October 1945 and postmarked, "Saint Louis MO." The letter was from Major Mark A. Renick. Upbeat and warm — the Major thanked Bill for his recent letter, "and the card signed by the Italians," talked about fixing up his "old house" and reported the highly anticipated discharge of a son from the Coast Guard. He also mentioned his "little bulldog" following him around and a party his daughter put on a few days earlier: "Just fifty-one girls were here so you can imagine the tough job I had. As bartender of course I had to taste quite a few before getting the right mixture."

Upon mustering out, Renick stated that the Army had given him eighty-seven days "accrued leave pay" plus an additional twenty days "recuperation leave pay." There is no mention of Mrs. Renick in his two-page letter, and one can only wonder: Was his wife, who had been ill, still alive?

McCutter

My name is McCutter,
One ear to the gutter,
I spread all the rumors for free.
If you have a question
On points of contention,
Ask Ridgeway, Howder or Me.

I rule on the policy,
The bad and the good,
I'm VIP, don't you see.
Confusion of others is
Not understood
By Ridgeway, Howder and Me.

The front office Colonel,
Sharp tongued eternal,
He knows all the rules A to Z.
But when there's trouble,
He comes on the double,
To Ridgeway, Howder and Me.

This story must end
While I've still got a friend,
Who will listen and reparteé.
For the forty-nine points,
We'll be home in six months,
Ridgeway and Howder, NOT me.

W.D. Allison 30 October 1945

Ridgeway is the aforementioned famed General Mathew C. Ridgeway who first gained his reputation in the Battle of Sicily, and then Salerno with his unit the 82nd Airborne Division. Colonel James D. Howder was the Chief of G-1 Division Personnel, MTOUSA. The name McCutter is not to be found among Bill's service documents, but it is a safe bet he was the recently arrived junior officer who awarded Bill the Adolf Hitler medal.

On November 4 Bill wrote Dotty, "All officers with eighty or more points are on their way to the depot tomorrow." He also reported attending the opera "La Boheme" and hating it: "The heroine wasted away from her normal 250 lbs. to a mere 220 pounds before she threw in the sponge. And I was itching all over when I left the place." It turned out that Bill's itching resulted from lice-infested "dirty plush chairs."

As his rotation date approached, Bill ironically expressed concern over who might do his job when he was gone. On November 8 he wrote, "… there is really quite a bit to do on the rail side." He was relieved to report that George had made it back from a trip somewhere, albeit four days late owing to travel snafus. "Our experienced personnel in Leghorn and Naples are gradually leaving and it gets increasingly difficult to get tonnage moved." He reported that he might be eligible for the Replacement Depot as early as the 10th. "I get a big kick out of packing," he wrote. "I can hardly wait. Now that George is back there are no more headaches for me and I can leave with no concern over the job. The experience is something like passing your final exams." On November 12, 1945, the anniversary of his departure for Europe Bill was authorized to wear two "hash marks" on the left lower sleeve of his blouse, symbolizing two six-month periods of overseas duty:

NOVEMBER 11, 1945

My thoughts in Church this morning,
Wandered far and near.
Most everything the preacher said
Was lost upon my ear.

A year ago tomorrow
I climbed the gangplank drear.
Into the side of a gray ship,
Its end did disappear.

My pack was heavy, with blankets rolled,
And soldier's tools with every part.
But the biggest load I carried,
Was the sadness in my heart.

My loving Wife and little Son,
Were praying for me then.
And looking forward to the day,
When I would come again.

And now I have my orders home.

W.D. Allison, Capt. T.C.

On November 13 Bill finally reported to the Naples Replacement Depot, the same outfit that lost him for a week the year earlier. His letter to Dotty that day expresses joy at the thought of soon being home, but also included this:

This morning I met one of the men who shared our tent a year ago when I arrived. Do you remember me writing about one officer who when he ran out of things to write to his wife, just figured out another way to tell her how much he loved her? Well the officer that I met this morning reports that [he] was killed in action, still a second is missing and probably killed and he himself was wounded.

Bill passed some of the time working in the hobby shop, where he built a small drawing board and T-square out of Lucite, a new material that fascinated him. He would write Dotty: "When heated it becomes almost as flexible as leather. It will stay in the shape in which it cools. It is the material I have in mind for the domed sleeping room in the ultramodern home."

Thurs, Nov 15, 1945
Letter No. 374

Darling, Davy and Dick:

I just came in from dinner to the lounge here in the hotel. The men are sitting around talking, playing cards, reading, a ping-pong game in the next room, checkers & chess. Most of the men seem to be smoking at least from the density of the air, and all of them have an eye on the bulletin board at the end of the room. I just heard there is a stack of orders in the orderly room that likely will be handed out in the morning. Quite a few headed out yesterday but none today… all are anxious…

Sunday, Nov, 18, 1945
Letter No. 376

Darling:

I can scarcely endure the disappointment of being left behind as the carrier loads. They say the orders for it are all issued now and mine have not arrived. It seems the group I've been assigned to escort home are scheduled for another ship, probably a Liberty. It will take about two weeks on the water. I guess when we have all of the rest of our lives together, another week or so apart can be endured but being unable to do anything about it or having any choice makes it so difficult…

It's wonderful to love and be loved by you.

Bill

Four days later, on Thanksgiving Day, November 22, 1945, Bill learned that he and the 108 enlisted men in his charge would return on one of the fastest ships, the aircraft carrier *USS Randolph*. One of Bill's favorite stories was how he had been detailed chief mess officer for a belated Thanksgiving dinner at sea involving thousands of embarked Army personnel. "It was the worst job I ever had in the service," he repeated proudly on more than one occasion. "We ran out of fresh turkey and opened greasy, canned stuff. The ship rolled and pitched, and the slop spilled down ladders and all over the hanger deck where we bunked. It was unbelievable, yuck!"

Upon arrival in Port of New York, the first thing Bill and his shipmates did, after phoning loved ones was to, "Drink milk. We craved it." Bill's Service Record shows he departed Camp Atterbury, Indiana (the Army separation activity he and his enlisted men had been railed to) on December 8. He traveled by train to Detroit, Michigan, a distance of 309 miles. The Army paid Bill accrued leave until 17 February 1946 and his muster-out physical examination shows he had gained eleven pounds in the service.

The reunion took place at Michigan Central Station in Detroit, with Bill, Dotty and Davy (with the newborn being at the Harding Road apartment being watched over by grandparents). Many decades later when traveling on I-75 to Toledo to visit Dave and his family, Bill would look up at the decayed and darkened shell of Michigan Central Station. He would never fail to reminisce about "that wonderful day."

One of Bill's favorite stories was about something Davy said at the Detroit apartment, in anticipation of receiving a gift from the locked footlocker Bill had mailed back on November 11. Bill could not find his trunk key immediately and was amazed to hear his three and one-half year old spout: "Daddy, do you have a duplicate key?" Twenty-three years later David, then a U.S. Army surgeon, would take this footlocker with him to Vietnam.

In Bill's trunk were treasures — two white marble carved elephants — a small one and a larger one for Davy. He had earlier mailed home two orange and white alabaster vases and a picture book entitled, "Scenic Wonders of Italy" (the photo of the statue of the naked Venus de Milo really caught the attention of a certain a young boy).

The "AUTHORITY FOR RETENTION OF WAR TROPHIES" documents issued to Bill indicate he brought home a pistol, compass, helmet, parka with fur liner, fur cap, bayonet and scabbard and pocket knife.

One of David's favorite stories about the homecoming is how Dotty and Bill both took "sick" at the same time. "They spent so much time in bed I got concerned," Dave remembered.

EPILOGUE

Harold Alexander 1891-1969

British Field Marshal The Honorable Sir Harold R.L.G. Alexander, Supreme Allied Commander of the Mediterranean Theater of Operations, later to be known as the Earl Alexander of Tunis, had the distinction of commanding the largest number of international delegations ever assembled in the history of warfare — twenty-six per his memoirs. Effectively managing coalition forces was not an easy task given the challenges presented by divergent languages and different organizational structures, weapon systems and training regimens, but Alexander did it.

Harold Alexander

Born as a third son to a noble London family, it was a normal progression for young Alexander to enter the Royal Military College, Sandhurst. In World War I Alexander served with distinction in units that were in the thick of battles, was twice wounded and decorated for bravery. Stints of international, empire and home duty followed between the world wars. In 1937 he served as an aide-de-camp to His Majesty King George VI during the coronation ceremony. When World War II broke out in 1939 Alexander held the rank of Major General.

As officer-in-charge of the British Expeditionary Force during the final evacuation of Dunkirk in early June 1940, Alexander departed on the last warship
after he got his men safely off the continent. After the fall of Singapore in February 1942 he proceeded to Burma where he fought a desperate holding action
against the advancing Japanese. In mid-August 1942 he was hastily summoned
to become Commander-in-Chief Middle East Command, replacing the sacked
Claude Auchinleck. In the year that followed Alexander earned his title Alexander
of Tunis for his contribution in bringing about the link-up with Anglo-American
forces from the Operation Torch landing, effectively dooming Rommel's Africa
Korps. One commentator observed, "Alexander's appointment owed much to
his ability to bring conflicting personalities together into an effective team."[528]
Truly he did this with Clark and Truscott.

No doubt Alexander had his detractors, and there were those who resented
his noble heritage. He earned his promotions through victory, however, and his
biography makes for a most interesting military history read.

Bill Allison 1908–1999

In Bill's military service record are the documents that corroborate a story that
Dotty often told, the documents that were both a source of angst and pride for
her, documents that are so representative of Bill's generation. On April 11, 1941
some eight months before Pearl Harbor, Bill flunked a routine military physical
for being eleven pounds underweight and having an enlarged spleen. The Army
letter he received gave Bill a choice: "If you do not desire transfer [to the Inactive
Reserve] you will be honorably discharged from the Officer's Reserve Corps."
Bill chose to stay in and requested the transfer.

A little over a year later and with our country at war, an Army doctor re-
examined Bill. His enlarged spleen was this time deemed medically OK, but Bill
was again disqualified for being underweight. Buried in the yellowed paperwork
is the form AFFIDAVIT Bill voluntarily signed on June 30, 1942 (at a time when
he had steady employment at Hudson Motor Car Company and a wife and
twenty-eight day-old son):

> I, WILLIAM DAVID ALLISON, 1st Lt,. Sig Res   , *being desirous*
> *of entering upon active military service during the current emergency,*
> *and being aware of the fact that I have the following physical defects:*

<u>Ten pounds underweight</u>, *do hereby acknowledge the existence of the above mentioned physical defects, and request that I be placed on extended active duty.*

—ᵚᵚᵚ—

It happened that the home Bill and Dotty built in 1947 had a basement workshop that witnessed considerable use. Replete with welding equipment, drill press, grinders, and other metal and woodworking equipment, over the decades Bill turned out model after model of automobile suspension systems, steerage linkages, tie and stabilizer rods, U-shaped torsion bars and a plethora of other innovations, all representative of new automotive technology. Bill tinkered incessantly in his workshop and at a time when a personal computer had yet to be invented, he would invariably use a drafting table in an adjoining room to formalize his concepts.

Over the period 1938-1992 Bill was awarded seventy-six U.S. patents and a number of his inventions ended up in production. He was proud to be seen working a slide-rule.

Among Bill's memorabilia is to be found a quote attributed to the financer Baron Rothschild (1840-1915). Bill relished the humor: "There are three ways of ruining oneself: women, gambling and inventors. The last is the least agreeable but the most certain."

Bill proved the Baron wrong.

"I have been blessed to live during the most exciting technological era the world has ever known," Bill was fond of saying. One of his earliest inventions was a winding device or winch for vehicles that he licensed to Garwood Industries for production. Filed in 1944 and issued in 1949 this wire spooling device ended-up being used extensively by military vehicles to pull out other vehicles that were (surprise!) stuck in the mud, and for numerous civilian applications as well.

Bill invented a power steering assist mechanism that was sold to General Motors in the late 1940s. He is perhaps best remembered however, for inventing the Torsion-Level Ride suspension system that went into production at Packard Motor Car Company in 1955. With great handling characteristics and an unequalled smoothness of ride, Torsion-Level Packards are still popular with antique automobile hobbyists. One recent TV commentator described the experience of driving a Packard Caribbean: "This thing rides like a cloud."

Following Packard, Bill worked in research and development at Ford Motor Company until his retirement in 1975, when he was awarded an honorary membership in Ford Executive Engineers. He produced scores of patents while at Ford — the most extensively built being a rear suspension system used on the Ford Aerostar minivan. In retirement Bill took a keen interest in developing clean energy, focusing on wind power as a substitute for burning fossil fuels. In addition to several multi-vane windmill and blade design patents, he also patented a new oil well pumping mechanism and even a suspension and braking system for in-line roller skates based upon the tandem-wheeled design employed in his 1945 multi-axle tank carrier. At age eighty Bill personally tried out his modified roller-blades on a bumpy section of sidewalk. His windmill, pump-jack and skate suspension inventions made little money but provided Bill with hours of joy.

In 1972 Bill and Dotty vacationed in Italy and Bill revisited several of the places and sights he had experienced during the war. Theirs was a ten-day trip, with bus tours in and around Rome, Naples and Florence. Bill's only diary entry from this vacation that referenced the war said, "Saw top of Palace of Caserta where I was stationed during World War II." Upon returning, Bill said, however, that Naples had bettered itself almost beyond recognition: "In the war, women carried large water jugs on their heads like in ancient times."

Bill's recollection of the water sellers of old was spot on. On February 28, 1944 British journalist Norman Lewis recorded from Naples: "These picturesque figures [the water sellers] and the equipment they carry are hardly changed from the representations of them in the frescoes of Pompeii." Lewis explained the reason that Lieutenant Dick Stroud never saw Italians drink water. A cup of water "costs three or four times the equivalent amount of wine," Lewis wrote.[529] During the war the Americans and the British soldiers could afford to purchase clean drinking water; many — most — natives could not. By 1972 all Italians could purchase water. And chocolates. And more.

Dotty died in 2006.

Edward Almond 1892-1979

Edward "Ned" Almond, a Virginia Military Institute graduate had a full and successful career in the U.S. Army. Following World War II he joined General MacArthur's staff in Tokyo and in 1949 rose to Chief of Staff, Far East Command.

Promoted to Lieutenant General, he served as a corps commander in Korea and later as commanding officer U.S. Army War College.

General Almond believed in racial segregation, as did many U.S. Army generals at the time.

> *"The white man… is willing to die for patriotic reasons. The Negro is not. No white man wants to be accused of leaving the battle line. The Negro doesn't care… people think being from the South we don't like Negroes. Not at all. But we understand his capabilities. And we don't want to sit at the table with them."* Edward Almond[530]

Pietro Badoglio 1871–1956

If a single accomplishment may be lauded for a lifetime achievement, then the Marshal and Prime Minister of Italy, 1st Duke of Addis Ababa, Pietro Badoglio ought to be honored highly for having died of natural causes at the ripe old age of eighty-five in 1956.

This man was a survivor.

If Badoglio had died before Shakespeare, there would have been a play written about him. To quote one contemporary pundit:

> *"His shifting loyalties have left him reviled by communists as well as fascists, by Italian patriots and the enemies of Italy and by republicans as well as well as monarchists. Certainly, others in history have been known for changing allegiance, fighting for one side and then later opposing it, but usually they were being loyal to some greater cause, some noble principle, even if evident only to themselves. In the case of Marshal Badoglio however, it is hard to see any motivation other than a self-serving effort to shift blame, avoid responsibility and survive the consequences of what were often his own mistakes."*[531]

Multiple sources confirm the accuracy of this sentiment. Rising in the military ranks Badoglio served as chief of Italian army general staff from 1919 to 1921, when the political situation involving Benito Mussolini and his fascist Black Shirts reared up. Initially not supporting Mussolini, Badoglio accepted an appointment as ambassador to Brazil. In 1925, with Mussolini in full control of Italy, Badoglio had a change of heart about Il Duce and accepted the dictator's appointment to his old military post. He subsequently governed Libya from 1928 to 1934, and the following year assumed command of Italian forces in Ethiopia, where he employed mustard gas, conquered Addis Ababa, expanded the Italian empire and acted as Viceroy of the country, being awarded the title Duke. Later, back again as army chief of staff, Badoglio counseled his Iron Prefect and King that Italy was ill prepared to enter World War II, but failed to object to them declaring it.

Pietro Badoglio

Then there is this ditty from *Encyclopedia Britannica*: "On Dec. 4, 1940, in the midst of Italy's disastrous campaign in Greece, he [Badoglio] resigned as chief of staff and disavowed responsibility for Mussolini's acts. It is not clear, however, whether his objections were tied to concerns over morals or military strategy."[532] In mid-1943 with Italy losing badly and the war getting closer to Italian shores, as related in this history Badoglio arranged to have King Victor Emmanuel III sack Mussolini and have himself appointed Prime Minister. What followed was the Gilbert & Sullivan-like comedy performance described in this book. The 1943 "switch in time" brought Badoglio under British protection, however. After the war Badoglio could have been prosecuted as a war criminal for having ordered mustard gas used on the Ethiopians. This crime was overlooked however, as the British (and to a lesser extent the Americans) found Badoglio "... instrumental in bringing Italian belligerency in the Second World War to a close."[533] Badoglio had successfully refashioned himself as an anti-Soviet Union stand-up leader for freedom, and in his transformation found a tasting for regular servings of British tea and cake.

Mary Bancroft 1903-1997

The daughter of a Boston Brahmin father who published the *Wall Street Journal*, Mary Bancroft chose to live a free-spirited life. Her 1983 book *Autobiography of a Spy* advertises "Debutante, writer, confidant, secret agent — the true story of her extraordinary life by Mary Bancroft." Dropping out of Smith College after a year and leaving New York City for Europe (following a high-society divorce) Bancroft settled in Zurich in 1934 where she became fluent in French and German, wrote for Swiss newspapers, attended lectures and formed a close friendship with psychotherapist Dr. Carl Jung and married a Swiss national. When the war broke out the U.S. Embassy in Berne introduced her to Allen Dulles who hired her first as an OSS analyst of articles written in the Nazi controlled press, and later as a secret agent. She fell in love with Dulles and also became infatuated with the German *Abwehr* officer who Dulles assigned her to work with regarding *Operation Valkyrie* — the July 20, 1944 assassination plot against Hitler. She wrote about this German spy: "...the attraction between us was like a high tension power line..." Finally divorcing her Swiss husband in 1947, Bancroft returned permanently to the United States in 1953 to live the life of a New York heiress, novelist and autobiographer. Dulles, who died in 1969, would have no doubt appreciated what Bancroft wrote about him — it reads like an action-thriller novel. While in New York, Bancroft befriended Norman Mailer, Woody Allen and other notable writers and artists. "She corresponded with publisher Henry R. Luce for a number of years," a biographical sketch noted.[534]

Mark Clark 1896-1984

Of all of the high U.S. commanders to be rated by historians after World War II, General Mark W. Clark arguably holds first place in both the "least likable" and "most militarily incompetent" categories. "He was cocky to the point of arrogant," wrote one modern day commentator "... dubbed Marcus Aurelius Clarkus..."[535] Truscott noted in a letter he wrote home at a time when he was subordinate to Clark, that Clark had, "plenty of ability, but is one of the most self-centered individuals I have ever known. He has always given me 100% support heretofore — and I had almost forgotten my inability to feel complete confidence in him — but it comes back in force." Always the optimist, Truscott, finished: "It will work out alright I'm sure."[536] It was General Patton, however — himself a candidate for a "not-a-nice-guy" award — who said it most succinctly about Clark: "Too damn slick," Old Blood and Guts blurted, "[he] made my flesh creep."[537]

For his part, Clark is on record as being derogatory about Alexander behind his back. Clark considered the British not aggressive enough, and on more than one occasion he referred to Alexander as a vacillating "feather duster,"[538] that is, someone who waivered between confidence and uncertainty. A Pulitzer Prize winning historian labeled Clark a "... tall, hawk nosed ... Anglophobe ..." noting he was "... a publicity and glory hound, a man ruthless towards subordinates ..."[539] It is no surprise that Alexander, with Churchill's backing, eventually found a way to work around Clark in the form of Lucien Truscott.

Mark W. Clark

Clark and Truscott did not respect each other professionally — that comes out in the writings of both by what was said and what was left unsaid. Clark hardly mentions Truscott towards the end of his World War II memoirs. As for Truscott's take on Clark, one only needs to read Truscott's negative opinion of Clark's Pianoro Plan. To Clark's credit he did not use his command position to hold back or tarnish Truscott's military career. On May 24, 1945 Clark wrote Truscott's final Efficiency Report "... rating him [Truscott] number one among seventy-one general officers for promotion ..."[540] Clark undoubtedly sensed that any lower rating of Truscott would not, could not, be supported by Eisenhower and Marshall given the hugely successful outcome of the North Apennines break-out. Clark was adept at Army politics, if nothing else, and that meant keeping controversial matters off the desks of superiors.

This assessment comes from a modern-day writer: "It was mostly because of General Clark's desire to be the first into Rome in May-June 1944 that a large portion of German forces escaped encirclement..."[541] More salt for the wound comes from yet another recently published historian: "The prospect of attacking through the passes [Gothic Line] appealed to Clark — it would give the Fifth Army the lion's share of the action, and for him the lion's share of the glory."[542]

The above noted, it should also be pointed out that the U.S. Army never lost confidence in General Mark W. Clark. Early in the war he had taken a personal risk that served his country extremely well. During the planning stage for *Operation Torch*, the 1942 invasion of North Africa, Clark led a dangerous pre-assault intelligence-gathering foray into French Morocco, arriving there in a submarine with only a handful of aides. The information that he gathered and provided to Eisenhower from this secret trip proved invaluable (of note one of the aides was Lemnitzer).

Moreover, it was Clark who trained and organized the U.S. Fifth Army, "the first American Army to invade Hitler's Fortress Europe," and no one questioned his competency in doing so. He participated in combat, survived close enemy shellfire hits, and at one-time personally led an attack against 18 German tanks; he also partook in other valorous actions. Clark's preference was to witness fluid operational situations rather than just rely on reports, and he was seen by G.I.s outside his command bunker often. As a tactician, however, he was justly criticized for launching unimaginative head-on attacks.

Asked about Mark Clark's reputation among the men, Jack King said, "General Clark didn't bother us at the 91st." Jack never recalled seeing him. Asked specifically about Anzio, Jack pointed out that it was "common knowledge" that Clark had botched the invasion there by failing to press the attack and allowing the Germans time to set up their defenses. "He always traveled with press," Jack laughed, again with a disclaimer he had not personally seen this. "To show he was a combat general."

Clark did not agree with what President Truman did in 1948 by integrating the U.S. Armed Forces. He wrote in 1950:

> Let me be clear that I am opposed to discrimination. I believe there is a way to work toward a solution of the problems that handicap the Negro soldier, although I do not feel at this stage of the game there should be an indiscriminate mixing of Negro and white soldiers in our Army.[543]

General Mark Clark stayed in the army following World War II and on July 27, 1953, as United Nations Commander he signed the armistice that ended the Korean War. The last years of his professional life were spent as president of The Citadel, the military college at Charleston, SC, and during the course of his tenure there met alumnus John Lesesne, M.D.

Should the cadets of The Citadel today be proud that General Clark served as their president given all of the negative things that have been written about him? Yes, they should. Mark W. Clark was a U.S. army general who entered the theatre of war as a leader at a time when there was no certainty that the United States would be victorious. Clark deserves credit for what he accomplished. Also, Clark personally had no illusions about what he fought for. His mother was a child of Romanian Jews.

Anton Dostler 1891-1945

Wehrmacht General of the Infantry Anton Dostler had served thirty-four years in the German Army at the time two U.S. soldiers tied him to a stake on the morning of December 1, 1945 preparatory to his execution by a firing squad consisting of twelve American soldiers. He had been found guilty by a five-officer U.S. Military Commission convened by General McNarney of ordering the summary execution of fifteen uniformed American servicemen. At his four-day trial Dostler argued that he had not issued the order but rather passed it on as a standing Führer order (a "Führerbefehl") and that, in any event, reprisal was legal against such OSS commando operatives. The Commission found otherwise, noting that the 1907 Hague Convention on Land Warfare permitted the execution of spies and saboteurs disguised in enemy uniforms or civilian clothes and also that the Geneva Convention prohibited reprisals against prisoners of war, which these fifteen military uniformed Americans clearly were. The Commission pointed out that the fifteen Americans "... were neither tried nor given a hearing"[544] and rejected the defense of following a Hitler order.

As a military courtesy of sorts Dostler was allowed to die in uniform wearing his insignia of rank; such a distinction was not afforded to subsequent condemned military war criminals.

Of interest today, the Commission ruled that McNarney had the power to appoint it and also accepted the prosecution arguments that a Military Commission "... for more than 100 years [had been] the proper method of trial" and that the United States was the "…injured belligerent who could bring the captured before a Military Commission."

As Commander-in-Chief President Truman was the last stop of an expedited review process. Truman was not troubled with the Commission's ruling — he allowed Dostler's execution to proceed.

Allen Dulles 1893-1969

"His ten years of service in the Central Intelligence Agency," President John F. Kennedy said into the microphone about Allen Dulles, "have been the climax of a lifetime of unprecedented and devoted public service beginning in the First World War…"

The date was November 28, 1961 and setting the CIA Building in Langley, VA. The President continued on about Dulles' "… outstanding contributions… profound knowledge… naturally keen judgment… zestful energy… undaunted integrity…" Concluding his remarks, Kennedy turned to Dulles and awarded him the National Security Medal. The following day Dulles (as ordered) turned in his letter of resignation as CIA Director.[545]

Someone had to be held accountable for the Bay of Pigs fiasco.

Although this was not the storybook ending that Dulles would have wanted for his career as a spy chief, Dulles was gracious about what Kennedy had done and he enjoyed his retirement by taking up writing again, something he liked to do and at which he excelled. His was an interesting career indeed!

As stated, out of college in 1916, Dulles worked for the U.S. diplomatic service in Istanbul, Vienna and Berne and acquired an appetite for international relations and all things European before returning home to become a lawyer in the mid-1920s. In the 1930s Dulles acted a legal adviser for arms limitations talks under the auspices of the League of Nations and in that capacity had occasion to meet leaders of many European nations including Hitler and Mussolini. Repelled by the Nazi treatment of the Jews, Dulles was instrumental in having his law firm Sullivan and Cromwell close its Berlin office in protest. In 1938 he made an unsuccessful attempt to secure the Republican nomination to run for New York States' 16th Congressional District, arguing vociferously that the United States should bolster its national defense forces. Although Dulles failed at his attempt for elected office, when the war came his public and long-standing antipathy toward the fascists and proven ability as a high-powered lawyer (one with connections all over Europe) put him top of the list for recruitment by the OSS.

Following World War II Dulles became an adviser to presidential candidate Thomas E. Dewey and kept his hand in Republican politics. His CIA directorship came under President Eisenhower in 1952 and during the Cold War Dulles put together a huge international spy network. He investigated *all* communists and other perceived threats to the U.S. and its interests. He championed the development and use of the U-2 spy plane during a period before spy satellites, and did scientific research on mind control. It was Allen W. Dulles who covertly "facilitated" the Shah of Iran coming into power in 1953 and he accomplished a coup d'état in Guatemala the following year. As CIA Director one might reasonably rate Dulles as "pro-active".

Allen Dulles

It was Jacqueline Kennedy who first recommended a James Bond book to Dulles, giving him a copy of the one he ended up enjoying the most, *From Russia with Love*. Soon thereafter Dulles was introduced to and befriended its author, Ian Fleming. "I knew Ian well and liked him," Dulles said in an interview after leaving the CIA. "If you didn't bore him he would probably like you. Ian was a real gourmet, particularly in exotic dishes from the Orient." Asked how James Bond would compare with actual secret agents, Dulles replied: "There is very little resemblance. The modern spy could not permit himself to become the target of luscious dames who approach him in bars or come out of closets in hotel rooms. Most of the great spies were modest in appearance, careful in their actions and their contacts ... I fear that James Bond in real life would have had a thick dossier in the Kremlin after his first exploit and would not have survived the second." Still, Dulles loved the Bond series and Fleming mailed him new books as they came out with clever personal inscriptions. In 1964, when Fleming did not look well to Dulles (and Dulles knew that his friend had refused to "take it easy" when medically advised to do so) he mailed Dulles his final book with the Japanese setting *You Only Live Twice*. Fleming inscribed in it: "To Celestial Dulles-san, from Miserable Fleming-san."[546] Fleming died shortly after at age fifty-six.

The two intelligence men apparently shared more than epicurean palates and a taste for expensive liquors, fine wines and the best tobaccos. Like Agent 007 both were unabashed womanizers. In Dulles' case, his tally of adultery was "a least a hundred" according to a letter his sister Eleanor wrote, per a *New York Times* article. His biographer, Stephen Kinzer, who wrote the article observed: "Dulles's behavior was well known in Washington and elsewhere, but never publicly reported. By the journalistic codes of the 1950s, it was not newsworthy." Apparently Dulles viewed seduction as a sport.

As an aside, undoubtedly hoping to motivate others to come forward with something akin to dirt, Kinzer adds, gratuitously: "... he [Dulles] was rumored to have become familiar with one of the highest-profile women of the era, Clare Boothe Luce, the wife of..."[547]

Like him or not, Allen Dulles was a key figure during an era when America was known to play hardball with foreign countries; he was a major persona and achieved a number of successes for his country.

In his exceptional but tailored book *The Secret Surrender* Dulles reveals the feedback that he was proudest of in regard to what he accomplished in wartime Italy and perhaps in his lifetime. One of the officers that worked for his boss William Donovan had a son in the U.S. Army in Italy poised to attack when the announcement of the German surrender broke. This father sent agent #110 (the OSS number for Dulles) a short note:

> *Countless thousands of parents would bless you were they privileged to know what you have done. As one of them privileged to know, and with a boy in the Mountain Division, I do bless you.*[548]

Doubtless many German parents would have blessed Dulles too had they known.

Victor Emmanuel III 1869-1947

In 1946 the Italian people abolished the *Kingdom of Italy* by a referendum vote that established a republic. Emmanuel III's reign (1900-1946) witnessed the beginning and end of Italian fascism. As monarch he accepted and embraced "... a totalitarian form of government..." essayist Umberto Eco observed, "based upon the idea of a charismatic ruler, on corporatism, on the utopia of the imperial fate of Rome, on an imperialistic will to conquer new territories, on an exacerbated nationalism, on the ideal of an entire nation regimented in black shirts, on anti-Semitism..."[549]

The result was a chain of events leading to a copycat Hitler and human disaster. Following being voted out, the former king took exile in Alexandra, Egypt. He died the following year. His son Umberto II took exile in Portugal and died in 1983, never having returned to Italy.

Gee-Haw 1835-1956

No mules were returned to America following the war in Italy. Some were shipped to CBI, others given to Italians and still others sent to Greece for use in its civil war. Some captured Nazi mules ended up being fed to their former masters. "The last U.S. Army mules were formally mustered out of service in December 1956," wrote history Professor Emmett M. Essen, "ending a 125 years of military reliance on the virtues of this singular animal." Reintroduction of the mule was considered by the Army in 1985 but not followed up on after *New York Times* columnist Tom Wicker reacted by sarcastically recommending that Congress name October 26 "Mule Appreciation Day." Replaced by the helicopter, the mule today remains the official mascot of the United States Military Academy. The animal serving in this capacity at West Point after World War II was originally named "Bud" but the Cadets changed his name to "Hannibal," undoubtedly a tie-in to Italy. Hannibal died in action in 1964, having been kicked by another mule.

Gero von Schulze Gaevernitz 1901-1970

There is little to relate about Gero Gaevernitz following the war. His close friendship with Allen Dulles remained solid for life and he never again was to have a crucial role on the world stage such as he briefly held at Ascona and Caserta in 1945. Gaevernitz was an economist and continued to maintain business holdings in Switzerland. He remained steadfast in his belief that there was goodness within the German people; that Hitler's following was never as strong as the Nazi propaganda apparatus reported it to be. Indeed, in 1947 Gaevernitz wrote a book about heroic Germans who paid dearly for trying to stop Hitler. In the book's introduction William Dovovan gave the reason Gaevernitz wrote it: "... [to] remind us of the self-sacrifice of brave men who died on the gallows, under torture or in concentration camps because they dared against hopeless odds to plot the downfall of a tyrant."[550]

Gero von Schultz Gaevernitz

Gaevernitz remained true to the teachings of his father Gerhart (1864–1943), a university professor and German citizen, who early in life wrote the book *Zum Sozial Frieden* ("Toward a Peaceful Society") and late in life became a Quaker.[551]

If Mary Bancroft's gossipy innuendo is by chance correct there exists a personal ambiguity about Gaevernitz's private life. The implications could be hilarious, depressing or both depending on one's perspective. After the surrender in Italy took effect Gaevernitz traveled to Bolzano palace to be with Wolff and Vietinghoff before Allied forces arrived to take them into custody. Peace had been achieved and Gaevernitz no doubt assuaged these nervous commanding generals by assuring them that they had done the right and honorable thing; also perhaps he intimated that they would treated decently in confinement. The German generals undoubtedly appreciated the role that Gaevernitz had performed to perfection. As the U.S. Army prepared to move into Bolzano they had this American intelligence officer (and a new found friend) at their side, supporting them.

In her catty autobiography Mary Bancroft wrote that Hungarian intelligence had determined (without evidence) that Gaevernitz was the lover of Allen Dulles.[552] Sizzle sells books but the possibility exists that Bancroft offered this gratuitous tittle-tattle as a not too subtle means to express *her* opinion of Gaevernitz's sexuality. Innuendo such as this normally is not worth repetition but imagine, reader, the incongruity and sweet irony of a kind-hearted gay man saving the life of at least one uber-Nazi who under different circumstances would not have hesitated to murder him for simply being the human being he had been born to be.

Ernst Kaltenbrunner 1903-1946

The highest-ranking SS officer to be tried after the war, *SS Obergruppenführer* Kaltenbrunner was hanged October 16, 1946 for war crimes and crimes against humanity.

Herbert Kappler 1907-1978

SS Obersturmbahnführer Kapplar, head of the German Police and Security Services Rome was fortunate to be tried by an Italian court at a time when Italy had abolished the death penalty. He had planned the minute details of the ten-for-one decimation roundup and reprisal murder of 335 Roman citizens in March 1944 known as the Ardeatine caves massacre. He acted as one of the triggermen. In 1976, terminally ill with cancer and weighing only 100 lbs., Kappler escaped when his wife carried him in a suitcase out of a military hospital in Rome. West German authorities declined to extradite him.

Albert Kesselring 1885-1960

"I am unhappy over Kesselring's death sentence," wrote the Governor General of Canada in 1947 to the former Prime Minister of Great Britain. "Personally as his old opponent on the battlefield I have no complaint against him. Kesselring and his soldiers fought against us hard and clean."[553]

In stating this to Churchill, Alexander had to be mindful that he, while in command had made BBC radio broadcasts to Italians on three occasions in June 1944 urging partisans to shoot "in the back" German soldiers who were left in the rear area following the German retreat from the Rome.[554]

A British Military Court convicted Kesselring of ordering the Ardeatine massacre and also the incitement of others to kill Italian citizens. But had not he, Alexander, urged Italian citizens not in uniform to kill (by "bushwhacking" no less) German soldiers? True, Alexander had never ordered a decimation reprisal (and this point is troubling for Kesselring) but when would this revenge of the victors over the vanquished be stopped?

Albert Kesselring

Churchill agreed with Alexander, and the two former leaders intervened on Kesselring's behalf with Prime Minister Clement Attlee, the upshot being the commutation of the death sentence to life imprisonment. In 1952 Kesselring was released from prison on the grounds of ill health — but the cancer he supposedly had remarkably went into remission and he died of a heart attack eighteen years later. "Uncle Albert" or "Smiling Albert" was popular with most post-war Germans and also many ranks of his former enemy. His legend as an intrepid and even gallant military commander continues to grow to this day. And there was nothing political to be gained by the West in 1952 from his continued confinement. A very real Cold War was on then and it was time to put the rancor caused by World War II in the past. Kesselring remained unrepentant and unabashedly defended the honor of German soldiers who served in World War II. At the same time he supported the "European Defense Community" against the Soviet Union. He wrote two military memoirs, and in one of them he states: "The battle of the Apennines can really be described as a famous page in German military history."[555]

Kesselring joined the Bavarian Army in 1904 and rose steadily through the ranks because of proven ability. He was in leadership positions in all the major campaigns of World War II — the invasions of Poland in 1939, France, 1940, the Battle of Britain 1940 and *Operation Barbarossa* — the attack on the Soviet Union in 1941. It is his operational record as a field marshal and defensive commander in Italy, however, that causes him to be remembered today in military history. With a Luftwaffe background, it is remarkable that he was able to do what he did in Italy — and largely without air power.

The photograph was taken at Kesselring's trial.

Lyman Lemnitzer 1899-1988

General Lemnitzer rose to the top of the U.S. military being appointed Chairman of the Joint Chiefs of Staff in September 1960, but his early Army career was not marked by rapid ascent to rank. Fifteen years as a lieutenant in the coast artillery followed graduation from the West Point class of 1920. Born to a Lutheran family in Honesdale, PA a small town in the Poconos not far from Scranton, he worked at menial jobs before his Academy appointment.

"Lem," as his friends called him, served tours at Army forts in Virginia and Corregidor and taught courses in physics, mechanics and other hard sciences at West Point. In 1940 he was selected to attend an all-important career enhancer — the Army War College. With duty afterwards in Washington D.C. in a planning capacity, promotions started coming and when the World War II broke out in December 1941, Lemnitzer was tapped. In June 1942 he was promoted to full colonel and two weeks later, brigadier general.[556]

His career following World War II included command of an infantry division in Korea and additional choice assignments, each involving increased responsibility. Shortly before leaving office, President Eisenhower appointed Lemnitzer Chairman of the Joint Chiefs of Staff. In a twist of fate Lemnitzer was not extended to a second term in this office by President Kennedy but rather appointed Supreme Commander of NATO (this happened after the Bay of Pigs failure).

Purportedly a regular guy who enjoyed his family and fishing in remote Pennsylvania with a barber friend, Lemnitzer typified the 1950s American Cold

Warrior. His biographer wrote about a culture that may have embraced a good portion of the U.S. military at the time:

> Lemnitzer would become a fervent foe of Communism during his years as a general, and his antipathy could well have had its roots in the times of the "Great Red Scare." The bloody 1917 Russian Revolution had horrified the world and, no doubt, the patriotic and impressionable young machinery inspector in peaceful Honesdale. Army troops were called out often in the early years of Lemnitzer's career to put down riots that most War Department officials considered Communist inspired. General Leonard Wood, a former Army chief of staff who led troops against particularly bad labor riots in Omaha, Nebraska and Gary, Indiana, undoubtedly spoke for many fellow military men when he said that all Bolsheviks should be deported "in ships of stone with sails of lead, with the wrath of God for a breeze and hell for their first port."[557]

Clare Boothe Luce 1903-1987

With a veddy proper High English accent Her Excellency Clare Boothe Luce, U.S. Ambassador to Italy, responded to the question put to her by one of her interviewers on the TV talk show *Longines Chronoscope*. The year was 1955 and Luce had served as ambassador for two years, the first woman "named or assigned to a first class European power," said the TV show host who introduced her. This gentleman also observed that some persons doubted the wisdom of President Eisenhower's choice in appointing a woman at a time Italy was in trouble over the advance of communism and also a crisis looming over the Italian port city of Trieste that was still claimed by Yugoslavia. "Well, two years have passed," the host continued, "and communism has become weaker. Italy is stronger, even the Trieste problem has been settled. In short, never underestimate the power of a woman."

Luce, dressed stylishly as ever, thin and wearing two strings of pearls, beamed when she said about the Italians, "... they are a very wise people and are beginning to see that communism really, really doesn't pay and doesn't produce the things that they expected..."

For an individual who had been born illegitimate to a tenement-raised mother and a father who was a traveling musician and piano salesman, Clare Boothe Luce used her considerable intellect and breathtaking good looks to ascend to heights that made the statement "this could only happen in America" ring true. Doors opened for her because she forced them open; she wanted it to happen.

Clare Boothe Luce

Growing up, young Clare worked in the theater district of New York City on various productions where her ambitious mother hoped for her to become an actress. For a brief period Clare was an understudy for Mary Pickford and she landed a small part in the movie produced in 1915 by Thomas Edison, *The Heart of a Waif*. Clare had only four years of formal schooling, but somewhere along the line, probably at Long Island's Cathedral School of St. Mary (where she was an excellent scholar but designated by her fellow students as the "most conceited girl in the school"[558]) or perhaps Miss Mason's School in Tarrytown, which was a finishing school, Clare developed a voracious appetite for reading and writing. If Clare was not to become an actress, her mother (who married a wealthy surgeon in 1919 after being lavishly supported for several years by another man she would not wed because he was Jewish) determined that Clare would marry well — and by that she meant secure a rich husband. This was accomplished in 1923 when Clare, age twenty, became Mrs. George Tuttle Brokaw. Brokaw, an heir to a clothing fortune, was twenty-two years older than his bride, and his passions in life were reported to be golf, multiple club memberships and alcohol. Their marriage lasted six years and produced a daughter, Ann born in 1924.

Not content to live off ample settlement and alimony money, Clare Boothe Brokaw, the witty "gay divorcée," as she was then labeled, wasted no time in becoming the toast of Manhattan. Everyone with eyesight appreciated her exquisite features and sense of high style; it was the infatuated publisher Conde Nast who discovered her writing ability. By 1933 Clare was managing editor of Nast's magazine *Vanity Fair* and by 1935 Clare had become Mrs. Henry Luce.

Politically Clare Boothe Luce started out as a Democrat but that changed when President Roosevelt began rolling out his New Deal economic programs. Her marriage to Luce, an ardent and unabashed Republican and anti-socialist, farther moved her to the political right, although she remained her own person in more than one way. Harry and Clare had an "open marriage" before that term came into usage. As stated, before her marriage to Harry Luce there had been notable lovers such as the Wall Street financer Bernard Baruch and Conde Nast; after her marriage to Luce there were Joe Kennedy, Lucien Truscott and others. In the mid-thirties she started writing Broadway plays, her greatest success being *The Women*, a satire on indolent wealthy women awaiting quickie Reno divorces. A prolific writer, she wrote eight plays, a number of movie scripts and three books, in addition to doing correspondent work for *Life* magazine and other publications. She served two consecutive terms as member of Congress, winning her seat in 1942 from a wealthy district that encompassed the town of Greenwich CT.

For a "conservative," Luce embraced a number of activist positions — she introduced a labor law to ensure women and minorities received equal pay for equal work, supported American involvement in the United Nations, the establishment of a strong Woman's Army Auxiliary Corps, war refuge relief, and other measures that were decidedly internationalist and not isolationist in nature. Above all Luce wanted World War II managed efficiently and to a far different conclusion than World War I. In reporting for the picture magazine *Life*, she became the voice for G.I.s serving all over the world. Chain-smoking, hard drinking and forever the penultimate party girl (who always somehow managed to keep her slim hourglass figure) she never missed a beat with lighthearted shameless self-promotion. One biographer reported that on her first inspection trip to the Italian Front, the all-male-except-Luce staid Military Affairs Committee posed for a photo wearing army issue green overcoats. At the last moment before the shutter snapped Luce reversed her coat to become the only one in the picture to sport a white camouflage snow coat.

Thinking of this one might remember that famous photo of a white-bloused Hitler standing in the middle of his dark-bloused army officers ringing Napoleon's tomb. There was a huge difference of course, that being Clare did hers while laughing. In short order Luce made Sergeant Bill Mauldin a devotee. It was Luce who famously coined, "No good deed goes unpunished." She was an ardent feminist and women's liberationist several decades before that "movement" supposedly started.

As stated, tragedy struck Luce a hard blow in early 1944. In January her daughter Ann, a student at Stanford University was killed in an automobile accident. This event, it is said, dampened Luce's appetite for politics and she decided not to run for a third term in Congress. With spiritual counseling from Bishop Fulton Sheen she converted to Roman Catholicism. This did not stop her affairs, however, and the fact that her new religion offered absolution from sin, may have played a part in her conversion.

Luce remained a national political firebrand giving 100 speeches endorsing Dwight Eisenhower in his 1952 run for the presidency. When Eisenhower interviewed her after his election victory, Luce told him straight out she wanted to be ambassador to Italy. She then quickly worked her new religion and gender into the conversation, pointing out why he should select her for Italy as opposed to someone else, and particularly a man. She reminded the president-elect that millions of Catholics had voted for him and that someone of her faith should properly be sent to the Vatican and finally, that American females "would be pleased that a woman had finally got a number one diplomatic post."[559] Eisenhower had been thinking maybe Mexico, but no more!

Once in Italy, at the behest of her boss U.S. Secretary of State John Foster Dulles (the older brother of Allen) Clare Boothe Luce stepped into a delicate diplomatic situation. On one hand the U.S. wanted to maintain good relations with Yugoslavia's Marshal Tito, the only communist strongman to stand up to the Soviet Union. On the other hand, the U.S. wanted to maintain good relations with an Italy that teetered on the brink of going communist. The problem was, both counties claimed ownership of the free city of Trieste on the Adriatic Sea and both rattled sabers to get it. It was Clare Boothe Luce as much as anyone else who got the two adversaries to accept a compromise agreement with each side gaining and giving up territory.

And how did Luce help prevent the left in Italy from being voted into power? According to a book written by Blanche Wiesen Cook entitled *The Declassified Eisenhower*, Italy was only a 4% swing away from what Luce referred to as the "Cominform Left" (socialist-communist political alliance) defeating the center and right parties, and it was Luce who determined that more foreign aid and payments (bribes) to the Christian Democratic Party would not help the cause of free market enterprise in Italy. Luce came up with a hardball tactic that worked: "... publicly withholding or withdrawing U.S. contracts from Communist-dominated labor unions..."[560]

There was another reason for the American success in Italy, however, and one difficult to measure. The austere communists could not hope to win against a second American invasion that Luce helped facilitate through high visibility. "600,000 American tourists visited Italy this year," Luce proudly announced during her TV interview. The unspoken truth was that no negative political force on earth, and particularly the humorless, drab left-wing ideologues could compete with the smash 1953 movie hit *Roman Holiday* starring Gregory Peck and pert newcomer Audrey Hepburn. A celebration had started in Italy and Luce and her husband Harry sensed it — they supported it with lavish social events and widespread press coverage. They celebrated a happy-again people who lived in a breathtakingly beautiful country with a rich heritage. This second American invasion, this time a peaceful one, was four times larger than the U.S. Fifth Army.

"For all their sins Italians are forgiven because of pasta" (unknown pundit).

"Let those at **H**ome see Rome" (and they did).

Her affected high English accent and Cleopatra-like lifestyle notwithstanding, by the end of her public career Clare Boothe Luce had made a difference.

Bill Mauldin 1921-2003

It was not easy for Bill Mauldin winning that second Pulitzer Prize in 1959. Cartooning was far more difficult without Willie and Joe; everyone in America loved those G.I. dogfaces that did their duty and won a war despite having to serve under vainglorious career militarists. It was one thing however to mock the brass hats and an entirely different thing to successfully take on the four-flushers who had been elected and not selected.

Mauldin won his second Pulitzer by playing to the center and addressing a subject matter that every thinking human being could agree upon. He then applied genius. Boris Pasternak and his novel *Doctor Zhivago* had been banned from the Soviet Union. Mauldin depicted Pasternak laboring in a gulag with another prisoner. "I won the Nobel Prize for Literature," Pasternak says. "What is your crime?"

An unapologetic lifelong liberal, Mauldin hailed from Mountain Park, New Mexico and took courses at the Chicago Academy of Fine Arts before enlisting in the Arizona National Guard in 1940. He ended up in combat infantry as a member of the 45th Division and saw action in Sicily and Italy. In his spare time, he drew cartoons for the *45th Division News*, and over a period the quality of his work got noticed. He was invited to join the staff of the *Stars and Stripes* newspaper during the early spring 1944. His periodic sedition against military authority was tacitly encouraged by Eisenhower, who wanted the average G.I. to remain American, that is, fiercely independent (read: not goose-stepping Nazi-thinking). Mauldin supplied the perfect channel for this.

The best way to describe Bill Mauldin is to quote him. This comes from his book *Up Front*:

> *To the dogface out on patrol, his platoon command post, with its machine gun emplacement, is rear echelon and home and the safest place in the world.*

> *The gunner in the platoon C.P. is itching to get the hell out of there and back to the safety of company headquarters, where the topkick is equally anxious to find an excuse to visit Battalion.*

> *The radio operators in Battalion like to go after extra tubes at Regimental supply, even though Regimental seldom stocks tubes, and the guys who work at field desks in Regimental hate the guts of those rear echelon bastards in Division. Division feels that way about Corps, Corps about Army, Army about Base Section, and, so help me Hannah, Base Section feels that way about soldiers in the States.561*

Wade McCree, Jr. 1920-1987

Lieutenant McCree, an African-American who served with the 365th Regiment, 92nd Infantry Division briefly experienced combat at Cinquale Canal in the Serchio Valley sector prior to the German assault in the area. Following the war McCree completed his JD degree at Harvard University Law School. His legal career was stellar — a successful private practice in Detroit followed by judicial positions culminating in his appointment to the U.S. Court of Appeals, Sixth Circuit. He subsequently served as Solicitor General of the United States under the Carter administration, arguing twenty-five cases before the U.S. Supreme Court. Following that, he became a law professor at the University of Michigan Law School.

McCree participated in the Wayne State University Press *Invisible Soldier* project. Although he did not himself witness the Serchio Valley plight (his unit the 365th served at the time in Central Italy with the British) he had served under General Almond long enough to know what it was like to experience a segregated army.

"I think the men of the 92nd Division, if asked, would have said they were a pretty sorry outfit," McCree opined for the WSU Press. "It seems to me that you cannot treat people as second-class citizens or second-class soldiers and expect them to behave in a first-class fashion ..."

"I share Ralph Ellison's concept of the invisibility of America's black citizens," McCree wrote. "Just as we are not consciously seen and hence are not considered when national domestic policy is made, neither were we seen or considered when the conduct of World War II was planned."[562] [Ed: Ellison wrote the novel *The Invisible Man* in 1952]

McCree told it as he remembered it and did not pull punches:

> I don't believe I ever saw my regimental commander as far forward as a company command post. To imagine him being in a platoon or company area was unthinkable. Our battalion commander was an utter coward. I never saw him in a company area. In one skirmish around Bebbio he panicked, and this had a tremendous demoralizing impact on the black officers. The rumor was out that our executive officer shot himself in the foot. All of these things added to the distrust of the orders coming down from higher command. Many of these officers saw only a map concerning their men and anything they knew was second hand.[563]

McCree also offered this insight as to the reason for the disharmony:

> There was no sense of mission. I found that the cause was the absence of any identification between the officers and men. When I say 'officers' I am speaking of the white officers because I believe the original design for

the 92nd had been the regular army pattern of white officers and black troops. However, with some black officers coming through Fort Benning there had to be a place for them, and this upset that design.[564]

He finished:

My four-year military stint was a horizon-expanding experience, and not just in a geographical sense. To see how different personalities react under stress was enlightening and sometimes frightening. And to witness what happens to spirited men who are forced to accommodate the unacceptable is soul-rending.[565]

Joseph T. McNarney 1893–1972

Hailing from Emporium, PA, Joe McNarney was a small town kid who made good. Thirty-six percent of his West Point class of 1915 (representing fifty-nine out of 164 graduates) ended-up being generals ("the class the stars fell on") and within that grouping McNarney, with four stars was only behind five star classmates Dwight Eisenhower and Omar Bradley.

Early on in his Army career McNarney became a pilot and in World War I was placed in various positions of command, attaining quickly the temporary wartime rank of lieutenant colonel. He was not a fighter pilot ace but rather a gifted leader and recognized organizer. In the battle of Meuse-Argonne he served as a corps commander. Choosing to make the Army Air Corps a career, he served stateside following the war and reverted to the peacetime rank of captain.

The period between the two world wars witnessed many choice military assignments and experiences — to name some — commanding a flying school, instructing at the Air Corps Tactical School, graduating with honors from the Command and General Staff School at Fort Leavenworth, KA, completing the Army War College course, commanding a Bomb Group and serving an undoubtedly prestigious position in Washington D.C. with the War Plans Division of the War Department General Staff. It was not until March 1940, however, that he was finally elevated above the rank that he held following World War I: he was promoted to colonel. Four years later McNarney would be a four-star general and an administrative theater commander; he had become MTOUSA. He retired from the military in 1952 after serving in other important capacities including a period as commander of the American army of occupation in Germany.

That McNarney could be feisty in defense of causes important to the Army and willing to take on issues with political implications, there can be no doubt. Telling perhaps is that he was promoted to full general in March 1945 — three months after the brouhaha involving home furloughs from Italy crested.

Primary Sources with Michigan Connections: John L. King (1924 –); John M. Lesesne M.D. (1920 – 2017); Richard E. Stroud (1905-1975)

Jack King finished college after the war, graduated from Ohio State University and the University of Michigan Law School in 1950. He was then employed in the Regional Counsel Office of the IRS as a trial attorney where he worked for three years before being recruited by the Detroit law firm of Berry Moorman as a litigating attorney in corporate tax law. As the years progressed Jack became managing partner, his name was added to the firm name and his practice gravitated to probate and trust law and serving as trustee of a number of trusts for various clients; he also acted as president of two charitable foundations in Detroit, and today still serves as president of one. "I married Eileen Hickey in 1950," Jack said. "We raised four children and now have nine grandchildren and eight great-grandchildren." Eileen died in 2011 and the following year Jack moved to Falls Church, VA "to be near my daughter and grandchildren." Jack has vivid and happy memories of Italy.

John Lesesne did go to medical school after the war, as he mentioned he might in his wartime dairy. After obtaining his medical degree from Duke University, he took his internship and residency in internal medicine at the University of Michigan and ended-up specializing as an allergist practicing in the Grosse Pointes for many years. He married Ann in 1953 and the couple had six children. Today they are blessed with seventeen grandchildren.

For many years John sail-raced to Mackinac and competed in international ocean races. John and Ann also shared a passion for tennis. "He didn't talk much about the war," Ann recently told, "but was proud that he served and remains keenly interested in world events and history." On a trip to Italy, John took Ann to places where Company "B" had been positioned and pointed to target areas fired upon. The Tuscan countryside was so peaceful and beautiful and the villages so pristine, Ann said she had difficulty envisioning that a war had taken place there.

In July 2015 the author had occasion to meet John's friend Paul Duker, age 101. Mr. Duker said he is forever indebted to John. Many decades earlier Mr. Duker had taken a young son to the emergency room at St. John's Hospital in Grosse Pointe Woods. Try as the ER technicians might, the child could not be brought out of asthmatic shock; Paul was cautioned to brace for tragedy. John Lesesne M.D. appeared at 3:00 a.m. and offered a wild card, last ditch remedy. Asked what Paul's son is doing today, Paul smiled and answered what his son was doing at that precise moment: "He's out on the water racing to Mackinac," the gracious old gentleman responded. He added, happily: "He's an Old Goat," meaning his son has participated in twenty-five plus races. Mr. Duker passed away in 2016.

For John Lesesne, saving lives became infinitely more rewarding than taking them. Later in life John sailed recreationally with his good friend Jack King — neither man ever brought up the subject of World War II Italy — they did not know until recently that there was a 91st Infantry Division connection.

John passed away in March 2017, as this book was in production.

Dick Stroud regained his health after the war, went back to work in the field of education and gravitated to the area of school administration. No doubt the skills and discipline that Dick acquired while serving as an officer in the USAAF helped him transition into management. Another child arrived to Sue and Dick following the war, Sarah, and this family blessing was followed by tragedy in 1951 when Sarah's older brother "Dickie" was killed while playing outside — a truck carelessly backed up. The knowledge of this horrendous event made the reading of the wartime letters which are so full of hope by the author all the more poignant and sadly impactful. The measure of the tragedy is gauged in these letters written six years before its occurrence.

The Stroud family persevered and that dreamed-of-home of their own materialized. In 1956 Dick Stroud was made principal of Thomas Jefferson High School, Dallas, with a student population of 2,200 covering grades nine to twelve. From a hardscrabble start, Dick had earned college degrees from the University of Texas and SMU and climbed to the top of his chosen profession.

One of Sarah's favorite "protective father stories" is about her application in the 1960s to become an American Field Service foreign exchange student. "Not Italy!" the stern but loving father said to his daughter.

Sarah's most precious possessions today include the letters and the small presents her parents exchanged before she was born. Sarah's mother Sue died in 2012 at age 100.

Josip Broz Tito 1892-1980

It is correct to state that Marshal Tito was incensed by what happened at Trieste in mid-1945 and over a year later, when most Allied troops had returned home, he acted out his temper. On August 9, 1946 Yugoslav fighters damaged a U.S. military C-47 transport plane and forced it to land near Ljubljana; the Yugoslav government then held the seven U.S. airmen and two Europeans aboard as hostages. This act was followed by the shooting down on August 19 of another C-47 where all aboard (five U.S. airmen) perished. Advised by the press that a U.S. "angry" ultimatum was going to be delivered, on August 22 Tito had the nine hostages released to U.S. military control and ordered his air force "... not to fire on foreign aircraft..."[566]

The Cold War was on and further perturbations followed, but in Tito's case, he proved not to be a minion of the Soviet Union. The story ends with a 1971 photograph of Tito and Nixon and spouses smiling happily together from a White House balcony.

Lucien Truscott, Jr. 1895-1965

In 2012 Truscott's grandson and fourth generation namesake wrote a piece appearing in the *Sunday New York Times* reminding readers, among other things, that Patton and his grandfather "... stormed the beaches... with blood in their eyes and military murder on their minds" and that "... they were nearly psychotic in their drive to kill enemy soldiers and subjugate enemy nations." He opined: "Thankfully, we will probably never have cause to go back to those blood-soaked days."[567]

Hopefully for the world Lucien IV will prove correct in his forecast.

If, however, the United States ever does need to replicate 1945, the likes of Lucien's grandfather might be a good military type to pattern oneself after. Patton achieved success through speed and finesse; so did Truscott.

On May 30, 1945 Truscott delivered a Memorial Day address at the temporary cemetery for 25,000 men killed south of Rome and earlier in Sicily. At the podium, Truscott surprised his audience with an abrupt about face. He turned and spoke to the dead men directly, many of whom he had led in battle. Mauldin, along with the rest of the audience was moved to tears and later opined that Truscott "... was incapable of planned dramatics."[568] Truscott hurt his family, yes, and abused his health. But in the end, Lucien Truscott was a success. Quite a number of young American men lived to old age because he was in charge.

Lucien Truscott, Jr.
*Photo credit: Courtesy of the West Point Museum
Collection, United States Military Academy*

Telling about how likable Truscott was, he befriended a young Army doctor in 1946 that wrote his military memoirs in 1989. A chapter pertains to Truscott. The two got off to a rocky start when Truscott crustily refused to enter a hospital after the doctor determined during a house call that the general likely had suffered a heart attack. This doctor had pluck; he quoted Army regulations to the effect that a military physician always outranks his patient in medical matters and that made him, a captain, temporarily a four-star general. The doctor became even less popular with Truscott when he ordered him to stop smoking. The ice between the two began to break a few days later when Truscott fessed-up that he had gone all the way to Ike to get the doctor "fired" and Ike shot back that there was no doctor "in the area as well-trained," request denied. What followed were long conversations between the general and the captain. Truscott drew the doctor out by asking about his hometown, and when he learned it was Cleveland, told about his experience there as a polo coach, which the army in the early days permitted him to do in order to generate a little more needed income. Words followed easily in the days and weeks to come, but the conversations were not one-sided. The doctor's wife had gone off and purchased an expensive home in Cleveland, the doctor was concerned, and the general wanted the details. General Truscott ended-up offering to the dumbstruck captain that he would rent a room; it was that kind of a relationship (the doctor declined the gift but never forgot the offer).

In turn the doctor learned about the cavalry days, the 3rd Infantry Division and what it had been like to disobey a direct order of General Patton.

"One night I reported to General Truscott and started to address him as 'Sir,'" wrote Gerald T. Kent, M.D. "He held up his hand and said, 'Please don't use that word again.'"

"I said, 'I thought I was supposed to say 'Sir.'"

" 'Well, maybe, but the way you pronounce it, it sounds like 'son-of-a-bitch.' ' "

"I never used it again with him."[569]

Eisenhower rated his two most effective World War II U.S. Army commanders to be Patton and Truscott.

Max Waibel 1901-1971

Major Waibel climbed the ranks in the Swiss Army and retired as *Oberstdivisonär* (Major-General) Chief of Infantry. In 1965 a twentieth anniversary reunion of Allied and Swiss participants in *Operation Sunrise* was held at the lakeside villa at Ascona. Dulles wrote: "Max Waibel was nearby, and several of us had an opportunity to see him."[570]

Heinrich von Vietinghoff 1887-1952

The last supreme commanding general of the German Army in Italy participated in the Adenauer government following the war in a military advisory capacity.

Leon Weckstein 1931-

Leon Weckstein wrote a second book about the Italian war in 2011 entitled *200,000 Heroes,* an anecdotal tribute to the partisans who fought so bravely to liberate their country from the hated *Tedeschis.* Weckstein resides in Thousand Oaks, CA, and "enjoys the pleasures he shares with his family."

Karl Wolff 1900-1984

Did Nazi SS General Karl Wolff bargain the surrender to the Americans and British in exchange for immunity from prosecution as a war criminal? As stated, historians, journalists and law professors have grappled with this issue over the years (after prosecutors did what they could against Wolff) and the question is reasonably settled today: yes.

Karl Wolff had a malevolent side to him that Allen Dulles failed to spot, or if he did, chose to ignore in his description of the man.

Wolff served in World War I as an infantry officer and was awarded the Iron Cross first class for bravery in battle. Attracted to the appeal of a reborn, militarily strong Germany, Wolff joined the Nazi Party in 1931 and applied for membership in the SS. Accepted, he rose quickly within SS ranks, and by 1937 had served as adjutant (chief of staff) to Heinrich Himmler and as high as "third in command" of the SS. He held the position SS Liaison Officer to Hitler and became close to the Führer. He fell out of favor with Himmler, however, in 1943, was briefly ill, and in September 1943, sent to Italy as "Highest SS and Police Leader." In July 1944 Hitler appointed him additionally to command Waffen-SS combat forces in Italy.

Karl Wolff

Wolff never fit the stereotype of a cold-eyed SS mass murderer, but given his high position within the SS and close working relationship with the Führer and one of the other most powerful leaders in the Third Reich, Himmler pre-1943, it seems implausible that he was unaware that institutional criminality was hugely afoot.

Wolff was arrested May 13, 1945, but not prosecuted at the Nuremburg Trials. Rather, while confined he gave evidence against his fellow Nazis at these trials. Released by the Allies in 1947, he was a year later prosecuted by German authorities as part of a de-nazification program his crime being membership in the SS for which he served seven months of a four-year sentence. Wolff subsequently earned a living in Germany managing a public relations (advertising) firm and was rumored to work for the CIA.

In 1962 that letter written by Wolfe twenty years earlier to the Reich Minister of Transport pertaining to the evacuation by rail of the Warsaw Ghetto to Treblinka re-surfaced in the aftermath of the Eichmann trial. On the basis of this letter and additional evidence implicating him in the deportation of Italian Jews to Auschwitz, in 1964 Wolff was convicted and sentenced to fifteen years in prison. At his trial Wolff adamantly denied knowledge that mass murder was taking place at SS run camps. Released from prison in 1969 due to poor health, Wolff lived another fifteen years and towards the end of his life lectured and did TV interviews about the SS.

Controversial but always assertive and (to a fault) congenial, Wolff was a pitchman for himself. An example of this is contained in the Dulles book, *The Secret Surrender*. Per Dulles, Wolff sweet-talked bunker resident Adolf Hitler into letting him off the hook for secretly meeting with the OSS on March 8. Requesting the meeting with his Führer to clear the air over treason accusations levied by Kaltenbrunner, Wolfe convinced his Führer (again per Dulles) that his motivation for acting alone was so Hitler could disown involvement if his enemy contact proved unproductive. Unsure whether his averment of loyalty would be believed, Wolff was greatly relieved on April 19, 1945 when Hitler warmly ordered him to carry on in Italy. The fact seems to be to the extent Hitler had any friends Wolff was among his closest.

In his book Dulles opines how Wolff finessed Hitler (it had been probably the same way that Wolff finessed Dulles only Dulles did not admit to that). "The old charm," Dulles wrote about Wolff's final face to face with Hitler, "so it seemed, the blue-eyed openness and frankness, that had helped him arrive in high places years before, even in the SS ranks, had worked again."[571]

Wolff never asked for *de jure* immunity (per Dulles) but his late-in-the-war association (and arguably even friendship) with the head of the OSS Berne office may have resulted in him receiving *de facto* immunity for a considerable period of time. Dulles had great influence following the war, and as stated, a very positive relationship with President Truman. Wolff provided testimony at criminal trials following war and the fact that he was not himself tried at Nuremburg was not the doing of the OSS. Dulles lacked prosecutorial authority.

The United States Holocaust Museum notes the following:

> In July 1942, the Operation Reinhard authorities [SS] completed the
> construction of a killing center, known as Treblinka II, approximately
> a mile from the labor camp ... Between late July and September 1942,
> the Germans deported around 265,000 Jews from the Warsaw ghetto to
> Treblinka.[572]

Practically all of these Jews ended up murdered by carbon monoxide after first
being shorn of their hair, stripped naked, and driven on the run into gas chambers.
The Holocaust Museum notes that a train to Treblinka consisted of about fifty or
sixty cars and was processed at the killing center in chains up to twenty cars at a
time. To paraphrase SS General Karl Wolff in his 1942 letter praising the Reich
Minister of Transport about his role in this operation: "... the smooth carrying
out of all these measures seems to be guaranteed."[573]

NOTES

FOREWORD

1 Lesesne, John M., diary entry dated November 24, 1944

2 Mauldin, Bill, *Up Front: Fiftieth Anniversary Edition*. New York & London: W.W. Norton & Company, 1995, p. 97

3 United States Army *100th Chemical Mortar Battalion*, as reported at http://www.4point2.org/100cmb.htm (date accessed 07/13/2015)

4 U.S. Army Office of Military History, *History of the 4.2" Chemical Mortar*, as reported at http://www.4point2.org/mortar42.htm (date accessed 07/02/2015)

5 War Department Technical Manual TM 9-1260, *Mortars, Light Field and Mounts (all types)* January 26, 1942

6 91st Division *August 1917–January 1945*, commemorative pamphlet dedicated by Major General William Livesay, Commanding, 15 April 1945, p. 51

7 Weller, Grant, *The Experience of Truck Operations in Italy* (PhD dissertation, Chapter 10 as provided by U.S. Army Transportation Corp historian Richard E. Kilblane February 10, 2015) p. 362

8 Weller, op. cit., p 225

9 Stroud, Richard E., letter to Sue dated January 28, 1945

10 Stroud, op, cit., December 22, 1944

CHAPTER ONE

11 Per information supplied by Sarah Stroud Ollison, daughter of Richard E. Stroud

12 Stroud, op. cit., October 29, 1944

13 Lesesne, op. cit., January 20, 1945

14 King, John L., diary entries dated March 10 1944 ("I have been selected along with S/Sgt Thompson to go on the Advanced Party.") and April 1, 1944 ("Left POE [Port of Entry] and boarded our troop ship, it is a Liberty ship.")

15 King, op. cit., tape-recorded interview April 19, 2015. Additional information (summarized): "I was born October 24, 1924. My father worked for the New York Central Railroad. The Army let me finish my first year of college at University of Dayton after I joined the enlisted reserves on October 28, 1942. I looked this up. On May 13, 1943 I went on active duty. I have two diaries but they really don't say much because I was very conscious at age eighteen of not putting any military information in there. I had basic training at Camp Roberts, CA in June 1943 and in November was assigned to Camp Adair, Oregon. I started out in an Army Specialized Training Program that was supposed to send me to a college for further education in subjects like engineering or languages and that kind of stuff but the ASPT program got closed and I was assigned to an infantry unit. I had hoped for a nice college dormitory at Yale, Harvard or the University of Michigan but ended up digging slit trenches instead!"

16 *Life* magazine, November 6, 1944: *The Whole Story: Our Foreign Policy Problem is not Solved by Mr. Roosevelt's Reading of History*, editorial p. 32

17 Stroud, op. cit., October 29, 1944

18 Dulles, Allen W., *The Secret Surrender*. Guilford, CT: The Lyons Press, 2006, originally published 1966, p. 7

19 Srodes, James, *Allen Dulles Master of Spies*. Washington DC: Regnery Publishing, Inc., 1999, p. 336

20 Kinzer, Stephen, *The Brothers*. New York: Time Books Henry Holt and Company, 2013, p. 63

21 Bancroft, Mary, *Autobiography of a Spy*. New York: William Morrow and Company, Inc., 1983, p. 242

22 Descendants of John Welsh Dulles: Allen Macy Dulles, as reported at http://www. auburnhistoricproperties.org/upload/pdf/Dulles%20AUB.pdf (date accessed 08/12/2014)

23 Srodes, op. cit., p. 313

24 Kinzer, op. cit., p. 72

25 Srodes, op. cit., (citing in endnote #1 for Chapter Eight the depository of the Dulles letter being OSS History Record Group 59, Box 52, File 103,918/744 Burns to Victor, National Archives) p. 242

26 *Life* magazine issues, 1944-45 front section notice

27 Weckstein, Leon, *Through My Eyes: 91st Infantry Division in the Italian Campaign*, 1942-1945. Central Port, OR: Hellgate Press, 1999, p. 103

28 Gordon, Richard and Robbins, Robert, *The 91st Infantry Division in World War II*. Washington D.C.: Washington Infantry Press, 1947 (comment of John L. King, May 31, 2015: "It was copyrighted in 1947 by Infantry Journal Inc., 1115 17th Street NW, Washington, DC. 20006. Major Richard Gordon, Division Education and Information Officer initiated the collection of source material. Upon the Division's arrival in the U.S. the work was taken over by Major Robert A. Robbins, 361st Infantry, who carried it to completion. Most source material came from G-2 records. There is no indication in the opening pages that the book was ever recorded or filed with the Library of Congress. I may have one of the few copies in existence."), p. 337

29 Lesesne, op. cit., November 15 and 19, December 4 and 5, 1944

30 Truscott, Lucien K., Jr., *Command Missions*. New York: E.P. Dutton and Co., 1954; reprinted Novato, CA: Presidio Press, 1990, p. 447

31 Lesesne, op. cit., November 15, 1944

32 Lesesne, op. cit., November 9, 1944

33 Lesesne, op. cit., November 10, 1944

34 Ibid

35 Lesesne, op. cit., November 11, 1944

36 Lesesne, op. cit., November 15, 1944

37 Weckstein, op. cit., p. 107

38 Lesesne, op. cit., November 16, 1944

39 Lesesne, op. cit., November 13, 1944

40 American Merchant Ships Sunk in WWII — Liberty Ships *S.S. Meyer London* and *S.S. Thomas G. Masaryk* torpedoed 16 April 1944; Liberty Ship *S.S Paul Hamilton* sunk by aircraft 20 April 1944, as reported at http://www.armed-guard.com/sunk.html (date accessed 01/02/2016)

41 King, op. cit., tape-recorded phone interview, April 19, 2015: "We landed in Algeria on April 19, 1944 and did invasion training there in a little town called Port Aux Poules. We went over to Naples on June 18 where we spent a couple of days sleeping on the floor at the University of Naples. One of our regiments had already gone in at Anzio and really got chopped up pretty badly. Happily, I was not involved with that."

42 Rosenblum, Gail, *Minneapolis survivor of WWII attack shares story of horrific Christmas Eve*, Star Tribune, December 21, 2002, as reported at http://www.startribune.com/lifestyle/11479016. html (date accessed 08/22/2014); also see The National WWII Museum, New Orleans, *70th Anniversary of the SS Leopoldville Troopship Disaster*, as reported at http://www.nww2m. com/2014/12/70th-anniversary-of-leopoldville-troopship-disaster/ (date accessed 01/04/2016)

43 Bykofsky, Joseph and Larson, Harold, *The Technical Services — The Transportation Corps: Operations Overseas*. Washington, D.C.: Center for Military History United States Army, 1957, reprinted 1990, p. 229

44 *Life* magazine, January 8, 1945: *War Inspection: Congressional committee gets data firsthand on the European fronts*, p. 27

45 Clark, Mark W., *Calculated Risk*. New York: Enigma Books — republished 2007, pp. 319-320

46 Clark, op. cit., pp. 244-245

47 Blackwell, Ian, *Fifth Army in Italy 1943-1945*. South Yorkshire, UK: Pen and Sword Military, 2012, p. 72

48 History Net, *African American 92 Infantry Division Fought in Italy During World War II*, as reported at http://www.historynet.com/african-american-92nd-infantry-division-fought-in-italy-during-world-war-ii.htm (date accessed 01/23/2016)

49 Miller, Donald L., *The Story of World War II*. New York: A Touchstone Book, Simon & Schuster, 2001, pp. 247-248; also Motley, Mary Penick, Editor, *The Invisible Soldier: The Experience of the Black Soldier, World War II*. Detroit: Wayne State University Press, 1975, republished paperback 1987, pp. 340-341

50 Lesesne, op. cit., December 4, 1944.

CHAPTER TWO

51 World War II Today, *Italy Declares War of Britain and France*, Mussolini quote recorded in diary of Count Ciano, Italian Foreign Minister, as reported at http://ww2today.com/10th-june-1940-italy-declares-war-on-britain-and-france (date accessed 01/04/2016)

52 Ibid

53 Kesselring, Albert, *The Memoirs of Field-Marshal Kesselring*. New York: Skyhorse Publishing, 2016 (written 1953), p. 169

54 Binder, L. James, *Lemnitzer, A Soldier for his Time*. Dallas, VA: Brassey's, Inc., 1997, p. 112

55 Salmaggi, Cesare and Pallavisini, Alfredo, *2194 Days of War*. New York: Barnes & Noble Books, 1977, p 414

56 Lamb, Richard, *War in Italy 1943-1945 A Brutal Story*. New York: St. Martin's Press, 1994, p. 176

57 Ibid

58 Lamb, op. cit., p. 177

59 Kesselring, op. cit., p. 184

60 Dulles, op. cit., p. 49

61 Tompkins, Peter, *Italy Betrayed*. New York: Simon & Schuster, 1966, pp. 228-229

62 Reid, Howard, *Dad's War*. London: Bantum Press, 2003, p 34

63 Churchill, Winston S., *Closing the Ring*. Boston: Houghton Mifflin, 1951, p.116

64 Salmaggi and Pallavisini, op. cit., p. 429

65 Miller, op. cit., p. 218

66 Tompkins, op. cit., p. 236

67 Dulles, op. cit., p. 45

68 Miller, op. cit., p. 218

69 D'Este, Carlo, *Fatal Decision: Anzio and the Battle for Rome*. New York: Harper, 1991, p. 39

70 Wallace, Robert and the Editors of Time-Life Books, *The Italian Campaign*. Alexandria, VA: Time-Life Books, 1978, p. 63

71 Katz, Robert, *The Battle for Rome*. New York: Simon & Schuster, 2003, pp. 47-48

72 Katz, op. cit., p. 139

73 Katz, op. cit., 150

74 Blackwell, op. cit., "Overseeing the Salerno planning he [Alexander] should have foreseen the difficulties of landing the American and British forces so far apart that the Germans were able to pose a serious threat of driving a wedge between them before dealing with them in a piecemeal fashion. Patton had seen the danger, but neither Alexander nor Clark recognized it…" p. 183

75 Blackwell, op. cit., p. 182

76 Blackwell, op. cit., p. 179

77 Katz, op. cit., p. 151

78 Katz, op. cit., p. 152

79 Laurie, Clayton D., *Anzio, 1944*, United States Army Center of Military History, as reported at http://www.history.army.mil/brochures/anzio/72-19.htm (date accessed 06/10/2014) p. 19

80 Laurie, op. cit., p. 2

81 Blackwell, op. cit., p. 193

82 Miller, op. cit., pp. 231-233

83 Dulles, op. cit., pp. 51-52

84 Laurie, Clayton D., *Rome-Arno 1944*, U.S. Army Center of Military History, as reported at http://www.history.army.mil/brochures/romar/72-20.htm date accessed 04/06/2015, p. 18

85 Dulles, op. cit., p. 47

86 TRIAL OF GENERAL ANTON DOSTLER, COMMANDER OF THE 75 GERMAN ARMY CORPS, as reported at http://www.worldcourts.com/ildc/eng/decisions/1945.10.12_United_States_v_Dostler.pdf (date accessed 06/26/2014)

87 Holland, James, *Italy's Sorrow, a Year of War, 1944-1945*. New York: St. Martin's Press, 2008, see photo insert between p. 338 and 339

88 Kesselring, op. cit., pp. 236-237

89 Holland, op. cit., p. 187

90 Holland, op. cit., photo caption write-up appearing between pp. 338-339; also pp. 444-445

91 Katz, op. cit., statement attributed to Eugen Dollmann, p. 291

92 Lamb, op. cit., pp. 99-100

93 Dulles, op. cit., p. 54

94 Dulles, op. cit., p. 52

95 Clark, op. cit., pp. 272-73

96 Truscott, op. cit., p. 370

97 Encyclopedia Britannica, *Ivanoe Bonomi, Prime minister of Italy*, as reported at http://www.britannica.com/biography/Ivanoe-Bonomi (date accessed 01/04/2015); also see Holland, op. cit., pp. 249-250

98 *New York Times* Obituaries March 19, 1983. Umberto II, King of Italy, the last of the House of Savoy monarchs who reigned from May 8 to June 7, 1946, when Italy voted for a republic abolishing the monarchy. Born Umberto Nicola Giovanni Maria of Savoy in 1904, the former king lived in exile in Portugal until his death in 1983.

99 Laurie, op. cit., p. 25

100 Newnan, William L., *Escape in Italy*. Ann Arbor, MI: The University of Michigan Press, 1945, p. 4; Email from William Krag dated 12/30/2014 "The next pass took out the bridge so the entire train, the rest of the POWs as well were lost. A good decision by BN!"

101 OnWar.com, *2 cm Flakvieriing 38, Technical Specifications* as reported at https://www.onwar.com/weapons/afv/data/2-cm-Flak-30-38-Flakvierling.htm (date accessed 01/05/2016)

102 Wyler, William, Director *Thunderbolt*, Monogram Pictures (1947) introduction by James Stewart, narrated by Lloyd Bridges, as reported at https://www.youtube.com/watch?v=ugFV-oo8Eyw (date accessed 01/03/2014)

103 Kesselring, op. cit., p. 209

104 Blackwell, op. cit., p. 215

105 Blackwell, op. cit., p. 243

106 Blackwell, op. cit., p. 186

107 Blackwell, op. cit., p. 241, 247

108 Kesselring, op. cit., p. 218

109 Miller, op. cit., p. 247

110 Motley, op. cit., p. 341; comment of Sergeant Willard A. Williams

111 Motley, op. cit., p. 318; comment of Warrant Officer Robert Millender

112 Miller, op. cit., p. 217

CHAPTER THREE

113 Wells, Bob, *The Milk Farm, Italy WWII*, as reported at http://milmag.com/2011/05/the-milk-farm-italy-wwii/ (date accessed 02/05/2015)

114 Allison William D., letter No. 5 to folks dated November 30, 1944

115 Lesesne, op. cit., November 26, 1944.

116 Allison, op. cit., letter No. 4 to folks dated November 28, 1944

117 Allison, op. cit., letter No. 6 to folks dated December 4, 1944

118 Allison, op. cit., letter No. 17 to Dotty dated November 27, 1944

119 Stroud, op. cit., December 20, 1944

120 Stroud, op. cit., December 12, 1944: "I'm much put out because you have not received the letter I wrote you from Bermuda preparing you for this long wait."

121 Lesesne, op. cit., December 13, 1944

122 Allison, op. cit., letter No. 22 to Dotty dated December 1, 1944

123 Comment of Jonathon T. Walton May 22, 2016: "Officers, including my brother Howard declined to carry the M-1 Carbine so as to not attract sniper fire." Walton served with the 78th Infantry ("Lightning") Division in Germay.

124 Allison, op. cit., letter to folks dated November 30, 1944

125 Stroud, op. cit., December 29, 1944

126 Stroud, op. cit., January 15, 1945

127 Allison, op cit., letter No. 20 to Dotty dated November 30, 1944

128 Allison. op. cit., letter No. 6 to folks dated December 4, 1944

129 Stroud, op. cit., January 2, 1945

130 Motley, op. cit., comment of Staff Sergeant David Cason, Jr., 370th Regiment transferred to 365th, p. 266

131 History Net, *African American 92 Infantry Division Fought in Italy During World War II*, op. cit.

132 Motley, op. cit., comment of Sergeant E. J. Wells, 365 Infantry Regiment, p.314

133 Motley, op. cit., comment of Second Lieutenant Jefferson Jordan, 370th Infantry Regiment, p. 284

134 Motley, op. cit., p. 268

135 Motley, op. cit., p. 273

136 Motley, op. cit., p. 316

137 Motley, op. cit., p. 297

138 Allison, op, cit., letter No. 94 to Dotty dated February 7, 1945

139 *Oxford English Dictionary*: repple-depple; Oxford University Press. 2002: n. "A replacement depot, a facility where troops are processed before being assigned to a unit or sent home after injury or a tour of duty."

140 Stroud, op. cit., January 22, 1945

141 Stroud, op. cit., January 19, 1945

142 Stroud, op. cit., December 9, 1945

143 Lesesne, op. cit., diary entry (undated) pp. 5-6

144 Dulles, op. cit., p. 38

145 Cook, Blanche Wiesen, *The Declassified Eisenhower.* New York: Penguin Books, 1984, "... the Cold War did not in fact begin in July 1945; it began in October 1917." p. 2

146 Wiesen, op. cit., p. 40

147 Delattre, Lucas, *A Spy at the Heart of the Third Reich: The Extraordinary Story of Fritz Kolbe, America's Most Important Spy in World War II.* New York: Gove Press, 2005, p. 115

148 Bancroft, op. cit., p 191

149 Bancroft, op. cit., p. 137

150 National Archives: *Allen Dulles and No. 23 Herrengasse, Bern, Switzerland, 1942-1945*, as reported at http://blogs.archives.gov/TextMessage/2012/11/09/allen-dulles-and-no-23-herrengasse-bern-switzerland-1942-1945/ (date accessed 11/28/2014)

151 Allison, op. cit., letter (unnumbered) to Dotty dated December 20, 1944

152 Abilo, Anthony C., Sergeant, U.S. Army Air Forces, 18th Depot Supply Squadron, Naples, WWII. Video transcript taken by New York State Military Museum in connection with its Oral History Program, as reported at https://www.youtube.com/watch?v=XXZ8zHpSdSQ&feature=youtu.be (16:51 minutes into the videotape; date accessed 01/22/16)

153 Howe, George F., *19 Days from the Apennines to the Alps.* Milan, Italy: Pizzi and Pizio, 1945. Note: a U.S. Fifth Army commemorative victory booklet, p. 22

154 Ferguson, op. cit., p. 319

155 Truscott, op. cit., p. 461

156 Blackwell, op. cit., pointing out additionally that the desertion problem was not unique to Italy. As of January 1, 1945, while the Battle of the Bulge raged, "... the U.S. Provost Marshal estimated that more than 18,000 American deserters were on the run in the European Theatre of Operations..." p. 219

157 Abilo, op. cit., time 17 minutes, 15 seconds

158 Truscott, op. cit., p.461

159 Lesesne, op. cit., December 5, 1944

160 Allison, op. cit., letter No. 7 to folks dated December 9, 1944

161 Truscott, op. cit., p. 463

162 Truscott, op. cit. (Truscott reported "Beetle" Smith telling him on November 24, 1944 at Versailles: "The PM personally asked for you."), p. 448

163 Sroud, op. cit., January 7, 1945

164 Stroud, op. cit., December 12, 1945

165 The poem *Panorama of Italy* may be found under the category "War Poems — Author Unknown" at http://www.warpoems.org/poem23.htm (date accessed 1l/11/2014)

166 Allison, op. cit., letter No. 330 to Dotty and folks dated October 2, 1945

167 Frazier, Ian, *Typewriter Man, Atlantic Magazine*, November 1997 Issue, as reported at http://www.theatlantic.com/magazine/archive/1997/11/typewriter-man/376988/ (date accessed 05/28/2015)

168 King, op. cit., May 17 1943

169 Truscott, op. cit., pp. 452-453

CHAPTER FOUR

170 Allison, op. cit., unnumbered letter dated December 20, 1944

171 Bykofsky and Larson, op. cit., p.187

172 The Tomb of Virgil was used as a code locator for First Lieutenant Richard E, Stroud and his wife Sue per Sarah Stroud Ollison.

173 Oland, Dwight D., *North Apennines 1944-4*, brochure prepared for U.S. Army Center of Military History, www.army.mil/cmh-pg/brochures/nap/72-34.htm (date accessed 08/10/2015), , p. 17

174 Lesesne, op. cit., November 6, 1944

175 Blackwell, op. cit., p. 224

176 Truscott, op. cit., p. 449

177 Salmaggi and Pallavisini, op. cit., pp. 636-37

178 King, op. cit. June 8, 1943

179 Stroud, op. cit., January 7, 1945

180 Motley, op. cit., comment of Second Lieutenant Jefferson L. Jordan, 370th, p. 285

181 Dulles, op. cit., pp. 35-36

182 Stroud, op. cit., December 22, 1944

183 *Life* magazine, January 8, 1945, op. cit., p. 27

184 Morris, Sylvia Jukes, *Price of Fame, the Honorable Clare Boothe Luce.* New York: Random House, 2014, p. 105 and 110

CHAPTER FIVE

185 Lesesne, op. cit., February 23, 1945

186 Lesesne, op. cit., December 14, 1944

187 Lesesne, op. cit., November 26, 1944: "I've started again to think about what I'll do when I go home. The field of medicine I find most attractive, but it will take so damned long — no shortcuts. I hate to think of going back to school for 6 years. On the other hand, I don't want to first "get a job"— something which wouldn't particularly interest me — only a means of making a living. I certainly wish I'd had pre-med and a couple of years of med school."

188 Salmaggi, op. cit., p. 641

189 Pitt, Barrie, Consultant Editor, *The Military History of World War II.* New York: The Military Press of New York, 1986, p 144

190 Weller, op. cit., p. 341

191 USAAF Chronology, December 1944, for Sunday, December 3, Mediterranean Theater of Operations (MTO) Tactical Operations as reported at http://paul.rutgers.edu/~mcgrew/ wwii/usaf/html/Dec.44.html (date accessed 05/27/2014)

192 Howe, op. cit., p. 14

193 Lesesne, op. cit., November 13, 1944

194 Lesesne, op. cit., December 10, 1944

195 Truscott, op. cit., p. 454

196 Truscott, op. cit., pp. 454-455

197 Morris, *Price of Fame,* op. cit., p. 106

198 Blackwell, op. cit., pp. 219-220

CHAPTER SIX

199 Motley, op. cit., p. 276

200 Truscott, op. cit., p. 455

201 Ibid

202 Truscott, op. cit., p. 454

203 Kesselring, op. cit., p. 220

204 Viviano, *San Francisco Chronicle*, July 13, 2000

205 Clark, op. cit., p. 325

206 Truscott, op. cit., p. 455

207 Lamb, op. cit., p 120

208 Wallace, Robert and the Editors of Time-Life Books, *The Italian Campaign World War II*; Alexandria, VA; Time-Life Books 1978, p. 183

209 Oland, op. cit., pp. 25-26

210 Lamb, op. cit., pp. 119-120

211 Lamb, op. cit., p. 120

212 Ibid; also *Combat Chronology of U.S. Army Air Forces December 1944, The United States Army Air Forces in World War II* as reported at http://www.usaaf.net/chron/44/dec44.htm

213 Lamb, op. cit., p. 120

214 Miller, op. cit., p. 248

215 Motley, op. cit., Wade McCree quote: "The officers of the 88th were very serious about their mission. They hanged one of their boys for desertion under fire." (author's note: he 88th Infantry was a U.S. division and it did not execute a U.S. serviceman. The likelihood is one of the British colonial units in the vicinity of McCree took the action he remembered), p. 302

216 Motley, op. cit., p. 346

217 Allison, op. cit., letter No. 311 to Dotty dated September 14, 1945 "I often think of the forty-four days I waited…"

218 Allison, op. cit., letter (unnumbered) to Dotty dated December 29, 1944

219 Truscott, op. cit., p. 454

220 Truscott, op. cit., p. 456

221 Allison, op. cit., letter to Dotty dated December 26, 1944

222 Allison, op. cit., letter to Dotty dated December 29, 1944

223 Motley, op. cit., p. 299

224 Allison, op. cit., letter to his folks dated December 29, 1944

225 Lesesne, op. cit., January 1, 1945

226 *Stars and Stripes*, January 4, 1945, *Tour of Duty' Home Leave Urged for Joes*, p.1 see: http://peggy-w.hubpages.com/hub/Clare-Boothe-Luce-Soldiers-Tour-of-Duty-1945-and-Today (date accessed 05/24/2014)

227 Lesesne, op. cit., January 16, 1945

228 YouTube: *Mussolini — the Last Days* as reported at https://www.youtube.com/watch?v=5V4t2pmT2Hs — sound newsreel of the December 16, 1945 Il Duce Milan speech (date accessed 12/10/2014)

229 Dulles, op. cit., p. 56

230 Holland, op. cit., pp. 448-449

231 Lamb, op. cit., p. 650

232 American Football *Italian Spaghetti Bowl*, as reported at http://www.spaghettibowl. americanfootballitalia.com/game.html (date accessed 04/23/2015)

233 Stroud, op. cit., January 7, 1944

234 Rottman, Gordon L, *World War II Axis Booby Traps and Sabotage Devices*. Oxford: Osprey Publishing Limited 2009, p. 12

235 Lesesne, op. cit., March 21, 1945

236 Lesesne, op. cit., January 1, 1945

CHAPTER SEVEN

237 Truscott, op. cit., p. 456

238 Clark, op. cit., p. 321

239 Motley, op. cit., p. 302

240 Salmaggi and Pallavisini, op. cit., p. 654

241 Salmaggi and Pallavisini, op. cit., pp. 66-67

242 World War II Italy: *Air War — Civilian Casualties* as reported at http://histclo.com/essay/war/ ww2/cou/ita/air/w2ia-cas.html (date accessed 01/05/2016); World War II Database, *Italy* as reported at http://ww2db.com/country/italy (date accessed 01/05/2016)

243 Lamb, op. cit., p. 90

244 Stroud, op. cit., January 11, 1945

245 Stroud, op. cit., January 14, 1945

246 Stroud, op. cit., February 3, 1945

247 Pogue, Forrest C., *Organizer of Victory 1943-1945: General George C. Marshall*. New York: The Viking Press, 1973, p. 536

248 *Life* magazine, January 8, 1945, op. cit., p. 27

249 Correspondence with Chairman of the Council of Ministers of the USSR and the Presidents of the USA during the Great Patriotic War of 1941–1945, Volume — 2, Correspondence with Franklin D. Roosevelt and Harry S. Truman 1945 (hereinafter referred to as "Leader Communications") No. 257 PERSONAL AND MOST SECRET FROM PREMIER J. V. STALIN TO THE PRESIDENT, Mr F. ROOSEVELT January 15, 1945 as reported at https://www.marxists. org/reference/archive/stalin/works/correspondence/02/45.htm (date accessed 06/04/2015)

250 Morris, *Price of Fame*, op. cit., p. 108

251 Lamb, op. cit., p. 120

252 Allison, op. cit., letter to Dotty dated January 7, 1945

253 Jenkins, McKay, *The Last Ridge*. New York: Random House, 2003, p. 141

254 Jenkins, op. cit., pp. 145-196

255 Clark, op. cit., caption from photo insert (page unnumbered)

256 Clark, op. cit., p. 328

257 Clark, op. cit., p. 140

258 Bykofsky and Larson, op. cit., p.229

259 Dole, Bob, *One Soldier's Story*. New York: HarperCollins, 2005, Dole, p. 8

260 Dole, op. cit., p. 142

261 Dole, op. cit., p. 141

CHAPTER EIGHT

262 Ollison, Sarah, recollection regarding her father First Lieutenant Richard E. Stroud (comments 01/20/2016)

263 Stroud, op. cit., January 14, 1945

264 *Time Magazine*, June 18, 1945

265 Allison, op. cit., letter No. 335 to Dotty dated October 6, 1945

266 Lesesne, op. cit., January 19, 1945

267 Lesesne, op. cit., November 21, 1944

268 Morris, *Price of Fame*, op. cit., p. 114

269 Morris, *Price of Fame*, op. cit., p. 111

270 Clark, op. cit., p 333

271 Bykofsky and Larson, op. cit., p.188

272 Allison, op. cit., letter No. 26 to folks dated February 23, 1945

273 *Life* magazine, op. cit., January 29, 1945, p. 28

274 Srodes, op. cit., p. 338

275 Bancroft, op. cit., p. 244

276 Stroud, op. cit., January 28, 1945

277 Lesesne, op. cit., February 6, 1945

278 Lamb, op. cit., p. 5

279 Ollison, Sarah, op. cit., recollection

280 Allison, op. cit., letter (unnumbered) to folks dated February 17, 1945

281 Stroud, op. cit., January 7, 1945

282 Stroud, op. cit., February 8, 1945

283 Stroud, op. cit., February 12, 1945

284 Allison, op. cit., letter No. 164 to Dotty dated April 18, 1945

285 Lewis, Norman, *Naples '44*. New York: Carroll & Graf Publishers, 1978, funeral pp. 36-37; dandelions p. 28

286 Bourke-White, Margaret, *They Called It "Purple Heart Valley."* New York: Simon and Schuster, 1944, p. 39

287 Mauldin, op. cit., p. 73

288 Lesesne, op. cit., February 9, 1945

289 Headquarters Special Service Army Air Forces Service Command Mediterranean Theater of Operations presents *Mediterranean Symphony Orchestra, "Popular Symphonic Selections"* Thursday February 22, 1945

290 Clark, op. cit., p. 334

291 King, op. cit., comments recorded May 17, 2015 reading from his diary entry of February 13, 1945

292 Holland, op. cit., p. 489

293 Clark, op. cit., pp. 331-332

294 The Avalon Project at Yale Law School, *The Yalta Conference, February 1945*, as reported at http://avalon.law.yale.edu/wwii/yalta.asp (date accessed 03/16/2015)

295 Dulles, op. cit., p. 123

296 Stroud, op. cit., February 8, 1945

297 Stroud, op. cit., February 24, 1945

298 Lesesne, op. cit., February 23, 1945

299 Bancroft, op. cit., p. 137

300 Dulles, op. cit., p. 60

301 Lesesne, op. cit., February 23, 1945

CHAPTER NINE

302 Allison, op. cit., letter No. 132 to Dotty dated March 17, 1945

303 Miller, op. cit., p. 217

304 Lamb, op. cit., p. 55

305 Miller, op. cit., p. 217

306 Dulles, op. cit., p. 18

307 Kesselring, op. cit., p. 231

308 Holland, op. cit., pp. 444-445

309 Katz, op. cit., p. 203

310 Holland, op. cit., p. 123

311 *Cayuga Mission Circa 1945 OSS Office of Strategic Services World War II Italy* film; YouTube at https://www.youtube.com/watch?v=XcSqdLk8gfA (date accessed 03/18/2016)

312 Lamb, op. cit., p. 160

313 Newnan, op. cit., p. 30

314 Lamb, op. cit., p. 164

315 Allison, op. cit., letter No. 211 to Dotty dated June 5, 1945

316 Mauldin, op. cit., p. 104

317 Lesesne, op. cit., February 2, 1945

318 Lesesne, op. cit., February 12, 1945

319 *New York Times*, February 14, 1945, by wireless from Milton Bracker, p. 5

320 Truscott, op. cit., p. 474

321 Truscott, op. cit., p. 475

322 Salmaggi and Pallavisini, op. cit., p. 676

323 Allison, op. cit., letter No. 90 to Dotty dated February 3, 1945: "Was very busy today. Am going back to work tonight."; V-Mail No. 92 to Dotty dated February 5, 1945: "[I] have just finished work at the office and I am so _ _ _ _ tired. Fourteen hours a day is too long."

324 Jenkins, op. cit., pp. 146-178

325 Jenkins, op. cit., pp. 179-196

326 Jenkins, op. cit., p. 179

327 Jenkins, op. cit., p. 196; also 10th Mountain Division (Light Infantry) "Climb to Glory" reported at www.globalsecurity.org/military/agency/army/10mtn.htm (date accessed 01/03/2014)

328 Truscott, op. cit., p. 468

329 Howe, op. cit., p.23

330 Howe, op. cit., p. 22

331 Lesesne, op. cit., November 15, 1944:"Jay just got a call from Col Reynolds saying that when Jay's platoon finished firing on C. Piana the Jerries hauled away several mule carts of casualties."; November 18, 1945 (quoted in Chapter Four)

332 Shelton, Peter, Climb to Conquer. New York: Scribner, 2003 (an account by German General Von Senger who opposed the U.S. Army 10th Mountain Division); pp. 213-219

333 Howe, op. cit., p. 15

334 Kesselring, op. cit., p. 220

335 Weckstein, op. cit., pp 106-107

336 Leader Communications, op. cit., No. 278 Received on March 4, 1945 PERSONAL AND SECRET FOR MARSHAL STALIN FROM PRESIDENT ROOSEVELT

337 New York Times, May 13, 1945 "Nearly half of the estimated 200,000 British and 76,000 prisoners of war still in Germany are believed to be within the Russian zone of occupation…"

338 See Tolstoy, Nikolai, Forced Repatriation to the Soviet Union: The Secret Betrayal, 1988 Hillsdale College presentation

339 Morris, Price of Fame, op. cit., p. 119

340 Pogue, op. cit., p. 537

341 Dulles, op. cit., p. 75

342 Dulles, op. cit., p. 79

343 Dulles.,op. cit., p. 76

344 Dulles, op. cit., p. 81

345 Dulles, op. cit., Chapter 3, "Roadblocks to Surrender" pp. 25-36

346 Dulles, op. cit., p. 30

347 Dulles, op. cit., p. 78

348 Bancroft, op. cit., p. 289

349 Dulles, op. cit., p. 124

350 Ibid

351 Dulles, op. cit., p. 77

352 Bancroft, op. cit., p. 289

353 Dulles, op. cit., "Within our office, knowledge of Sunrise was restricted to two other officers besides Gaevernitz and me." (Dulles identifies one of the officers as Captain Tracy Barnes, leaving open the possibility that the other was Mary Bancroft), p. 121

354 Dulles, op. cit., pp. 89-90

355 Dulles, op. cit., p. 102

356 Howe, op. cit., p. 14

357 Truscott, op. cit., p. 501

358 Morris, *Price of Fame*, op. cit., p. 119

359 Morris, *Price of Fame*, op. cit., p. 120

360 Lesesne, op. cit., March 7, 1945

361 Ibid

362 Allison, op. cit., letter No. 42 to folks dated May 5, 1945

363 Allison, op. cit., unnumbered letter to Dotty dated March 15, 1945

364 Allison, op. cit., letter No. 131 to Dotty dated March 16, 1945

365 Allison, op. cit., letter No. 210 to Dotty dated June 3, 1945

366 Allison, op. cit., letter No. 30 to folks dated March 13, 1945

367 Allison, op. cit., letter No. 30 to folks dated March 13, 1945

CHAPTER TEN

368 Howe, op. cit., pp. 20-21

369 Truscott, op. cit., p. 482

370 Howe, op. cit., p. 28

371 Howe, op. cit., p. 18

372 Dulles, op. cit., pp. 123-124

373 Morris, *Price of Fame*, op. cit., p. 120 and 124

374 Morris, *Price of Fame*, op. cit., p. 122

375 Howe, op. cit., p. 32

376 Leader Communications, op. cit., No. 281 PERSONAL AND TOP SECRET FOR MARSHAL STALIN FROM PRESIDENT ROOSEVELT (see footnote 87) March 25, 1945

377 Dulles, op. cit., p. 98

378 Leader Communications, op. cit., No. 282 PERSONAL AND SECRET FROM PREMIER J. V. STALIN TO THE PRESIDENT, Mr F. ROOSEVELT March 25, 1945

379 Dulles, op. cit., p. 98

380 Dulles, op. cit., p. 99

381 Dulles, op. cit., pp. 98-102

382 Dulles, op. cit., p. 100

383 Dulles, op. cit., p. 103

384 Dulles, op. cit., p. 90

385 Dulles, op. cit., p. 104

386 Halbrook, Stephen P., *Operation Sunrise: America's OSS, Swiss Intelligence, and the German Surrender 1945*, "Conversations between Critic, 110 and 476, who was later joined by G. 19 March, 11.00–13.00 hours. Record Group 226, Entry 110, Box 2, Folder 16 — misc. memoranda [U.S. National Archives] as reported at http://www.stephenhalbrook.com/law_review_articles/sunrise.pdf (date accessed 06/19/2015), p. 7, footnote 26

387 Leader Communications, op. cit., No. 280 Received on March 25, 1945 PERSONAL AND SECRET FOR MARSHAL STALIN FROM PRESIDENT ROOSEVELT

388 Binder, op. cit., p. 133

389 Motley, op. cit., p. 344

390 Leader Communications, op. cit., No. 283 PERSONAL AND SECRET FROM PREMIER J. V. STALIN TO THE PRESIDENT, Mr F. ROOSEVELT March 29, 1945

391 Stroud, op. cit., March 22, 1945

392 Headquarters Mediterranean Theater of Operations United States Army APO 512: Travel Orders dated 31 March 1945 to Captains William D. Allison, Leland P. Christensen and Gerald E. Hynan and First Lieutenant Ross O. Nichols

393 Dulles, op. cit., p. 109

394 Leader Communications, op. cit., No. 284 Received on April 1, 1945 PERSONAL AND TOP SECRET FOR MARSHAL STALIN FROM PRESIDENT ROOSEVELT

395 Srodes, op. cit., p. 346

396 Leader Communications, op. cit., No. 285 PERSONAL AND TOP SECRET FOR MARSHAL STALIN FROM PRESIDENT ROOSEVELT

397 History, Art & Archives, United States House of Representatives, Rogers, Edith Nourse 1881-1960, as reported at http://history.house.gov/People/Listing/R/ROGERS,-Edith-Nourse-(R000392)/ (date accessed 05/25/2014)

398 U.S. Congressional Record — House of Representatives, April 2, 1945, p. 3050

399 *New York Times*, "Mrs. Luce Demands Heavy Tax on Rich," April 18, 1943, p. 40

400 Leader Communications, op. cit., April 3, 1945 No. 286 PERSONAL, MOST SECRET FROM MARSHAL J. V. STALIN TO THE PRESIDENT, Mr ROOSEVELT

401 Leader Communications, op. cit., No. 287 Received on April 5, 1945 PERSONAL AND TOP SECRET FOR MARSHAL STALIN FROM PRESIDENT ROOSEVELT

402 Leader Communications, op. cit., No. 288 PERSONAL AND SECRET FROM PREMIER J. V. STALIN TO THE PRESIDENT, Mr F. ROOSEVELT April 7, 1945

403 Atkinson, Rick, *The Guns at Last Light*. New York: Henry Holt and Company, 2013, p. 513

404 Atkinson, op. cit., p. 512

405 The History Learning Site, *Military Casualties of World War Two* as reported at http://www.historylearningsite.co.uk/world-war-two/military-casualties-of-world-war-two/ (date accessed 01/05/2016)

406 Congressional Research Service *American War and Military Operations Casualties: Lists and Statistics*, compiled as of January 2, 2015, as reported at https://www.fas.org/sgp/crs/natsec/RL32492.pdf (date accessed 01/05/2016)

407 The History Learning Site, *Military Casualties of World War Two*, op. cit.

408 THE WAR *Life in the Infantry*, as reported at https://www.pbs.org/thewar/at_war_infantry.htm (date accessed 07/07/2015)

409 Weller, op. cit., pp. 340-341

410 Stroud, op. cit., April 6, 1945

411 Lesesne, op. cit., diary entry believed written March 30, 1945, the day before Easter Sunday

412 Truscott, op. cit., p. 480

413 Howe, op. cit., p. 31

414 Weckstein, op. cit., p. 120

415 Photo Archives, United States Holocaust Memorial Museum, *Passover Seder Services*, as reported at http://digitalassets.ushmm.org/photoarchives/detail.aspx?id=1140360 (date accessed 10/12.2015)

416 USAAF Chronology for April 1945 as reported at http://paul.rutgers.edu/~mcgrew/wwii/usaf/html/Apr.45.html (date accessed 02/23/2015)

417 Howe, op. cit., pp. 31-32

418 Ibid, p. 33

419 *Middle East Stares and Stripes* April 6, 1945, page 4/8

420 Reilly, William A., M.D., Escamilla, Roberto F., M.D. and Long, Perrin H., M.D., *Sand Fly Fever*, http://history.amedd.army.mil/booksdocs/wwii/infectiousdisvolii/chapter2.htm (date accessed 01/04/2015)

421 Reilly, op. cit., p.1

422 Dulles, op. cit., p. 117

423 Papa, Thomas A., *Po Valley 1945*, p. 5: brochure prepared for U.S. Army Center of Military History reported at http://www.history.army.mil/brochures/po/72-33.htm (date accessed 01/04/2015)

424 Shelton, op. cit., p 217

425 Fort Drum, United States Army, 10th Mountain Division History, as reported at http://www.drum.army.mil/AboutFortDrum/Pages/hist_10thMountainHistory_lv3.aspx (date accessed 02/06.2016)

426 Fort Drum, op. cit., p. 3

427 Ibid

428 Miller, op. cit., pp. 241-249

CHAPTER ELEVEN

429 Stroud, op. cit., April 24, 1945

430 Leader Communications, op. cit. No. 290 Received on April 13, 1945 PERSONAL AND TOP SECRET FOR MARSHAL STALIN FROM PRESIDENT ROOSEVELT

431 Dulles, op. cit., p. 123

432 Papa, op. cit., p. 7

433 Weckstein, op. cit., p. 123

434 Howe, op. cit., p. 57

435 Howe, op. cit., p. 59

436 Dulles, op. cit., p. 136

437 Dulles, op. cit., p. 137

438 Kesselring, op. cit., p. 213

439 Kesselring, op. cit., p. 280

440 Kesselring, op. cit., pp. 213-214

441 United States Army *100th Chemical Mortar Battalion*, op. cit.

442 Stroud, op. cit., April 22, 1945

443 Dulles, op. cit., pp. 137, 138

444 Dulles, op. cit., p. 140

445 Dulles, op. cit., p 157

446 Stroud, op. cit., April 27, 1945

447 Stroud, op. cit., April 30, 1945

448 Lesesne, op. cit., November 18, 1944

449 Howe, op. cit., pp. 75-76

450 Howe, op. cit., p. 77

451 Howe, op. cit., p. 80

452 Miller, op. cit., p. 13

453 Lamb, op. cit., p. 293 and photo insert #21

454 Dulles, op. cit., p 171

455 Dulles, op. cit., pp. 174-175

456 Papa, op. cit., p. 14

457 Pitt, op. cit., p. 284

458 Truscott, op. cit., p. 500

459 Howe, op. cit., p. 71

460 The Avalon Project at Yale Law School, *Instrument of Local Surrender of German and Other Forces Under the Command or Control of the German Commander-In-Chief Southwest; April 29, 1945*, as reported at http://www.yale.edu/lawweb/avalon/wwii/gs9.htm (date accessed 01/04/2015)

461 The Avalon Project, op. cit., Section 13, *Disposal of Prisoners of War and of Persons in Custody*

462 The Avalon Project, op. cit., Paragraph 8 of *Appendix A — Orders for German Land Forces ("Status of Surrendered Personnel")* states, "At the Supreme Allied Commander's discretion, some or all of such personnel may be declared to be prisoners of war."

463 Gaevernitz, Gero von Schultz, *They Almost Killed Hitler: Based on the Personal Account of Fabian von Schlabrendorff*, New York: The Macmillan Company, 1947 (reprinted 2014 as part of the *Uncommon Valor Series*, Steve W. Chadde, Series Editor) p. vi

464 Weckstein, op. cit., p. 132

465 Howe, op. cit., pp. 88-89

466 Papa, op. cit., pp. 15-16

467 Shelton, op. cit., p 217

468 Dulles, op. cit., pp. 205-206

469 Bykofsky and Larson, op., cit., p. 208-209

470 Bykofsky and Larson, op., cit., p. 214

471 Atkinson, op. cit., p. 617

CHAPTER TWELVE

472 Gordon and Robbins, op. cit., p. 335

473 Weckstein, op. cit., p. 159

474 Ibid

475 Allison, op. cit., letter No. 42 to folks dated May 5, 1945

476 Gordon and Robbins, op. cit., p. 339

477 Gordon and Robbins, op. cit., p. 340

478 Gordon and Robbins, op. cit., p. 341

479 Gordon and Robbins, op. cit., p. 343

480 Kaplan, Robert D., *The Greek Crisis Is About More Than Money*, Opinion, *Wall Street Journal*, July 1, 2015, p A13

481 Gordon and Robbins, op. cit., p. 357

482 Von Lingen, Kerstin, *Allen Dulles, the OSS, and Nazi War Criminals*. New York: Cambridge University Press, 2013, p. 1

483 Atkinson, op. cit., p. 519

484 BBC *On This Day January 27, 1945*, as reported at http://news.bbc.co.uk/onthisday/hi/dates/stories/january/27/newsid_3520000/3520986.stm (date accessed 11/12/2015)

485 Reitlinger, Gerald, *The Final Solution: The Attempt to Exterminate the Jews of Europe 1939-1945*. New York: A.S. Barnes & Company, Inc., A Perpetua Book, 1961; first American edition New York: Beechhurst Press, Inc., 1953, p. 257

486 Yale Law School, *The Avalon Project: The Reich Foreign Minister to the German Foreign Office*, as reported at http://avalon.law.yale.edu/20th_century/ns051.asp (date accessed 02/07/2016)

487 Bettina, Elizabeth, *It Happened in Italy: Untold Stories of How the People in Italy Defied the Horrors of the Holocaust* (Nashville: Thomas Nelson, 2009) p. xv

488 Miller, op. cit., p. 217

489 Bettina, op. cit., p. xv

490 Medical Department, United States Army, *Personnel in World War II*, Washington D.C.: Office of the Surgeon General, 1963, p. 487

491 Adjusted Service Rating Score calculations as of May 12, 1945: John L. King: 24 months active duty + 10 months overseas duty + 15 battle participation awards (Rome, Arno, North Apennine campaigns) = 49 points

John M. Lesesne: 38 months active duty + 10 months overseas + 5 battle participation awards (North Apennine campaign) = 57 points (note: Panama duty excluded from "overseas")

492 Miller, op. cit., p. 590

493 The Charleston Evening Post, Charleston, S.C., *Captain Lesesne Cited for 183 Days of Combat*, June 18, 1945, p. 16

494 Allison, op. cit., letter No. 197 to Dotty dated May 21, 1945

495 Headquarters Mediterranean Theater of Operations United States Army APO 512 ("MTOUSA") *Travel Orders* dated 22 May 1945 to Captain William D. Allison…"On or about 23 May 1945, to Verona and such other places in Italy as may be necessary."

496 Howe, op. cit., pp. 15-16

497 Bykofsky and Larson, op. cit., p. 230

498 Ibid

499 Ollison, op. cit., recollection January 20, 2016

500 Allison, op. cit., letter No. 210 to Dotty dated June 3, 1945

501 Letter dated 21 September 1945 from JOSEPH T. McNARNEY, General, U.S. Army, to Capt. William D. Allison, "…The new system of measure which you developed to obtain a standard scale for evaluation of production capacity of all truck companies has been proved sound in operation. Your original study and subsequent work have contributed greatly to the development of sound experience data which in turn has been very valuable as a basis for determination of transportation requirements. Your originality of thought and devotion to duty reflect great credit on yourself and the military service."

502 Heefner, Wilson A., *Dogface Soldier: The Life of General Lucian K. Truscott, Jr.* Columbia and London: University of Missouri Press, 2010, pp. 247-48

503 *The Stars and Stripes*, Friday March 23, 1945, p.8

504 Miller, op. cit., p. 230

505 The History Reader — Dispatches in History from St. Martin's Press: *Goodbye OSS and Hello CIA: National Security Act of 1946*, as reported at http://www.thehistoryreader.com/contemporary-history/goodbye-oss-hello-cia-national-security-act-1947/ (date accessed 11/26/2014); also Srodes, op. cit., p. 355

506 Kinzer, op. cit., p. 74

507 Bykofsky and Larson, op. cit., p. 230

508 Allison, op. cit., letter No. 314 dated September 15, 1945

509 Stroud, op. cit., January 29, 1945; Ollison, op. cit., recollection January 20, 2016: "White Rock Lake was a destination for young lovers."

510 Lesesne, op. cit., January 9-12, 1945

511 King, op. cit., week beginning June 17, 1945

512 Bykofsky and Larson, op. cit., p. 231

513 Ibid

514 Ibid

515 Heefner, op. cit., pp. 252-253

516 Srodes, op. cit., p. 363

517 *Mediterranean Theatre, Outline of POW Command Activities*, as reported at www.milhist.net

518 Delany, John P., *The Blue Devils in Italy: A History of the 88th Infantry Division in World War II* (The Battery Press Nashville, 1988) pp 359-360 as reported on www.milhist.net

519 King, op. cit., August 4, 1945

CHAPTER THIRTEEN

520 Allison, op. cit., letter (unnumbered) to Dotty dated March 19, 1945

521 Allison, op. cit., letter No. 209 to Dotty dated June 2, 1945

522 Allison, op. cit., letter to folks dated April 10, 1945

523 Stroud, op. cit., February 3, 1945

CHAPTER FOURTEEN

524 Allison, op. cit., letter No. 319 dated September 21, 1945 to "Hon., Folks & Boys"

525 Stroud, op. cit., April 26, 1945

526 Allison, op. cit., letter No. 343 to Dotty dated October 13, 1945

527 Allison, op. cit., letter No. 344 to Dotty dated October 14, 1945

EPILOGUE

528 Blackwell, op. cit., p 123

529 Lewis, op. cit., pp. 85-86

530 Atkinson, Rick, The Day of Battle, New York: Henry Holt and Company, 2007, p. 383

531 The Italian Monarch as reported at http://italianmonarchist.blogspot.com/2012/09/marshal-of-italy-pietro-badoglio-1st.html (date accessed 06/04/2015)

532 Encyclopedia Britannica, Pietro Badoglio — Italian General and Statesman, as reported at http://www.britannica.com/biography/Pietro-Badoglio (date accessed 01/05/2016)

533 Carey, John, Dunlap, William V. and Pritchard, R. John, editors, International Humanitarian Law. (Ardsley, NY: Transnational Publishers, Inc., 2003, p. 54, footnote 96

534 Harvard University Library Papers of Mary Bancroft… a Finding Aid as reported at http://oasis.lib.harvard.edu/oasis/deliver/~sch00042 (date accessed 01/05/2016)

535 Weider History, Mark W. Clark: a General Reappraisal, as reported at Historynet.com at http://www.historynet.com/mark-w-clark-a-general-reappraisal.htm (date accessed 06/10/2014)

536 Heefner, op. cit., p. 219

537 Blackwell, op. cit., p. 118

538 Blackwell, op. cit., p. 72

539 Unger, Debi and Irwin, George Marshall: a Biography. New York: Harper Collins, 2014, p. 280

540 Heefner, op., cit., p. 253

541 Battistelli, Pier Paolo, Albert Kesselring, Leadership — Strategy — Conflict. Oxford, UK: Osprey Publishing, 2012, p. 12

542 Blackwell, op. cit., p. 220

543 Clark, op. cit., p. 326

544 TRIAL OF GENERAL ANTON DOSTLER, COMMANDER OF THE 75 GERMAN ARMY CORPS, op. cit.

545 The American Presidency Project, John F. Kennedy, #485 Remarks Upon Presenting an Award to Allen W. Dulles, as reported at http://www.presidency.ucsb.edu/ws/?pid=8461 (date accessed 07/22/2014)

546 Basinger, Stuart, Dr. Shatterhand's A Conversation with Allen Dulles as reported at http://www.hmss.com/firstbond/dullesinterview/index.html (date accessed 07/17/2014)

547 Kinzer, Stephen, When a C.I.A. Director Had Scores of Affairs, New York Times The Opinion Pages, November 10, 2012, as reported at http://www.nytimes.com/2012/11/10/opinion/when-a-cia-director-had-scores-of-affairs.html?_r=0 (date accessed 07/22/2014)

548 Dulles, op. cit., (the officer who submitted the note to Dulles was Brigadier General John Magruder), pp. 217-218.

549 Eco, Umberto, Ur-Fascism, The New York Review of Books, June 22, 1995, as reported at http://www.pegc.us/archive/Articles/eco_ur-fascism.pdf date accessed 03/13/2016

550 Gaevernitz, op. cit., p. vi

551 Oxford Dictionary of National Biography: Gaevernitz, Gerhart von Schulze — (1864–1943), first published May 2005; online edition, Jan 2011, locatable at http://www.oxforddnb.com/index/93/101093049/ (index accessed 01/06/2005)

552 Bancroft, op. cit., "He [Gisevius] was particularly pleased when he reported that the Hungarians, in despair because they had been unable to document with whom Allen was sleeping — for of course, in their eyes everyone had to be sleeping with someone — had concluded that Allen and Gero von Gaevernitz, his assistant, must be having and affair because they were constantly together and Gero was so extremely handsome!"; p. 191.

553 Lamb, op. cit., p 76

554 Lamb, op. cit., p. 65

555 Kesselring, op. cit., p. 213

556 Binder, op. cit., p. 71

557 Binder, op. cit., p. 37 citing James, D. Clayton, *The Years of MacArthur* (Boston, Houghton Mifflin Company 1970), Vol. 1, p. 260

558 Morris, Sylvia Jukes, *Rage for Fame, the Ascent of Clare Boothe Luce*. New York: Random House, 1997, p. 57

559 Morris, op. cit., *Clare, in Love and War, Vanity Fair*, as reported at http://.vanityfair.com/society/2014/07/clare-booth-luce (date accessed 07/10/2014)

560 Cook, op. cit., p. 194

561 Mauldin, op. cit., p. 135

562 Motley, op. cit., p. 304

563 Ibid

564 Motley, op. cit., p. 297

565 Motley, op. cit., p. 305

566 Chicago Tribune, August 23, 1945, headline *TITO'S STORY! FLYERS FREED*, p. 1 as reported at http://archives.chicagotribune.com/1946/08/23/page/1/article/titos-story-flyers-freed (date accessed 06/03/2015)

567 Truscott IV, Lucien, *A Phony Hero for a Phony War*, New York Times Sunday Review, November 18, 2012, as reported at http://www.nytimes.com/2012/11/18/opinion/sunday/a-phony-hero-for-a-phony-war.html?_r=0 (date accessed 07/01/2014)

568 Heefner, op. cit., p. 246

569 Kent, Gerald T., *A Doctor's Memoirs of World War II*. Cleveland, OH: The Cobham and Heatherton Press, 1989, pp. 123-124

570 Dulles, op. cit., pp. 213-214

571 Dulles, op. cit., p 146

572 Holocaust Encyclopedia, Treblinka, as reported at http://www.ushmm.org/wlc/en/article.php?ModuleId=10005193 (date accessed 01/19/2014)

573 Reitlinger, op. cit., p.257

SELECTED BIBLIOGRAPHY

Alexander of Tunis, Field Marshall the Earl, *The Alexander Memoirs 1940-1945*. Barnsley, UK: Pen & Sword, 2010.

Arnold-Forster, Mark, *The World at War*. New York: Stein and Day, 1973.

Atkinson, Rick, The Day of Battle, New York: Henry Holt and Company, 2007

Atkinson, Rick, *The Guns at Last Light*. New York: Henry Holt and Company, 2013.

Battistelli, Pier Paolo, *Albert Kesselring, Leadership — Strategy — Conflict*. Oxford, UK: Osprey Publishing, 2012.

Binder, L. James, *Lemnitzer, A Soldier for his Time*. Dallas, VA: Brassey's, Inc., 1997.

Blackwell, Ian, *Fifth Army in Italy 1943-1945*. South Yorkshire, UK: Pen and Sword Military, 2012.

Bourke-White, Margaret, *They Called It "Purple Heart Valley."* New York: Simon and Schuster, 1944.

Bykofsky, Joseph and Larson, Harold, *The Technical Services — The Transportation Corps: Operations Overseas*. Washington, D.C.: Center for Military History United States Army, 1957, reprinted 1990.

Carey, John, Dunlap, William V. and Pritchard, R. John, editors, *International Humanitarian Law*. (Ardsley, NY: Transnational Publishers, Inc., 2003.

Churchill, Winston S., *Closing the Ring*. Boston: Houghton Mifflin, 1951.

Clark, Mark W., *Calculated Risk*. New York: Enigma Books — republished 2007.

Cook, Blanche Wiesen, *The Declassified Eisenhower*. New York: Penguin Books, 1984.

D'Este, C., *Fatal Decision: Anzio and the Battle for Rome*. New York: Harper, 1991.

Dole, Bob, *One Soldier's Story*, New York: HarperCollins Publishers, 2005.

Dulles, Allen W., *The Secret Surrender*. Guilford, CT: The Lyons Press, 2006, originally published 1966.

Ferguson, Harvey, *The Last Cavalryman: The Life of General Lucian K. Truscott, Jr.* Norman, OK: University of Oklahoma Press, 2015.

Gaevernitz, Gero von Schultz, *They Almost Killed Hitler: Based on the Personal Account of Fabian von Schlabrendorff*, New York: The Macmillan Company, 1947 (reprinted 2014 as part of the *Uncommon Valor Series*, Steve W. Chadde, Series Editor)

Heefner, Wilson A., *Dogface Soldier: The Life of General Lucian K. Truscott, Jr.* Columbia and London: University of Missouri Press, 2010.

Holland, James, *Italy's Sorrow, a Year of War, 1944-1945*. New York: St. Martin's Press, 2008.

Howe, George F., *19 Days from the Apennines to the Alps*. Milan, Italy: Pizzi and Pizio, 1945. Note: a U.S. Fifth Army commemorative victory booklet.

Jenkins, McKay, *The Last Ridge*. New York: Random House, 2003.

Katz, Robert, *The Battle for Rome*. New York: Simon & Schuster, 2003.

Kesselring, Albert, *The Memoirs of Field-Marshal Kesselring*. New York: Skyhorse Publishing, 2016 (written 1953).

Kent, Gerald T., *A Doctor's Memoirs of World War II*. Cleveland, OH: The Cobham and Heatherton Press, 1989.

Kinzer, Stephen, *The Brothers*. New York: Time Books Henry Holt and Company, 2013.

Lamb, Richard, *War in Italy 1943-1945 A Brutal Story*. New York: St. Martin's Press, 1994.

Mauldin, Bill, *Up Front: Fiftieth Anniversary Edition*. New York & London: W.W. Norton & Company, 1995.

Miller, Donald L., *The Story of World War II*. New York: A Touchstone Book, Simon & Schuster, 2001.

Morris, Sylvia Jukes, *Rage for Fame, the Ascent of Clare Boothe Luce*. New York: Random House, 1997.

Morris, Sylvia Jukes, *Price of Fame, the Honorable Clare Boothe Luce*. New York: Random House, 2014.

Motley, Mary Penick, Editor, *The Invisible Soldier: The Experience of the Black Soldier, World War II*. Detroit: Wayne State University Press, 1987.

Newnan, William L., *Escape in Italy*. Ann Arbor, MI: The University of Michigan Press, 1945.

Patton, George S. Jr., *War As I Knew It*. New York: A Bantum Book, edition 1980.

Pitt, Barrie, Consultant Editor, *The Military History of World War II*. New York: The Military Press of New York, 1986.

Pogue, Forrest C., *Organizer of Victory 1943-1945: General George C. Marshall*. New York: The Viking Press, 1973.

Reid, Howard, *Dad's War*. London: Bantum Press, 2003.

Reitlinger, Gerald, *The Final Solution: The Attempt to Exterminate the Jews of Europe 1939-1945*. New York: A.S. Barnes & Company, Inc., A Perpetua Book, 1961; first American edition New York: Beechhurst Press, Inc., 1953.

Salmaggi, Cesare and Pallavisini, Alfredo, *2194 Days of War*. New York: Barnes & Noble Books, 1977.

Shelton, Peter, *Climb to Conquer*. New York: Scribner, 2003.

Srodes, James, *Allen Dulles Master of Spies*. Washington DC: Regnery Publishing, Inc., 1999.

Tompkins, Peter, *Italy Betrayed*. New York: Simon & Schuster, 1966.

Truscott, Lucien K., Jr., *Command Missions*. New York: E.P. Dutton and Co., 1954; reprinted Novato, CA: Presidio Press, 1990.

Unger, Debi and Irwin, *George Marshall: a Biography*. New York: Harper Collins, 2014.

Von Lingen, Kerstin, *Allen Dulles, the OSS, and Nazi War Criminals*. New York: Cambridge University Press, 2013.

Wallace, Robert and the Editors of Time-Life Books, *The Italian Campaign*. Alexandria, VA: Time-Life Books, 1978.

Weckstein, Leon, *Through My Eyes: 91st Infantry Division in the Italian Campaign, 1942-1945*. Central Port, OR: Hellgate Press, 1999.

APPRECIATIONS

I wish to express gratitude to those who furnished me with unpublished World War II era personal writings and passed down oral accounts, the first being Sarah Ollison, the daughter of the late Dick Stroud (Sarah also made much appreciated editorial suggestions). Jack King allowed me to use excerpts from his wartime diary and permitted me to interview him in tape-recorded phone sessions. Ann Lesesne, John's wife agreed to my usage of her husband's wartime journal (and with my encouragement offered this important historical record to John's alma mater The Citadel for use by its Archives and Museum).

Jon Walton edited my book in a micro and macro manner, spotting corrections and recommending substantial revisions to tighten the storyline. Bill Allen also worked on my manuscript and I very much appreciate his contribution. Mick Hanou, President of the 91st Bomb Group Memorial Association, reviewed my manuscript primarily for military history accuracy but also ended-up making excellent suggestions for narrative placements. My brother Mark Allison assisted with map-making, editing and photo layouts.

I express appreciation to the Centro Incontri Umani-Ascona, a Swiss foundation dedicated to the promotion of peace and the memory of members of the von Gaevernitz family, for allowing me the use of their website photograph of Gero von Schultz Gaevernitz.

I thank those members of the Witenagemote Club (a gentlemen's literary association that I joined in 2002) who assisted me with the making of this book. Member Bill Krag introduced me to Dr. and Mrs. Lesesne and also provided me with the book *Escape in Italy* written in 1945 by late "WIT" member/army ranger William Newnan. Bill also introduced me to Paul Duker who contributed to the Epilogue. I thank members Tom Cliff for editing and Bill Ball who cued me in on the tragic story of the torpedoing, on Christmas eve 1944, of the troopship SS *Léopoldville*. As an aside, the Witenagemote Club was founded in 1885 in Detroit and has never missed a season.

Lastly, I express appreciation to Leon Weckstein for permitting me to use excerpts from his compelling combat infantry narrative about the Italian war entitled *Through my Eyes*. I felt I needed a "doggie" to round out the cast of American soldiers depicted, and Mr. Weckstein provided well!

Richard Allison, 2017

ABOUT THE AUTHOR

RICHARD ALLISON's interest in military history stems from both his ancestry and personal experience. His forebears fought in a number of U.S. wars. In 1968 he was commissioned in the U.S. Naval Reserve through OCS. He served three year's active duty, first as a watch officer aboard the aircraft carrier *USS Intrepid* *(CVS-11)* and following that, on an admiral's staff in a national command authority watch-standing and administrative capacity. Afterwards he became a lawyer and affiliated with the Navy JAG Corps drilling reserve. He retired from the Navy in 1996 as a captain.

As a civilian Allison worked 35 years as a bank trust lawyer both in estate and personal trust administration. In 1999 he served as chairman of the Michigan Banker's Association Trust Executive Committee. A lifelong resident of Grosse Pointe, Michigan, Allison served as president of the Rotary Club there and also as chairman of the non-profit Grosse Pointe War Memorial Association. He is married and has a daughter who is married to a Navy helicopter rescue swimmer. Retired from both careers now, he enjoys mountain hiking, reading, researching military history and writing.

INDEX

ALPHABETICAL: